THE BRITISH ISLES
0
100 Miles
0
200 km
M3 motorways
A3 main through routes
National parks
Mainland
Orkney Islands
Wick
Lewis
Outer Hebrides
Skye
Inner Hebrides
Mull
Islay
Moray Firth
Elgin
Inverness
Peterhead
Loch Ness
Aberdeen
Fort William
Ben Nevis
Grampian Mountains
Scotland
North Sea
Dundee
Perth
St. Andrews
Firth of Forth
Glasgow
Edinburgh
Firth of Clyde
Ayr
Southern Uplands
Tweed
Northumberland National Park
Gretna Green
Stranraer
Carlisle
Solway Firth
Newcastle
Sunderland
Middlesbrough
Londonderry
Northern Ireland
Belfast
Enniskillen
Sligo
Isle of Man
Lake District National Park
North York Moors National Park
Yorkshire Dales National Park
York
Blackpool
Blackburn
Bradford
Hull
Irish Sea
Galway
Dublin
IRELAND
Isle of Anglesey
Holyhead
Liverpool
Kirkby
Manchester
Leeds
Grimsby
Speke
Sheffield
Snowdon
Chester
Peak District NP
Derbyshire
England
Limerick
Snowdonia National Park
Cambrian Mountains
Stoke-on-Trent
Nottingham
Shrewsbury
Derby
Norwich
Leicester
Great Yarmouth
Waterford
Rosslare
Wales
Peterborough
Birmingham
Aberystwyth
Coventry
Cork
St. George's Channel
Pembrokeshire Coast National Park
Fishguard
Worcester
Stratford-upon-Avon
Northampton
Cambridge
Ipswich
Brecon Beacons National Park
Luton
Hatfield
Braintree
Harwich
Colchester
Essex
Gloucester
Oxford
London
Pembroke
Swansea
Newport
Wembley
Swindon
Southend on Sea
Thames
Cardiff
Bristol
Bath
Greenwich
Bristol Channel
Windsor
Exmoor NP
Canterbury
Stonehenge
Dover
Tunnel
Salisbury
Sussex
Ashford
Southampton
Calais
Exeter
Portsmouth
Brighton
Hastings
Eastbourne
Bournemouth
Paris
Dartmoor National Park
Cornwall
Isle of Wight
Plymouth
Strait of Dover
Penzance
English Channel
Land's End
Scilly Is.
Lizard Point

Learning English

Swift 1

Lehrwerk für Englisch als 2. Fremdsprache

von

Stephanie Ashford
Noreen O'Donovan
Helmut Reisener

Ernst Klett Verlag
Stuttgart Düsseldorf Leipzig

Learning English Swift 1

für Englisch als 2. Fremdsprache

von
Stephanie Ashford, Villingen-Schwenningen; Noreen O'Donovan, Pforzheim;
Dr. Helmut Reisener, Lüneburg sowie Wolfgang Funk, Bamberg

Beratende Mitarbeit
Wolfgang Funk, Bamberg; Axel Plitsch, Wülfrath; Klaus-Peter Thieser, Dillingen/Saar; Traute Werner, Heidelberg

Visuelle Gestaltung
Christian Dekelver, Weinstadt (Layout + Grafik); Elsie Lennox, London (Zeichnungen) sowie
Peter Gray, London

Kassetten und CDs

SB Begleitkassette zum Schülerbuch für zu Hause und für den Unterricht mit Texten, Liedern, Ausspracheübungen (Klettnummer 547018)
Begleit-CD zum Schülerbuch mit gleichem Inhalt (Klettnummer 547058)

HV Kassette mit den Hörtexten für den Unterricht (Klettnummer 547019)
CD mit gleichem Inhalt (Klettnummer 547059)

Lernsoftware
Zu diesem Band gibt es ein Vokabel- und ein Grammatikprogramm. Diese Programme bieten abwechslungsreiche Übungsformen, Leistungs- und Lernzielkontrollen und ein Lexikon mit dem Wortschatz des Lehrwerks.

1. Auflage A 1 5 4 3 2 1 | 2003 2002 2001 2000 1999

Alle Drucke dieser Auflage können im Unterricht nebeneinander benutzt werden, sie sind untereinander unverändert. Die letzte Zahl bezeichnet das Jahr des Druckes.

Internetadresse: http://www.klett-verlag.de

Redaktion: Redaktionsdienst ETS, Stuart Amor, Stuttgart;
Lektorat Projekte, Gaby Bauer-Negenborn, Starnberg

Verlagsredakteur: Andrew Hutchins
Herstellung: Eckhard Schultze

Umschlaggestaltung: Christian Dekelver, Weinstadt
Reproduktion: Repro Maurer GmbH, Tübingen
Druck: Druckerei Appl, Wemding
ISBN 3-12-547010-2

Gedruckt auf Papier aus chlorfrei gebleichtem Zellstoff, säurefrei.

Vorwort

Hallo und herzlich willkommen bei **Swift 1!**

Damit du dich in deinem neuen Englischlehrbuch gut zurecht findest, erfährst du jetzt erst einmal, was alles in ihm steckt.

Dieser 1. Band enthält neun *Units* mit interessanten Themen und Situationen. Jede *Unit* beginnt mit *Check-in.* In diesem Abschnitt lernst du vorwiegend die neuen Wörter und Wendungen kennen, die du für die *Unit,* und natürlich auch für später, brauchst. Nach *Check-in* folgen drei *Steps: Step* A führt die neue Grammatik der *Unit* ein, *Step* B enthält den oder die Haupttext(e), *Step* C bietet verschiedene weiterführende Übungen und spielerische Aktivitäten, die den Stoff der *Unit* vertiefen. Es folgen zwei *Tracks: Track* 1 festigt das bisher Gelernte, ohne neue Strukturen einzuführen. *Track* 2 führt zusätzliche Wörter und Grammatik ein und folgt dem bayerischen Lehrplan. Den neuen Wortschatz aus *Track* 2 erkennst du auf den Vokabelseiten an dem hochgestellten $^{+}$. Den Abschluss jeder *Unit* bildet *Check-out.* In diesem Abschnitt können einzelne Schwerpunkte der *Unit* noch einmal geübt werden. Direkt nach *Check-out* findest du die neuen Wörter der *Unit* auf den Vokabularseiten. Sie sind nach dem Auftreten in den Abschnitten der *Unit* angeordnet. Am Ende der Vokabularseiten gibt es einen Kasten mit den neuen Wörtern der *Unit,* die du bereits kennst und jeden Tag anwendest. Diese Wörter sind alphabetisch sortiert.

Soviel zu den neun *Units.* Im Anschluss findest du in *Extra* ab Seite 158 interessante Originaltexte als Zusatzlektüre. Dort gibt es auch zwei Projekte. Auf *Extra* folgt das Kapitel *Translation* mit Übungen zur Übersetzung deutscher Texte ins Englische. Auf Seite 180 beginnt *Grammar.* Die Punkte in der Grammatik folgen den *Units.* Alle neuen Strukturen sind in Übersichten zusammengefasst und leicht verständlich erklärt. Schau einfach mal rein! Und damit du schnell nachschlagen kannst, wenn du wirklich mal ein Wort vergessen hast, gibt es am Ende von **Swift** noch ein *Dictionary.* In dieser alphabetischen Liste sind alle Wörter mit Angabe der *Unit,* in der sie neu vorkommen, aufgenommen.

So, nun weißt du bereits alles Wesentliche. Zur raschen Orientierung hier noch alle Symbole, die dir in **Swift** begegnen werden. Dann kann es wirklich losgehen. Viel Spaß!

SB — Alle Texte, Lieder, Gedichte und Ausspracheübungen, die auf der Begleitkassette/-CD zum Schülerbuch (SB) aufgezeichnet sind, erkennst du an diesem Zeichen.

HV — Übungen mit diesem Symbol verweisen auf die Kassette/CD zum Hörverstehen (HV). Die Hörtexte sind nicht im Schülerbuch abgedruckt.

G 1 — In den Übungen, die mit diesem Symbol gekennzeichnet sind, wird neue Grammatik eingeführt. Du findest die Erklärungen unter dem entsprechenden Punkt im Grammatikanhang.

Dieses Piktogramm verweist auf schriftliche Übungen. Lege dir einen Ordner *(folder)* an, in den du alle deine schriftlichen Arbeiten und Textprodukte aus **Swift** einheftest.

WP — Dieses Piktogramm kennzeichnet alle Wortschatzübungen. WP steht für *word power.*

YOU — In Übungen, die mit diesem Symbol versehen sind, kannst du über dich und deine persönlichen Erfahrungen sprechen.

Inhalt

UNIT 1

1 At the airport

Check-in
Arrivals
Departures
Baggage

Terminal 2
Bus stop
Taxi
Underground

Car park 1

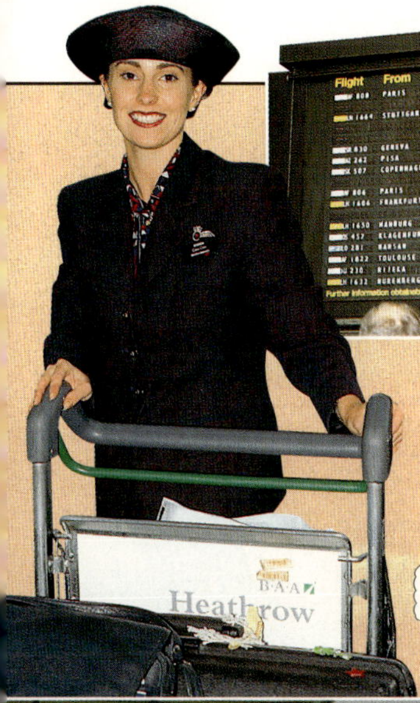
B·A·A
Heathrow

Flight
Arrivals
Flight
From
Last stop
Information

City shuttle
Coffee bar
Snacks
Car rentals

Information ?

Hello! I'm Maike.
Hi! I'm Sandra.
Hello, I'm Sebastian.
Hello, I'm Tessa.
Hi! I'm Tarkan.
Welcome to England. I'm Tony Clifton.
Hi, I'm Max.
Good to have you here, Jean.
I'm Jean Harrison-Haber.
OK. Let's go to Islington.

1

1 Careful with the instruments!

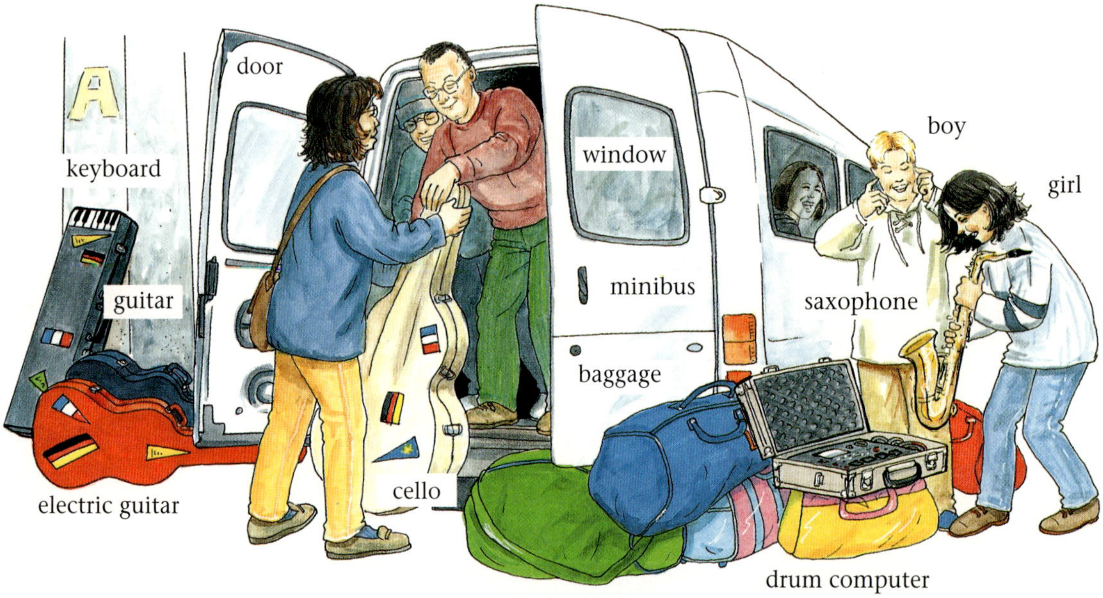

G 1

2 a [ə] or an [ən]?

pilot
check-in
airport
girl
instrument
guitar
coffee bar

open window
boy
bus
door

Example: a pilot

3 Scherzfrage: Wie heißen diese Wörter auf Deutsch?

check-in
keyboard
interview
mountain bike
drum computer
cello
band
hot dog

Be careful here:

pilot
instrument
magazine
saxophone

G 2

4 the [ðə] or the [ði]?

Let's go to the ...

Hello, everybody!

1 And what about you?

a) I'm Max. And what about you? → I'm Tina. And what about you? → I'm … And what about you?

b) I'm from Neunkirchen. And what about you? → I'm from … And what about you? → ???

2 Are you …?

Are you Sandra?

Are you …

… OK?
… German?
… English?
… from Xstadt?
… Svenja?
… Thomas?
… the guitar player?

Yes, I am.

No, I'm not. I'm …

G 3/4

3 The friends

Hello,
my name's
Tessa Clifton.
I'm from
Islington.
And what
about you?

Hello,
my name's
Maike.
I'm from …

Hello,
my name's
Tarkan.
I'm from …

Go on.

I'm = I am
My name's = My name is

"My name's BAD DOG. And what about you?"

4 One thing – two words

Example: mountain bike *Go on.*

mountain	computer
drum	stop
hot	player
car	bike
snack	shuttle
school	guitar
bus	park
guitar	bar
electric	magazine
city	dog

G 3 5 He, she or it?

	he	she	he / she	it
keyboarder			✓	
pilot			✓	
Maike		✓		
instrument				✓
Tarkan	✓			
window				✓

minibus Sandra friend hot dog
girl Mr Clifton Max door name

6 Sound check

Say:

check‿in ['tʃekɪn]
from‿a picture ['frɒmə]
she's‿a singer ['ʃi:zə]
an‿electric guitar [ənɪ'lektrɪk]

I'm‿English [aɪm'ɪŋglɪʃ]
it's‿about you [ɪtsə'baʊt]
one‿instrument [wʌn'ɪnstrəmənt]
at‿an‿airport [ætən'eəpɔ:t]

7 Numbers

Listen and say the numbers.

0	zero	['zɪərəʊ]
1	one	[wʌn]
2	two	[tu:]
3	three	[θri:]
4	four	[fɔ:]
5	five	[faɪv]
6	six	[sɪks]
7	seven	['sevn]
8	eight	[eɪt]
9	nine	[naɪn]
10	ten	[ten]
11	eleven	[ɪ'levn]
12	twelve	[twelv]
13	thirteen	[ˌθɜ:'ti:n]
14	fourteen	[ˌfɔ:'ti:n]
15	fifteen	[ˌfɪf'ti:n]
16	sixteen	[ˌsɪks'ti:n]
17	seventeen	[ˌsevn'ti:n]
18	eighteen	[ˌeɪ'ti:n]
19	nineteen	[ˌnaɪn'ti:n]
20	twenty	['twenti]

8 Sound check

G 5

Listen and say the sentences.

a) 1. I'm from London.
2. She's a singer.
3. They're here.
4. You're OK.
5. He's a friend.
6. We're from Germany.
7. It's my instrument.
8. I'm German.

b) 1. Are you from Islington?
2. Is he a saxophone player?
3. Is she a singer?
4. Are you Mr Clifton?
5. Is she in the minibus?
6. Are they OK?
7. Is it about you?
8. Are we in the picture?

SAVE

short	long	–
I'm	I am	Am I …?
you're	you are	Are you …?
he's	he is	Is he …?
she's	she is	Is she …?
it's	it is	Is it …?
we're	we are	Are we …?
you're	you are	Are you …?
they're	they are	Are they …?

G 6

9 One or more

a)

1 one: car park, pilot, bus stop, airport, snack, instrument, mountain bike

but …

2	3	4
5	6	7
8	9	10
11	12	13
14	15	…

car parks
pilots
bus stops
…
Go on.

[ssssss]

b)

1 one: girl, magazine, taxi, guitar, hotel, boy, window, door

but lots of …

girls
magazines
taxis
…
Go on.

[zzzzzz]

c) *And what about these?*

arrival terminal step saxophone name keyboard unit thing

10 Sound check: [s] or [z] ?

Listen and make two lists:

[s]	[z]

please sentence listen these music instrument is this ask

11 A quiz with instruments

These pictures are from a picture dictionary.

You say: "I know no. … . It's a(n) … ."
Or you ask: "What's no. …?"

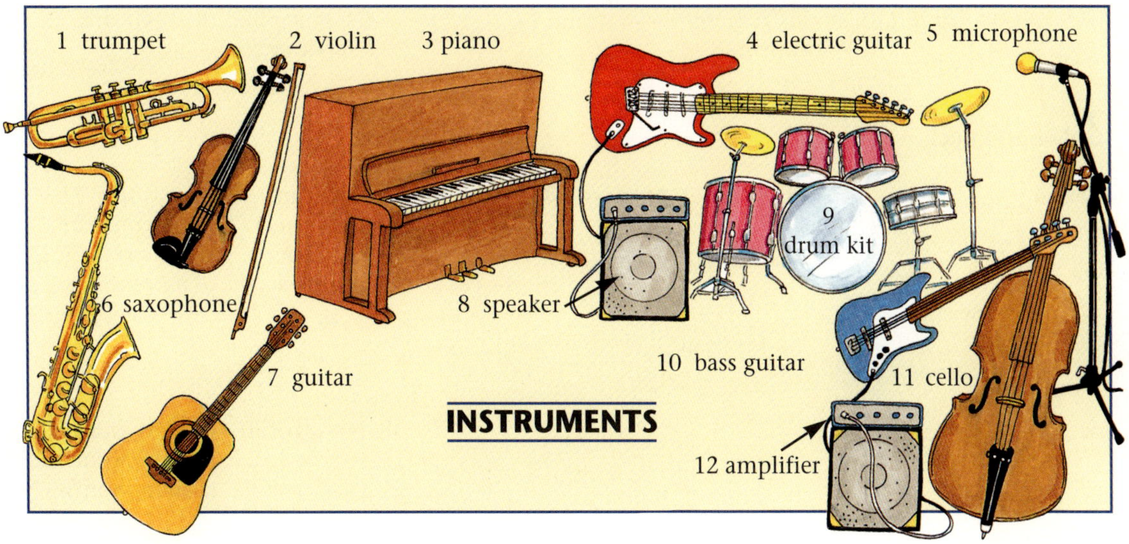

1

An interview

Nicola is the reporter for the school magazine.

Nicola: Oh, our German friends! Welcome to Islington. Just a little interview for our school magazine, please. Your names are on your T-shirts. That's good. Are you all from Neunkirchen?
Tarkan: No, I'm not. I'm from Langenfeld.
Nicola: But you are all from one school?
Maike: Yes, we are.
Nicola: What about you, Maike?
Maike: Er … it's Maike.
Nicola: Danke, Maike.
Maike: Well, I'm the bandleader and a singer.
Nicola: Max, what's your instrument?
Max: Er … two instruments: I'm the saxophone player and I'm on the cello.
Nicola: The cello, wow! And what about you, Sandra?
Sandra: Two instruments too. I'm the guitar player and the keyboarder.

Nicola: Thank you. And Sebastian, what are your instruments?
Sebastian: Just one instrument: the electric guitar. But I'm a singer too.
Nicola: Tarkan – is that a German name?
Tarkan: No, it isn't. It's a Turkish name. My instrument is the drum computer.
Nicola: Thank you all for the interview. Have a good time here. Just one more question: What's the name of your band?
Maike: Oh, we're 'The Good Vibes'.
Nicola: 'The Good Vibes'! Thank you.
Germans: Bye.

1 What we know

Make sentences.

1. Nicola
2. Tarkan
3. The names
4. The German friends
5. Maike
6. Max
7. Sandra's instruments
8. Sebastian
9. Tarkan's instrument
10. The instruments

is / are

a singer too.
the bandleader and a singer.
the drum computer.
in the bus.
a Turkish name.
on the T-shirts.
all from one school.
the saxophone player.
the guitar and the keyboard.
a reporter.

2 Sound check

a) [u:]: two, you, too, school, interview

[ɔ:]: reporter, four, all, for, your, more, airport, keyboard

b) [ɪ] or [i:]? *Make two lists.*

little, instrument, please, leader, guitar, is, singer, she, keyboard, magazine, list

[ɪ]	[i:]
it's	we

c) [aɪ] : I'm (2 more words) ??
[eɪ] : name (2 more words) ??
[æ] : band (5 more words) ?????
[e] : welcome (8 more words) ????????

d) [v] : arrival (2 more words) ??
[w] : welcome (4 more words) ????
[f] : careful (2 more words) ??

The Good Vibes

Hello!

Let's say HELLO to our German friends! (From left to right): One girl (Maike) is the bandleader, and she's a singer. The other girl is Sandra. Sandra's two instruments are the guitar and the keyboard. Max is the boy with two instruments, the cello and the saxophone. Sebastian's instrument is the electric guitar. The boy on the right is Tarkan. (That's a Turkish name.) Tarkan's instrument is the drum computer. Have a good time here in Islington. And let the 'good vibes' get a lot stronger!

G 7

3 Yes or no? – Is or are?

1. Tarkan ... the boy with an English name. No, he ...n't. He's the boy with a Turkish name.
2. Sebastian's instruments ... the guitar and the keyboard. No, they ...n't. They ... Sandra's instruments.
3. Max ...n't a singer. Yes, that's right. He ...n't a singer.
4. Maike ... a singer and Sebastian ... a singer too. Yes, that's right. Maike and Sebastian ... singers.

	yes	no
one:	is	isn't
two or more:	are	aren't

G 8

4 His or her?

1. Maike's name. – Her name.
2. Nicola's interview. – ...
3. The boy's instrument. – ...
4. Tony's bus. – ...
5. The girl's friend. – ...
6. Tessa's T-shirt. – ...

Maike / Nicola / the girl → she	Maike's / Nicola's / the girl's → her	Sebastian / Tony / the boy → he	Sebastian's / Tony's / the boy's → his

5 My – your – his – her?

1. "Hello, I'm the bandleader. ... name is Maike."
2. This is the boy with the drum computer. ... name is Tarkan.
3. And this is Sandra. ... instruments are the guitar and the keyboard.
4. This is Max. ... instruments are the saxophone and the cello.
5. "Hello, Sebastian! What is ... instrument?"
6. This is Tony Clifton. He is in ... bus.
7. And here is Nicola with ... school magazine.

6 The odd one out

1	2	3	4	5	6
cello	Islington	Heathrow Airport	Tessa	one	Maike
guitar	Tarkan	Munich Airport	Sebastian	six	Michael Jackson
window	Nicola	Düsseldorf Airport	Maike	picture	Sebastian
keyboard	electric	Islington	Sandra	nine	Nicola
saxophone	Heathrow	Stuttgart Airport	Nicola	eleven	Madonna

Example: 1. The odd one out in list one is window. A window isn't an instrument. *Go on.*

1 ⟨A song: Sunshine[1] reggae[2]⟩

Words and music by J.Guldberg / T. Stahl

Don't worry[3], don't hurry[4].
Take it easy[5].
Let the good vibes
get a lot stronger.

Gimme[6], gimme
Gimme just a little smile.
That's all I ask[7] of you.
We got[8] a message[9] for you.

[1]['sʌnʃaɪn] *Sonnenschein* [2]['regeɪ] *aus Jamaika stammende Popmusikrichtung* [3](= do not) [dəʊnt 'wʌri] *mach dir keine Sorgen*
[4]['hʌri] *(sich be)eilen* [5][ˌteɪk‿ɪt‿'i:zi] *nimm's leicht* [6](= give me) ['gɪmi] *gib mir* [7]['ɑ:sk‿əv] *verlangen, bitten (um)*
[8](= we have got) [gɒt] *wir haben* [9]['mesɪdʒ] *Nachricht*

2 An 'I can see' game

No. 1: "At an airport I can see lots of taxis."
No. 2: "At an airport I can see lots of taxis and magazines."
No. 3: "At an airport I can see lots of taxis and magazines and pilots."
No. 4: "At an airport I can see ..."

3 Listening comprehension: Instruments

Listen and say the names and numbers of the instruments.

4 A buzz-game

a) *Careful with the 3:*

one (1) – two (2) – *buzz* – four (4) – five (5) – *buzz* – seven (7) – eight (8) – *buzz* – ten (10) – eleven (11) – *buzz* – *buzz* – ...

b) *Careful with the 4:*

one (1) – two (2) – three (3) – buzz – ...

5 How are you?

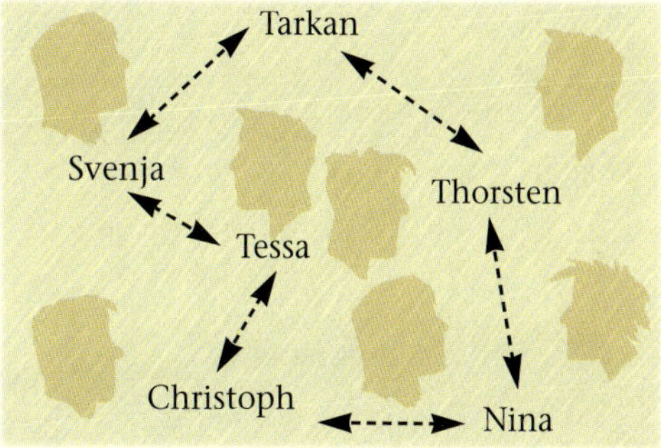

6 Music in your class

YOU

Make a list.

name	his / her instrument	his / her band	his / her singer(s)	his / her music
Svenja K.	saxophone	Top Girls	Jennifer Kolby	jazz / classical music
Alexander S.	–			

7 Cartoon fun

"Where's the piccolo player?"

"Let's play it again! Lots of time – lots of time!"

WP 1 Words – words – words

a) Words with two letters — anweisitinmyontoatno ...

b) Words with three letters — twobutheronesaycarhisyesareyouandthenotalltoofun ...

c) Words with double letters — doorcoffeegoodhellowellbookallcelloschool ...

2 A quiz

1. Max is the  with two instruments.
2. Sandra is the  with two instruments.
3.  is the bandleader.
4.  's drum computer is OK.
5. Nicola is the reporter for her  .
6. Sebastian's instrument is the 
7. And this is Tony Clifton's  .

WP 3 Let's make word pairs

Example: play – say *Go on.*

play	one	band	say
you	we	two	fun
and	what	not	game
door	name	he	four

4 Lots of ...

and

2 ...
3 ...
4 ...
5 ...
6 ...
7 ...
8 ...
9 ...

?

5 At an airport

Say lots of sentences.

At an airport you can	say hello to lots of see lots of get lots of	pilots. hot dogs. friends. taxis. instruments. arrivals. magazines. singers. snack bars. ...

WP 6 Word games

KEY**B**OARD
S**A**XOPHONE
I**N**STRUMENTS
LEA**D**ER

ARRIVALS
P**I**LOTS
TE**R**MINALS
DE**P**ARTURES
H**O**TELS
REPO**R**TERS
TICKE**T**S

What about more word games?

WP 1 Make more word pairs

Girl and boy, you and I,
Yes and no, hello – goodbye,
His and her, water and air,
Words are easy in a pair.

hot dog / snack
go on / stop
I / my
check-in / check-out
the first / the last
football / tennis
baggage / ticket

taxi	air	arrivals	eleven	window	cello	English
guitar	bus	door	German	water	twelve	departures

WP 2 What are the last two words?

1. The magazine for a school is a … .
2. A bike for the mountains is a … .
3. A ticket for the Underground is an … .
4. A bar in a hotel is a … .
5. A shop at an airport is an … .
6. The window of a shop is a … .
7. A dictionary with pictures is a … .

3 Make a mind map

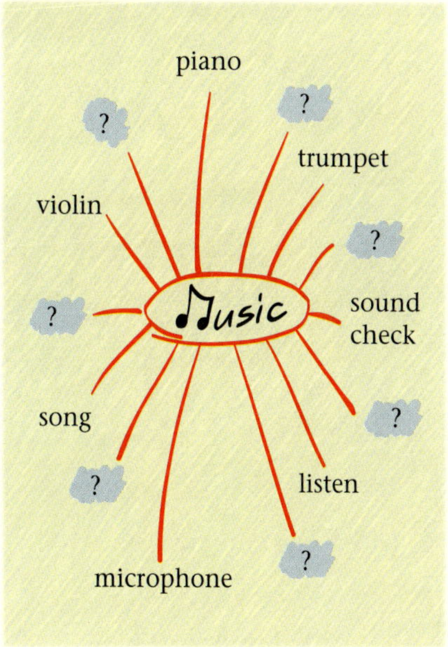

SB 4 Sound check: Words with an [æ] sound

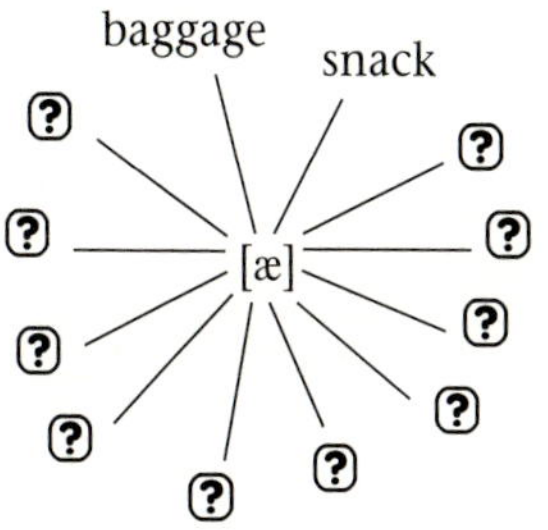

t-xi	-m	m-p
m-gazine		th-t
pi-no		b-nd
h-ve	-t	-nd

5 Fun poems and poem fun

a) An 'up and down' poem *© June Factor*

↑	↓	↑	↓	↑	↓	↑	↓
down	and	you	if	find	you	you	will
and	you	love	you	I	love	for	be
up	will	I	love	if	me	love	forgot.
Read	see	that	me.	And	not	my	

b) Two poems for friends

Make new friends
But keep the old,
New friends are silver,
Old friends are gold.

There are gold ships,
There are silver ships,
But the best ship
Is friendship.

WP 1 Words with the letter i

Make two lists, one with the [ɪ] *words and one with the* [aɪ] *words.*

[ɪ]	[aɪ]
ticket	pilot

instrument	pilot	find	six	nine	arrivals	mind map
ticket	window	bike	list	singer	fine	guitar

2 One and more

Example: One guitar, two girls, three …

WP 3 Words with y

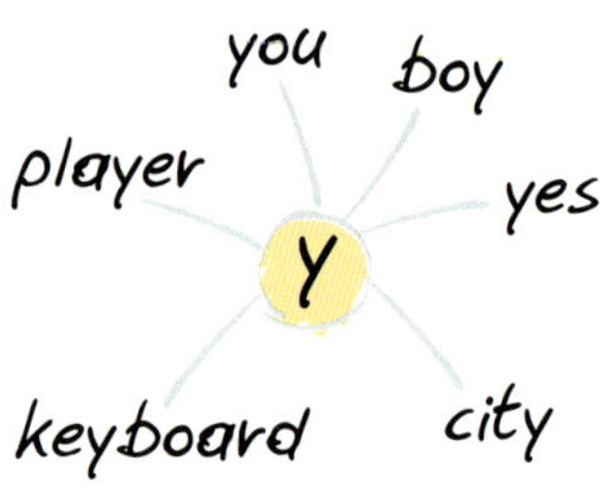

More words with y?

10 words = ☺
11 words or more = Super!

4 Questions and answers

a)

	Is she …?	
I'm …	Are we …?	
You're …		from …
He's …	Are they …?	in …
She's …	Am I …?	a …
It's …		the …
We're …	Is he …?	…
They're …	Are you …?	
	Is it …?	

?

b)

Yes, they are.

Are we at Terminal 3?

Yes, she is.

Are the cello and the guitar your instruments?

Are they from Islington?

No, we aren't.

No, it isn't.

Are you all from one school?

Are you 15, Tessa?

No, they aren't.

Yes, we are.

Yes, I am.

Is she a singer?

Is it a keyboard?

Vocabulary

Nach jeder *Unit* findest du eine Liste mit den neuen Vokabeln. In der linken Spalte sind die englischen Wörter in der Reihenfolge, in der sie in der *Unit* vorkommen. Dahinter steht die Phonetik in eckigen Klammern. Sie zeigt dir, wie das Wort ausgesprochen und betont wird. Wie du die Lautschrift liest, siehst du im nächsten Abschnitt (*The phonetic symbols*).
In der mittleren Spalte ist die deutsche Übersetzung der englischen Wörter. Oft lassen sich Wörter aus einer Sprache nicht direkt in die andere übertragen. Deshalb stehen manchmal mehrere Ausdrücke in der Mittelspalte.
In der rechten Spalte findest du Lernhilfen in Form von Beispielsätzen, Definitionen, Illustrationen usw., die dir das Behalten der neuen Vokabeln erleichtern sollen. Merken musst du dir jetzt nur noch:

Symbole

〈 〉	=	fakultativer (nicht obligatorischer) Wortschatz
°	=	rezeptiver (passiver) Wortschatz
+	=	*Track* 2-Wortschatz
*	=	unregelmäßiges Verb (siehe Seite 228)
[ˈ]	=	Hauptbetonung
[ˌ]	=	Nebenbetonung
[‿]	=	enge Verbindung zweier Wörter
~	=	Auslassung des zu erklärenden Wortes

Abkürzungen

BE	=	*British English*
AE	=	*American English*
so.	=	*someone* = jmd(m/n) / jemand(em/en)
sth.	=	*something* = etw / etwas
sing.	=	Singular
pl.	=	Plural
coll.	=	*colloquial* = umgangssprachlich

The phonetic symbols

Konsonanten		**Vokale**		[ʊ]	book
[ŋ]	morni**ng**	[ɑː]	f**a**ther	[u]	ann**u**al
[r]	**r**ed	[ʌ]	b**u**t	[uː]	tw**o**, t**oo**
[s]	cla**ss**	[e]	p**e**n	**Diphthonge (Doppellaute)**	
[z]	i**s**	[ə]	**a** sist**er**	[aɪ]	m**y**, **I**
[dʒ]	**G**erman	[ɜː]	g**ir**l	[aʊ]	h**ou**se, n**ow**
[ʃ]	**sh**e	[æ]	b**a**nd	[eə]	th**ere**, p**air**
[tʃ]	**ch**air, sandw**ich**	[ɪ]	**i**t	[eɪ]	n**a**me, th**ey**
[ð]	**th**e, wi**th**	[i]	happ**y**	[ɪə]	h**ere**, id**ea**
[θ]	**th**anks	[iː]	w**e**, r**ea**d	[ɔɪ]	b**oy**
[v]	ha**v**e, **v**ideo	[ɒ]	**o**n, g**o**t	[əʊ]	hell**o**, g**o**
[w]	**w**ord, **o**ne	[ɔː]	b**a**ll	[ʊə]	y**ou're**

Alle anderen Zeichen werden wie im Deutschen ausgesprochen: [j], [k], [l] usw.

The alphabet

a [eɪ]	**b** [biː]	**c** [siː]	**d** [diː]	**e** [iː]	**f** [ef]	**g** [dʒiː]	**h** [eɪtʃ]	**i** [aɪ]
j [dʒeɪ]	**k** [keɪ]	**l** [el]	**m** [em]	**n** [en]	**o** [əʊ]	**p** [piː]	**q** [kjuː]	**r** [ɑː]
s [es]	**t** [tiː]	**u** [juː]	**v** [viː]	**w** [ˈdʌbljuː]	**x** [eks]	**y** [waɪ]	**z** [zed]	

1

CHECK-IN

	unit ['ju:nɪt]	Lektion, Einheit
	at [æt/ət]	an / am, in / im, bei
	the [ðə/ði]	der / die / das
	airport ['eəpɔ:t]	Flughafen
	arrival [ə'raɪvl]	Ankunft
	departure [dɪ'pɑ:tʃə]	Abflug, Abfahrt
	baggage ['bægɪdʒ]	Gepäck
	Underground ['ʌndəgraʊnd]	U-Bahn
	car park ['kɑ: pɑ:k]	Parkplatz
	city shuttle ['sɪti ˌʃʌtl]	Pendelverkehr zur Innenstadt
	car rental ['kɑ: ˌrentl]	Autovermietung
	hello / hi [hə'ləʊ/haɪ]	hallo
	I'm (I am) [aɪm]	ich bin
	welcome ['welkəm]	willkommen
	to [tʊ/tu]	in / im, zu
	England ['ɪŋglənd]	England
	good [gʊd]	gut
	to **have*** [hæv]	haben
	you [ju:]	du, ihr, Sie
	here ['hɪə]	hier
	let's (let us) [lets]	lass(t) uns
	to **go*** [gəʊ]	gehen
	Islington ['ɪzlɪŋtən]	*Stadtteil in London*
1	**careful** ['keəfʊl]	vorsichtig
	with [wɪð]	mit
	door [dɔ:]	Tür
	window ['wɪndəʊ]	Fenster
	boy [bɔɪ]	Junge
	girl [gɜ:l]	Mädchen
	electric [ɪ'lektrɪk]	elektrisch
	guitar [gɪ'tɑ:]	Gitarre
	drum computer ['drʌm kəmˌpju:tə]	Rhythmusgerät
2	**a(n)** [ə(n)]	ein / eine
	or [ɔ:]	oder
	example [ɪg'zɑ:mpl]	Beispiel
	open ['əʊpn]	offen
3	to **be*** [bi:]	sein
	magazine [ˌmægə'zi:n]	Zeitschrift

London — England
Let's go to ...
Welcome to ...
Islington — ???

a boy or a girl?
a door or a window?
... or ...?

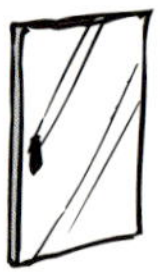

electric

a departure or an arrival?
a saxophone or an electric guitar?

franz exemple *lat* exemplum
engl example

an open magazine

STEP A

	step [step]	Schritt, Stufe, Abschnitt
1	**everybody** ['evriˌbɒdi]	jeder, alle (zusammen)
	and [ænd/ənd]	und
	what [wɒt]	was?
	What about ...? [ˌwɒt‿ə'baʊt]	Was ist mit ...?
	from [frɒm]	von
2	**are** [ɑ:]	sind

Are you from Neunkirchen?
Yes, we are.

	yes [jes]	ja
	German ['dʒɜ:mən]	deutsch, Deutsch
	English ['ɪŋglɪʃ]	englisch, Englisch
	player ['pleɪə]	Spieler(in)
	no [nəʊ]	nein; kein / keine
	not [nɒt]	nicht
3	**friend** [frend]	Freund(in)
	my [maɪ]	mein / meine
	's (is) [ɪz]	ist
	bad dog [ˌbæd 'dɒg]	böser Hund
	to **save** [seɪv]	sichern, abspeichern
4	**one** [wʌn]	eins
	thing [θɪŋ]	Sache, Ding
	two [tu:]	zwei
	word [wɜ:d]	Wort
	to **go on** [ˌgəʊ‿'ɒn]	weitermachen, fortsetzen
	school [sku:l]	Schule
	city ['sɪti]	Großstadt, Innenstadt
5	**keyboarder** ['ki:bɔ:də]	Keyboardspieler(in)
	he / she / it [hi: / ʃi: / ɪt]	er / sie (*sing.*) / es
	Mr ['mɪstə]	Herr (*Anrede*)
6	**sound check** ['saʊn(d) tʃek]	Klang-, Tonkontrolle
	to **say*** [seɪ]	sagen, reden
	picture ['pɪktʃə]	Bild
	singer ['sɪŋə]	Sänger(in)
7	**number (No.)** ['nʌmbə]	Zahl, Nummer (Nr.)
	to **listen** ['lɪsn]	zuhören
8	**sentence** ['sentns]	Satz
	London ['lʌndən]	London
	they [ðeɪ]	sie (*pl.*)
	Germany ['dʒɜ:məni]	Deutschland
	we [wi:]	wir
	in [ɪn]	in/im
	about [ə'baʊt]	über (etw), von (etw)
	short [ʃɔ:t]	kurz
	long [lɒŋ]	lang
9	**more** [mɔ:]	mehr
	but [bʌt]	aber
	lots of ['lɒts‿əv]	viele (von)
	these [ði:z]	dies / das (sind); diese(r/s) (*pl.*)
10	to **make*** [meɪk]	machen
11	to **know*** [nəʊ]	wissen, kennen
	please [pli:z]	bitte
	to **ask** [ɑ:sk]	fragen
	dictionary ['dɪkʃənəri]	Wörterbuch
	°**speaker** ['spi:kə]	Lautsprecher
	°**drum kit** ['drʌm kɪt]	Schlagzeugausrüstung
	°**amplifier** ['æmplɪfaɪə]	Verstärker

STEP B

A	**just** [dʒʌst]	gerade, eben
	to **give*** [gɪv]	geben

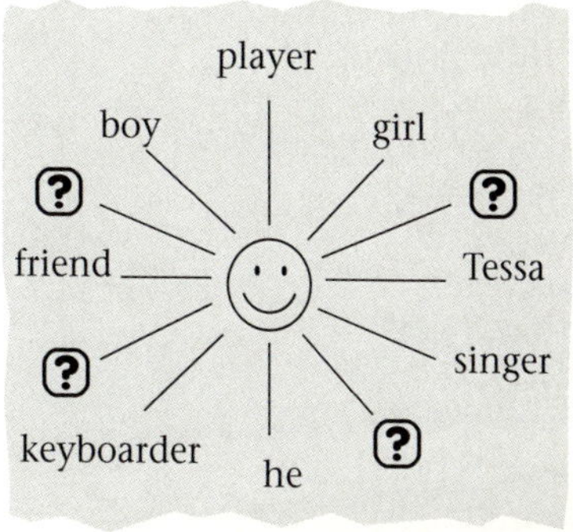

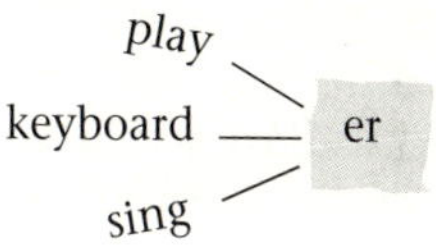

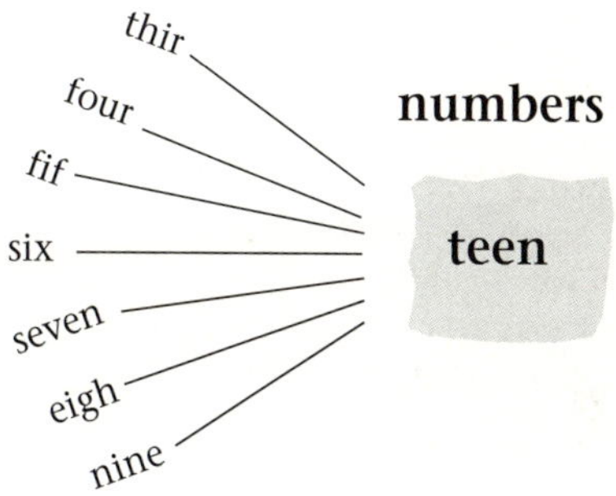

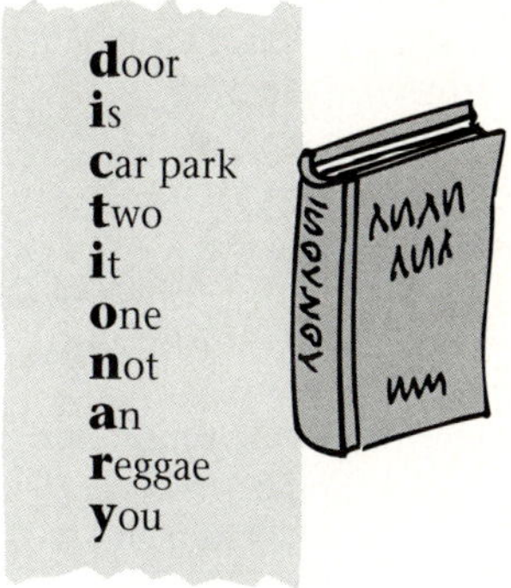

Words with o

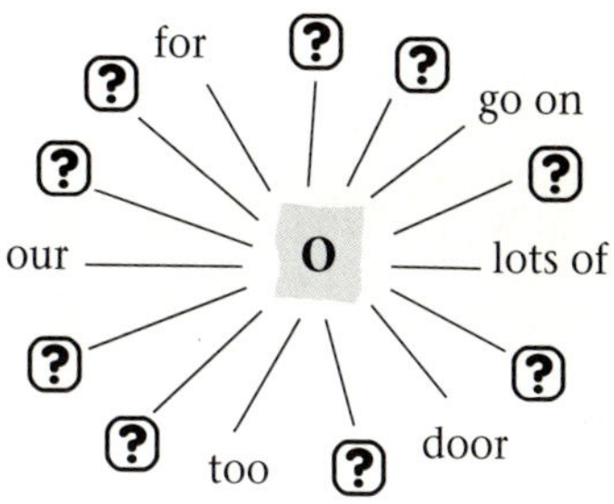

1

	little ['lɪtl]	klein
	smile [smaɪl]	Lächeln
	for [fɔː]	für
	thank you ['θæŋk jʊ]	danke
	our ['aʊə]	unser
	your [jɔː]	dein / deine, euer / eure, Ihr / Ihre
	on [ɒn]	auf, an / am
	that [ðæt]	das; dass
	all [ɔːl]	alle(s)
	well [wel]	nun gut, na ja
	wow! [waʊ]	*Ausruf der Bewunderung*
	too [tuː]	auch, ebenfalls
	isn't (is not) ['ɪznt]	ist nicht
	Turkish ['tɜːkɪʃ]	türkisch, Türkisch
	time [taɪm]	(Uhr-)Zeit
	question ['kwestʃən]	Frage
	vibes (vibrations) ['vaɪbz (vaɪ'breɪʃnz)]	Schwingungen, Vibrationen
	(good)bye [(ˌgʊd)'baɪ]	(auf) Wiedersehen, tschüs
B	**left** [left]	links
	right [raɪt]	rechts; richtig
	other ['ʌðə]	andere(r / s)
	to get* [get]	bekommen, haben
	a lot [ə 'lɒt]	viel, eine Menge
	stronger ['strɒŋgə]	stärker
3	**aren't (are not)** [ɑːnt]	sind nicht
4	**his** [hɪz]	sein / seine
	her [hɜː]	ihr / ihre
5	**this** [ðɪs]	dies / das (ist); diese(r / s) (*sing.*)
6	**odd one out** [ˌɒd wʌn‿'aʊt]	das Nichtdazupassende
	Heathrow [ˌhiːθ'rəʊ]	*Name eines Londoner Flughafens*
	Munich ['mjuːnɪk]	München

STEP C

2	**can** [kæn]	kann
	to see* [siː]	sehen, erblicken
	game [geɪm]	Spiel
3	**listening comprehension** ['lɪsnɪŋ ˌkɒmprɪ'henʃn]	Hörverstehen
4	**buzz-game** ['bʌzˌgeɪm]	*Name eines Spiels*
5	**How are you?** [ˌhaʊ‿'ɑː juː]	Wie geht's (dir / euch / Ihnen)?
	fine [faɪn]	gut, fein, prima
7	**fun** [fʌn]	Spaß
	where [weə]	wo, wohin
	to play [pleɪ]	spielen
	again [ə'gen]	wieder

TRACK 1

	track [træk]	Spur, Weg, Pfad
1	**letter** ['letə]	Buchstabe; Brief
	double ['dʌbl]	doppelt(e / r)
3	**pair** [peə]	Paar

Tessa is an English name.
Max is a German name.
Tarkan is a Turkish name.

The Unit 1 alphabet

are
band
check-in
dictionary
electric
fun
good
he
is
just
keyboard
left
mother
...

A musical mind map for your folder

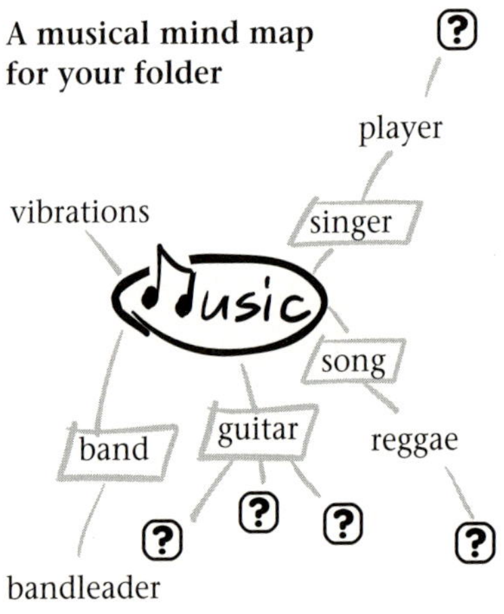

again and again and again ...

franz double *lat* duplex
engl double

TRACK 2

1	+**air** [eə]	Luft
	+**easy** [i:zi]	leicht, einfach
	+**the first** [ðə 'fɜ:st]	erste(r / s), der / die Erste
	+**the last** [ðə 'lɑ:st]	letzte(r / s), der / die Letzte
2	+**shop** [ʃɒp]	Geschäft, Laden
3	+**mind map** ['maɪnd ˌmæp]	*etwa:* Gedankennetz
5	+**poem** ['pəʊɪm]	Gedicht
	+**up** [ʌp]	(hin)auf
	+**down** [daʊn]	herunter, nieder
	+to **read*** [ri:d]	lesen
	+**will** [wɪl]	werden
	+**if** [ɪf]	wenn, falls
	+**me** [mi:]	mich
	+to **find*** [faɪnd]	finden
	+to **forget*** [fə'get]	vergessen
	+**new** [nju:]	neu
	+to **keep*** [ki:p]	(be)halten
	+**old** [əʊld]	alt
	+**there are** [ðeə(r)‿'ɑ:]	es gibt, da sind
	+**ship** [ʃɪp]	Schiff
	+**friendship** ['fren(d)ʃɪp]	Freundschaft

CHECK-OUT

1	**mind map** ['maɪnd ˌmæp]	*etwa:* Gedankennetz
4	**answer** ['ɑ:nsə]	Antwort

COGNATE WORDS

band [bænd]	Musikgruppe, Band
bandleader ['bændˌli:də]	Leiter(in) einer Musikgruppe
°**bass** [beɪs]	Bass
+**best** [best]	beste(r / s), der / die Beste
bus stop ['bʌs stɒp]	Bushaltestelle
cartoon [kɑ:'tu:n]	Witzzeichnung
cello ['tʃeləʊ]	Cello
check-in ['tʃekɪn]	Abfertigungsschalter (am Flughafen), Einchecken
check-out ['tʃekaʊt]	Abschlusskontrolle, Auschecken
class [klɑ:s]	Klasse
classical music ['klæsɪkl 'mju:zɪk]	klassische Musik
coffee bar ['kɒfi ˌbɑ:]	(kleines) Café
+**football** ['fʊtbɔ:l]	Fußball
gold [gəʊld]	Gold
hot dog ['hɒt dɒg]	Hotdog *(langes weiches Brötchen mit Würstchen)*
hotel [həʊ'tel]	Hotel
instrument ['ɪnstrəmənt]	Instrument
interview ['ɪntəvju:]	Interview
jazz [dʒæz]	Jazz *(Musikrichtung)*
keyboard ['ki:bɔ:d]	elektronische Orgel, Keyboard
list [lɪst]	Liste
+to **love** [lʌv]	lieben, gern haben, mögen
°+**microphone** ['maɪkrəfəʊn]	Mikrofon
minibus [('mɪnɪ)bʌs]	Kleinbus
mountain bike ['maʊntɪn ˌbaɪk]	Geländefahrrad, Mountainbike
music ['mju:zɪk]	Musik
name [neɪm]	Name
OK [əʊ'keɪ]	in Ordnung, okay
photo ['fəʊtəʊ]	Foto
°+**piano** [pi'ænəʊ]	Klavier
piccolo ['pɪkələʊ]	Piccolo(-Flöte)
pilot ['paɪlət]	Pilot(in)
quiz [kwɪz]	Fragespiel, Quiz
reporter [rɪ'pɔ:tə]	Reporter(in), Journalist(in)
saxophone ['sæksəfəʊn]	Saxophon
+**silver** ['sɪlvə]	silber
snack [snæk]	Imbiss
song [sɒŋ]	Lied, Song
taxi ['tæksi]	Taxi
tennis ['tenɪs]	Tennis
terminal ['tɜ:mɪnl]	Terminal
ticket ['tɪkət]	Flugschein, Fahrkarte
°+**trumpet** ['trʌmpɪt]	Trompete
T-shirt ['ti:ʃɜ:t]	T-Shirt
°+**violin** [ˌvaɪə'lɪn]	Geige
+**water** ['wɔ:tə]	Wasser

UNIT 2

Welcome to Islington!

The five friends are with families in Islington, in North London.
Why? Well, their English teacher is from London.
She has got friends at an Islington school.

1 Who are they with?

Maike is in a garden flat. There are nice red flowers in the front garden. – She is with the …
Sebastian is in a new house with a small front garden. The door is white. – He …
Sandra is in a house with a red door. There are flowers in a window. – …
Max is in a flat. There is a big old tree in front. – …
Tarkan is in a house with a brown roof. – …

2 What about you?

YOU

a) *Talk about your house or flat. Start:*

It's a … with …
There is a … / There are … in the …
There isn't … but …
The door / roof is …

yellow | black | red | green | blue | brown | white

b) *Ask and answer:*

What colour is your …?
It's …

c) *Write down five sentences about your house or flat.*

At home with the Bradens

This is Sandra's room. It's a little room under the roof. The wall is blue. There is a table, a chair, a high cupboard and a bed. It's Mr Braden's hobby room too. He has got an interesting hobby.

G 9

1 Look and see

a)

Is there a Are there	picture window computer flowers magazines	in Sandra's room?	– Yes, there is. – Yes, there are. – No, there isn't. – No, there aren't.

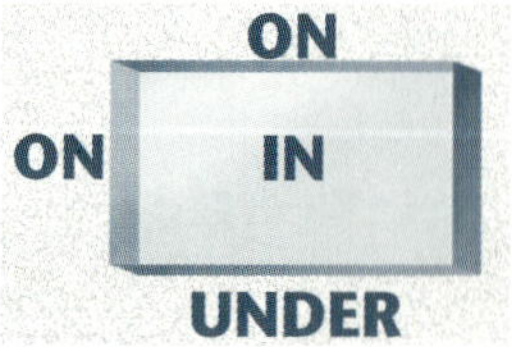

b) Where is the ...? – It's ...
Where are the ...? – They are ...

c) And what about her guitar?
And her T-shirts?
And her ...?

SAVE

There is ... There are ...	There isn't ... There aren't ...	Is there ...? Are there ...?

G 10/11

2 Hobbies

All of the Bradens have got interesting hobbies. *Look at the pictures and say what they are.*

Start: Mr Braden's hobby is astronomy. Liz's hobby is ...

Can you find the rule?

hobby – hobb*ies*
family – famil*ies*

but: boy – boys

And what about:
city – London and Berlin are big ...
dictionary – Sandra has got two ...

B

Sandra isn't in her room. She's in the Bradens' living room. The two Braden children are there too.

Sandra: This is a nice living room. It's – different.
Liam: Different?
Sandra: Well, there are lots of old things in it.
Liam: Huh! All from Dad's shop in Islington High Street.
Sandra: And there's a – er, what's the word for this?
Liz: A fireplace? Of course there's a fireplace.
Sandra: Oh, this is a nice picture of a baby. Is it you, Elizabeth?
Liz: Yes, it is. But it isn't nice – it's silly! And please call me Liz. Elizabeth is too long.
Sandra: OK, Liz is nice too. Er … can I see the other rooms?
Liz: Sure, but we can do that later – here are Mum and Dad …

3 Listening comprehension: Names

Listen to Mr and Mrs Braden and Sandra. Find out:

1. Is Sandra a German or an English name?
2. What's Mr Braden's name? And Mrs Braden's?
3. What is their cat's name?

4 The other rooms

Sandra can see lots of doors – but what are the rooms? *Ask and answer questions in pairs. You are Sandra and Liz.*

5 Sound check with th

Listen and say: [θ] or [ð] ?

Elizabeth is in the bathroom.
There are three trees in the garden.
This is my brother in the other picture.

Max is with the Smith family.
Their things are in the van.
The van is at the airport.

… and be careful here: [ði]

SB

C In one of the rooms Sandra can see a computer. She has got an idea.

Sandra: Can I send an e-mail to my mum and dad from your computer?
Liz: Yes, but that's not our computer. It's Mum's. She's a reporter.
Sandra: You've got two computers?
Liz: Yes. The other computer is in Liam's room.
Sandra: And he's got a modem too?
Liz: Oh, of course – he's a computer freak.

And my sister is a pop music freak!

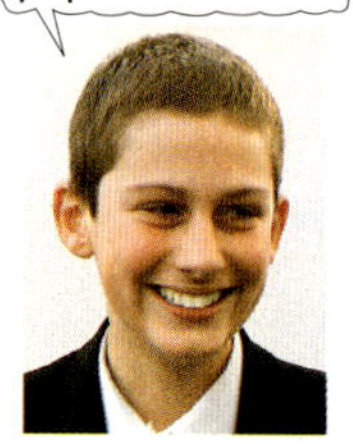

SAVE

you've got = you have got
he's got = he has got

Have (= *haben, besitzen*) *steht meistens mit* got.

I / you / we / they	**have**	got …
he / she / it	**has**	

G 12/13

6 What have they got?

a) *Look at the list and say what the people have got and what they haven't got.* (✓ = yes, ✗ = no)

house		fireplace	garden	garage	computer	van
the Bradens	✓	✓	✓ (small)	✗	✓ (new)	✗
the Cliftons	✓	✓	✓ (big)	✓ (big)	✗	✓ (white)
the Wilsons	✗	✓	✓ (big)	✓ (big)	✗	✓ (green)
Sandra's family	✗	✗	✗	✓ (small)	✓ (old)	✗

b) *Write down what the things are: big, small, green, etc.*

Examples: Liam's computer is new.
The Cliftons' garage is big.

Can you find out when it's … 's or … s'?

c) *Work in pairs and talk about what you've got or haven't got.*

Have you got a …? – No, I / we haven't got a …, but I / we've … .
– Yes, I / we've got a (big / small / new / …) … .

G 14

7 Liz has got a problem

Put in 'my', 'your', 'his', etc.

SAVE

I	– my		we	–	our
you	– your		you	–	your
he	– his		they	–	their
she	– her				
it	– its				

1 … house is very nice, Liz.

2 Yes, it is – … house is nice. But we can't stay here. We've got ten more weeks in this house.

3 What? But that's terrible! Why?

4 You see, … Mum has got a new job, and it isn't in London. It's in Cornwall. Yes, it's terrible! It's OK for Mum – … new job is interesting. And for Dad: he can do … work with old things in the country too. It's OK for … brother – … friends are on the Internet. All of the others can do … hobbies in the country too. Even the cat is happy about … new home! But … hobby is pop music, and London is the place for that. All … friends are here! What can I do in Cornwall?

5 Oh dear!

WHAT'S THAT FUNNY SOUND?

(End of part one)

1 The people in the story

a) There are … people in the story. *Make a list.*

b) *And what's the number of:*

(Mr Clifton is a man,
Mrs Braden is a woman.)

men	women	children
	boys	girls

?

c) *Can you say/guess what is in the box?*

SAVE

man		men
woman	*but lots of:*	women
child		children

G 15

2 Problems, problems

1. The band … play their music in the Cliftons' garage.
2. Mr Clifton has a problem: he … find a place where the Germans … play.
3. Tessa isn't sure about her Uncle Hassan's garage but she … ask.
4. Uncle Hassan … do the work in the garage but the children …
5. There is a hole in the box, but the girls … see what's in it.
6. … Liz look after the dog? – We … say. Ask her mum and dad!

3 Who can say what?

Here are more sentences from the story, but they are not in the pictures.
Who can say what – and when?

Example: Sandra can say this, in / after picture number … / after the story.

- What's the problem?
- The Clifton's have got a new baby.
- We've got a German reggae band here. Can they play in your garage?
- Is your uncle Turkish? He's got a Turkish name.
- No, he's from India. It's an Indian name too. There are lots of Indians in London.
- It's a girl dog, so let's call her Milly. That's a good name.
- No problem, Mrs Braden. She's a nice little dog.
- I can't wait to go to Cornwall!

1 Lost or found

Make ads for these things or animals.

2 Role play: At the Indian restaurant

Dr Modi's brother has got a restaurant in North Islington. It is very good! Liam, Liz and Tessa are there with Tarkan and Sandra. *Play the roles.*

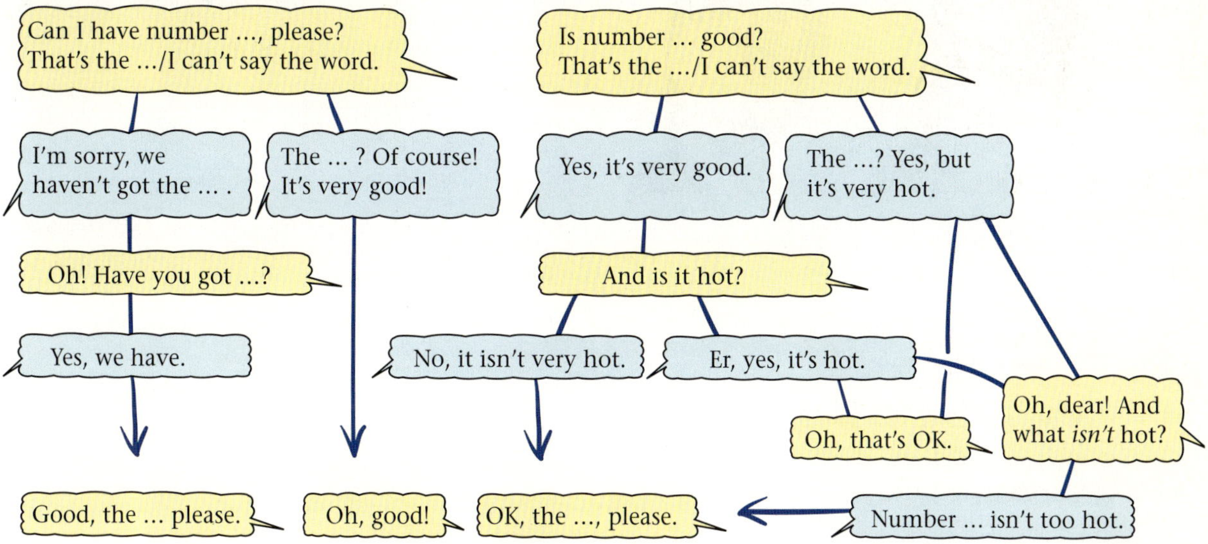

3 ⟨A Beatles song: Hello – Goodbye⟩

a) *Can you remember the story? Say who these people are:*

b) The Beatles have got a song about this.
The words are easy, so sing along with the Beatles.

You say yes, I say no,
You say stop, and I say go, go, go!
Oh. Oh, no!
You say goodbye, and I say hello.

Hello, hello!
I don't know why you say goodbye,
I say hello!

I say high, you say low[1],
You say, why? – and I say I don't know!
Oh. Oh, no!
You say goodbye, and I say hello.

Hello, hello!
I don't know why you say goodbye,
I say hello!

[1] [ləʊ] *niedrig*

4 Your kind of music?

Talk in groups about your kind of music:

- My kind of music is ...
- ... is great / nice / terrible / boring / ...

"I'm into classical music now.
You know, Rolling Stones, Beatles, ..."

"Please turn it down!"

1 Make a mind map

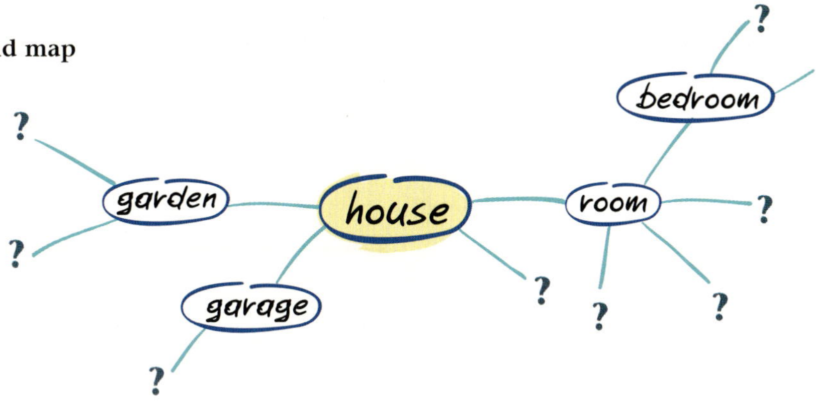

2 This picture – that picture

There … boy in this picture, →
but there … in that picture. ↓

There … girl in this picture, →
but there … in that picture. ↓

There … child in this picture, →
but there … in that picture. ↓

← There … baby in this picture,
↓ but there … in that picture.

← There … man in this picture,
↓ but there … in that picture.

← There … woman in this picture,
↓ but there … in that picture.

3 What can you do?

Work in pairs.

Can you …

say 'How are you?' in Turkish

sing

play the saxophone / the keyboard / …

listen to classical music

fix computers / mountain bikes / …

?

Yes, I can.
No, I can't.

2

1 Upstairs and downstairs

a) *Work in pairs. Ask and answer questions about the Bradens' house. You can ask about:*
- *the rooms,*
- *the things in the rooms,*
- *the garden, etc.*

Where's ...?	It's ...
Where are ...?	They are ...

upstairs | next to ... | in ... | downstairs

How many (things) are there in the ...?
What colour is / are ...?

And where is the cellar?

Oh, we haven't got a cellar!

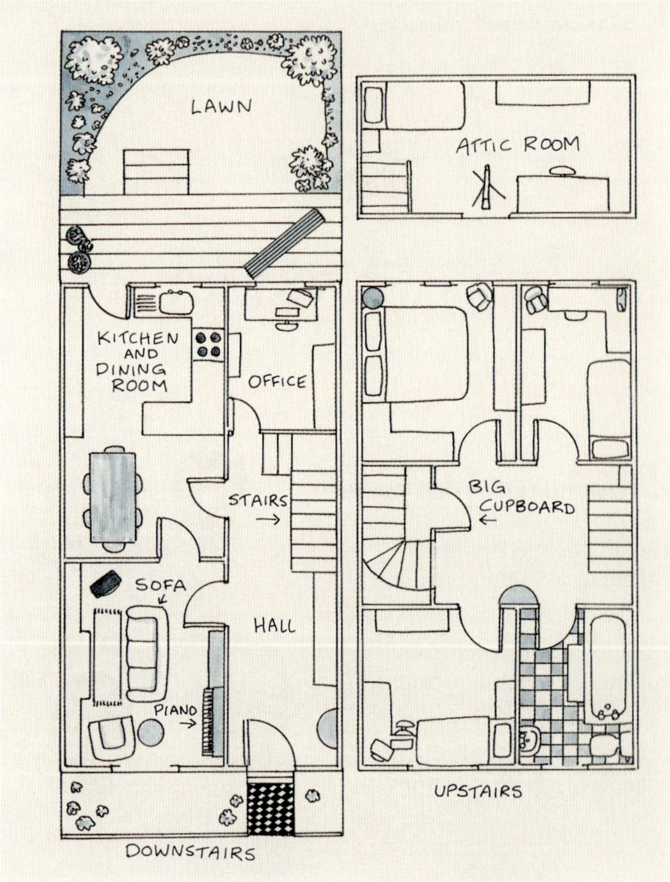

b) *Write a short text about the Bradens' house.*

2 Mr Braden's hobby

Put in the right words. You can find the new words on this page.

Mr Braden's hobby is ... . His hobby room is ... in the ... . He's got a ... there. When Sandra isn't there, he can go ... to his room and look at the ... or at the ... or the ... .

But the ... of London are very bright and sometimes he can't ... a lot of stars. So he is happy to leave the city and go to the ... . The ... can be very good in Cornwall!

1 Find the odd one out

1 red, blue, green, small, yellow

2 table, tree, chair, bed, cupboard

3 music, computer, garden, brother, astronomy

4 girl, boy, animal, man, woman

5 vet, teacher, pilot, flower, reporter

6 London, Berlin, New York, Stuttgart, Islington

1. The odd one out is … . The others are … .
2. … You can put the others … .
3. … The others are … .
4. … The others … .
5. …
6. …

2 What's different?

Use these words to say what is different in picture A and picture B.

have/has got

his/her/their … is/are

there is/are

3 An e-mail to a friend in America

Liz hasn't got a lot of friends on the Internet like Liam, just two or three. But Liam is a computer freak and can do funny things to his sister's e-mail. *Can you put in the words again?*

funny small your dog vet
cat can week music
garage happy her uncle

Hi, Susie,
We've got a German girl with us for two … . She's nice. … name's Sandra. She's in a reggae band. (That's … : a German reggae band! Ha! Ha! But why not? Their … is OK.)
And now, the big story: I've got a dog! She's sweet and I'm … again! (Yes, Max the cat is OK. But Mum and Liam are the 'cat people' in our family; Dad and I are '… people'!)
I can't have her at home. Our house is too … for a dog and a … . But I … look after her in Dr Modi's … . Dr Modi is a … , he's my friend Tessa's … . But that's a long story.
How are things with you?
… English friend, Liz ;–)

4 Listening comprehension: Jimmy who?

HV

Jimmy is on the phone to a friend. *Listen and find out:*

1. Has Jimmy's family got a house or a flat?
2. Has Jimmy got a brother or a sister?
3. What German boy or girl is with Jimmy's family?

Now can you say what Jimmy's family name is?

2

CHECK-IN

	family, *pl.* **-ies** ['fæməli]	Familie(n)
	north [nɔ:θ]	Norden, nördlich
	why [waɪ]	warum
	their [ðeə]	ihr / ihre *(pl.)*
	teacher ['ti:tʃə]	Lehrer(in)
	to **have* got** [ˌhæv 'gɒt]	haben
	front [frʌnt]	Vor-, Vorder-
	tree [tri:]	Baum
	flower ['flaʊə]	Blume
	flat [flæt]	(Etagen-)Wohnung
1	**who** [hu:]	wer
	there is / are [ðeə(r)‿'ɪz / 'ɑ:]	da ist / sind, es gibt
	nice [naɪs]	hübsch, nett
	red [red]	rot
	new [nju:]	neu
	small [smɔ:l]	klein
	white [waɪt]	weiß
	big [bɪg]	groß
	old [əʊld]	alt
	in front [ɪn 'frʌnt]	davor, vorn
	brown [braʊn]	braun
	roof [ru:f]	Dach
2	to **talk (about)** ['tɔ:k‿əˌbaʊt]	sprechen, reden (über)
	to **answer** ['ɑnsə]	antworten
	colour ['kʌlə]	Farbe
	yellow ['jeləʊ]	gelb
	blue [blu:]	blau
	black [blæk]	schwarz
	green [gri:n]	grün
	to **write* (down)** [ˌraɪt 'daʊn]	(auf)schreiben

STEP A

A	**at home** [ət‿'həʊm]	zu Hause, daheim
	room [rʊm]	Zimmer
	under ['ʌndə]	unter
	wall [wɔ:l]	Wand
	table ['teɪbl]	Tisch
	chair ['tʃeə]	Stuhl
	high [haɪ]	hoch
	cupboard ['kʌbəd]	Schrank
	interesting ['ɪntrəstɪŋ]	interessant
1	to **look** [lʊk]	schauen, betrachten
2	to **find*** [ˌfaɪnd‿'aʊt]	finden
	rule [ru:l]	Regel
	Mrs ['mɪsɪz]	Frau *(Anrede für verheiratete Frauen)*
B	**living room** ['lɪvɪŋ rʊm]	Wohnzimmer
	child(ren) [tʃaɪld / 'tʃɪldrn]	Kind(er)
	different ['dɪfrnt]	verschieden, anders(artig)

The Smiths / Wilsons / Mannings / Bradens / Modis are families.

franz famille *lat* familia
engl family

A house in a tree is a tree house.
A flower from a garden is a garden flower.

franz couleur *lat* color
engl colour

Flowers can be red. / yellow. / blue. / white. / …

Here and there,
Who and where …
Words are easy in a pair.

We can talk about interesting houses. / teachers. / hobbies. / gardens. / …

franz différent *lat* differens
engl different

	dad [dæd]	Papa, Vati
	shop [ʃɒp]	Geschäft, Laden
	High Street ['haɪ stri:t]	*Straßenname*
	fireplace ['faɪəpleɪs]	(offener) Kamin
	of course [əv 'kɔ:s]	natürlich, selbstverständlich
	silly ['sɪli]	dumm, kindisch
	to call [kɔ:l]	nennen, (an)rufen
	me [mi:]	mich
	sure [ʃʊə]	sicher, klar
	to do* [du:]	tun, machen
	later ['leɪtə]	später
	to come* [kʌm]	kommen
	mum [mʌm]	Mama, Mutti
3	**cat** [kæt]	Katze
4	**to work** [wɜ:k]	arbeiten
	kitchen ['kɪtʃɪn]	Küche
	office ['ɒfɪs]	Arbeitszimmer, Büro
	bathroom ['bɑ:θrʊm]	Bad, Badezimmer
	bedroom ['bedrʊm]	Schlafzimmer
	van [væn]	Kleinlaster, Lieferwagen
C	**idea** [aɪ'dɪə]	Idee, Einfall
	to send* [send]	schicken, senden
	sister ['sɪstə]	Schwester
6	**garage** ['gærɑ:ʒ]	Garage
7	**terrible** ['terəbl]	schrecklich, furchtbar
	Oh, dear! [əʊ 'dɪə]	Oh je!
	to stay [steɪ]	bleiben
	week [wi:k]	Woche
	to put* [pʊt]	setzen, stellen, legen
	Cornwall ['kɔ:nwɔ:l]	*Region in Südengland*
	country ['kʌntri]	Land
	brother ['brʌðə]	Bruder
	even ['i:vn]	sogar
	happy ['hæpi]	froh, glücklich
	place [pleɪs]	Ort, Platz

STEP B

A	**sound** [saʊnd]	Klang, Ton
	sorry ['sɒri]	(es) tut mir Leid
	early ['ɜ:li]	früh
	to try [traɪ]	versuchen, probieren
	electricity [ˌelɪk'trɪsəti]	Elektrizität, Strom
	uncle ['ʌŋkl]	Onkel
	work [wɜ:k]	Arbeit
	hey! [heɪ]	He!
	to fix [fɪks]	befestigen, reparieren
	box [bɒks]	Kiste, Schachtel
	over there [ˌəʊvə 'ðeə]	da drüben
	hole [həʊl]	Loch
	I don't know [aɪ ˌdəʊnt 'nəʊ]	ich weiß (es) nicht
	to open ['əʊpn]	öffnen, aufmachen

listen	say
come	go
boy	girl
cat	dog
brother	sister
mum	dad
old	new
question	answer
?	?

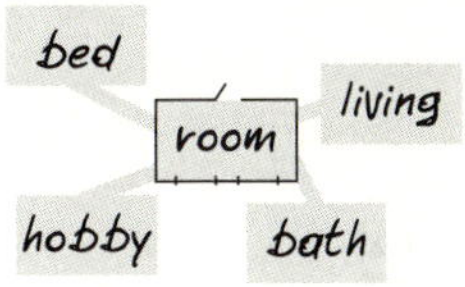

... an idea?

Britain and Germany are countries. Cornwall is part of Britain.

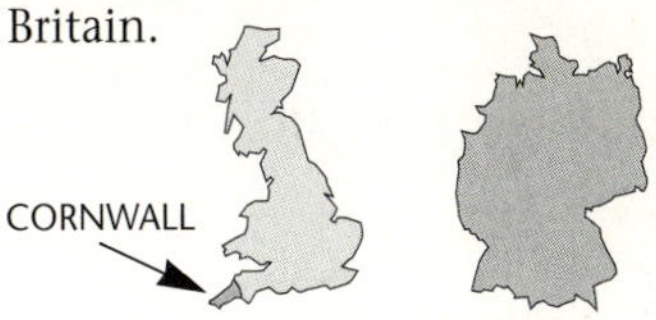

happy unhappy

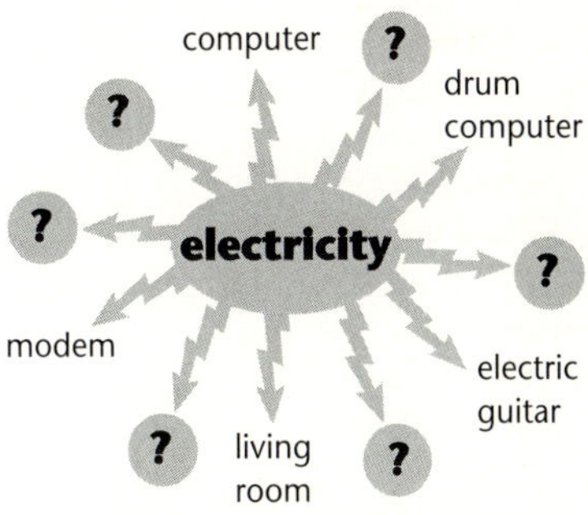

What can you open?
I can open a | door. / window. / book.

	straw [strɔ:]	Stroh
	of [ɒv/əv]	von / vom
	part [pɑ:t]	Teil
1	**people** ['pi:pl]	Leute, Menschen
	story ['stɔ:ri]	Geschichte
	man, *pl.* **men** [mæn / men]	Mann/Männer
	woman, *pl.* **women** ['wʊmən / 'wɪmɪn]	Frau(en)
	to **guess** [ges]	raten, vermuten
B	**dog** [dɒg]	Hund
	food [fu:d]	Essen, Nahrung
	gone [gɒn]	ausgegangen, zu Ende gegangen
	vet (veterinarian) [vet (ˌvetrɪ'neəriən)]	Tierarzt / -ärztin
	hungry ['hʌŋgri]	hungrig
	some [sʌm]	einige
	how [haʊ]	wie
	owner ['əʊnə]	Eigentümer(in), Besitzer(in)
	to **put up** [ˌpʊt‿'ʌp]	aufgeben, aufhängen
	ad (advertisement) [æd (əd'vɜ:tɪsmənt)]	Anzeige
	to **look after** [ˌlʊk‿'ɑ:ftə]	schauen nach, sorgen für
	her [hɜ:]	sie *(Akk.)*; ihr *(Dat.)*
	Dr Modi [ˌdɒktə 'məʊdi]	*Personenname*
	too [tu:]	zu (sehr, viel)
	to **wait** [weɪt]	warten
	if [ɪf]	wenn, falls
	perhaps [pə'hæps]	vielleicht
	bad [bæd]	schlecht
	(not) after all [ˌɑ:ftə‿'ɔ:l]	doch (nicht)
3	**when** [wen]	wenn; wann
	India ['ɪndiə]	Indien
	Indian ['ɪndiən]	Inder(in)
	Milly ['mɪli]	*Hundename (weiblich)*

STEP C

1	**lost** [lɒst]	verloren
	found [faʊnd]	gefunden
	animal ['ænɪml]	Tier
	to **phone** [fəʊn]	telefonieren, anrufen
2	**role play** ['rəʊlpleɪ]	Rollenspiel
	very ['verɪ]	sehr
	hot [hɒt]	heiß; *hier:* scharf (gewürzt)
⟨3⟩	**Beatles** ['bi:tlz]	*bekannte Rockgruppe*
	to **remember** [rɪ'membə]	sich erinnern (an)
	along (with) [ə'lɒŋ]	zusammen (mit)
4	**What kind (of) ...?**	Was für eine/welche Art ...?
	great [greɪt]	großartig, spitze
	boring ['bɔ:rɪŋ]	langweilig
	I'm into ... ['ɪntə]	*hier:* ich stehe auf ... / ich bin begeistert von ...
	Rolling Stones [ˌrəʊlɪŋ 'stəʊnz]	*bekannte Rockgruppe*
	to **turn down** [ˌtɜ:n 'daʊn]	herunterdrehen, leiser stellen

double trouble

di..erent	sw..t
si..y	r..m
ca..	te..ible
fu..y	gr..n
wa..	ye..ow
ho..y	sma..
tr..	r..f

You've got a dog?
So you are a
dog owner.

A woman
from India
is an Indian.

Milly is a dog.
A dog is an animal.

franz animal *lat* animal
engl animal

A
BORING
STORY

C D-ROM
o nline
m odem
p roblem
u se
t each
e -mail
r ule

TRACK 2

1	+**upstairs** [ˌʌp'steəz]	oben; Obergeschoss
	+**downstairs** [ˌdaʊn'steəz]	unten; Erdgeschoss
	+**next to** ['nekst tu:]	neben, in der Nähe von
	+**attic** ['ætɪk]	Dachboden
	+**lawn** [lɔ:n]	Rasen
	+**dining room** ['daɪnɪŋ ˌrʊm]	Esszimmer
	+**stairs** [steəz]	Treppe
	+**hall** [hɔ:l]	Diele, Eingangshalle
	+**cellar** ['selə]	Keller
	+**how many?** ['haʊ ˌmeni]	wie viele?
2	+**page** [peɪdʒ]	Seite
	+**bright** [braɪt]	hell, leuchtend
	+**sometimes** ['sʌmtaɪmz]	manchmal
	+to **leave*** [li:v]	verlassen
	+**sky** [skaɪ]	Himmel
	+**star** [stɑ:]	Stern
	+**moon** [mu:n]	Mond
	+**light** [laɪt]	Licht

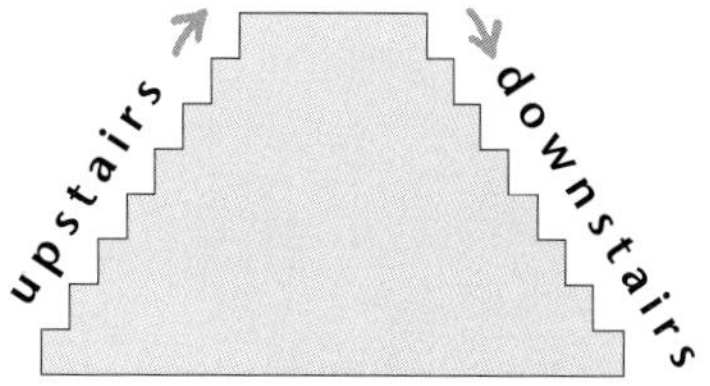

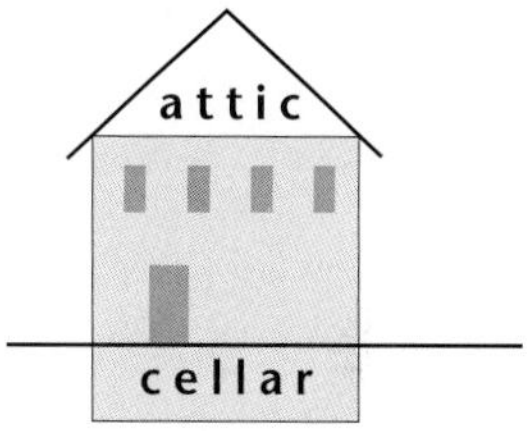

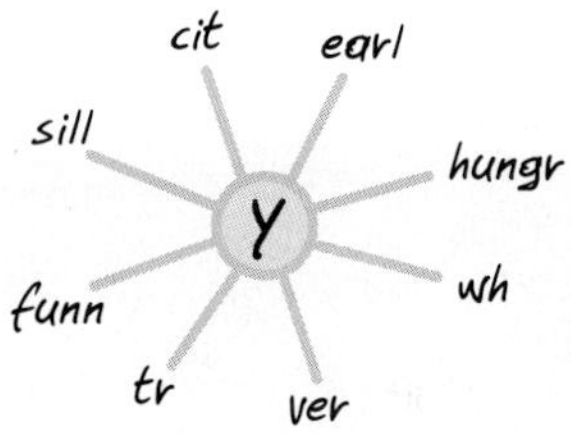

CHECK-OUT

2	**New York** [ˌnju: 'jɔ:k]	New York
	to **use** [ju:z]	benutzen, gebrauchen
3	**America** [ə'merɪkə]	Amerika
	like [laɪk]	(ebenso) wie
	funny ['fʌni]	witzig, spaßig
	us [ʌs]	uns
	sweet [swi:t]	süß, niedlich
4	**phone** [fəʊn]	Telefon
	now [naʊ]	nun, jetzt

franz problème *lat* problema
engl problem

COGNATE WORDS

astronomy [ə'strɒnəmi]	Astronomie	**job** [dʒɒb]	Job, Arbeit, Stelle
baby ['beɪbi]	Baby	**modem** ['məʊdem]	Modem
bed [bed]	Bett	**planet** ['plænɪt]	Planet
computer [kəm'pju:tə]	Computer, Rechner	**pop music** ['pɒp ˌmju:zɪk]	Popmusik
e-mail ['i:meɪl]	elektronische Post, E-Mail	**problem** ['prɒbləm]	Problem
end [end]	Ende, Schluss	**restaurant** ['restrɔ:ŋ]	Restaurant
freak [fri:k]	Fan, Anhänger(in)	**so** [səʊ]	so, also
garden ['gɑ:dn]	Garten	**sofa** ['səʊfə]	Sofa, Couch
group [gru:p]	Gruppe	to **start** [stɑ:t]	anfangen, beginnen
hobby, *pl.* **-ies** ['hɒbi]	Hobby(s)	**telescope** ['telɪskəʊp]	Teleskop, Fernrohr
house [haʊs]	Haus	**text** [tekst]	Text
Internet ['ɪntənet]	Internet	**TV** [ˌti:'vi:]	Fernseher
		version [vɜ:ʃn]	Version, Fassung

UNIT 3

At Islington Green

1 Listening comprehension: Welcome and thanks

Mr Todd (headteacher): Well, let's give a big thank you to our German friends. Their music is a great way to start assembly this week. Welcome to our school and thanks for 'The Good Vibes'. (*Cheers and clapping*) Perhaps you want to ask the Germans some questions. … Yes, Pamela Kwang from Year 7?

Listen and note down some key words. What are the questions about?

ASSEMBLY					
	MONDAY	TUESDAY	WEDNESDAY	THURSDAY	FRIDAY
8.55 – 9.45	Science	PE	Art	English	Maths
9.45 – 10.35	Science	Drama	French	French	PE
10.35 – 10.50			BREAK		
10.50 – 11.40	IT	Geography	History	Science	Geography
11.40 – 12.30	Maths	English	Maths	Music	English
12.30 – 1.25			LUNCH		
1.30 – 2.25	History	French	Games	IT	Science
2.25 – 3.15	English	PE	Games	Design + Technology	Health

G 16 2 Year 7's timetable

a) *Ask and answer questions about Year 7's timetable. Here are some examples. Work with a partner.*

1. What's the first lesson after assembly on ...?
2. What's the subject before lunch on ...?
3. What's the last lesson on ...?
4. What's before / after break on ...?
5. How many ... lessons have they got?

b) *Write down your timetable in English. What is the same? What is different?*

21	twenty-one	[ˌtwentiˈwʌn]
22	twenty-two	[ˌtwentiˈtuː]
23	twenty-three	[ˌtwentiˈθriː]
...		
30	thirty	[ˈθɜːti]
31	thirty-one	[ˌθɜːtiˈwʌn]
...		
40	forty	[ˈfɔːti]
50	fifty	[ˈfɪfti]
60	sixty	[ˈsɪksti]
70	seventy	[ˈsevnti]
80	eighty	[ˈeɪti]
90	ninety	[ˈnaɪnti]
100	a / one hundred	[ˈhʌndrəd]

G 17 3 What time is it?

a) *What time is Science on Monday morning?*

You can say: Science is at eight fifty-five. *Or:* Science is at five to nine.
Go on with: What time is ... on ... morning / afternoon?

eight o'clock | five past eight | quarter past eight | half past eight | twenty-five to nine | quarter to nine

b) *What time is it now?* 7.00 12.30 10.20 8.45 11.50 8.05 9.55 6.15

3

Tarkan

A Tarkan tells Tessa Clifton a bit about school and homework in Germany.

I go to school in Neunkirchen. I usually go there on my bike – it's only ten minutes from home. At school I like Maths and IT. I don't get much homework, only about 30 minutes. I always do it in the kitchen and listen to music at the same time. My parents don't like that. After that, I often work on my computer.

At break the next morning Tessa talks to Jimmy Wilson. Jimmy wants to know all about Tarkan.

Jimmy: What's Tarkan like, Tessa? Tell me more about him. Is he OK?
Tessa: Well, you know he plays the drum computer for 'The Good Vibes'. He doesn't sing for them. He lives in Langenfeld with his mum and dad and his two sisters. They don't like his reggae music. They like Turkish music.
Jimmy: And what about his school in Germany?
Tessa: He usually goes to school on his bike. He likes Maths and IT. He doesn't get much homework. He usually does it in the kitchen. After that he works on his computer.
Jimmy: What are his other hobbies?
Tessa: He says he doesn't watch TV but he likes kung fu films. He also likes football and backgammon. He sometimes plays football for Neunkirchen football club. He doesn't smoke and he never drinks. And later on, he wants to get a job in a big city and work with computers.
Jimmy: He seems OK. Can I come round some time and have a game of backgammon with him?
Tessa: Yes, why not? Any time!

G 18/19

1 What Tarkan does

What can you say about Tarkan?

		does	music in the kitchen.
	sometimes	sings	football for a club.
	often	works	to school on his bike.
Tarkan	usually	goes	for 'The Good Vibes'.
	always	listens to	kung fu films on TV.
	never	plays	on his computer.
		watches	his homework in the kitchen.

YOU

2 And what about you?

a) *Say where you go to school, how you usually get there, what you like/don't like at school, where and when you do your homework, etc.*

b) *Write a short article about your best friend. Start like this:* My best friend is in Year … . His/her name …

SAVE

want	wants			listen	listens			go	goes	[z]
work	works	[s]		play	plays	[z]		watch	watches	[ɪz]
like	likes			sing	sings			do	does	[ʌz]

B Later that morning Liz takes Milly back to Dr Modi's house.

Dr Modi: Hello, Liz. Ah, you've got Milly with you. ... Yes, thank you for your phone call. I'm sorry about assembly. But I sometimes forget to shut that garage door. Is everything all right at school now? Does your headteacher like dogs?

Liz: Yes, he does, very much. And Milly is a very friendly dog. So everything's OK. Dr Modi, don't you have problems with Milly here? Is she a good dog? Doesn't she bark a lot?

Dr Modi: No, she doesn't, not really. And anyway I understand her now. But what about Liam's cat when you take Milly to your house? Don't they fight?

Liz: No, they don't. Not now. Milly still chases Max all the time, but it's only for fun. I think Max likes Milly.

Dr Modi: And what about your parents? Do they like Milly?

Liz: Yes, they do. They really love her.

Dr Modi: And what do you want to do with Milly when you move to Cornwall?

Liz: Take her for long walks by the sea, of course.

Dr Modi: Would you like to play with her a bit now?

Liz: Yes, but I can't. ... Oh no, look at the time! I must get back to school. Bye, Dr Modi. And thank you.

SAVE

do [du:] + not = don't
does [dʌz] + not = doesn't

Do	I need ...?	Don't	I take ...?
Do	you think ...?	Don't	you want ...?
	he		he
Does	she like ...?	Doesn't	she eat ...?
	it		it
Do	we know ...?	Don't	we play ...?
Do	you hate ...?	Don't	you drink ...?
Do	they chase ...?	Don't	they need ...?

3 People in your class

Compare two people in your class. Start like this:

Martin likes rock music but Thomas doesn't like it.
Stephanie doesn't play ... but ... *Go on.*

G 19/20

4 Sometimes, never

Make sentences. Be careful with word order.

1. a new CD / Liz / has got
2. the computer / can use / Sandra
3. bullies / the boy / the girls
4. often / Tarkan / on his computer / works
5. to school / he / always / on his bike / goes
6. Milly / understands / Dr Modi / usually
7. the garage door / sometimes / forgets to shut / he
8. chases / Max / Milly / all the time

G 21/22

5 Questions with 'do', 'does', 'don't' and 'doesn't'

	you	work					
	your friend	chase					
Do	your parents	eat			Yes,	I	do.
Does	cats	drink				he, she, it	does.
Don't	dogs	like	...	?		we	don't.
Doesn't	teachers	play			No,	they	doesn't.
	vets	live					
	Max	want to					

6 A quiz

Write down ten questions for an interview with a boy or girl in your class. Start with 'does' or 'do'.

Examples: Does your friend / sister / brother play ...? – No, he / she doesn't.
Do your friends / parents like ...? – Yes, they do.

Sandra's recordings

The next morning Sandra goes to Islington Green again with Liz and Liam. Sandra wants to write an article for her school magazine in Neunkirchen. Liam has got a good idea. Sandra interviews some pupils from his class after lunch. The cafeteria is a good place for the recordings.

I'm James. 14 years old. I live with my mum. Most of my friends know that my parents are split up, I think. But I don't know how many others at school have parents who are split up.
Nobody seems to talk about it.
My mum works shift. So she's not always at home. I do most of the practical jobs around the house. We've got a dog. So I spend two or three hours a night with him. I like animals. I want to be a vet one day.
Drugs? Yes, I think there are drugs at school. They always talk about them. But I spend my money on our dog.

I'm Joanna. I'm 14 too. I live with my mum and dad and my baby brother. Well, at school I like Maths and Sports. But we get too much homework – 50 minutes a night!
Bullies? Yes, there are three or four boys who are bullies. Sometimes they push me over. And one of these silly boys chases me around all the time! And then he rings me up at home.

Hi, I'm Gina and I'm 14. I live with my mum and dad, my brother, twelve, and my baby sister, four.
Bullies? Yes, of course there are some bullies here. But it's better here than in my old school.
Smoking? Well, lots of kids smoke at school. Most of the girls smoke, not so many boys. But I hate it. It makes me sick.

I'm Ben. I'm 15. I'm sport mad – football, basketball, hockey, …
Homework? Yes, I do my homework the night I get it. I plan it round what's on the telly.
Drugs? Our teachers try to teach us about drugs. But they're not very up to date. We know more about drugs than the teachers.
I don't take drugs because of my sports. I want to stay fit.
And I don't drink. But some of my friends do.
Girlfriend? No, I haven't got the time for a girlfriend. It's because of my sports, you know.

Hello, I'm Stephanie. I'm 15. I live with my mum and my brother. This school is OK. I've got my friends here. I like English and Music.
Homework? Yes, I do about one hour at night.
When I'm not at school I like to play volleyball and watch sports on TV.
My best friend – he's not my boyfriend – lives over the road. And his baby sister gets on with my baby brother. So we all go out and play together in the evening. Mum makes sure we're in by nine o'clock.
Pocket money? Well, I get £2.50 a week from my grandma and a bit more for extra jobs. Later I want a job round here and I want to look after my mum when she's old.

1 A mind map

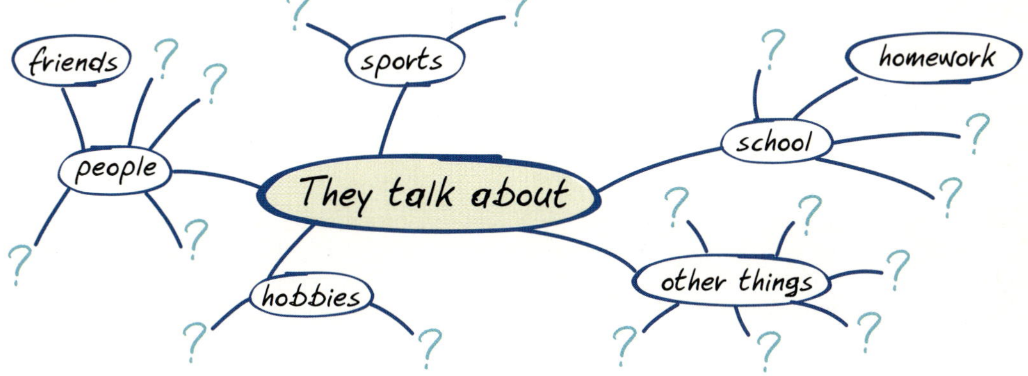

2 Who says what?

Go through the recordings and find out who says what.

Example: "My mum works shift." – James says that.

- I like Maths and Sports.
- Most of the girls smoke.
- I like English and Music.
- And then he rings me up at home.
- I don't drink.
- Sometimes they push me over.
- I do my homework at night.

3 What do they like?

G 23

a) *Answer the questions.*

What does	James Joanna Gina Ben Stephanie	like love hate want	?

b) *And what about you?*
What do you like/love/hate/want?

4 More questions

Can you ask and answer these questions?

Example: Who wants to be a vet? – That's James. He wants to be a vet one day.

Who	lives likes hates wants plays watches chases works gives rings	music? with his mum? the pocket money? with her best friend? Joanna around all the time? animals? to be a vet? sports on TV? smoking? shift? with her baby brother? Joanna up at home? volleyball?

5 What they often do

YOU

*Say what your family sometimes, often, usually, always, never does. Be careful: sometimes, often, etc. always go **before** the verb!*

Examples: At night my sister always watches TV.
My parents sometimes work at weekends.

At night ... After school ... ... around the house. ... with the dog.

(?) At the weekends ... At home ... ... with friends. (?)

6 What teachers often say

A good pupil ...

his or her / homework / does / always
books / forgets / his or her / never
smoke / doesn't / school / at
good / books / reads / always
takes / drugs / never

never / girls / bullies / boys / other / and
does / say / teachers / always / what
drinks / never / alcohol
other / the / kids / always / helps
at night / doesn't / watch / TV

1 Bullies and bullying

Read the text, look at the pictures and answer the questions.

a) *What is this boy's problem?*

b) *Write a new text for the pictures. You can start like this:*

I bet my brother has got more pocket money than me. *Or:*
I bet my friend has got more computer games than me.

c) "Inside every bully there is a small helpless person."
What do you think? Do bullies have problems too? Discuss.

[1] letting (to let) *lassen* [2] she'll (she will) *sie wird*

YOU

2 And what about you?

Talk about your school. Here are some ideas to help you.

Example: I like my school but ...
My teachers ...

My favourite subjects ...

I hate ...

My friends are ...

Xday is a good day for me because ...

G 24

3 This/that – these/those

Put in the right words.

1. Is ... your dog over there?
2. Look at ... instrument here.
3. Let's look at ... computers over there.
4. Oh yes, ... computer here is interesting.
5. Look at ... picture of my brothers: ... is Pete and ... is Dave.
6. Can you see ... bullies over there? I hate them.
7. Sometimes they push me over. I don't like ... .

3

3 Learning tip: Working with words

a) *Pictures can help you to learn new words.*

b) *Slogans can help you to learn grammar.*

Example: He – she – it: *Das ‚s' muss mit!*

c) *Grids can help you.*

	Nähe	*Ferne*
singular	this	that
plural	these	those

d) *Acrostics can help you.*

SOMETIMES
CHILDREN
HOMEWORK
OVER
OFTEN
LEARN

4 ⟨A song: Respect yourself[1]⟩

[1] [rɪ'spekt jɔː'self] *respektiere dich (selbst)* [2] ['tʃeɪndʒ jɔː 'maɪnd] *deine Meinung ändern* [3] [blaɪnd] *blind* [4] [laɪt] *Licht* [5] [ˌiːtʃ_'ʌðə] *einander, sich (gegenseitig)* [6] ['præktɪs] *ausführen, praktizieren* [7] [preɪ] *beten, erbitten* [8] ['reɪnbəʊ] *Regenbogen* [9] ['mɪs jɔː_'eɪm] *dein Ziel verfehlen* [10] [ˌʃəʊ 'wiːknəs] *Schwäche zeigen* [11] (= got to) ['gɒtə] *müssen* [12] (= want to) ['wɒnə] *wollen* [13] [grəʊ] *wachsen*

1 Max the cat

Liam's cat Max is funny. He likes Liam's bedroom but not the kitchen. His favourite food is hot dogs, not cat food. He loves guitar music but not the cello. In the evening Max always sits on the telly, not on the sofa. And he plays with dogs, not with other cats. He runs after children, not after a ball. Sandra doesn't understand him.

Sandra: Doesn't Max like the kitchen?
Liam: No, he doesn't. He likes …

Go on.

WP

2 Words in pairs

Write down the pairs in groups. One pair means nearly the same. One pair is singular and plural. Five pairs are opposites. Seven pairs are words of the same group.

talk	boyfriend	before	teacher
day	basketball	lesson	
always	microphone	eleven	sing
him	the first	different	

speak	pupil	break	her
girlfriend	the same		football
never	song	twelve	after
night	the last		cassette

3 Graffiti fun

Can you translate them? Use the word list at the end of your book.

A guide dog in New York

Hello, everybody! I'm Mark Morton.
But let my dog speak first:

1 My name is Blacky. I'm a German shepherd and I work as a guide dog for Mark Morton here in New York City. I wear a leather harness. It's like a uniform for me. It lets everybody know that I'm a special dog.

2 Well, yes, Blacky is always with me. We make a good team. At night she sleeps on the floor next to my bed. Blacky obeys my commands of 'forward', 'right', 'left', 'sit', and 'come'. I always say 'good girl' to her. But sometimes she does things wrong because she doesn't pay attention or doesn't understand. Then I say the German word 'pfui' to her. And then she knows she must try again. She sees what is dangerous to a blind person: bicycles, stones, doorsteps … Well, what else can Blacky tell you? Let her do it for me.

3 Yes. These things are very important for us:

1. Don't touch us. You confuse us and we can't pay attention then.
2. Don't say 'come here' to us. We must stay together.
3. But you must tell us when the traffic lights are green. We are colour-blind.
4. And please tell us the numbers of the buses. We can't read.
5. Please give way.
6. Keep your own dogs back. We don't play when we are at work.
7. Don't give us a shock with loud music or mopeds.
8. And don't be afraid of us.

Thank you.

1 That's why!

Put the right parts of the sentences together.

1. Blacky sleeps on the floor next to Mark's bed
2. Sometimes Blacky does things wrong
3. Mark says 'pfui' to her
4. Don't touch guide dogs
5. Tell a blind person when the traffic lights are green
6. And also tell them the numbers of the buses
7. Be careful with loud noises

because

- that confuses them.
- she doesn't pay attention.
- dogs are colour-blind.
- she must always be with him.
- that gives them a shock.
- dogs can't read.
- she must try again.

1 What do we know now?

A headteacher Teachers A bully A friend Baby brothers and baby sisters Parents A good pupil	sometimes always usually never often	like want take watch do go	play drink get on well know smoke	drugs. to school. to assembly. alcohol. sports on TV. with friends. his / her homework. games. how to learn.

2 My favourite day at school

My My friend's Our My friends'	favourite day at school is	MON TUE WED THUR FRI	because	I he / she we they	can	play ... talk about ...
					like love	Maths, ...

3 Crack the code

	1	2	3	4	5	6	7
1	A	B	C	D	E	F	G
2	H	I	J	K	L	M	N
3	O	P	Q	R	S	T	U
4	V	W	X	Y	Z		

A = 1/1, B = 1/2, C = 1/3, ...,
V = 4/1, W = 4/2, and so on.

Now read these names:

3/5, 1/5, 1/2, 1/1, 3/5, 3/6, 2/2, 1/1, 2/7
3/5, 1/1, 2/7, 1/4, 3/4, 1/1
1/3, 2/5, 2/2, 1/6, 3/6, 3/1, 2/7

And now write these words down in code:
headteacher, boyfriend, computer, ...

4 How to ask questions

Du möchtest wissen ...

- ob es *bullies* an englischen Schulen gibt.
- ob dein(e) Gesprächspartner(in) Musik mag.
- wie viel Taschengeld die anderen pro Woche erhalten.
- wie viele Stunden pro Woche jemand fernsieht.
- wo jemand wohnt.

What's ...?
How many ...?
How much ...?
Do you ...?
Where do you ...?
Are there ...?

3

CHECK-IN

1	**Islington Green** [ˌɪslɪŋtən ˈgriːn]	*Name einer Schule*
	headteacher [ˌhedˈtiːtʃə]	Schulleiter(in)
	way [weɪ]	Art und Weise, Weg
	assembly [əˈsembli]	(Schul-)Versammlung
	thanks [θæŋks]	danke
	cheer [tʃɪə]	Jubel, Beifall
	clapping [ˈklæpɪŋ]	Klatschen, Applaus
	to **want** [wɒnt]	wollen, wünschen
	year [jɪə]	(Schul-)Jahr; Jahrgang, Klasse
	to **note (down)** [ˌnəʊt ˈdaʊn]	notieren, (auf)schreiben
	key word [ˈkiː wɜːd]	Schlüsselwort
	°**Science** [ˈsaɪəns]	(Natur-)Wissenschaften
	°**IT (Information Technology)** [ˌaɪˈtiː (ˌɪnfəˈmeɪʃn tekˈnɒlədʒi)]	Informatik
	°**History** [ˈhɪstri]	Geschichte
	°**PE (Physical Education)** [ˌpiːˈiː (ˈfɪzɪkl ˌedʒʊˈkeɪʃn)]	Sport, Turnen
	°**French** [ˈfrentʃ]	französisch, Französisch
	°**Art** [ɑːt]	Kunst
	break [breɪk]	Pause
	lunch [lʌntʃ]	Mittagessen
	°**Health** [helθ]	Gesundheitslehre
2	**timetable** [ˈtaɪmˌteɪbl]	Stundenplan
	first [ˈfɜːst]	erste(r / s), der / die Erste
	lesson [ˈlesn]	Unterrichtsstunde
	subject [ˈsʌbdʒɪkt]	(Unterrichts-)Fach; Thema
	after [ˈɑːftə]	nach
	before [bɪˈfɔː]	vor
	last [lɑːst]	letzte(r / s), der / die Letzte
	how many? [ˈhaʊ ˌmeni]	wie viele?
	same [seɪm]	gleich, dasselbe
3	**morning** [ˈmɔːnɪŋ]	Morgen, Vormittag
	afternoon [ˌɑːftəˈnuːn]	Nachmittag
	10 **o'clock** [əˈklɒk]	10 Uhr
	past [pɑːst]	nach
	quarter (to/past) [ˈkwɔːtə]	Viertel (vor / nach)
	half [hɑːf]	halb

STEP A

A	to **tell*** [tel]	erzählen
	a bit [ə ˈbɪt]	ein wenig, ein bisschen
	homework *sing.* [ˈhəʊmwɜːk]	Hausaufgaben
	usually [ˈjuːʒli]	gewöhnlich, normalerweise
	only [ˈəʊnli]	nur
	to **like** [laɪk]	mögen, gerne haben
	much [mʌtʃ]	viel
	always [ˈɔːlweɪz]	immer
	parents [ˈpeərnts]	Eltern

The boys, girls and teachers of a school start the day or the week with assembly.

Pamela is in year 7.
It's her seventh year at school.

franz noter *lat* notare
engl to note

The days of the week

Mon	Tue	Wed	Thu	Fri	Sat	Sun

Monday	[ˈmʌndeɪ]	*Montag*
Tuesday	[ˈtjuːzdeɪ]	*Dienstag*
Wednesday	[ˈwenzdeɪ]	*Mittwoch*
Thursday	[ˈθɜːzdeɪ]	*Donnerstag*
Friday	[ˈfraɪdeɪ]	*Freitag*
Saturday	[ˈsætədeɪ]	*Samstag*
Sunday	[ˈsʌndeɪ]	*Sonntag*

learn
early
sit
still
over
number

In schools in Britain there is a lunch break.

franz leçon *lat* lectio
engl lesson

A man and a woman are parents when they have a child or children.

franz parents *lat* parentes
engl parents

	often ['ɒfn]	oft, öfters
	him [hɪm]	ihn, ihm
	next [nekst]	nächste(r / s), der / die Nächste
	to live [lɪv]	wohnen, leben
	to watch [wɒtʃ]	anschauen, zuschauen
	to watch TV [ˌwɒtʃ tiː'viː]	fernsehen
	also ['ɔːlsəʊ]	auch, ebenfalls
	sometimes ['sʌmtaɪmz]	manchmal
	to smoke [sməʊk]	rauchen
	never ['nevə]	nie(mals)
	to drink* [drɪŋk]	trinken
	to seem [siːm]	(er)scheinen
	to come round [ˌkʌm 'raʊnd]	vorbeikommen, herüberkommen
	any time [ˌeni 'taɪm]	jederzeit
1	**to take*** [teɪk]	nehmen, (hin)bringen
B	**back** [bæk]	zurück, Hinter-
	(phone) call [('fəʊn) kɔːl]	Anruf
	to forget* [fə'get]	vergessen
	to shut* [ʃʌt]	schließen
	everything ['evriθɪŋ]	alles
	all right [ˌɔːl 'raɪt]	in Ordnung
	friendly ['frendli]	freundlich, angenehm
	to bark [bɑːk]	bellen
	really ['rɪəli]	wirklich
	anyway ['eniweɪ]	ohnehin, sowieso
	to understand* [ˌʌndə'stænd]	verstehen
	to fight* [faɪt]	streiten, kämpfen
	still [stɪl]	noch
	to chase [tʃeɪs]	(herum)jagen
	to think* [θɪŋk]	denken, glauben, meinen
	to move [muːv]	(sich) bewegen, *hier:* umziehen
	walk [wɔːk]	Spaziergang
	sea [siː]	Meer, (die) See
	would you like to? [wʊd ˌjuː 'laɪk tə]	möchtest du? / möchtet ihr / möchten Sie?
	must [mʌst]	müssen
3	**to compare** [kəm'peə]	vergleichen
4	**pupil** ['pjuːpl]	Schüler(in)
5	**to eat*** [iːt]	essen

STEP B

recording [rɪ'kɔːdɪŋ]	Aufzeichnung, (Ton-)Aufnahme
most (of) ['məʊst‿əv]	meiste(r / s)
to split* up [ˌsplɪt‿'ʌp]	sich (voneinander) trennen
who [huː]	der / die / das, welche(r / s)
nobody ['nəʊbədi]	niemand
to work shift [ˌwɜːk 'ʃɪft]	Schicht arbeiten, Schichtdienst machen
hour ['aʊə]	Stunde
night [naɪt]	Nacht
day [deɪ]	Tag
drug [drʌg]	Droge

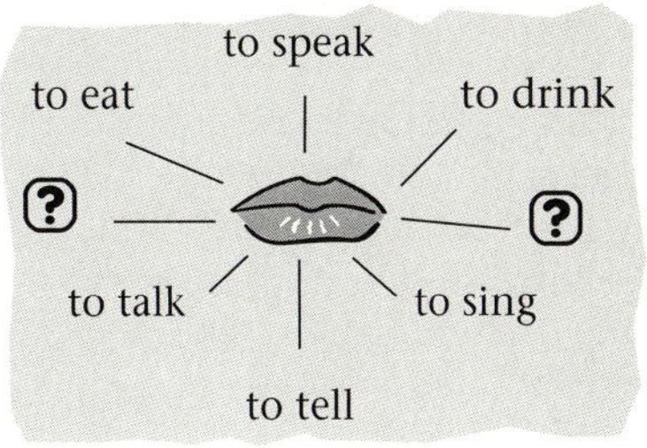

the first	the last
before	after
morning	afternoon
always	sometimes
a bit	a lot
brother	sister
pupil	teacher
boy	girl
to open	to shut

b**a**rk
dri**n**k
s**i**t
move
e**a**t
love

franz comparer *lat* comparare
engl to compare

child
brot**h**er
pup**i**l
gir**l**
frien**d**
gi**r**lfriend
sist**e**r
boyfrie**n**d

Most people think day shifts are better than night shifts.

franz heure *lat* hora
engl hour

3

	to spend* [spend]	verbrauchen, ausgeben; verbringen
	money ['mʌni]	Geld
	bully, *pl.* **-ies** ['bʊli]	Schlägertyp, Angeber(in)
	to push so. over [ˌpʊʃ‿'əʊvə]	jmdn umstoßen
	to ring* so. up [ˌrɪŋ‿'ʌp]	jmdn anrufen
	baby sister [ˌbeɪbi 'sɪstə]	(ganz) kleine Schwester
	better ['betə]	besser
	smoking ['sməʊkɪŋ]	(das) Rauchen
	kid [kɪd]	Kind
	to hate [heɪt]	nicht mögen, hassen
	sick [sɪk]	krank, übel
	mad [mæd]	verrückt, wahnsinnig
	telly ['teli]	Fernseher
	girlfriend ['gɜ:lfrend]	Freundin
	boyfriend ['bɔɪfrend]	Freund
	over ['əʊvə]	hinüber
	road [rəʊd]	Straße
	to get on (well with so.) [ˌget‿ɒn 'wel]	(gut mit jmdm) zurechtkommen
	together [tə'geðə]	zusammen
	evening ['i:vnɪŋ]	Abend
	to make sure [ˌmeɪk 'ʃʊə]	sicherstellen
	by [baɪ]	an, neben, bis
	pocket money ['pɒkɪt ˌmʌni]	Taschengeld
	grandma ['grænmɑ:]	Großmutter, Oma
2	**through** [θru:]	durch, über
5	**weekend** [ˌwi:k'end]	Wochenende
6	**book** [bʊk]	Buch

STEP C

1	**to bet*** [bet]	wetten
	inside [ˌɪn'saɪd]	im Innern (von)
	every ['evri]	jede(r / s)
	helpless ['helpləs]	hilflos
	to discuss [dɪ'skʌs]	diskutieren, besprechen
2	**favourite** ['feɪvrɪt]	bevorzugt, Lieblings-
3	**learning tip** ['lɜ:nɪŋ ˌtɪp]	Lerntipp
	°**grid** [grɪd]	Netz, Gitter
	those [ðəʊz]	jene, diese (*pl.*)
	°**acrostic** [ə'krɒstɪk]	Akrostichon (*nacheinander zu lesende Buchstaben, die ein Wort ergeben*)

TRACK 1

1	**to lie*** [laɪ]	liegen
	to run* [rʌn]	rennen, laufen
	to be **surprised** [sə'praɪzd]	überrascht sein
2	**down** [daʊn]	hinunter, unten
	to mean* [mi:n]	bedeuten; meinen
	nearly ['nɪəli]	fast, beinahe

I hate smoking and alcohol.

Drugs make you sick.

Some people are sport mad. / TV mad. / music mad.

My boyfriend lives over the road.

My grandma and grandpa always get on well together.

pocket money: magazine, hot dogs, hobbies, job, music, computer, shopping, phone, pet, books, extra money

Fun with letters

He <u>b</u>arks <u>a</u>t a <u>b</u>ully.
I <u>h</u>ear you are <u>h</u>elpless.
We <u>r</u>un <u>r</u>ound a <u>r</u>oom.
Go on.

Noun and verb

magazine	–	look at
hot dog	–	..t
article	–	r..d
cafeteria	–	s.t
sport	–	d.
hockey	–	pl.y
coffee	–	dr.nk
homework	–	d.
cassette	–	l.st.n t.
e-mail	–	wr.t.
shock	–	g.v.

	opposite ['ɒpəzɪt]	Gegenteil; gegenüber
	to **speak*** [spi:k]	sprechen
3	to **translate** [træns'leɪt]	übersetzen

TRACK 2

	+**guide dog** ['gaɪd dɒg]	Blindenhund
	+**New York City** [ˌnju: jɔ:k 'sɪti]	New York
	+**Blacky** ['blæki]	*Hundename*
	+**shepherd** *AE* ['ʃepəd]	Schäferhund
	+to **wear*** [weə]	tragen
	+**leather harness** [ˌleðə 'hɑ:nɪs]	Ledergeschirr, -gurtwerk
	+**floor** [flɔ:]	Fußboden
	+to **obey** [ə'beɪ]	gehorchen
	+**forward** ['fɔ:wəd]	vorwärts
	+to **sit*** [sɪt]	sitzen
	+to **pay attention** [ˌpeɪ‿ə'tenʃn]	aufmerksam sein, achtsam sein
	+**then** [ðen]	dann
	+**dangerous** ['deɪndʒrəs]	gefährlich
	+**important** [ɪm'pɔ:tnt]	wichtig
	+to **touch** [tʌtʃ]	berühren, anfassen
	+to **confuse** [kən'fju:z]	verwirren, irritieren
	+**traffic light** ['træfɪk ˌlaɪt]	Ampel
	+to **show*** [ʃəʊ]	zeigen
	+**colour-blind** ['kʌləblaɪnd]	farbenblind
	+**loud** [laʊd]	laut
	+to **be afraid** [ə'freɪd]	Angst haben, sich fürchten
1	+to **connect** [kə'nekt]	verbinden, zusammenfügen
	+**noise** [nɔɪz]	Geräusch, Lärm
	+**because** [bɪ'kɒz]	weil, da

CHECK-OUT

1	to **learn*** [lɜ:n]	lernen
2	**because** [bɪ'kɒz]	weil, da
3	to **crack** [kræk]	knacken, aufbrechen
4	**how much?** ['haʊ ˌmʌtʃ]	wie viel?

COGNATE WORDS

alcohol ['ælkəhɒl]	Alkohol
article ['ɑ:tɪkl]	(Zeitungs-)Artikel
backgammon ['bækgæmn]	*Name eines Brettspiels*
ball [bɔ:l]	Ball
basketball ['bɑ:skɪtbɔ:l]	Basketball
best [best]	beste(r / s), der / die Beste
blind [blaɪnd]	blind
cafeteria [ˌkæfə'tɪəriə]	Cafeteria
cassette [kə'set]	Kassette
club [klʌb]	Klub, Verein
code [kəʊd]	Kode
command [kə'mɑ:nd]	Befehl, Kommando
°**Design and Technology** [dɪ'zaɪn‿ən tek'nɒlədʒi)]	Gestalten und Technik
°**Drama** ['drɑ:mə]	Theaterspielen *(Fach)*
extra ['ekstrə]	zusätzlich, extra
fit [fɪt]	gesund, in Form
football ['fʊtbɔ:l]	Fußball
°**Games** [geɪmz]	Sport
°**Geography** [dʒi'ɒgrəfi]	Erdkunde, Geographie
graffiti [grə'fi:ti]	Graffiti
to **help** [help]	helfen
hockey ['hɒki]	Hockey
to **interview** ['ɪntəvju:]	interviewen, befragen
kung fu film [ˌkʊŋ 'fu: fɪlm]	Kung-Fu-Film
to **love** [lʌv]	lieben, gern haben, mögen
Maths [mæθs]	Mathe(matik)
minute ['mɪnɪt]	Minute
moped ['məʊped]	Moped, Kleinkraftrad
partner ['pɑ:tnə]	Partner(in)
person ['pɜ:sn]	Person
to **plan** [plæn]	planen, vorhaben
practical ['præktɪkl]	praktisch
rock music ['rɒk ˌmju:zɪk]	Rockmusik
shock [ʃɒk]	Schreck, Schock
to **sing*** [sɪŋ]	singen
°**slogan** ['sləʊgən]	Slogan, Wahlspruch
sofa ['səʊfə]	Sofa, Couch
+**special** ['speʃl]	besondere(r/s)
sport [spɔ:t]	Sport
team [ti:m]	Mannschaft, Team
TV ['ti:'vi:]	Fernseher
uniform ['ju:nɪfɔ:m]	Uniform
up to date [ˌʌp tə 'deɪt]	modern, aktuell
volleyball ['vɒlibɔ:l]	Volleyball

UNIT 4

Seeing the sights

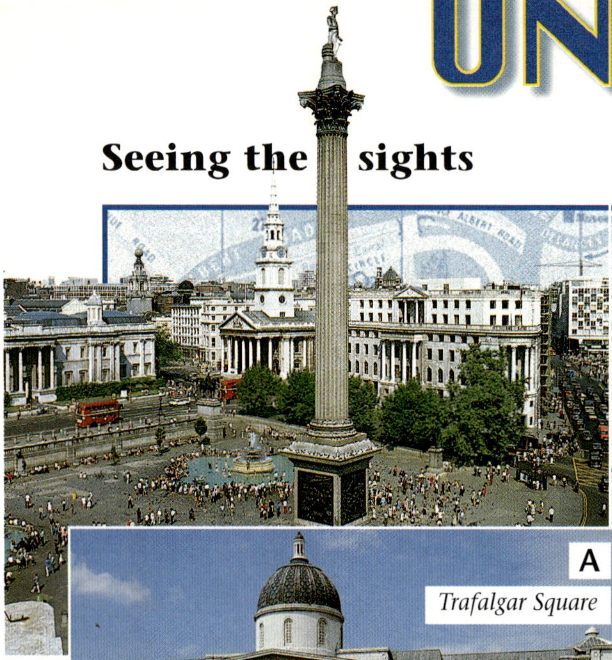

A Trafalgar Square

B Covent Garden tube station

C The West End – London's theatreland

D Hampstead Heath

E Harrods – a famous department store

F Big Ben

1 Listen and look

Listen to the sounds of London and match them with the photos.

Example: Sound one goes with picture F.

2 About London

a) *Which picture goes with which number?*

LONDON

1. It gets its name from the big bell inside the clock.
2. The Underground, or the tube, is a quick, cheap way to get around London, but you can see more from the top of a double decker bus.
3. It's expensive, but it sells everything!
4. There are plays and musicals around every corner.
5. London isn't only shops and traffic. Here you can have a picnic under the trees or just lie and do nothing.
6. In summer lots of tourists feed the birds.

b) *What else do you know about London? Make a list.*

3 Words – words – words

Which of these forms of transport can you see in the pictures?

bike – taxi – plane – train – boat
double decker bus – motorbike

Covent Garden

Liam, Maike and Jimmy are walking around Covent Garden. There are lots of interesting things to see and do, and people are having fun. Some people are standing in a group and clapping.

Maike: What are all those people looking at?
Liam: Come on. Let's find out.
Jimmy: I can't see anything. There are too many people.
Liam: Wait! I can see his head.
Maike: Who? What's he doing? Is he juggling?
Liam: No, he isn't. He's ... Oh! He's eating fire!
Maike: Really? Hey, can I sit on your shoulders, Liam? Please!
Liam: OK ... phew! You're heavy!
Maike: Thanks. Ah, this is better. Wow!
Jimmy: I can't see! What's happening, Maike?
Maike: He's walking on a bed of nails, and he isn't wearing shoes!
Jimmy: Ouch! That hurts!
Liam: Don't worry, Jimmy. He's smiling – he's OK.
Jimmy: I'm not talking about him! You're standing on my foot, Liam! Get off!
Liam: Oh, sorry Jimmy! Hey, look – some people are leaving. Now you can see more.
Maike: Too late. It's all over now. He's going around with a hat and collecting money.

G 25

1 What's happening?

Match the sentence parts.

What **are they** do**ing**? – **They are** watch**ing** a man.
What **is he** do**ing**? – **He is** walk**ing** on a bed of nails.
Is he wear**ing** shoes? – No, he isn't.

1. A man in Covent Garden
2. The people in the big group
3. Jimmy
4. Liam and Maike
5. Maike
6. Liam
7. The man

are
is

standing on Jimmy's foot.
clapping.
collecting money.
sitting on Liam's shoulders.
telling Jimmy about the man.
walking on a bed of nails.
waiting to see the man.

2 Verbs with -ing

Write the -ing form of the verbs and put them in three groups.

listen	write	play	stop	sit
make	go	come	clap	wait
run	put	leave	sing	get

SAVE

+ ing	no 'e' + ing	double letter + ing
listening	making	running

G 25

3 Who is doing what?

play – juggle – drink – write – eat – listen to – sell – read

Put in 'is' or 'are' and the verb.

Example: 1. A boy ... a postcard.
A boy is writing a postcard.

2. A girl and her mother ... ice cream.
3. A man ... guitar.
4. A woman ... coffee.
5. Two boys ... comics.
6. A man and a woman ... flowers.
7. Two women ... music.
8. Three men ... balls.

4 In your classroom

We / I Our teacher Some pupils The person next to me	am is / are (not)	read play do write sleep sit on sing open eat listen to	a newspaper. homework. the table. in the classroom. the windows. football. a snack. an English song. our teacher.

4

5 What is different?

a) *Work with a partner. One of you looks at picture A, the other looks at picture B. (Don't look at your partner's picture!). Five things are different. Talk about the pictures to find out what they are.*

Example: A girl is writing a postcard. What about in your picture?

b) *Write sentences about what is different.*

A

B

6 Listening comprehension: Who is who?

Liz and Liam are having a birthday party. Their parents are just back from a restaurant, and are watching the party through the window.

a) *Listen and match the names and numbers.*

Lance:	
Tessa:	2
Tarkan:	1
William:	
Diana:	

b) *Say who is doing what.*

Example: Tarkan is playing the piano.

7 What are they doing now?

Think of five famous people. What do you think they are doing now? Write two sentences about each person.

Example: Michael Jackson is singing an old song.
Michael Jackson is playing a new guitar.

8 Guess what I'm doing

Think of an action like 'play the piano', 'eat an ice cream' or 'walk on a bed of nails', and act it to your group. The others have one minute to guess what you are doing.

G 26

9 Spies

The people in the picture are spies. What are they doing? *Write questions and answers.*

Example: 1. Is the young woman pulling the man?
No, she's really giving him money.

1. young woman
2. man in T-shirt
3. old woman
4. old man
5. girl
6. boy

eat ice cream – take photo of Big Ben
pull man – talk into microphone
sleep – read newspaper – write code
talk to woman in green jacket
give money – watch old woman
take photo of girl – write postcard

The City

"You can see the whole City from up here," says Mr Wilson. He is with Jimmy and Maike at the top of the Monument.
"The whole city?" asks Maike.
"No, Maike. This is the City with a big C. It's where all the banks are. Right now people are phoning New York and Tokyo and Frankfurt, and buying and selling dollars and gold. See that building with the name *Gosforth & Sons* in big letters? That's where I work. And now I must go back because my lunch break is nearly over!"
So they run down the 311 steps. Mr Wilson takes a taxi to the bank, and Maike and Jimmy start to walk to Bank tube station.
"Let's go to the Tower of London," says Jimmy. "It's only one stop, and ... Hey, – we can go from Monument. It's just around the corner!"
But when they go into the next street, two men are coming the other way. They are running.
"Be careful!" cries Jimmy. But it's too late. Maike and one of the men fall. "You idiot!" he says to Maike. He stands up, but doesn't help her.
"Hey, what are you doing, man?" asks Jimmy.
The men are trying to get into a car. A woman is driving it. In a flash they are gone.
"Anyway, I've got your Harrods bag," says Jimmy. "Are you OK?"
"Er, yes, I think so. And thanks. But look – the car is stopping. I think they're coming back."
"Don't worry," Jimmy tells her. "Let's just go."

* * *

At the Tower of London, Jimmy and Maike are waiting to see the Crown Jewels.
"See that man with red hair, about twenty people behind us?" says Maike. "He looks like that man in the City. You know, the one in a big hurry!"
But Jimmy is sure it's a different person. "There are lots of other men like that!"
"Maybe you're right," says Maike, and they go inside.

* * *

"Where are we going now?" asks Maike.

"What about the London Aquarium?" says Jimmy. "It's great. We take the Circle Line from here."
And off they go.
After four stops on the train, Maike says, "Look – there he is again!"
"I can't see him," says Jimmy.
"He's hiding behind a newspaper!"
"OK, let's get out here," says Jimmy. "It's a nice walk along the river anyway."
They get out, but the man gets out too.
"Is he following us?" asks Jimmy.
"No, but he's talking on his mobile phone."

* * *

"Look, Maike, you can see Big Ben from the river!" says Jimmy. But Maike is tired. "This bag is too heavy!" she says.
"That's because of all those maps and guide books!" Jimmy smiles. "Why bring them when you've got me?"
But Maike isn't listening. "Hey, Jimmy, look at that car. I'm sure it's the one from the City. The woman is the same, and that other man in the green jacket ..."
Now Jimmy is worried too. "Come on – to the next tube station!" But the car is there first, and the man in the green jacket is getting out.

1 What happens next?

Why are these people following them? And what can Maike and Jimmy do now?

"Don't look at them – just walk!" says Jimmy, and then in a loud voice, "That's enough sightseeing for one day. Let's go home. We take the next train to Victoria and change for Islington." At Victoria they get out and go to the Victoria Line. The man is behind them.
"He's still following us. Do just what I say."
They are getting into the train to Islington.
The doors are closing. "Quick! Jump!" says Jimmy. He pulls Maike with him.
The train starts, but they can see the man inside. He is trying to open the door but it is too late. The train is moving out of the station.
"Now, quick – into the other train!"
"But it's going the wrong way! It's going to Brixton!" says Maike.
"No, that's the right way! We can go to the market and listen to some good reggae. But first look inside your bag – if it is your bag."
Maike doesn't understand, but she opens it anyway. "Where are my maps and ... what's this?" She pulls out a box with *Gosforth & Sons* on it. It is full of money – lots and lots of money!
"What do we do now?" asks Maike.
"Those bank robbers aren't the only ones with a mobile phone!" says Jimmy. He takes one out of his pocket and dials 999.

2 Opposites

a) *Find the opposites of these words in the text.*

Part	*Opposite*
1 (ll. 1-33)	part, small, early, answers (v), starting
2 (ll. 34-46)	in front of, the same
3 (ll. 47-60)	before, terrible
4 (ll. 61-102)	opening, right, bad, out of, push

b) *Look for one more opposite in each part.*

3 Right or wrong?

Three of these sentences aren't right. *Say what is wrong.*

1. Mr Wilson works in the City.
2. He isn't working at *Gosforth & Sons* this afternoon.
3. Maike and Jimmy don't see the Crown Jewels because a woman is following them.
4. Jimmy and Maike get off the Circle Line train at the fifth stop.
5. The woman in the car is wearing a green jacket.
6. Maike hasn't got her bag on the train to Brixton.

4 Who says what?

Who says these things on the phone? And when in the story do they say them?

a) They're walking back to Tower Hill station. We can see them from the car. Follow them, but be more careful this time!

b) They're looking at the Crown Jewels. – Yes, the girl has still got the bag. – I can't because there are too many people!

c) What's happening, Mr Gosforth? What are the police doing here? – Bank robbers? I don't believe it! In my lunch break? Well, how much money ...?

d) I'm on the Victoria Line. This train is going to Islington, but the boy and the girl are gone! – No, I don't know which way. Maybe ...

e) Is that the police? Good! I've got some ...

f) They're going west on the Circle Line. – No, I don't think they can see me. – Now we're at Temple. They're getting off. Get them when they come out of the station, OK?

1 Asking the way

Three people want to know the way to different places. a) *Find out which streets they are in now.*

A Excuse me, please. Can you tell me the way to the tube station?
B Yes, of course. Go left at the traffic lights, then take the first left into Queen Street. The station is on the right, after the pub.
A Thank you.

C Excuse me, is there a telephone around here?
D Yes, go left at the computer shop, then right into Church Street. It's opposite the video shop, between the sports centre and the church.
C Thanks.

E Excuse me, where's the bus stop for the 38 to Islington?
F Go straight on. At the end of Queen Street go right. The bus stop for Islington is on your right, opposite the school.
E Thank you.

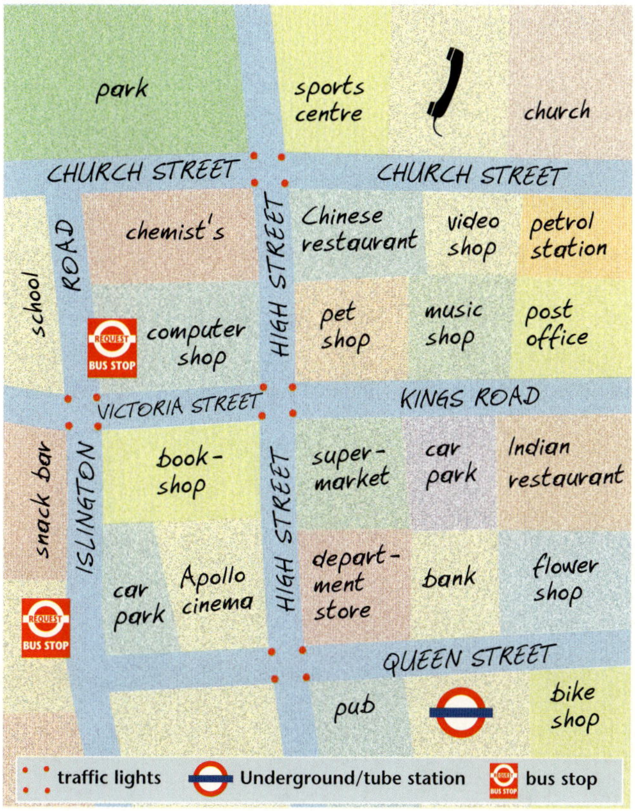

b) *Three people outside the post office are asking the way. Put in the words.*

right	go	me	Excuse	straight	can	before
opposite	through	way	chemist's	around	traffic	course
there	left	car park	on	Victoria Street		

1. A ... me, where's the ... ?
   B Go right at the ... lights, then go left into Church Street, and it's ... the left.
2. C Excuse ..., ... you tell me the ... to the Apollo Cinema?
   B Yes, of ... . Go ... into the High Street, and it's on your ..., ... the department store.
3. D Hello, is ... a snack bar ... here?
   B Yes, go ... on ... the traffic lights into ... and then ... left. It's opposite the ..., ... the sports shop.

c) *Work with a partner. Ask and answer questions about how to find places on the map.*

G 27

2 Learning tip: Where?

Collect prepositions for your vocabulary notebook. Make pictures for the words.

the High Street
Islington High Street *(no 'the')*
Queen Street *(no 'the')*

3 ⟨Crazy chains[1]⟩

Learn this crazy chain. Then close your books and practise[2] it in groups.

This is the key of the kingdom.
In that kingdom there is a city.
In that city there is a town[5].
In that town there is a street.
In that street there is a lane[6].
In that lane there is a yard[7].
In that yard there is a house.
In that house there is a room.
In that room there is a bed.
On that bed there is a basket[8].
In that basket there are some flowers.
Flowers in a basket.
Basket on the bed.
Bed in the room.
Room in the house.
House in the yard.
Yard in the lane.
Lane in the street.
Street in the town.
Town in the city.
City in the kingdom.
Of the kingdom this is the key.
This is the key of the kingdom.

1['kreɪzi‿tʃeɪn] *verrückte Kette* 2['præktɪs] *üben* 3[ki:] *Schlüssel* 4['kɪŋdəm] *Königreich* 5[taʊn] *(Klein-)Stadt* 6[leɪn] *Gasse, schmale Straße* 7[jɑ:d] *Hof* 8['bɑ:skɪt] *Korb*

4

4 A full house

The Modis' house is full this afternoon. What does Dr Modi say when people phone for people in his family or their friends? *Work in pairs.*

WP 1 Words – words – words

a) *Look at the picture and find:*

One thing with 's' as the first letter, one thing with 'f', two things with 'p', three things with 't', four things with 'b', and five things with 'c'.

b) *Write a story with the words from a). You can start like this:*

A *boy* is sitting on a *chair* in his *boat*. He …

2 Writing a postcard

Maike is writing a postcard to her penfriend in America.
Can you put in the adjectives?

Dear Abby,

I'm having a gr... time here in London. It's my f... city and really i...g! There's so much to do. The weather is go... – it isn't raining! The food isn't too ba..., but the coffee is te... – it's like br... water! I love the I... curries, but they can be very h... . At the moment I'm sitting in a n... café and writing postcards. My G... friends are buying s...y souvenirs in Oxford Street, but I'm staying here. Shopping is so bo...! Tonight the Wilsons want to take me to Starlight Express. The tickets are exp..., so I think they're for the front row.
I can't wait!

Love, Maike

by airmail

4

1 A view from the plane

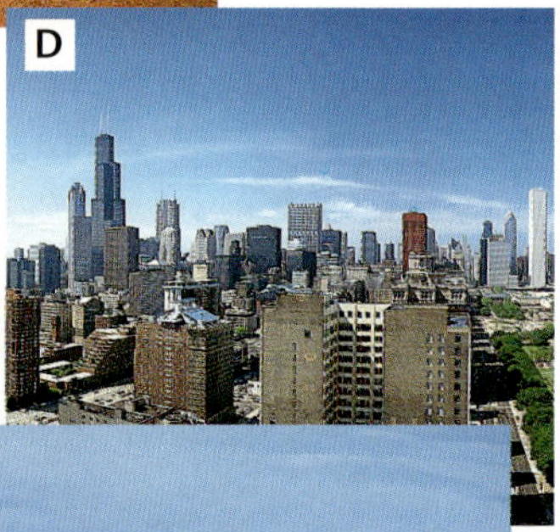

"Ladies and gentlemen, this is your captain speaking. There's a lot of air traffic at O'Hare, so we're still waiting to land. Well, it looks like another cold day down in Chicago. The temperature at O'Hare is zero degrees. That's about minus eighteen degrees Celsius. If you look out on the right, you can see Lake Michigan, and on the left there's a great view of the Chicago skyline. That tall building is the famous Sears Tower – a hundred and ten floors high. But don't worry – it's got a fast elevator! As you can see, Chicago has got a lot of parks. Its motto is 'Urbs in Horto'. That's Latin for 'city in a garden'. Anyway, we can land now, so thank you for flying with American Airlines, and have a nice day."

a) *Which pictures show what the people see when they look out of the window?*

b) *What can people see from a plane over your town or city?*

2 City and town words

Start a mind map of 'city and town' words.

3 What's the weather like over there?

a) *Collect words to talk about the weather and seasons.*

b) *Talk about the weather where you live. What is it like at different times of year? When is the best time of year to visit your town or city? What is it like today?*

I don't like London in the summer. The weather is usually warm and sunny at that time of year, but there are too many tourists. A good time to visit London is in spring or autumn. People think it rains all the time in England, but it doesn't. It can rain a lot in winter. Sometimes it snows, but only a bit.

People call Chicago the windy city. The wind can be really strong here! Summers are always hot, and we get cold winters – usually with a lot of snow. Temperatures can go down to minus thirty. I love fall because that's when the football season starts! The weather today? Cold and cloudy.

1 Words – words – words

Put two more words in each list.

1. train, car, …
2. green, yellow, …
3. chair, bed, …
4. bedroom, kitchen, …

2 Make sentences

Some of the sentences are questions.

1. wearing / hat / a / Maike / silly / is
2. what / they / watching / are (?)
3. making / Liz / hat / Liam / newspaper / a / dad's / are / their / and / with
4. in / sitting / who / my / is / chair (?)
5. your / doing / why / you / aren't / homework / now (?)
6. man / there / wearing / not / over / the / is / shoes

3 Questions and answers

Example: 1. Nicola / play tennis? – No / football.
Is Nicola playing tennis? –
No, she isn't. She's playing football.

2. Tarkan / write postcards? – Yes.
3. Liam and Liz / play computer game? – Yes.
4. Mr Wilson / work in the bank? – No / have lunch break.
5. Maike and Jimmy / feed the birds? – Yes.
6. Mr and Mrs Modi / make pizza? – No / snacks.

4

G 28

4 What are they doing – and where?

Put in the present progressive form of the verbs (v) and the prepositions (p).

(v)	(p)
hide, read, get (2x), stand, run, sit, sleep	behind, around, next to, between, on, out of, into

Example: 1. Some people (v) (p) a bus.
Some people are getting out of a bus.

2. A little girl (v) (p) her father's shoulders.
3. Two girls (v) (p) a tree.
4. A man (v) a newspaper (p) two women.
5. A dog (v) (p) woman in the yellow T-shirt.
6. A bird (v) (p) on a man's head.
7. A boy (v) (p) the tree.
8. A man (v) (p) a taxi.

SB

5 Sound check

Listen and note down the 'odd sound out'.

1. those know stop go
2. watch hat match flat
3. how now row wow
4. break really here year
5. nice why try way
6. cheap street great eat

1. The odd sound out in No. 1 is … .
2. The odd sound out in … . *Go on.*

4

CHECK-IN

	sight [saɪt]	Sehenswürdigkeit
	Trafalgar Square [trəˌfælgə 'skweə]	*berühmter Platz in London*
	Covent Garden [ˌkɒvnt 'gɑ:dn]	*Platz in London*
	tube [tju:b]	*Name der Londoner U-Bahn* (*wörtlich:* Röhre)
	the **West End** [ˌwest‿'end]	*Theaterviertel in London*
	Hampstead Heath [ˌhæmstəd 'hi:θ]	*Park im Nordwesten Londons*
	Harrods ['hærədz]	*Kaufhaus in London*
	famous ['feɪməs]	berühmt
	department store [dɪ'pɑ:tmənt ˌstɔ:]	Kaufhaus
	Big Ben [ˌbɪg 'ben]	*Glockenturm in London*
1	to **match** [mætʃ]	zuordnen
2	**which** [wɪtʃ]	welche(r/s)
	bell [bel]	Glocke
	clock [klɒk]	Uhr
	quick [kwɪk]	schnell, rasch
	cheap [tʃi:p]	billig
	around [ə'raʊnd]	um ... herum, umher
	expensive [ɪk'spensɪv]	teuer
	to **sell*** [sel]	verkaufen
	play [pleɪ]	Theaterstück
	corner ['kɔ:nə]	Ecke
	traffic ['træfɪk]	Verkehr
	nothing ['nʌθɪŋ]	nichts
	to **feed*** [fi:d]	füttern
	bird [bɜ:d]	Vogel
	else [els]	(sonst) noch, außerdem
3	**plane** [pleɪn]	Flugzeug
	train [treɪn]	(U-Bahn-)Zug

STEP A

to **walk** [wɔ:k]	spazierengehen
to **stand*** [stænd]	stehen
to **clap** [klæp]	klatschen, applaudieren
anything ['eniθɪŋ]	etwas
head [hed]	Kopf
to **juggle** ['dʒʌgl]	jonglieren
fire ['faɪə]	Feuer
to **sit*** [sɪt]	sitzen
shoulder ['ʃəʊldə]	Schulter
phew! [fju:]	puh!
heavy ['hevi]	schwer
to **happen** ['hæpn]	geschehen, passieren
nail [neɪl]	Nagel
to **wear*** [weə]	anhaben, tragen
shoe [ʃu:]	Schuh

Do you know?

Hampstead Heath
Big Ben
Harrods
Covent Garden

is / **isn't**

a big department store.
a famous clock.
in London.
in New York.

franz fameux *lat* famosus
engl famous

Quick, go on!

play – ? – day
sell – ? – well
shoe – ? – you
feed – ? – read
rap – ? – map
fat – ? – cat

2 places in London:
Trafalgar Square, ...
3 famous buildings in London:
Big Ben, ..., ...
4 traffic words:
bus, ..., ..., ...
5 'foot' words:
shoe, go, ..., ..., ...
4 subjects:
Maths, ..., ..., ...
3 big cities:
Tokyo, ..., ...
2 animals:
bird, ...

hat
hair
head

foot
shoe

	ouch! [aʊtʃ]	au!, autsch!
	to **hurt*** [hɜ:t]	wehtun, schmerzen
	to **worry** ['wʌri]	sich Sorgen machen
	to **smile** [smaɪl]	lächeln
	foot [fʊt]	Fuß
	off [ɒf]	weg, fort
	to **leave*** [li:v]	weggehen, verlassen
	late [leɪt]	spät
	hat [hæt]	Hut
	to **collect** [kə'lekt]	sammeln
3	to **read*** [ri:d]	lesen
	mother ['mʌðə]	Mutter
4	to **sleep*** [sli:p]	schlafen
	newspaper ['nju:speɪpə]	Zeitung
6	**guest** [gest]	Gast
7	to **act** [ækt]	darstellen, vorführen
8	**each** [i:tʃ]	jede(r/s) Einzelne
9	°**spy**, *pl.* **spies** [spaɪ]	Spion(in), Spitzel

STEP B

whole [həʊl]	ganz, komplett
up [ʌp]	oben (auf); hinauf
the **Monument** ['mɒnjəmənt]	*Denkmal in London*
Tokyo ['təʊkiəʊ]	Tokio
to **buy*** [baɪ]	kaufen
building ['bɪldɪŋ]	Gebäude
Gosforth & Sons ['gɒsfɔ:θ‿ən ˌsʌnz]	*Name einer Bank*
Tower of London [ˌtaʊə‿əv 'lʌndən]	*Museum mit Schatzkammer (ehemaliges Gefängnis)*
into ['ɪntə]	in … hinein
street [stri:t]	Straße
to **cry** [kraɪ]	rufen, schreien; weinen
to **fall*** [fɔ:l]	fallen, stürzen
to **drive*** [draɪv]	fahren
in a flash [flæʃ]	blitzschnell
bag [bæg]	Tüte, Tasche
crown jewels [ˌkraʊn 'dʒu:əlz]	Kronjuwelen
hair [heə]	Haar
about [ə'baʊt]	ungefähr, etwa
behind [bɪ'haɪnd]	hinter
in a hurry ['hʌri]	in Eile, eilig
maybe ['meɪbi]	vielleicht
Circle Line ['sɜ:kl ˌlaɪn]	*Ringlinie der U-Bahn*
to **hide*** [haɪd]	verstecken, verbergen
along [ə'lɒŋ]	entlang, längs
river ['rɪvə]	Fluss
to **follow** ['fɒləʊ]	folgen
mobile phone [ˌməʊbaɪl 'fəʊn]	Mobiltelefon, Handy
to be tired ['taɪəd]	müde (sein)
map [mæp]	Stadtplan, Landkarte

Ouch, there's a nail in my shoe. It hurts!

People and what they do

A player	plays.
A driver	drives.
A fighter	fights.
A helper	helps.
A listener	listens.
A writer	writes.
A juggler	juggles.

Go on.

What spies like to do

They hide behind newspapers.
They never smile.
They follow people.
They watch the traffic.
They use mobile phones.
They wear hats.
They jump out of trains.

The  is in front of … / behind … / between … / under … / on …

I put a box in my bag.
I put a box and a map in my bag.
I put a box, a map and a … in my bag.

franz mobile *lat* mobilis
engl mobile

Opposites

good	–	bad
cheap	–	?
early	–	?
in front of	–	?
to sell	–	?
right	–	?

4

	guide book ['gaɪd bʊk]	Reiseführer *(Buch)*
	to **bring*** [brɪŋ]	bringen
	loud [laʊd]	laut
	voice [vɔɪs]	Stimme
	enough [ɪ'nʌf]	genug, ausreichend
	Victoria Line [vɪk'tɔ:riə ˌlaɪn]	*U-Bahn-Linie in London*
	to **change** [tʃeɪndʒ]	ändern, *hier:* umsteigen
	to **close** [kləʊz]	schließen
	to **jump** [dʒʌmp]	springen
	to **pull** [pʊl]	ziehen
	out (of) [aʊt]	hinaus, heraus
	wrong [rɒŋ]	falsch
	Brixton ['brɪkstn]	*Stadtteil in London*
	full [fʊl]	voll
	bank robber ['bæŋk ˌrɒbə]	Bankräuber(in)
	the **only ones** [wʌnz]	die Einzigen
	pocket ['pɒkət]	(Hosen-/Jacken-)Tasche
	to **dial** ['daɪəl]	wählen
2	**ll. (= lines)** [laɪnz]	Zeilen
4	**Tower Hill station** ['taʊə ˌhɪl 'steɪʃn]	*U-Bahn-Station*
	to **believe** [bɪ'li:v]	glauben
	Temple ['templ]	*U-Bahn-Station*

STEP C

1	**excuse me** [ɪk'skju:z mi:]	entschuldigen Sie
	traffic light ['træfɪk ˌlaɪt]	Ampel
	then [ðen]	dann, danach
	church [tʃɜ:tʃ]	Kirche
	between [bɪ'twi:n]	zwischen
	straight ['streɪt]	geradeaus
	chemist's ['kemɪsts]	Apotheke, Drogerie
	cinema ['sɪnəmə]	Kino
	petrol station ['petrl ˌsteɪʃn]	Tankstelle
2	**vocabulary notebook** [vəʊˌkæbjəlri 'nəʊtbʊk]	Vokabelheft

TRACK 1

2	**weather** ['weðə]	Wetter
	to **rain** ['reɪn]	regnen
	Oxford Street ['ɒksfəd ˌstri:t]	*Einkaufsstraße in London*
	tonight [tə'naɪt]	heute Abend, heute Nacht
	Starlight Express [ˌstɑ:laɪtˌɪk'spres]	*Name eines Musicals*
	row [rəʊ]	Reihe

TRACK 2

1	+**view** [vju:]	Blick, Ansicht
	+to **speak*** [spi:k]	sprechen
	+**O'Hare** [əʊ'heə]	*Flughafen in Chicago*

franz voix *lat* vox
engl voice

I pull a book out of my pocket.
I pull a box and a mobile phone out of my pocket.
I pull a box, a mobile phone and a ... out of my pocket.

franz ligne *lat* linea
engl line

Excuse me, is there a ... near here?

chemist's	department store
cinema	bus stop
petrol station	tube station
school	flower shop
bank	restaurant
shoe shop	...

Yes, go along ... Road,
... Street,

then go straight on.
go left / right.

+ ny = sunny

+ y = cloudy

I scream, you scream,
everybody wants  cream

+**another** [ə'nʌðə]	ein(e) andere(r / s)
+**cold** [kəʊld]	kalt
+**Chicago** [ʃɪ'kɑ:gəʊ]	Chicago
+**degree** [dɪ'gri:]	Grad
+**Lake Michigan** [ˌleɪk 'mɪʃɪgən]	Michigansee
+**tall** [tɔ:l]	hohe(r / s)
+**Sears Tower** [ˌsɪəz 'taʊə]	*höchstes Gebäude der Welt*
+**floor** [flɔ:]	Stockwerk, Etage
+**fast** [fɑ:st]	schnell, rasch
+**elevator** *AE* ['elɪveɪtə]	Aufzug, Fahrstuhl
+**Latin** ['lætɪn]	lateinisch, Latein
+to **fly*** [flaɪ]	fliegen
+**American Airlines** [əˌmerɪkən‿'eəˌlaɪnz]	*amerikanische Fluggesellschaft*
+**town** [taʊn]	(Klein-)Stadt
3 +**season** ['si:zn]	Jahreszeit
+**to visit** ['vɪzɪt]	besuchen
+**today** [tə'deɪ]	heute
+**strong** [strɒŋ]	streng, rauh
+**snow** [snəʊ]	Schnee
+**fall** *AE* [fɔ:l]	Herbst
+**cloudy** ['klaʊdi]	wolkig
+**sunny** ['sʌni]	sonnig
+**spring** [sprɪŋ]	Frühling
+**autumn** *BE* ['ɔ:təm]	Herbst
+to **snow** [snəʊ]	schneien

CHECK-OUT

4 **father** ['fɑ:ðə]	Vater

COGNATE WORDS

action ['ækʃn]	Aktion, Handlung
aquarium [ə'kweəriəm]	Aquarium
at the moment ['məʊmənt]	im Moment, zur Zeit
bank [bæŋk]	Bank, Geldinstitut
bike [baɪk]	(Fahr-)Rad
birthday ['bɜ:θdeɪ]	Geburtstag
boat [bəʊt]	Boot
café ['kæfeɪ]	Café
+**captain** ['kæptɪn]	(Flug-)Kapitän
+**Celsius** ['selsiəs]	Celsius
classroom ['klɑ:srʊm]	Klassenzimmer
coffee ['kɒfi]	Kaffee
comic ['kɒmɪk]	Comic(heft)
curry ['kʌri]	Curry(gericht)
dollar ['dɒlə]	*amerikanische Währung*
double decker bus [ˌdʌbl dekə 'bʌs]	Doppeldeckerbus
form [fɔ:m]	Form, Art
ice cream [aɪs 'kri:m]	Eiskrem, (Speise-)Eis
idiot ['ɪdiət]	Idiot
jacket ['dʒækɪt]	Jacke, Jackett
king [kɪŋ]	König
+**ladies and gentlemen** ['leɪdiz‿ən 'dʒentlmən]	(meine) Damen und Herren
+to **land** [lænd]	landen
love [lʌv]	(in) Liebe, *hier*: herzlichst
market ['mɑ:kɪt]	Markt
+**minus** ['maɪnəs]	minus
motorbike ['məʊtəˌbaɪk]	Motorrad
+**motto** ['mɒtəʊ]	Motto, Leitsatz
musical ['mju:zɪkl]	Musical
official [ə'fɪʃl]	offiziell
partner ['pɑ:tnə]	Partner(in)
party ['pɑ:ti]	Party, Fest
picnic ['pɪknɪk]	Picknick
police [pə'li:s]	Polizei
postcard ['pəʊstkɑ:d]	Postkarte
pub [pʌb]	Lokal, Gaststätte
queen [kwi:n]	Königin
shopping ['ʃɒpɪŋ]	Einkaufen
sightseeing ['saɪtˌsi:ɪŋ]	Besichtigung von Sehenswürdigkeiten
+**skyline** ['skaɪlaɪn]	(Stadt-)Silhouette, Skyline
sports centre ['spɔ:ts ˌsentə]	Sportzentrum, Sportanlage
station ['steɪʃn]	Haltestelle, Station
stop [stɒp]	Halt, Stopp
to stop [stɒp]	anhalten, stoppen
+**summer** ['sʌmə]	Sommer
telephone ['telɪfəʊn]	Telefon
+**temperature** ['temprətʃə]	Temperatur
theatreland ['θɪətəˌlænd]	Theaterviertel
top [tɒp]	oben
tourist ['tʊərɪst]	Tourist(in)
transport ['trænspɔ:t]	Transport, Beförderung
video shop ['vɪdiəʊ ˌʃɒp]	Videothek
+**warm** [wɔ:m]	warm
water ['wɔ:tə]	Wasser
west [west]	westlich, Westen
+**wind** [wɪnd]	Wind
+**windy** ['wɪndi]	windig
+**winter** ['wɪntə]	Winter

UNIT 5

Let's go shopping!

London is a great place for shopping. Here are some famous – or interesting – London shops.

BOND STREET

HMV, Oxford Street: A great number of CDs, records, videos of all kinds.

COVENT GARDEN

Dr Martens, Covent Garden: Doc Martens boots and shoes, of course, but also T-shirts, bags, etc.

KNIGHTSBRIDGE

Harrods, Brompton Road: London's most famous department store sells everything. The Queen gets lots of her clothes here.

5

1 Where can I get it?

Work in pairs.

a pair of Doc Martens shoes
a nice scarf for my mother
the latest Girlzone CD
a book about Jack the Ripper
an old Beano comic book
an old English frame for a photo
a collar for Liz's dog
the London Marathon computer game

Where can I get … find …
Where's that?
How do I get there?
Have they got … too?

Try …
It's in … near …
You can go by … Or …

Yes, they've got lots of … things like … all kinds of …
No, they haven't got …
I don't know. Ask …

music books records hats
handbags T-shirts
other kinds of … pet food
books about astronomy /…
reggae CDs new comics

HOLBORN

Books etc., Kingsway: As the name tells you, not only books of all kinds, but also magazines, postcards, calendars …

ANGEL

Out of the Attic, Islington High Street: Beautiful but expensive old things.

PICCADILLY CIRCUS

Mighty World of Comicana, Shaftesbury Avenue: All kinds of comics, old and new.

GOODGE STREET

Tempo, Tottenham Court Road: Computers, software, games – but also mobile phones, TVs, video recorders.

FINSBURY PARK

Silvester's Pet Supplies, Salisbury Road: Everything for your dog or cat or bird …

2 Listening comprehension: Where are they?

1. Tessa and her mother are in a …
2. Liam and Sebastian are …
3. Jimmy and Maike …
4. Mrs Braden is …
5. Sandra …
6. Tarkan …
7. Liz and Tessa …
8. Mr Braden and Mrs Clifton are in their …

pet shop	clothes shop
record store	department store
antique shop	food store
bookshop	computer store

It's more fun at the market

A London is famous for its markets. There are two great street markets quite near where the German friends are. Both of them have 'Camden' in their names, but only one is in Camden. Camden Passage is in the centre of Islington. You can find all kinds of old things there. The market stalls are open on Tuesdays, Wednesdays and Saturdays.

1 Asking for things

Read the dialogues – at both markets. How do the people ask for things? Make a list of all the different ways.

G 29/30

2 How to be nice

Hey – I want three of these knives. And give me a bag for them!

Some of the phrases are not so friendly, like these, for example:

1. "I want an old Superman comic."
2. "Give me a silver knife. These knives aren't silver."
3. "Not that one! The other one over there!"
4. "I want a white T-shirt with Madonna on it in black."
5. "I want two scarves in different colours."
6. "This is too small. Give me a size XL."
7. "A vanilla ice cream. And make it quick!"
8. "I want it in red, not green."

Look at your list. Can you find nice ways to say these things?

G 31

3 Look at these things

Work in pairs.

Start: Look at these …
Yes, they're nice/…

knive box
scarf watch glass

SAVE

box [-ks]
watch [-tʃ] | + -es *(always)*
glass [-s]

knife
scarf | -ves *(but not all -f/-fe words)*

B Camden Lock market really is in Camden. But it's near Islington. You can go there by train, or on the Underground, or even by boat! (Yes, the market is next to a canal.) Or you can walk ... But don't get too tired on the way: there are lots and lots of stalls to look at every Saturday and Sunday. What can you find there? – Nearly everything!

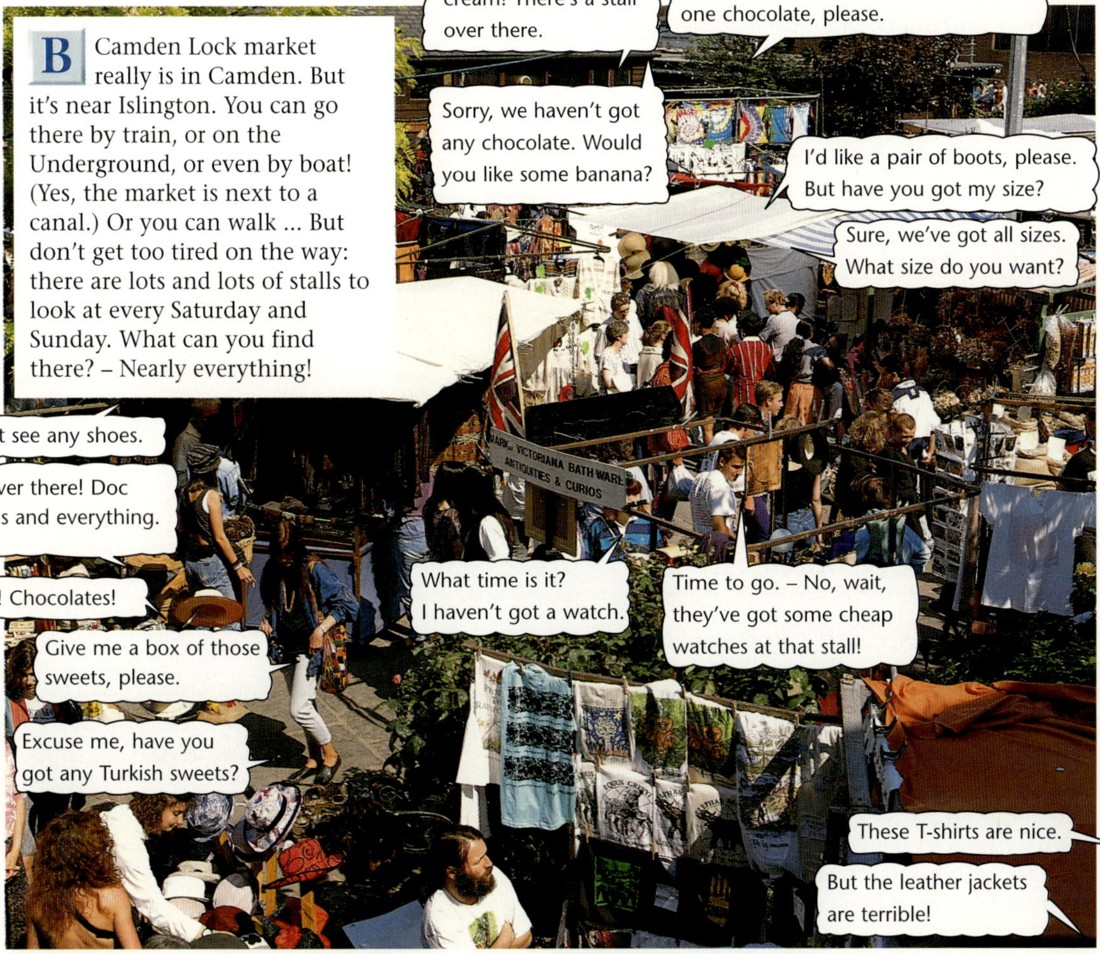

G 32

4 Some and any

a) *Look at the words 'some' and 'any' in the dialogues. Which words do the people use in positive sentences?*
in negative sentences?
in questions?

b) *Now put in the right words in these dialogues:*

– I'd like … salt on my chips, please.
– The salt's over there. Would you like … vinegar? Here it is!
– Oh, no thanks. I don't want … vinegar.

***

– Hm, they've got … reggae and lots of Irish folk, but no Indian music here. Excuse me, have you got … Indian music?
– Well, we've got … bhangra records over there.
– Oh, good. But what about CDs?
– Sorry, we haven't got … bhangra CDs.

G 33

5 Much, many and lots of

a) *Now look at these sentences from Units 2–5. How do people use 'much', 'many' and 'lots of'?*

– The bag is full of lots and lots of money.
– I don't get much homework.
– How much are those boxes?
– There are lots of old things in the garage.
– Most of the girls smoke, not so many boys.
– How many lessons have they got?

b) *Now put the right words in these sentences:*

1. There are ... stalls on the market.
2. How ... souvenirs have you got?
3. They haven't got ... shoes in my size.
4. They've got ... CDs at this stall.
5. How ... are these watches?
6. It's OK – I've got ... money.
7. Let's go. We haven't got ... time.

G 34

5 Tessa's birthday calendar

a) *Work in pairs. Ask and answer questions.*

Example: When is Tessa's birthday? –
It's in January. / It's on the nineteenth of January. /
It's on January the nineteenth.

Go on: … her father's / her … / Liz's … / …

JANUARY Me – 19th	MAY Tara M. – 2nd Mum – 17th	SEPTEMBER Baby Tim – 21st
FEBRUARY Aunt Hilary – 23rd	JUNE Hamida M. – 8th	OCTOBER Liz + Liam – 28th
MARCH Dad – 1st	JULY	NOVEMBER Jake (brother) – 12th
APRIL Uncle Hassan – 7th	AUGUST Rizwan M. – 30th	DECEMBER Tarkan – 5th

b) When is your birthday? *Talk about birthdays and make a birthday calendar for your class.*

5

6 Role play: When can we practise?

Two musicians are looking at this page from a calendar. They are talking about their plans for January.
Play the roles.

JANUARY

Sun	Mon	Tue	Wed	Thu	Fri	Sat
	1	2	3	4	5	6
7	8	9	10	11	12	13
14	15	16	17	18	19	20
21	22	23	24	25	26	27
28	29	30	31			

Let's practise together on the fourth.

That's a Thursday. Sorry, I've got … on that evening.

tennis yoga
German class

What about the …?

That's a … . Sorry, …

The … then?

Oh no, that's …'s 60th birthday.

my mother (50)
my father (60)
my grandma (80)

Oh dear! What about the …?

That's OK.

Good. And let's do it again on the …

Well, …

1st	first [fɜ:st]
2nd	second ['seknd]
3rd	third [θɜ:d]
4th	fourth [fɔ:θ]
5th	fifth [fɪfθ]
6th	sixth [sɪksθ]
7th	seventh ['sevnθ]
8th	eighth [eɪtθ]
9th	ninth [naɪnθ]
10th	tenth [tenθ]
11th	eleventh [ɪ'levnθ]
12th	twelfth [twelfθ]
13th	thirteenth [ˌθɜ:'ti:nθ]
14th	fourteenth [ˌfɔ:'ti:nθ]
15th	fifteenth [ˌfɪf'ti:nθ]
16th	sixteenth [ˌsɪks'ti:nθ]
17th	seventeenth [ˌsevn'ti:nθ]
18th	eighteenth [ˌeɪ'ti:nθ]
19th	nineteenth [ˌnaɪn'ti:nθ]
20th	twentieth ['twentiəθ]
21st	twenty-first [ˌtwenti'fɜ:st]
22nd	twenty-second
23rd	twenty-third
24th	twenty-fourth
25th	twenty-fifth
26th	twenty-sixth
27th	twenty-seventh
28th	twenty-eighth
29th	twenty-ninth
30th	thirtieth ['θɜ:tiəθ]
31st	thirty-first [ˌθɜ:ti'fɜ:st]
…	

Can you work out the rules for these numbers? And which numbers don't *follow the rules?*

40th	fortieth ['fɔ:tiəθ]
50th	fiftieth ['fɪftiəθ]
…	
100th	(a / one) hundredth ['hʌndrədθ]

Souvenirs of London

On Monday, Sebastian and Sandra go shopping in the centre of London. They are just going into a big computer store on Tottenham Court Road when they meet Liam. "Hi, you two," says Liam, "what are you doing here?"

"Oh, just looking around," says Sebastian.

"Sebastian's a real computer freak, just like you, Liam," says Sandra. "He wants to look at some computer games."

"Not again, Sebastian!" says Liam. "Or do you want to buy that game after all? You know, the really nice one – what's its name again?"

"London Marathon. No, Liam, you know I'd like to buy it, but I can't. It's much too expensive. Just look at those prices!" They are now in the games department. "I really am just looking."

"So have you got all your souvenirs, Sandra?" asks Liam.

"Well, some of them," she answers. "I can show them to you." She takes out a funny teapot. "This is for my mum. She usually drinks coffee, but now I can show her how to make some really good tea." Liam laughs.

"I haven't got a present for my dad yet, but I've got this for my sister." She pulls a little teddy bear out of her bag. "It sings 'London Bridge is Falling Down' when you pull this string."

"Not here, Sandra – look, we're on TV." They look at the TV high up on the wall. "Oh dear," says Sandra. "I think all the people in the store are laughing at us."

"And what about you, Sebastian?" asks Liam, but Sebastian doesn't hear. He is still looking at the computer games on CD-ROM.

Ding dong ding dong! "What's that?" asks Liam, and Sandra laughs. "I can show you," she says, "but not on TV, please." They move away. "He's got this model of Big Ben for his mum and dad." Liam looks at the clock on top of the model. "Wow! A quarter past two – it works!"

"And he's got this T-shirt with a map of the London Underground on it."

"Who is it for?" asks Liam.

"I think Sebastian wants to wear it. But it isn't much good as a map if you're wearing it, is it?"

"Now what is Sebastian doing over there?" They go over to him, but Sebastian doesn't see them. He has got a computer CD in his hand. He puts it in his pocket quickly. Then he turns around. "I want to go now," he tells Sandra and Liam.

1 What happens

Does Sebastian a) keep the CD?
b) buy the CD?
c) put the CD back?

Can you guess? Listen if you want to find out now.

They try to leave the shop, but a man and a woman are waiting for them at the door. The man puts his hand on Sebastian. "Excuse me, young man," he says. "Come this way, please."

Store detectives! All the people in the shop are looking at them! Sebastian's face is red. The woman looks at Sandra and Liam. "You must come too."

"You're making a terrible mistake," says Liam. "We haven't got anything from your store."

"Maybe not," says the woman, "but your friend has. And we think you are working as a team. We can see it all on TV."

They go into a small room. There is a table with five chairs, and a big TV on the wall. "Sit down." The man puts on the video. "That's us," says Liam. They can see the funny scene with the souvenirs. But they are not laughing at it.

Then they can see the scene where they go over to Sebastian. "There you can see it," says the man. He stops the video. "Look, he's putting it in his pocket!"

"Why are you hiding him like that?" asks the woman. It looks bad for the friends.

"Show us your bags, and everything in your pockets," the woman says.
They put all their things on the table – the silly teapot, the teddy bear, the model of Big Ben, the T-shirt, their money, maps, tickets and sweets.
But there is no CD. The detectives check the friends' pockets. Still no CD.
The woman looks at the man. "I think they're OK." The man says nothing for some time.
But then he stands up and opens the door.
"OK, kids, you can go now. Sorry for the mistake."
When they are out of the store, Sebastian starts to cry. "I'm really sorry," he says.
"That's OK," says Liam. "Just don't try that again! And if you want a computer game, I can show you how to download some great ones from the Internet."
"Yeah, thanks. But that's no good as a present for my brother. It's his birthday on 7th November."
"Give him that T-shirt. That way you can read the map on it." Even Sebastian laughs at that.
"OK, OK," he says. "My souvenir of London is a shock – and a lesson." Sandra and Liam have nothing to say to that.
"So where are you going now?" asks Liam.
"We're meeting the others," explains Sandra, "to go to the London Dungeon."
Liam laughs. "The London Dungeon? Just the right place for you, Sebastian. Have fun!"

2 Right or wrong?

Six sentences are wrong. *Find and correct them.*

1. Liam meets Sandra and Sebastian in an Oxford Street store.
2. Sebastian hasn't got a present for his parents.
3. Liam thinks the model of Big Ben is silly.
4. Sebastian puts a computer game in his pocket.
5. Sebastian tries to take the CD out of the store.
6. The detectives take them to a big room.
7. They put all their things on the table.
8. Sebastian is sorry.
9. Liam is going to the London Dungeon.

3 What do you think?

a) *Do you like the story? Say what you think.*

The first part is ...
The ending is ...
I don't like it when ...

terrible, nice, boring, funny, exciting, silly, interesting

b) *Talk about what the people do and say.*

Liam is right / wrong when he ...
Sebastian ...
Sandra ...

4 More of the story

Use these pictures to write some more of the story – but do not write out the children's words.

You can start like this: They say goodbye to ... / Then they want to ... / But ... / ... asks the way ... / ... takes ...

1 Your shopping day in London

Plan a shopping day in London:

a) *First say where you'd like to go. Here are some ideas (don't take too many – you only have time for two or three):*

King's Road (latest fashions!), ⊖ Sloane Square
Camden Lock Market, ⊖ Camden Town
Brixton Market, ⊖ Brixton
Petticoat Lane, ⊖ Liverpool Street
and see pages 74 / 75.

Say what you'd like to buy at these shops and markets.

b) *Look at the map of the London Underground. Find where you are starting (⊖ Angel), and then say how you get from there to the shops and markets.*

Start: We can take the ... Line to ... .
We can change to the ... Line there,
and go to ... . That's the station near ... .
After that ...

c) *Now look at the street map on the next page and compare how far it is on foot.*

d) *At the end, you must explain how you get back to Islington on the Underground.*

5

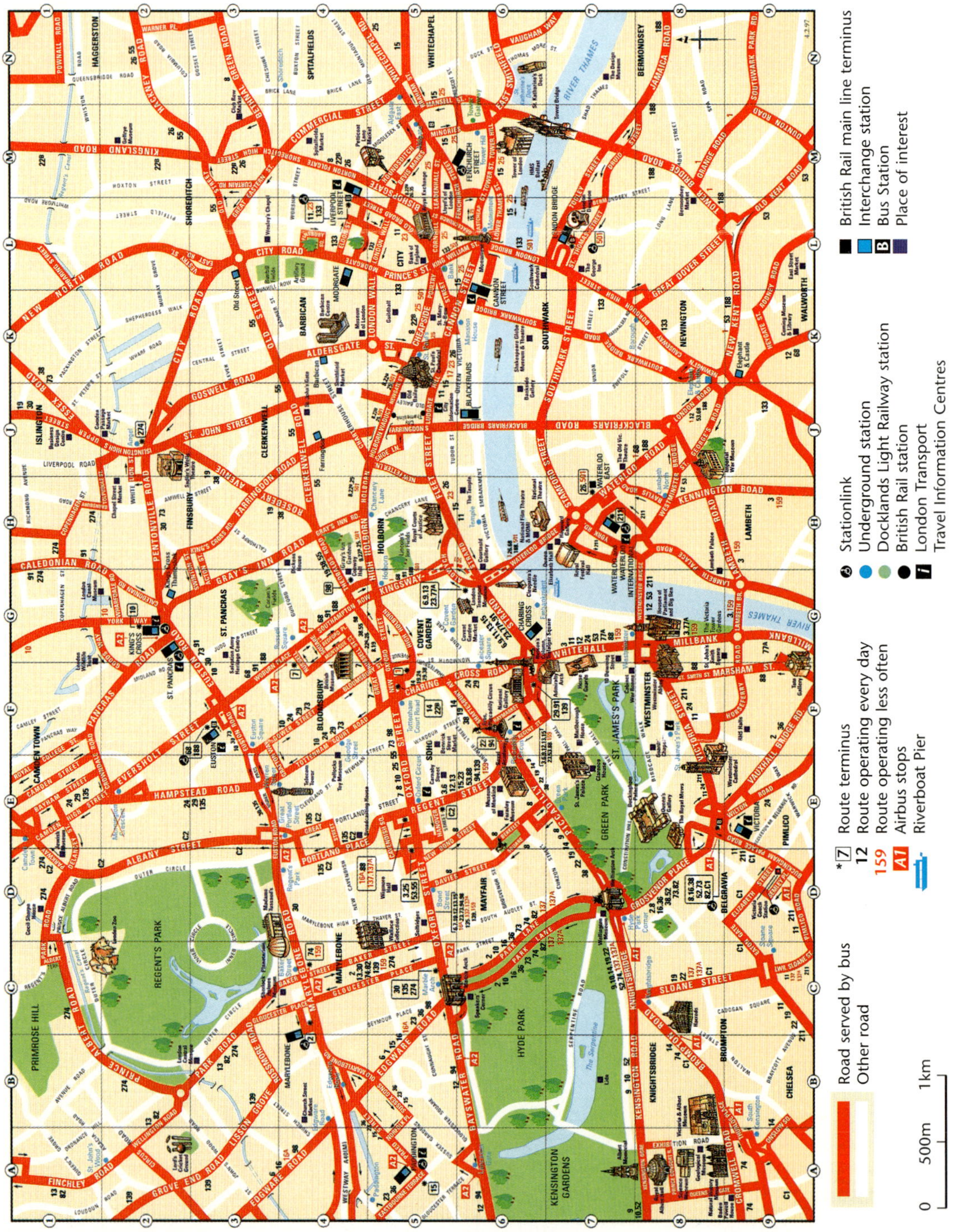

More about London

Choose five sights from the London street map and find some more information about them. You can try to find a London guide at your library or you can use the Internet. Write a short article about your London sightseeing tour.

2 Role play: Market scenes

Look at the picture of a stall at Camden Market. Pick out what you'd like to buy. Now work in pairs: one of you is buying and one of you is selling.

I'd like ..., please.

Which ...?

Sure, here it is. / Sorry, we haven't got ... .

I want the one with .... / The blue / ... one, please. / Have you got it in red / ...? Have you got (a) size ...?

3 ⟨A song: In Camden Town⟩

Listen to the song about Camden Town.

a) Here are the words of one verse[1] and the chorus[2].

(Sing up, tourists, sing!)
There's a crowd[3] of tourists and they're coming down the street,
Pleased as Punch[4] with their brand[5] new Doc Martens on their feet[6],
Past[7] stalls of leather jackets, old bric-a-brac[8],
Indian sunglasses[9] or a Chinese[10] bobble[11] hat.
Tramps[12] stare[13] in the window of the local[14] butcher's[15] shop,
Like a pack[16] of wild[17] dogs, they'd run off with the lot[18]!
In Primrose Hill[19], an angry[20] man, his hair[21] standing on end[22],
Shouts[23] and rants[24] in the ear[25] of his imaginary[26] friend.

Chorus:
In Camden Town, I'll[27] meet you by the Underground,
In Camden Town, we'll walk there as the sun[28] goes down,
In Camden Town –
In Camden Town, you can do anything you want to (do).

b) *Now learn the chorus and sing it.*

[1][vɜːs] *Strophe* [2]['kɔːrəs] *Refrain* [3][kraʊd] *Menschenmenge* [4][ˌpliːzd‿əz 'pʌntʃ] *hochzufrieden* [5][brænd] *brand (neu)* [6][fiːt] *Füße* [7][pɑːst] *vorbei (an)* [8]['brɪkəˌbræk] *Nippes, Kram* [9]['sʌnˌglɑːsɪz] *Sonnenbrille(n)* [10][tʃaɪ'niːz] *chinesisch* [11]['bɒbl] *(mit) Bommel* [12][træmp] *Landstreicher(in), Obdachlose(r)* [13][steə] *glotzen* [14]['ləʊkl] *örtlich* [15]['bʊtʃə] *Metzger* [16][pæk] *Rudel* [17][waɪld] *wild* [18] *sie würden mit dem ganzen Zeug weglaufen* [19][ˌprɪmrəʊz 'hɪl] *Gegend im Norden Londons* [20]['æŋgri] *wütend, böse* [21][heə] *Haar* [22][end] *hochstehen, zu Berge stehen* [23][ʃaʊt] *brüllen* [24][rænt] *schimpfen* [25][ɪə] *Ohr* [26][ɪ'mædʒɪnri] *unsichtbar, imaginär* [27](= I will) *ich werde* [28][sʌn] *Sonne*

4 Goodbye to London

The German friends are getting ready to go back to Germany. It is their last day in London.
Look at Maike's plan for that day and the next morning and then say what happens at what time.

Start: At four o'clock they pack their bags. At quarter to ...

16:00	Pack our bags
16:45	Take bags to school
17:20	Set up instruments
17:35	Give last concert
19:15	Put instruments + bags in Cliftons' van
19:50	Go to Wilsons' for small party
22:25	Go to bed

Tomorrow morning (Saturday)

6:40	Get up, pack small bags
7:00	Have breakfast
7:20 – 7:35	Put bags in Mr Clifton's van
8:15	Drive to airport
9:30	Check in
10:55	Take off
12:05	(local time) Arrive Frankfurt

1 Make a market mind map

2 How many do you want?

Work in pairs and make dialogues. Start like this:

I'd like one of those ..., please.

Sure, here it is. / Which ... do you want?

...

Or like this:

I'd like some ..., please.

Sure, how many do you want?

Six of them, please. / Three / ... and two / ..., please.

eight — three (2 white, 1 red) — four (2 blue, 2 black)

six — two — five (3 small, 2 big)

3 How old are they?

Work in pairs.

Example: How old is Mr Jones?
He's fifty. It's his fiftieth birthday today / in May / ... / on ...

Mr Jones (50)
May 26th

Mrs Jones (51)
April 9th

Uncle George (65)
November 30th

Aunt Stella (46)
February 12th

Mrs Wilson (35)
July 2nd

Jimmy Wilson (14)
January 1st

1 They still can't understand it!

G 35-37

It is the next day. The store detectives are still talking about their 'mistake'.

Hm. The three kids walked into the store together and talked for a while. We waited while the German boy looked at the games. Then we watched it all on TV. It's clear that the others tried to hide him. So we stopped them at the door and played them the video. But when we asked them to open their bags, they showed us everything. The boy even opened that silly model of Big Ben!
I can't understand it.

Yes. We saw what he did: he took the game, then he put it in his pocket. The others went nearer to him. But why? It was too late.
Wait – I think I understand! They told him to put the game back, and they hid him while he took it out of his pocket and put it back on the shelf. Then they went to the door where we met them. Now I know why the boy had nothing from the store in his pocket!
Well, we thought they were shoplifters. But I was right when I said, "The kids are OK" – even if one of them did something silly at first.

a) *Look at what the man says. Make a list of the verbs in the past tense.*

to walk	–	walked [t]
to talk	–	
to wait	–	waited [ɪd]
to try	–	tried [d]
…		

These forms are regular. Can you find the rule? How do you make regular past forms? Are they the same for different persons?

b) *Now look at what the woman says. Make a list of the verbs in the past tense. These forms don't follow your rule – they are irregular. Can you guess what verbs they are from?*

Example: 'saw' is from 'to see'

There is no rule – learn them by heart, and keep a list for new ones.

5

2 Liam's e-mail

Can you read Liam's e-mail to his friends? It isn't very easy because he is using a code for some of the words. His friends have got a computer program to break the code. But you don't need it because
a) *you know what happened,* b) *you know that all the words in code are the past forms of these verbs:*

have	do	show	stop	take	try	think	meet	be
see	go	put	ask	play	open	tell	say	

Hi, guys!
I glx a little adventure yesterday. I jkb this friend in a computer store (no name here, because he xvx something silly!). He rle with Sandra, our German guest. Sandra egcrkx me their funny souvenirs until we elr that we rkhk on the store's TV. Then we ebcaakx and rkyb over to this other friend. We elr what he xvx: he bccw a game from the shelf, asb it in his pocket and bhvkx to leave the store. But Sandra and I ebcaakx him, and he asb it back. At the door, two store detectives lewkx us to come with them to a small room. They bgcsngb our friend still glx the game. They adlukx the video of the scene in the games department. We cakykx our bags and egcrkx them everything we gl in our pockets. In the end, they bcdx us to go home and elvx they rkhk sorry. Phew!
Your friend, Liam

G 38

3 A shopping day in New York

One of Liam's American friends, B. J. Osceola of Florida, answered Liam's e-mail with his own shopping adventure. *Look at the pictures and say what B. J., his mother, and Mark did – or didn't do – there.*

I was in New York last week on a shopping trip. (Mom took me along to carry her bags!) We first did the big mid-town department stores.

At Saks Fifth Avenue we got scarves and gloves (my first pair – you never need gloves in Florida). Then Calvin Klein (three pairs of designer jeans), Tiffany's (silver jewelry), Barnes and Noble (bargain books – very heavy!). We didn't buy anything at Macy's (good!). We walked past the famous Empire State Building, but we didn't go up. No time for sightseeing – the antique market at 26th Street and Sixth Avenue was more important. At last we got back to our hotel on 23rd Street. Then we wanted to go downtown to a famous second-hand market, but weren't sure which subway to take.

At the street corner, we helped a blind man with a guide dog across the road, and he wanted to help us in return. He couldn't show us on the map, of course, but he could take us there, he said. We said OK, and off we went. On the way, he explained that he lived on the Lower East Side and played the piano in a jazz band in different bars there every night. His name was Mark Morton. At every street corner, he knew exactly where we were.

In the artists' district of SoHo, he knew what gallery we were near because of the smell of the paint. Mom stopped there to buy a painting. Mark's hobby was Chinese cooking, so he took us through Chinatown, where he wanted to buy some Chinese vegetables. We bought some too. Then through Little Italy (Mark knew by the smell of the pizzas) and into the Jewish district. That's where the market was. But before we said goodbye to Mark and his dog, he took us to a Jewish deli where we ate a huge pastrami sandwich. We were really very hungry after the long walk, but happy to see so many different parts of New York. The Orchard Street market was fun. I got a great, heavy leather jacket there, really cheap. (So what if I don't need it in Florida?) We took the subway back, of course, we were so tired. And the next day – OUCH!

Yours,
B. J. Osceola

SAVE

They were – They weren't ...
They could – They couldn't ...

But most verbs are like this:

They walked – They didn't walk ...
They bought – They didn't buy ...

1 Find the odd one out

1	2	3	4	5
shop	jeans	clock	handbag	knife
dungeon	shirt	watch	dog-collar	watch
store	jacket	video	glass	picture frame
stall	box	phone	jacket	box
market	scarf	magazine	boots	ice cream

1. The odd one out is ... . You don't ... in a ... .
2. ... You can't ... a ... / You can ... all the others.
3. ... A ... can't tell ...
4. ... The others are often ...
5. ... The others can be ...

2 The top twenty

At the Islington school, they sometimes put up lists like this. This one gives the names of the twenty best boys and girls from one year in all subjects.

You know some of the names here. *Find them and say what place they are in the 'top twenty'.*

Start: Tessa is first on the list. ...

1. Tessa Clifton	11. Angela Dawson
2. John Blake	12. Rizwan Modi
3. Tara Modi	13. Peter O'Brien
4. Mary Ann Mills	14. Nicola Smith-Norton
5. Liam Braden	15. Linda Wong
6. Rukshana Kapadia	16. Lauren McBride
7. Hassan Patel	17. Jimmy Wilson
8. Jonathan Grimsby	18. Kevin Harrington
9. Trevor James	19. Timothy Dawson
10. Karen Macintosh	20. Elizabeth Braden

3 The T-shirt stall

Look at the picture and make dialogues. Use 'some', 'any', 'one / ones' in the right way. One person asks for these things:

- a size XL 'London Underground' T-shirt in red
- a yellow T-shirt with a London scene on it, size M
- something with a London pop group on it, in a nice colour, size L
- a 'Spice Girls' T-shirt, size XS

The other person can sell it – or wants to sell something else. Write out your dialogues.

4 More birthdays

Look at Tara Modi's birthday list. Say what it tells you.

Start: Her father's birthday is on ...
It is his ... birthday this year.

Dad	7/4	(39)	Uncle Tony	1/3	(35)
Mum	23/2	(38)	Aunt Molly	17/5	(36)
Pramila	18/12	(18)	Tessa	19/1	(13)
Hamida	8/6	(16)	Jake	12/11	(5)
Rizwan	30/8	(14)	Baby Tim	21/9	(1)
Me	2/5	(13)	Uncle Farrukh	3/7	(30)
Parveen					
Shamira					

5

CHECK-IN

	record ['rekɔ:d]	Schallplatte
	kind [kaɪnd]	Art, Sorte
	clothes ['kləʊðz]	Kleidung, Kleider
	Doc Martens [ˌdɒk 'mɑ:tɪnz]	*Schuhmarke*
	boot [bu:t]	Stiefel
1	**scarf**, *pl.* **-ves** [skɑ:f]	Schal, Halstuch
	latest ['leɪtɪst]	neueste(r/s), zuletzt erschienene(r/s)
	Girlzone ['gɜ:lzəʊn]	*Name einer Musikgruppe*
	Jack the Ripper [ˌdʒæk ðə 'rɪpə]	*berüchtigter Frauenmörder in London im Jahr 1888*
	Beano ['bi:nəʊ]	*Name einer Comicserie*
	frame [freɪm]	(Bilder-)Rahmen
	collar ['kɒlə]	Hundehalsband
	handbag ['hændbæg]	Handtasche
	near [nɪə]	in der Nähe, nah
	beautiful ['bju:tɪfʊl]	schön
2	**store** ['stɔ:]	(großes) Geschäft, Laden
	bookshop ['bʊkʃɒp]	Buchhandlung

Shoes and boots come in pairs.

franz collier *lat* collare
engl collar

STEP A

A	**quite** [kwaɪt]	ziemlich
	both [bəʊθ]	beide
	Camden Passage [ˌkæmdən 'pæsɪdʒ]	*Markt im Londoner Stadtteil Islington*
	stall [stɔ:l]	(Verkauf-)Stand
	£ (pound sterling) [paʊnd]	*britische Währung*
	I'd (= I would) like [aɪd 'laɪk]	ich hätte gerne
	p (pence, *pl. of* **penny)** [pens]	*britische Währung (100 pence = £1)*
	any ['eni]	irgendeine(r/s), etwas
2	**knife**, *pl.* **-ves** [naɪf]	Messer
	phrase [freɪz]	Phrase, kurzer Satz
	them [ðem]	sie *(Akk.)*; ihnen *(Dat.)*
	Superman ['su:pəmæn]	*Name eines Comichelden*
	size [saɪz]	Größe
3	**watch** [wɒtʃ]	Armbanduhr
B	**Camden Lock** [ˌkæmdən 'lɒk]	*Schleuse im Londoner Stadtteil Camden*
	sweets [swi:ts]	Süßigkeiten
	leather ['leðə]	Leder
	chips [tʃɪps]	Pommes frites
	vinegar ['vɪnɪgə]	Essig
	Irish folk [ˌaɪərɪʃ 'fəʊk]	*Musikrichtung aus Irland*
	bhangra ['bæŋgrə]	*Musikrichtung aus Indien*
5	**aunt** [ɑ:nt]	Tante

Most dog collars, handbags and boots are made of leather.

a watch

sweets
meet
feet

In Great Britain people put vinegar on their fish and chips.

6	**to practise** ['præktɪs]	üben, proben
	musician [mju:'zɪʃn]	Musiker(in)
	page [peɪdʒ]	Seite

To be a good musician you must practise a lot.

STEP B

	to go shopping [ˌgəʊ 'ʃɒpɪŋ]	Einkaufen gehen
	Tottenham Court Road [ˌtɒtnəm kɔ:t 'rəʊd]	*Straßenname*
	to meet* [mi:t]	treffen, begegnen
	real [rɪəl]	echt, wirklich
	after all [ˌɑ:ftə 'ɔ:l]	schließlich, letztendlich
	price [praɪs]	Preis
	department [dɪ'pɑ:tmənt]	Abteilung
	to show* [ʃəʊ]	zeigen
	teapot ['ti:pɒt]	Teekanne
	to laugh [lɑ:f]	lachen
	present ['preznt]	Geschenk
	not … yet [jet]	noch nicht
	bridge [brɪdʒ]	Brücke
	string [strɪŋ]	Faden; Saite
	to hear* [hɪə]	hören
	away [ə'weɪ]	weg, fort
	to turn [tɜ:n]	(um)drehen, wenden
	to keep* [ki:p]	behalten
	young [jʌŋg]	jung
	face [feɪs]	Gesicht
	mistake [mɪ'steɪk]	Fehler
	yeah [jeə]	ja
	to explain [ɪk'spleɪn]	erklären
	London Dungeon [ˌlʌndən 'dʌndʒn]	*Museum in London (wörtl.: Verlies)*
2	**to correct** [kə'rekt]	korrigieren, verbessern
3	**exciting** [ɪk'saɪtɪŋ]	aufregend, spannend

franz musicien *lat* musicus
engl musician

Are you ready to go shopping?

January	['dʒænjuri]	*Januar*
February	['februri]	*Februar*
March	[mɑ:tʃ]	*März*
April	['eɪprl]	*April*
May	[meɪ]	*Mai*
June	[dʒu:n]	*Juni*
July	[dʒʊ'laɪ]	*Juli*
August	['ɔ:gəst]	*August*
September	[sep'tembə]	*September*
October	[ɒk'təʊbə]	*Oktober*
November	[nəʊ'vembə]	*November*
December	[dɪ'sembə]	*Dezember*

A pot for tea is a teapot.

from		to	
	musician		instrument
	penny		pound
	book		page
	picture		frame
	bridge		water
	birthday		present
	…		…

STEP C

1	**fashion** ['fæʃn]	Mode
	Sloane Square [ˌsləʊn 'skweə]	*Name eines Platzes*
	Petticoat Lane [ˌpetɪkəʊt 'leɪn]	*Straßenname und Markt*
	Liverpool ['lɪvəpu:l]	*Industriestadt in Nordwestengland*
	Angel ['eɪndʒl]	*U-Bahn-Station*
4	**ready** ['redi]	fertig, bereit (sein)
	to set* (up) [ˌset‿'ʌp]	(auf)stellen, (auf)bauen
	tomorrow [tə'mɒrəʊ]	morgen
	breakfast ['brekfəst]	Frühstück
	to take off [ˌteɪk‿'ɒf]	starten, abheben

Look at his clothes – the latest fashion.

Breakfast at Tiffany's is a famous American movie.

TRACK 2

1	+**while** [waɪl]	(eine) Weile; während
	+**clear** [klɪə]	klar, einleuchtend
	+**nearer** ['nɪərə]	näher
	+**shelf**, *pl.* **-ves** [ʃelf]	Regal(brett)
	+**shoplifter** ['ʃɒpˌlɪftə]	Ladendieb(in)
	+**something** ['sʌmθɪŋ]	etwas
	+**regular** ['regjələ]	regelmäßig
	+**irregular** [ɪ'regjələ]	unregelmäßig
	+to **learn* by heart** [ˌlɜ:n baɪ 'hɑ:t]	auswendig lernen
	+to **break*** [breɪk]	brechen, knacken
	+to **need** [ni:d]	brauchen
	+**guy** [gaɪ]	Freund, Kumpel
	+**adventure** [əd'ventʃə]	Abenteuer
	+**yesterday** ['jestədeɪ]	gestern
	+**until** [ən'tɪl]	bis
	+**American** [ə'merɪkən]	amerikanisch, Amerikaner(in)
3	+**Florida** ['flɒrɪdə]	*amerikanischer Bundesstaat*
	+**own** [əʊn]	eigene(r / s)
	+to **carry** ['kæri]	tragen
	+**mid-town** ['mɪdtaʊn]	*mittlerer Teil der Insel Manhattan in New York*
	+**Saks Fifth Avenue** ['sæks ˌfɪfθ 'ævənju:]	*Name eines Geschäftes*
	+**avenue** ['ævənju:]	Allee, (breite) Straße
	+**glove** [glʌv]	Handschuh
	+**Calvin Klein** [ˌkælvɪn 'klaɪn]	*Name eines Geschäftes*
	+**Tiffany's** ['tɪfniz]	*Name eines Geschäftes*
	+**jewelry** *AE* ['dʒu:əlri]	Schmuck
	+**Barnes and Noble** ['bɑ:nz‿ən 'nəʊbl]	*Name einer Buchhandlung*
	+**bargain** ['bɑ:gɪn]	günstiges Angebot, Gelegenheitskauf
	+**Macy's** ['meɪsiz]	*berühmtes Kaufhaus in New York*
	+**past** [pɑ:st]	vorbei (an)
	+**Empire State Building** [ˌempaɪə 'steɪt ˌbɪldɪŋ]	*berühmtes Hochhaus in New York*
	+**downtown** *AE* [ˌdaʊn'taʊn]	*südlicher Teil der Insel Manhattan in New York; sonst:* Stadtzentrum
	+**subway** *AE* ['sʌbweɪ]	U-Bahn
	+**across** [ə'krɒs]	darüber, über
	+**in return** [ɪn rɪ'tɜ:n]	dafür
	+**could** [kʊd]	konnte(n), könnte(n)
	+**Lower East Side** [ˌləʊə‿'i:st saɪd]	*Stadtviertel in New York*
	+**night** [naɪt]	Nacht
	+**district** ['dɪstrɪkt]	Bezirk, (Stadt-)Viertel
	+**SoHo** ['səʊhəʊ]	*Künstlerviertel in New York*
	+**smell** [smel]	Geruch

Is that a shoplifter over there? She took something from a shelf and put it in her pocket.

thing – **some** – one / times

Rhyme time

buy – bought	bring – brought
sell – sold	tell – told
know – knew	fly – flew
ring – rang	sing – sang
stand – stood	take – took

night – tonight | day – today
yesterday – today – tomorrow

Did you know?

Charlie Chaplin wasn't American, he was British.

Gloves are for your hands as shoes are for your feet.

Tiffany's is a famous jewelry shop (not only in New York).

Macy's is one of the biggest department stores in America.

'Downtown' is the American word for 'city centre'.

Never sit alone in a New York subway car.

Chinatown and Little Italy are districts in New York.

I ♥ N.Y.!

+**paint** [peɪnt]	Farbe	
+**painting** ['peɪntɪŋ]	Gemälde, Bild	
+**Chinese** [tʃaɪ'ni:z]	chinesisch, Chinesisch	
+**cooking** ['kʊkɪŋ]	Kochen, Essen	
+**Chinatown** ['tʃaɪnətaʊn]	*Stadtviertel in New York*	
+**vegetable** ['vedʒtəbl]	Gemüse	
+**Little Italy** [ˌlɪtl 'ɪtli]	*Stadtviertel in New York*	
+**Jewish** ['dʒu:ɪʃ]	jüdisch	
+**deli(catessen)** ['deli]	Delikatessengeschäft, -lokal	
+**huge** [hju:dʒ]	riesig	
+**pastrami** [pəs'trɑ:mi]	geräuchertes Rindfleisch	
+**Orchard Street** ['ɔ:tʃəd ˌstri:t]	*Straßenname*	
+**yours** [jɔ:z]	deine(r / s), eure(r / s), Ihre(r / s)	

Are you interested in paintings? Then you must go to a gallery.

to paint	paint	painting
to cook	cook	cooking

Chinese cooking ⇒ Chinatown
pastrami and pizza ⇒ Little Italy

There are exciting smells in that deli.

COGNATE WORDS

antique [æn'ti:k]	Antik-, Antiquitäten-
+**artist** ['ɑ:tɪst]	Künstler(in)
banana [bə'nɑ:nə]	Banane
+**bar** [bɑ:]	Bar
calendar ['kæləndə]	Kalender
canal [kə'næl]	Kanal
centre ['sentə]	Zentrum
to **check** [tʃek]	kontrollieren, überprüfen
chocolate ['tʃɒklət]	Schokolade
concert ['kɒnsət]	Konzert
+**designer** [dɪ'zaɪnə]	Designer(in)
detective [dɪ'tektɪv]	Detektiv(in)
dialogue ['daɪəlɒg]	Dialog, Gespräch
to **download** [ˌdaʊn'ləʊd]	herunterladen
+**exact** [ɪg'zækt]	exakt, genau
+**gallery** ['gælri]	Galerie
glass ['glɑ:s]	Glas
hand [hænd]	Hand
+**jeans** [dʒi:nz]	Jeans
local ['ləʊkl]	lokal, örtlich, Orts-
Marathon ['mærəθn]	Marathon
model ['mɒdl]	Modell
negative ['negətɪv]	negativ, verneinend
to **pack** [pæk]	packen
to **pick (out)** [ˌpɪkˌ'aʊt]	(heraus)picken, (heraus)suchen
plan [plæn]	Plan
positive ['pɒzətɪv]	positiv, bejahend
+**program(me)** ['prəʊgræm]	Programm
recorder [rɪ'kɔ:də]	(Video- / Kassetten-) Rekorder
role [rəʊl]	Rolle
salt [sɔ:lt]	Salz
+**sandwich** ['sænwɪdʒ]	Sandwich, belegtes Brot
scene [si:n]	Szene
+**second-hand** ['sekndˌhænd]	gebraucht, aus zweiter Hand
shock [ʃɒk]	Schock
silver ['sɪlvə]	Silber
sir [sɜ:]	mein Herr *(Anrede)*
software ['sɒftweə]	Software
souvenir [ˌsu:vn'ɪə]	Souvenir, Andenken
tea [ti:]	Tee
teddy bear ['tedi ˌbeə]	Teddybär
+**trip** [trɪp]	Kurzreise, Trip
vanilla [və'nɪlə]	Vanille
yoga ['jəʊgə]	Joga

5

UNIT 6

A new start

A

6th February

Dear Diary,

The heating isn't working and our house is like a fridge, so I'm wearing tights under my jeans, a sweatshirt, two jumpers, my red jacket and my old school scarf. And they call Cornwall the 'Riviera of England'!

But life in the country is fun and our new house is great. Liam can see the sea from his bedroom window, and I've got a view of fields and hills and woods. When I wake up in the morning I hear the birds in the trees. In London you just hear traffic. Right now it isn't so quiet because Liam is playing a new computer game again. I don't understand why those games are so noisy. Oh good, he's stopping now. My bedroom is really nice now. I'm painting it yellow and blue – my favourite colours – but now I've got paint on my clothes, in my hair, everywhere.

We start at Penryn College on Monday and we still haven't got our uniform. Mum wants to buy it for us tomorrow. I like shopping, but the uniform is AWFUL!

That's all for now. It's snowing and Milly wants to play with me outside.

B

To: mike@seaview.aol.uk
Subject: From London to Penryn
cc: steve@socks.netulike.com

Hi! How are you, Mike? Thanks for the Christmas presents. Better late than never! The Chicago Cubs sweatshirt is just the right size.
Well, we're in our new house now. I can't write much because my fingers are like ice and I'm wearing gloves! Mum is trying to fix the heating downstairs, but she isn't having much luck. That's the problem with old houses. Nothing works.
My room isn't bad, but there are pink flowers on the walls! I want to paint them black, but Dad says no. Liz can choose the colour of her walls, but I can't. Typical, isn't it? One rule for girls, one rule for boys.
Mum and Dad are busy with their new jobs, so now we've got this mad cleaning lady, Mrs Minns. She comes twice a week and says there are ghosts in the woods near our house. I hope she's right because it's so BORING here. In the summer we can go to the beach, but there's nothing to do in the winter.
At the moment I can't go out on my bike because of the snow. We're three miles from the village and there are not many buses. Help!!! I can't go anywhere!!!
Well, school starts on Monday, and

1 What do they like?

Make a list and write down what Liz and Liam like/don't like.

	Liz	Liam
likes		
doesn't like		

2 I can see ...

a) *Talk about what you can see in the pictures.*

b) *Look at the words on the right. Which of the things can you see from your bedroom window?*

river – car park
beach – hill
bridge – woods
night club
field – church
traffic – shops
disco – the sea
castle – farm

C

Penryn College: Our School Uniform

GIRLS
Plain black skirt or trousers
Plain white shirt or polo shirt with school logo
Plain black sweatshirt with school logo
Black and red school tie
Black footwear

BOYS
Plain black trousers
Plain white shirt or polo shirt with school logo
Plain black sweatshirt with school logo
Black and red school tie
Black footwear

Pupils who wear the school polo shirt do not need to wear a tie.

PE and GAMES
Plain red sports T-shirt
Black hockey socks with red tops

PE and GAMES
Black shorts
Football boots and trainers

3 Clothes for school

a) *What are Liz and Liam wearing? What have they* not *got yet?*

b) *Do you like their school uniform? Why or why not? What do you usually wear to school?*

4 Those are nice jeans!

Look at the people in the rest of the book and talk about their clothes. Examples:

Do you like Jimmy's trainers?
What do you think of that baseball cap?
I love Maike's sweatshirt / Tessa's shoes / ...
Those jeans look nice / funny / ...
That jacket is too big / a boring colour / ...

5 Guess why

1. Why do we say 'these trousers'?
2. Why do we call this a T-shirt?
3. Why do we call these shorts?

The skirt is an awful colour.
These trousers are too short.

6 Who is wearing what?

Describe what someone in your class is wearing. The others must guess who the person is.

The new school

It is Liz and Liam's first day at Penryn College.
A pupil is showing them around.

Pete: This is where we have assembly. The drama group sometimes comes here in the breaks. They're rehearsing for the school play at the moment.
Liz: When do we have assembly?
Pete: You're in Year 8, so you always have it on Tuesdays and Fridays.

Pete: That's the staffroom over there.
Liam: Oh – are you taking us inside?
Pete: Don't worry, Liam. Pupils never go in there!

Pete: Here's the library. I often work here, or just read.
Liam: Wow – look at all those computers!
Liz: Be quiet, Liam! People are reading, can't you see?

Pete: This is the cafeteria. The meals aren't too bad.
Liz: The teachers are having lunch now! It's only half past ten!
Pete: Oh, those people work in the cafeteria. I think they're just having a snack.

Liam: Why are they playing football outside? It's raining!
Pete: We usually play football in the gym when it rains, but not today. We're getting the gym ready for Red Nose Day! Come on – I can show you.

G 39

1 What's the rule?

a) *What do we call these tenses?*

They**'re** play**ing** football outside.
We usually **play** football in the gym.

b) *Look for more examples of the tenses and list the signal words that go with them.*

c) *Try to find a rule for when you use each tense. You can explain it in German.*

2 Red Nose Day

On Red Nose Day some people in Britain wear funny red noses and do things for charity.
Compare what happens on a typical day at Penryn College with what is happening now/today/at the moment.

Example: 1. The pupils **usually wear** uniform but **today** they **are wearing** crazy clothes.

3 What you do at school

Work in pairs. Ask your partner questions with 'Do you ...?'. If the answer is 'Yes, I do', ask if he or she is doing it now.

Example:

Do you play football at school?

No, I don't.

Yes, I do.

Are you playing football now?

No, I'm not.

Yes, I am.

play football	have lunch	wear jeans
wear a tie	eat sweets	learn French
sleep	do tests	read comics
do homework	send notes to friends	
smoke	use a computer	

4 A letter from Liz

Put in the verbs. Use the right forms of the present tense.

Dear Sandra,
Thanks a lot for your band's demo tape. I (listen) to it now and it's good! I (make) a copy for Liam too. I (send) you these photos of me in my new uniform. Isn't it awful? I'm sure you (laugh) now. We (not wear) that stupid hat all the time, of course!
Our new school isn't too bad. The teachers are OK, but they (give) us too much homework. In some subjects we (do) a lot of projects. At the moment we (do) a project on the sea.
It's fun because sometimes we (go) to the beach in our Biology lessons. (No, we (not go) in the water. It's too cold in winter!)
There's a Computer Club so Liam (spend) all his breaks there with the other computer freaks. They sometimes (meet) after school too. I think something is wrong with him at the moment because he (not play) computer games in his room. He's (do) his homework!
Everything is white outside. (snow) like crazy at the moment. Usually it (not snow) much in England. What about Germany?

Liz

5 Listening comprehension: A fashion show

Some pupils are putting on a fashion show for a Design and Technology project "A new school uniform".

a) *Listen to the four descriptions and match them with the picture.*

b) *How do you think Pete describes the fifth uniform?*

6 Your design

Draw your idea of a 'perfect' school uniform. Write about it and then describe your design to your class.

The girl in the woods

An ugly old woman with a green face walks into Liam's room.
"Why aren't you wearing your costume, Liz?" he asks his sister. "You look normal!"
"Ha ha, very funny!" says Liz. She is going to the King Arthur party as the bad witch, Morgan le Fay, and her brother is going as King Arthur's friend, Merlin the Magician. "Hurry up," she says. "The bus goes in five minutes!"
Liam puts on his hat and scarf, and they run downstairs.
Mrs Braden asks: "Have you got enough money for the bus?"
Liz checks her purse. "Yes, Mum. But, er ... can you or Dad fetch us from the party? The last bus is at nine o'clock."
"Well, I can't because my glasses are broken, but Dad can. He's at the Astronomy Club in Helston at the moment and he says he can fetch you from the party on his way back at eleven."
"But, Mum, that's too early," cries Liam.
Liz pulls his arm. "Don't be silly. You know Dad can't wait for us in the car all night! Come on, Liam, let's go!" She doesn't want to miss the bus.
Mrs Braden goes with them to the door.
"Be careful!" she shouts as they run down the road.
When they get to the bus stop, they are too late.
"What do we do now?" asks Liam.
Liz looks at her watch. "We can get the next bus in an hour. Or we can go home and forget the party."

INVITATION

Please come to my
KING ARTHUR PARTY
on Saturday, 15th January at 7 pm
at the village hall in Canbury
Come as your favourite character from the
Legends of King Arthur

Then Liam has an idea."Why don't we take a short-cut through the fields? I don't want to go by bus anyway. We look silly in these costumes."
"Are you sure you know the way?" Liz asks.
"I think so. We just follow the footpath, that's all."

Stop and think! What should they do now?
Go home?
Wait for the next bus?
Take the short-cut through the fields?

They follow the footpath through the fields, up the hill, and then into the woods.
"It's very dark," says Liz. "Remember what Mrs Minns always says about the ghosts in the woods. Let's just go back."
"Wait!" says Liam. A broken signpost is lying in the snow. "It's only one mile to Edgecombe now. Come on, this way."
They walk through the woods and into another field. Thick fog comes up from the sea and moves around them. Everything is white and very quiet.
"I think we're lost," says Liz. Then suddenly she stops.
"Look, Liam! Someone is walking in front of us. Look at those footprints in the snow." Then they see a dark shape. It is coming towards them out of the fog.

Stop and think! What should they do now?
Stay where they are?
Run away?

It is a girl of 15 or 16, in a long white dress. She smiles at them. "Merlin! Morgan le Fay!" Liz and Liam laugh. So it isn't a ghost after all! "Are you going to the party too?" asks Liam. The girl is quiet for a moment. Then she says: "I am looking for my Lancelot." "Ah, so you're Princess Elaine!" says Liz. She knows all the King Arthur legends. Elaine loves the knight, Sir Lancelot. But he loves someone else. "Yes, I am Elaine. But you are lost, I see. Come, I can show you the way."
They follow the girl down the other side of the hill, and then to the village hall in Edgecombe. Later, when it is time to go, Liam remembers Elaine.
"We must say thank you," he tells Liz. They go and look for her. Everywhere there are girls in Princess Elaine costumes, but they cannot find the right one – the girl from the woods.

Outside, Mr Braden is sitting in his car. He can't see Liz and Liam yet, but he can see a sad princess near the door. She is waiting for someone. Then a young man with golden hair comes ... and they leave together. In the fog they seem to be on a horse. Or is it a bike? Mr Braden takes off his glasses and cleans them. When he puts them on again, they are gone.

1 Spot the mistake

Example: Liz and Liam are wearing funny clothes because it is Red Nose Day.
Liz and Liam are wearing funny clothes because they're going to a costume party.

1. Liam is going as King Arthur and Liz is wearing a witch costume.
2. They can't get home by bus, but Mrs Braden can fetch them.
3. They miss the train so they decide to walk to the party.
4. Liam wants to go back home because of Mrs Minns's stories about ghosts.
5. They walk down the hill and then they go into the woods.
6. Elaine, the girl in the woods, loves King Arthur.
7. Elaine is lost so Liz and Liam show her the way.
8. Liam wants to say thank you to all the girls in Princess Elaine costumes.

2 Test your partner

Write five questions about the story and test your partner. Then answer your partner's questions.

3 The right word

Work in groups of three or four. Take turns and read out parts of the story. When you get to a new word, don't say it. Just say 'Buzz!' and finish the sentence. The others must fill in the right word.

4 Writing a story

Write your own (ghost) story in about 100 words. Use ten or more of these words and think of a good title.

shout	dark	ghost	white	run	fog	night
black	wait	fight	quiet	footprints	hill	broken
loud	old	terrible	chase	follow	careful	stop
push over	bad	helpless	nail	woods	cry	fire

1 Classroom language

Work in pairs. Look at the picture for one minute. Then test your partner's memory.

Example:

How many biros are there on Liam's desk?

There are three.

Where's the ruler?

It's in the pencil case on Liz's desk.

WP 2 Word pairs

Find pairs and make sentences with them.

Example: Please can I borrow your dictionary? I want to look up a word.

do repeat take clean
look up open make borrow

+

a sentence mistake dictionary
board test turns word books
homework pencil sharpener

YOU 3 Classroom talk

Work in pairs. Choose from the things in exercise one and make little dialogues.

Please can I use your …?
May I borrow your …?
Can you lend me your …?
Have you got a / some …?

Sorry, but I'm using it at the moment.
Sure, here you are.
Yes, of course.
I'm afraid I haven't. / Yes, I have.

SAVE

You lend something to someone ... *(like 'give').*
You borrow something from someone ... *(like 'take').*

6

HV 4 Listening comprehension: Please

Listen to five short dialogues and match them with the pictures.

WP 5 Keeping a vocabulary notebook

a) *You can put words in groups or headings:*

colours
red pink

b) *You can draw pictures:*

a pair of scissors 

c) *You can make a mind map:*

d) *You can give opposites:*

big – small lend – borrow

e) *You can explain words:*

library (n): You read or borrow books here.
awful (adj): terrible, bad

f) *You can translate words:*

snow (v / n): schneien; Schnee

Choose the best way (for you!) to put these words in your vocabulary notebook.

1. words for clothes (shirt, boots, …)
2. school words (assembly, teacher, …)
3. fog
4. nouns with 'have' (lunch, a break, …)
5. bad
6. gym

SB 6 ⟨A school poem[1]: Yaketty-yak[2]⟩ by Jack Ousbey

Why does my teacher talk all the time?
The talking begins at a minute to nine
When we're outside the door standing neatly[3] in line.
Yakketty-yakketty-yak

Each lesson begins with a speech[4] from the floor,
We think he has finished but then comes some more;
One thing is clear – he knows how to jaw[5].
Yakketty-yakketty-yak

Then come the questions as rapid[6] as rain.
Why does he ask them again and again?
When I don't understand, why won't he explain?
Yakketty-yakketty-yak

Our room has computers, there's no sign of chalk[7],
Just twenty-eight pupils forbidden[8] to talk,
With a teacher who watches us just like a hawk[9].
Yakketty-yakketty-yak

You will listen to me. You will not answer back.
Write neatly; in silence[10]; in biro; in black.
No chewing[11], no talking and no one will slack[12].
Yakketty-yakketty-yak

When the kids stay at home (I'm not really complaining[13]),
The days when the teachers go off for their training,
Who stands at the door and does all the explaining?
Yakketty-yakketty-yak

But listen to this – it's a kind of confession[14] –
When I grow up[15] and work in my chosen profession[16],
A teacher I'll be, and I'll speak with expression[17],
Yakketty-yakketty-yak

What do you think? Put in 'should' or 'shouldn't'.

1. The teacher … talk all the time.
2. The pupils … talk all the time.
3. Pupils … ask questions.
4. The teacher … explain if you don't understand.
5. Classrooms … have a blackboard and chalk.
6. Classrooms … have lots of computers.
7. Pupils … always write with a black biro.
8. All teachers … go off for training on the same day.
9. Jack Ousbey … be a teacher when he grows up.

[1]['pəʊɪm] *Gedicht*
[2][ˌjækəti'jæk] *Gequassel*
[3]['ni:tli] *ordentlich (in einer Reihe stehen)*
[4][spi:tʃ] *(offizielle) Rede*
[5][dʒɔ:] *endlos reden, ‚predigen'*
[6]['ræpɪd] *schnell*
[7][nəʊ‿'saɪn‿əv'tʃɔ:k] *keine Spur von Kreide*
[8][fə'bɪdn] *verboten (sein)*
[9][ˌlaɪk‿ə‿'hɔ:k] *mit Adleraugen*
[10][ɪn 'saɪləns] *schweigsam, still*
[11]['tʃu:ɪŋ] *(das) Kauen*
[12][slæk] *trödeln, nachlassen*
[13][kəm'pleɪn] *beklagen*
[14][ˌgrəʊ‿'ʌp] *erwachsen werden*
[15][kən'feʃn] *Geständnis*
[16][prə'feʃn] *Beruf*
[17][ɪk'spreʃn] *(mit) Gefühl, ausdrucksvoll*

6

1 Who am I?

a) *Work in groups of five or six. Write the name of a person in your class on a piece of paper and stick it on the head of someone in your group. Don't look at the name on your head.*

b) *Now you must all find out who you are. Choose the person in your groups who should start. This person asks yes/no questions, for example: "Am I a girl?" / "Am I wearing jeans?" If the answer is 'yes', he or she can ask another question. If the answer is 'no', then another person can ask a question. Go on until everyone knows who he/she is.*

YOU

2 A report about yourself

Liam makes friends from all over the world through the Internet. In this e-mail, Steve from Chicago is describing himself.

a) *Draw a picture of Steve.*

b) *Write a short report about what you look like, about your family and your hobbies.*

I usually wear glasses but I don't like them.
Right now I'm wearing my Chicago Cubs T-shirt and black jeans. I'm not wearing any shoes!
I've got two older brothers, Bruce and Wayne, and a baby sister, Kate.
My hobbies are baseball and computers, and I also like astronomy. My favorite movie is King Kong – the 1933 version.

3 A spelling game

Play this game in groups. Choose a word from your vocabulary book and spell it to the others. The first person who guesses the right word gets a point. The first person with twenty points wins the game.

1 King Kong

New York City has the legend of King Kong.
Put the parts of the King Kong story in the right order.

A natives took Ann from the ship and gave her to King Kong. But Ann won his heart. King Kong didn't kill her because he loved her so

B to put him in a freak show and make lots of money, but he ran away. He went crazy and the people of New York City were

C women. A group of Americans heard about this gorilla and wanted to see him, so they went to

D much. But he didn't want to give her back. The Americans fought him and saved Ann. Then they took King Kong back to New York. They wanted

E A giant gorilla lived on a secret island. His name was King Kong. When he got hungry – or angry – the natives fed him with young

F scared. King Kong climbed to the top of the Empire State Building with Ann. In the end planes came and killed him. But they didn't kill Ann.

G the island by ship. One of the Americans was a pretty young woman. Her name was Ann. When they landed at the island, the

2 Asking questions in the simple past

> King Kong loved *her*. – Who did he love? (*wen?*)
> *She* loved King Kong. – Who loved him? (*wer?*)

a) *Find the answers.*

1. Where was King Kong from?
2. What did the natives sometimes give him?
3. Who took Ann from the ship?
4. Who killed King Kong in the end?

b) *Ask and answer more questions about the story with these question words:*

What ...? Where ...? Who ...? Whose ...? Why ...? How ...? When ...?

3 Missing words

One word is missing from each sentence. *Choose a word that fits, say where it goes and what kind of word it is.*

Example: 1. King Kong was a very *big* gorilla. 'Big' is an adjective.

1. King Kong was a very gorilla.
2. How did the Americans to the island?
3. What the natives give King Kong when he got angry?
4. The Americans put King Kong a big cage.
5. They hoped to make lots of from him.
6. Everyone was when King Kong ran through New York City.

"No one, but no one, is safe on New York's streets these days."

WP 1 Country words

Can you find the words?

levgila dlfei verri gfo
esa owosd lihl rafm hbeca

2 Country life

Write six sentences about life in the country.

In the country	there are ...	there aren't ...
	you can ...	you can't ...
	you should ...	you shouldn't ...

WP 3 What can you do?

Think of three nouns for each verb.

You can ...

1. play ...
2. listen to ...
3. watch ...
4. have ...
5. earn ...
7. read ...
8. eat ...
9. miss ...
10. do ...
11. make ...

YOU 4 All about me

Complete the sentences.

1. I usually wear ... to school.
2. I never wear ... .
3. I wear ... .
4. I don't wear ... .
5. I am wearing ... .
6. I can't wear ... because ... .

5 What does he do? – What is he doing?

a) *Write three sentences about what Mr Braden is doing now.*

b) *Write three sentences about what Mr Braden does but isn't doing now.*

play ride eat
listen to look through

6 Excuse me ...

Put in the words.

afraid lend course Please but
half borrow dictionary here time

1. Can I ... your ruler, please? – Yes, ... you are.
2. Can you ... me your red pen? – I'm sorry, ... I'm using it at the moment.
3. What's the ...? – It's ... past twelve.
4. ... can I go to the toilet? – Yes, of ... .
5. Excuse me. Have you got a ...? – I'm ... I haven't.

CHECK-IN

A	**heating** ['hi:tɪŋ]	Heizung
	fridge [frɪdʒ]	Kühlschrank
	tights [taɪts]	Strumpfhose
	jumper ['dʒʌmpə]	Strickjacke
	Riviera [ˌrɪvi'eərə]	Riviera
	view [vju:]	Aussicht, Blick
	hill [hɪl]	Hügel
	woods [wʊdz]	Wald
	to **wake* (up)** [ˌweɪk'ʌp]	(auf)wachen
	quiet ['kwaɪət]	ruhig
	noisy [nɔɪzi]	laut, geräuschvoll
	to **paint** [peɪnt]	anmalen, streichen
	paint [peɪnt]	Farbe
	everywhere ['evriweə]	überall
	Penryn College [penˌrɪn 'kɒlɪdʒ]	*Name einer Schule in Penryn, Cornwall*
	awful ['ɔ:fl]	scheußlich, fürchterlich
	to **snow** [snəʊ]	schneien
	outside [ˌaʊt'saɪd]	draußen
B	**than** [ðæn/ðn]	als
	Chicago Cub [ʃɪ'kɑ:gəʊ 'kʌb]	*Name einer Baseballmannschaft*
	glove [glʌv]	Handschuh
	downstairs [ˌdaʊn'steəz]	unten
	luck [lʌk]	Glück
	to **choose*** [tʃu:z]	wählen, aussuchen
	to **be busy** ['bɪzi]	beschäftigt sein
	cleaning lady ['kli:nɪŋ ˌleɪdi]	Zugehfrau, Putzfrau
	twice [twaɪs]	zweimal
	beach [bi:tʃ]	Strand
	mile [maɪl]	Meile *(Längenmaß = 1,61 km)*
	village ['vɪlɪdʒ]	Dorf, kleine Ortschaft
	anywhere ['eniweə]	irgendwohin
	castle ['kɑ:sl]	Burg, Schloss
C	**plain** [pleɪn]	schlicht, einfach
	skirt [skɜ:t]	Rock
	trousers ['traʊzəz]	Hose(n)
	tie [taɪ]	Krawatte
	footwear ['fʊtweə]	Schuhe
	to **need** [ni:d]	brauchen
	trainer ['treɪnə]	Turnschuh
	to **fit** [fɪt]	passen
6	to **describe** [dɪ'skraɪb]	beschreiben
	someone ['sʌmwʌn]	jemand

In England they say:
as old as the hills.

franz vue *lat* visus
engl view

where / way / **any** / one / thing

d o w n s t a i r s

There are lots of castles in Britain.

Trainers are footwear.
Jeans are trousers.

Footwear, footwear, they
always come in a pair.

franz décrire *lat* describere
engl to describe

STEP A

to **rehearse** [rɪ'hɜ:s]	proben, üben
staffroom ['stɑ:frʊm]	Lehrerzimmer

The staffroom is for the teachers.
They are the staff.

6

	library ['laɪbri]	Bibliothek, Bücherei
	meal [mi:l]	Mahlzeit, Essen
	to **rain** [reɪn]	regnen
	gym(nasium) [dʒɪm('neɪziəm)]	Sporthalle
	today [tə'dei]	heute
	Red Nose Day [ˌred 'nəʊz ˌdeɪ]	*Tag, an dem Spenden für karitative Zwecke gesammelt werden*
2	**Britain** ['brɪtn]	Großbritannien
	charity ['tʃærɪti]	Wohltätigkeit
	crazy ['kreɪzi]	verrückt
	to **clean** [kli:n]	reinigen, putzen
3	**French** [frentʃ]	französisch, Französisch
4	**demo tape** ['deməʊ ˌteɪp]	Demo(nstrations)band
	stupid ['stju:pɪd]	dumm, dämlich
	cold [kəʊld]	kalt
5	**description** [dɪ'skrɪpʃn]	Beschreibung
6	to **draw*** [drɔ:]	zeichnen

STEP B

King Arthur [ˌkɪŋ 'ɑ:θə]	König Arthur *(berühmte Sagengestalt)*
pm [ˌpi:'em]	nachmittags *(12–24 Uhr)*
village hall [ˌvɪlɪdʒ 'hɔ:l]	Gemeindehaus
Edgecombe ['edʒkəm]	*Ort in Cornwall*
ugly ['ʌgli]	häßlich
witch [wɪtʃ]	Hexe
Morgan le Fay [ˌmɔ:gn lə 'feɪ]	*Figur der Arthursage*
Merlin the Magician [ˌmɜ:lɪn ðə mə'dʒɪʃn]	*Zauberer in der Arthursage*
to **hurry (up)** [ˌhʌriˌ'ʌp]	(sich) beeilen
purse [pɜ:s]	Geldbörse, Portmonee
to **fetch** [fetʃ]	(ab)holen
Helston ['helstən]	*Ort in Cornwall*
to **miss** [mɪs]	verpassen, versäumen
to **shout** [ʃaʊt]	rufen
short-cut ['ʃɔ:tkʌt]	Abkürzung
footpath ['fʊtpɑ:θ]	Fußweg, Pfad
should [ʃʊd/ʃəd]	sollen
dark [dɑ:k]	dunkel
to **remember** [rɪ'membə]	sich erinnern (an), denken (an)
signpost ['saɪnpəʊst]	Wegweiser
another [ə'nʌðə]	ein(e) andere(r/s)
thick [θɪk]	dick, dicht
fog [fɒg]	Nebel
to **lose*** [lu:z]	verlieren
to **be lost** [lɒst]	sich verlaufen
suddenly ['sʌdnli]	plötzlich
footprint ['fʊtprɪnt]	Fußstapfen
shape [ʃeɪp]	Gestalt, (äußere) Form
toward(s) [tə'wɔ:d(z)]	auf … zu, in Richtung auf, (ent)gegen

yesterday – today – tomorrow

GB GB is for Great Britain.
D is for Germany.

People often collect money for charity.

franz charité *lat* caritas
engl charity

am = *lat* ante meridiem
pm = *lat* post meridiem

Short for ?

m	pm	CD-ROM
km	USA	GB
TV	ad	e-mail
£	p	ft (foot/feet)
Mr	Ms	Mrs

A short-cut makes the way shorter.

Do you believe in magicians?
And what about witches?

6

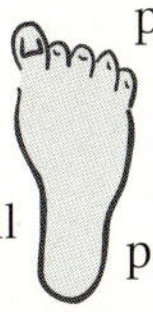

What is a fingerprint?

In thick fog you can lose your way, then you are lost.

These are different shapes:

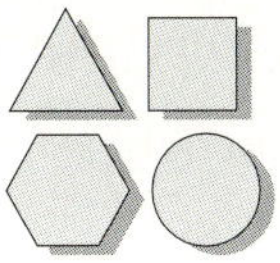

	dress [dres]	Kleid
	Lancelot ['lɑːntsəlɒt]	*Figur der Arthursage*
	Princess Elaine [prɪn'ses ɪ'leɪn]	*Figur der Arthursage*
	knight [naɪt]	Ritter
	side [saɪd]	Seite
	sad [sæd]	traurig
	horse [hɔːs]	Pferd
1	to **spot** [spɒt]	entdecken
	to **decide** [dɪ'saɪd]	entscheiden
3	to **take turns** [tɜːnz]	(sich) miteinander abwechseln
	to **finish** ['fɪnɪʃ]	beenden
	to **fill** [fɪl]	einfügen, auffüllen
4	**own** [əʊn]	eigene(r/s)

Pull up your socks! *(Streng dich an!)*

STEP C

1	**desk** [desk]	Schreibtisch
	ruler [ruːlə]	Lineal
	pencil case ['pensl ˌkeɪs]	Federmäppchen
	folder ['fəʊldə]	Mappe, Ordner
	scissors ['sɪzəz]	Schere
	pencil sharpener ['pensl ˌʃɑːpnə]	Bleistiftspitzer
	rubber ['rʌbə]	Radiergummi
	pen [pen]	Füller, Füllfederhalter
	pencil ['pensl]	Bleistift
	exercise book ['eksəsaɪz ˌbʊk]	Übungsheft, Heft
	(black)board [('blæk)bɔːd]	Tafel
	chalk [tʃɔːk]	Kreide
	sponge [spʌndʒ]	Schwamm
	biro ['baɪərəʊ]	Kuli, Kugelschreiber
2	to **borrow** ['bɒrəʊ]	(aus)leihen
	to **repeat** [rɪ'piːt]	wiederholen
3	**talk** [tɔːk]	Gespräch
	may [meɪ]	dürfen, können
	to **lend*** [lend]	(ver)leihen
5	**heading** ['hedɪŋ]	Überschrift

Let's take turns.
First it's my turn,
then it's your turn.

People and characters in history

jugglers	kings
witches	princesses
magicians	King Arthur
knights	Robin Hood
ghosts	...

Yes, you may, yes, you may,
but never in the month of May.

to repeat = to say it again

Lend your money and
lose your friends.

TRACK 1

1	to **stick*** [stɪk]	kleben
2	**yourself** [jɔː'self]	dich (selbst)
	himself [hɪm'self]	sich (selbst)
	older ['əʊldə]	älter(e/r/s)
	favorite *AE* ['feɪvrɪt]	bevorzugt, Lieblings-
	movie *AE* ['muːvi]	Film
	King Kong [ˌkɪŋ 'kɒŋ]	*Riesengorilla in einem berühmten Hollywood-Film*
3	to **spell** [spel]	buchstabieren
	point [pɔɪnt]	Punkt

I – myself	he – himself
you – yourself	she – herself

Don't do it yourself!

Who is older – Madonna or
Michael Jackson?

Can you spell your name?

TRACK 2

1	+**order** ['ɔ:də]	Reihenfolge
	+**native** ['neɪtɪv]	Eingeborene(r), Ureinwohner(in)
	+**heart** [hɑ:t]	Herz
	+to **kill** [kɪl]	töten, umbringen
	+to **save** [seɪv]	retten
	+**giant** ['dʒaɪənt]	Riese, Gigant
	+**secret** ['si:krət]	heimlich, Geheim-
2	+**whose** [hu:z]	wessen
3	+**island** ['aɪlənd]	Insel
	+**angry** ['æŋgri]	wütend, ärgerlich
	+to **be scared** ['skeəd]	Angst haben, verschreckt sein
	+to **climb** [klaɪm]	hochklettern
	+**pretty** ['prɪti]	hübsch, nett
	+**cage** [keɪdʒ]	Käfig

They go together

describe	description
trainers	footwear
hand	glove
beach	water
to clean	cleaning lady
to snow	to rain
summer	winter
magicians	witches
heading	story
King Kong	New York

Let's test your memory.

franz mémoire *lat* memoria
engl memory

CHECK-OUT

2	**life**, *pl.* **-ves** [laɪf]	Leben
5	to **ride*** [raɪd]	fahren, reiten

Xmas is short for Christmas.

A baseball team needs a baseball field.

COGNATE WORDS

arm [ɑ:m]	Arm	**nose** [nəʊz]	Nase
baseball ['beɪsbɔ:l]	Baseball	**perfect** ['pɜ:fɪkt]	perfekt, vollkommen
Biology [baɪ'ɒlədʒi]	Biologie	**pink** [pɪŋk]	pink
cap [kæp]	Kappe, (Schirm-) Mütze	**polo shirt** ['pəʊləʊ ˌʃɜ:t]	Polohemd
		project ['prɒdʒekt]	Projekt
character ['kærəktə]	Charakter	**report** [rɪ'pɔ:t]	Bericht
Christmas ['krɪstməs]	Weihnachten	**shorts** [ʃɔ:ts]	kurze Hose, Shorts
copy ['kɒpi]	Kopie	**show** [ʃəʊ]	Show
costume ['kɒstju:m]	Kostüm	**signal** ['sɪgnl]	Signal
design [dɪ'zaɪn]	Design	**snow** [snəʊ]	Schnee
disco ['dɪskəʊ]	Disko(thek)	**sock** [sɒk]	Socke
farm [fɑ:m]	Bauernhof, Farm	**sportsfield** ['spɔ:tsfi:ld]	Sportplatz
field ['fi:ld]	Feld	**summer** ['sʌmə]	Sommer
finger ['fɪŋgə]	Finger	**sweatshirt** ['swetʃɜ:t]	Sweatshirt
ghost [gəʊst]	Geist, Gespenst	**test** [test]	Test
golden ['gəʊldn]	golden	to **test** [test]	testen
+**gorilla** [gə'rɪlə]	Gorilla	**title** [taɪtl]	Titel, Überschrift
help [help]	Hilfe	**toilet** ['tɔɪlɪt]	Toilette
to **hope** [həʊp]	hoffen	**top** [tɒp]	ärmelloses T-Shirt
ice [aɪs]	Eis	**typical** ['tɪpɪkl]	typisch
legend ['ledʒənd]	Legende	**uniform** ['ju:nɪfɔ:m]	(Schul-)Uniform
logo ['ləʊgəʊ]	Logo, Emblem	to **wash** [wɒʃ]	waschen, putzen
memory ['memri]	Gedächtnis	**water** ['wɔ:tə]	Wasser
night club ['naɪt klʌb]	Nachtclub	to **win*** [wɪn]	gewinnen
normal ['nɔ:ml]	normal	**winter** ['wɪntə]	Winter

UNIT 7

News from the coast

Reporter: Bad news from the Cornish coast today. Beachgoers and holidaymakers report that there are lots of seabirds in big oil slicks along the Cornish coast. People are trying to rescue the birds and clean their feathers. But lots of birds are already dead. Here is what Ms Howard from *Friends of the Earth* can tell us about it.

Ms Howard: Well, yes. We must try to find the ships and tankers. The captains know it's illegal to spill the oil. What we can do now is to rescue as many birds as possible. We take them to places near the coast where we can clean them. But we can't rescue the birds in the oil slicks out at sea. And we can't reach those in the rocky bays. We need lots of volunteers to help us with this work. And we can't wait.

Reporter: Thank you, Ms Howard. And here on the phone we have Mr Cummings from the local coastguard team. Mr Cummings, why is the oil so dangerous?

Mr Cummings: Well, the very high wax content in the oil from the ships destroys the natural oil in the feathers. This is terrible for the birds and thousands die. We are now looking for the tanker. There are a number of ships around here along our coast. We must check their oil and ask: Is their oil the same as the oil in the sea?

Reporter: Thank you, Mr Cummings.

1 Bad news from the Cornish coast

Match the right parts of the sentences.

1. The radio reporter gives
2. People are trying
3. The radio reporter first talks
4. Ms Howard works for
5. The captains know that
6. The oil from the ships
7. The people and volunteers
8. Thousands of seabirds
9. Mr Cummings is

destroys the birds' feathers.

spilling oil is illegal.

to Ms Howard.

from the local coastguard team.

can't rescue all the birds.

to rescue the seabirds.

a report about the oil slicks.

Friends of the Earth.

must die.

At Penryn College

The day after the bad news there are lots of boys and girls in the Assembly Hall because Mr Clifford, the Biology teacher, wants volunteers for the seabird rescue. And he wants to start a 'Cornish Coast Project'. First he gives some more information. He starts with some slides.

OK then. Can everybody see all right? Britain has got more than 2,500 miles of coast. In many places, like here in Cornwall, there are high cliffs and rocky bays. And there are also lovely beaches, of course. But lots of beaches are full of rubbish. The Beachwatch volunteers try to clean up the beaches. They collect waste. We are going to help them.

Lots of tourists and beachgoers walk along the Cornwall Coast Path, up on the cliffs. We are going to do that too. And we are going to look at the dangerous places. Perhaps we can do more for the safety of the tourists.

Lighthouses are there to warn ships that land is near. You all know their signals in the dark. We are going to visit the Lighthouse Museum in Penzance – by bus, of course. I'm going to drive the bus!

Hundreds of lifeboats – big and small – help to save lives all around the British coast. We're going to visit the Coastguard in Falmouth and we're going to talk to the lifeboat teams there. And – there's a great fish and chip shop in Falmouth! Who's going to have fish and chips?

7

G 40

1 The Cornish coast project

a) *What are the volunteers going to do? Use the ideas in the box and write down the sentences.*

Example: The boys and girls are going to …

The boys and girls Mr Clifford The group The volunteers	is / are …	… the dirty beaches. … the lifeboat teams. … in Falmouth. … the Cornwall Coast Path. … the helpless birds. … in Penzance. … the rubbish. … information in newspapers and magazines.

b) *Can you think of some more plans for the project? Write them down.*

G 40

2 What are they going to do?

Look at these pictures and say what the people are going to do. You can start like this:

The boy with the ball is going to play football with his friends.

SAVE

The present progressive with going to

The action is right now.
They are going to Penzance by bus now.
(They are on their way.)

The going to-future

The going to-future is for intentions.
They are going to visit the lighthouse there.
(It is their intention.)

YOU

3 And what about your plans?

Work with a partner and talk about your plans. They can be fantasy plans too.

Example: What are you going to do at the weekend? – I'm going to interview Michael Jackson.

	at the weekend?		interview …
	tomorrow?		visit …
What are you going to do	in the summer holidays?	I'm going to	play …
	next week?		see …
	…?		…

4 Safety by the sea

The sea can be dangerous. Here are some rules for what you must or mustn't do at the sea or in the water. *Use the words 'must' or 'mustn't' to say the rules in a different way.*

Example:
1. Don't play on the rocks. They are dangerous when they are wet.
   – You **mustn't** play on the rocks.
2. Keep away from the cliffs. They can be dangerous too.
   – You **must** …
3. Don't go up on the cliffs.
   – You …
4. Watch out for the waves. They can push you over.
5. Don't swim when you are cold or tired.
6. Don't swim out to sea. The waves can pull you out into the open sea.
7. Always swim near the beach.
8. Don't stay in the water too long.
9. Always look out for warning signals.

7

SB

Britain's beaches – the best and the worst

Britain's beaches are full of rubbish. The annual Beachwatch report of Britain's beaches says:

There is an average of 1,500 pieces of waste per kilometre of beach. Cornwall has the dirtiest but also the cleanest beaches. Sennen Cove near Land's End is the cleanest in Britain.

Most of the rubbish comes from beachgoers and holidaymakers, over ten million people a year. Other waste comes from ships and boats and from the towns and villages all around Britain's coast. The Beachwatch volunteers – 2,500 men and women and young people in 1997 – try to clean up Britain's beaches every year. They say that the rubbish on Britain's coasts is international. Ships from many countries all over the world dump their rubbish overboard. The waste drifts to the coast, and there it is a danger to the people and to the wildlife.

Among the pieces of waste like food and shoes, fishing lines and thousands of other things are dead animals, mostly dead seabirds. If we find dead seabirds on the beaches, we can be sure that many more are dead out at sea. Usually only one percent of all dead seabirds are on the beaches. All the others die out at sea. Chemicals may be responsible, and oil from the ships, of course.

More than 50% of the waste is plastics. Plastic is cheap to produce, easy to use and easy to throw away. But it is difficult to dispose of.

Throwing plastic over the side or dropping it on the beach causes lots of problems because it doesn't rot away. It may be there on the beaches for years and years. So boat owners and captains must take their waste back to land and dispose of it.

Samantha Pollard from *Friends of the Earth* says: "Ships must stop dumping overboard and people must not drop waste on the beaches. Rubbish causes problems and can be dangerous."

Adapted from *The Guardian*, 6/5/1998

7

1 Right or wrong?

Find the wrong sentences and correct them.

1. On Britain's coasts there is an average of ten million beachgoers and holidaymakers.
2. Sennen Cove is the dirtiest beach in Britain.
3. Most of the rubbish comes from British ships.
4. Beachwatch volunteers try to clean up the beaches every week.
5. Most of the dead animals on the beaches are seabirds.
6. The waste drifts out to sea.
7. Boat owners must stop throwing captains overboard.
8. Plastic is cheap to produce.

2 A fantasy trip

a) *Go on a fantasy trip around your town or village (through a park, to a river, to famous buildings, ...). What kind of waste can you find there? Make a list.*

b) *Now think of a summer holiday on the coast. What kind of rubbish can you find there? And where does it come from?*

c) *What about the rubbish in and around your school? Be a 'schoolwatch' volunteer and collect the waste. Discuss the results and make an 'art' exhibition of the waste.*

3 Listening comprehension: The volunteers

After the meeting six of the volunteers talk about Mr Clifford's idea of a Cornish Coast Project.
a) *Say what they are going to do (or want to do).*

1. Melanie is going to / wants to ...
2. Andy ...
3. Dave ...
4. Jo ...
5. Liz ...
6. Liam ...

b) *And what about you? What would you like to do for the project? Maybe you need some more information about Cornwall and the British coast. You can use the Internet.*

4 Working with a scrapbook

The boys and girls in Mr Clifford's group keep a scrapbook of the Cornish Coast Project. You can do lots of things with or in a scrapbook: draw / write / collect texts / stick in pictures / photos / stickers / ...
Think about a scrapbook about the sea or the coast for your class. What can you put in it?

We can	write draw stick in collect	pictures photos texts words slogans information stories ...	about of	?

5 A 'sea words' mind map

Work with a partner and complete this mind map. You can make a big poster for your classroom.

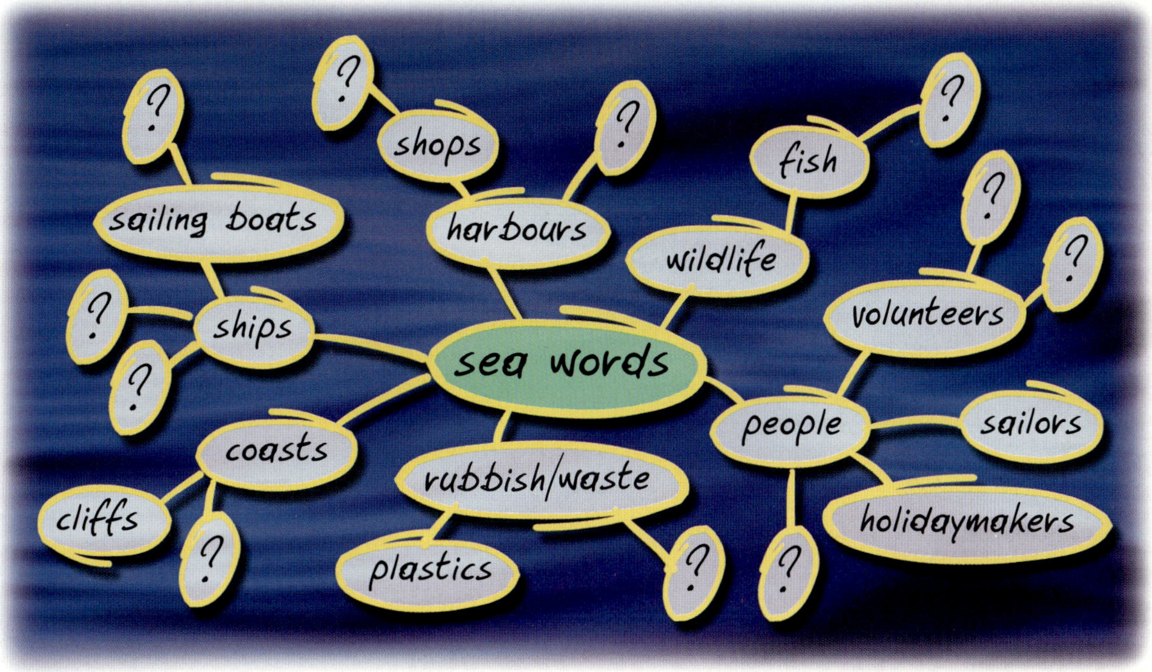

6 Where are you from?

Make sentences.

Where Who Which What	are you	talking listening proud looking waiting going good afraid	from at of for to at about	?

1 The going to-game

Go through the alphabet and make little dialogues.

A I'm going to go to America.
What are you going to do in America?
I'm going to ask Americans about assembly.

B I'm going to go to Britain.
What are you going to do in Britain?
I'm going to buy some boring books in bookshops.

C I'm going to go to Cornwall.
What are you going to do in Cornwall?
I'm going to chase some crazy cats.

D Denmark – drink – disco

E England – eat – ? *Go on.*

2 ⟨A song: Sailing[1]⟩

by Rod Stewart Words and music by G. Sutherland
© Island Musik Ltd., polygram Songs Musikverlag GmbH, Hamburg

1. I am sailing, I am sailing
Home again 'cross[2] the sea.
I am sailing stormy[3] waters
To be near you, to be free[4].

2. I am flying[5], I am flying
Like a bird 'cross the sky[6].
I am flying, passing[7] high clouds[8],
To be near you, to be free.

3. Can you hear me, can you hear me,
Through the dark night far away?
I am dying, forever[9] crying,
To be with you. Who can say?

4. We are sailing, we are sailing
Home again 'cross the sea.
We are sailing stormy waters,
To be near you, to be free.

[1][seɪlɪŋ] *segeln* [2]= across [krɒs] *über* [3]['stɔ:mi] *stürmisch* [4][fri:] *frei* [5]['flaɪɪŋ] *fliegen* [6][skaɪ] *Himmel* [7][pɑ:sɪŋ] *vorbeiziehen (an)* [8][klaʊd] *Wolke* [9][fɔ:(r)'evə] *für immer, ewig*

7

3 Cartoon fun

"I'm not going to be rescued by Bob and Vera Harrington."

"Navigation's easy – just follow the sewage back home."

4 Map reading

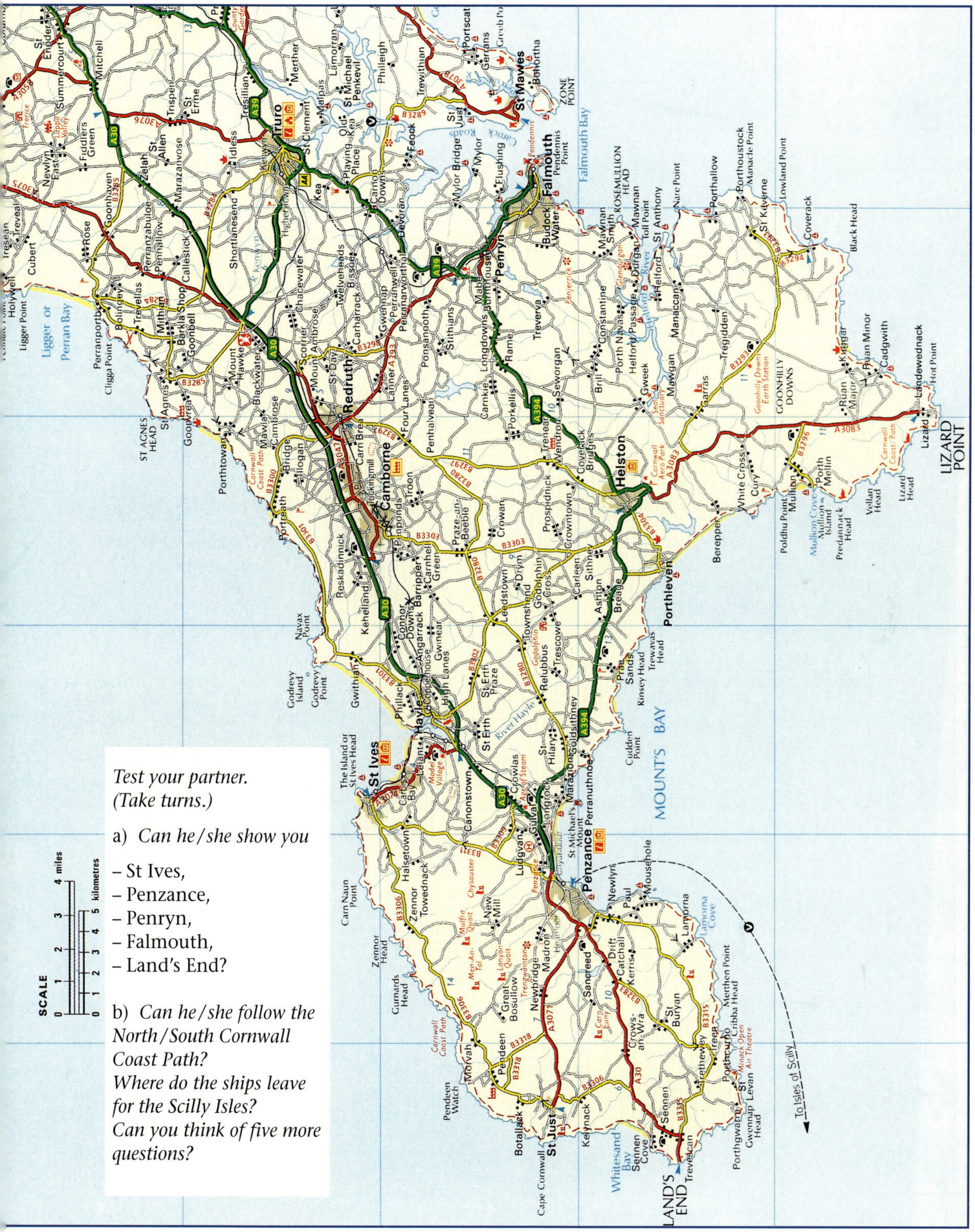

Test your partner. (Take turns.)

a) *Can he/she show you*

– St Ives,
– Penzance,
– Penryn,
– Falmouth,
– Land's End?

b) *Can he/she follow the North/South Cornwall Coast Path?*
Where do the ships leave for the Scilly Isles?
Can you think of five more questions?

1 Holidays on the coast

Talk about the pros and cons of holidays on the coast. What do these people think? And what about you? Write down two more pros and cons.

The wet rocks and the cliffs are dangerous. You can fall into the water. And it isn't so easy to get out again.

There is a lot of rubbish on Britain's coast. I would never go on holiday there.

I've got a boat and I love the boat trips out to sea, even in bad weather.

I love holidays on the coast. You can just lie on the beach and do nothing.

For me the coast is the place for a holiday. The beaches and the waves are great. And I love water sports.

I don't swim in the sea. Even the seabirds die because of the oil slicks along the coast.

2 Who is it?

Think of one boy or girl in your class and talk about him or her. But don't say the name and don't look at him or her. The others must guess who it is. Here are some ideas:

He / she
- has got a baby brother (two cats, …).
- is quiet (funny, sport mad, …).
- loves animals (music, …).
- hates sports (homework, …).
- often plays … (goes …, does …, eats …).
- …

3 Sea words with the letter i

Put these words into sound families. Make two lists.

lighthouse	ship	to die
lifeboat	to swim	cliffs
to find	fish	wildlife
signals	chips	high
trip	to drift	time
to drive	shift	right

[ɪ]	[aɪ]
ship	lighthouse

7

4 ⟨Two tongue twisters⟩

[1]= shell ['si:ʃel] *Muschel* [2]['si:ʃɔ:] *Strand* [3][swɒn] *Schwan* [4][swʌm] *geschwommen*

G 42

1 The sea and me

Just say what you think and give reasons. Example: I think watching seabirds is great because I like animals.

I think / I don't think

- walking along the beach …
- watching seabirds …
- being a captain of an oil tanker …
- helping *Friends of the Earth* or other teams …
- working as a radio reporter …
- visiting a coastguard station …
- rescuing seabirds …

… would make a good school project …
… is OK for boys but not for girls …
… must be interesting …
… is dangerous … … is for me …
… can be boring … … can be fun …
… is useful … … is great …

because

2 More nouns with -ing

to birdwatch to visit to talk to play
to explain to listen to work to climb

a) *Find and put in the right nouns with -ing.*

Example: 1. My dad enjoys … to radio reports.
My dad enjoys listening to radio reports.

2. … a lighthouse can be fun.
3. My brother is good at … things.
4. My friends like … in the cliffs.
5. A reporter must be good at … to people.
6. Our teacher is proud of … for *Greenpeace*.
7. My sister is very good at … .
8. Our friends know a lot about … .

Against killing whales

Against chemical discharges

Greenpeace stands for fresh air, clean water, respect for the earth, its creatures and their natural habitats.

b) *Now ask or interview other pupils in your class: What are they good at, proud of, …?*

c) *Write down what you are good at, not so good at, proud of, interested in, and what you enjoy, like, hate, …*

7

YOU

3 Good at swimming?

Example: My brother is good at swimming.
I'm crazy about …

Write down what	you your friend(s) your brother your baby sister your family your grandma …	is are	interested in. (not so) good at. famous for. proud of. afraid of. crazy about. …

SAVE

verb + -ing = noun *or* gerund

A gerund can be an object:
My sister enjoys swimming.

A gerund can be a subject:
Swimming helps you to keep fit.

4 Hurricane warning

Good morning. It's time now for our weather service again. We have the latest news about Hurricane Jessica. The storm is coming from the Bahamas and is now churning toward Florida's Atlantic coast at a speed of 100 miles per hour. But our experts say the storm will hit the east coast near Miami Beach at a speed of 110 to 120 miles per hour by two p.m. We want to warn residents that there will be bad damage due to the winds and very big waves. Jessica may flood roads, upturn cars, boats and mobile homes, and will damage roofs and break windows. It may also uproot trees and damage electric supply lines. Please be prepared. We hope that the damage won't be too bad. Evacuation may be necessary and there will be emergency services at all the evacuation points along the coast. Please help elderly people. As the hurricane moves north it will turn east and churn into the open Atlantic, or it will turn west, cross Florida and move towards the Gulf of Mexico. But our experts think that Jessica won't change direction in the next five or six hours.

Now stop listening. What's the radio report all about? What do we learn about Jessica? What will happen? Go on listening.

Ladies and gentlemen, we are now going to give you some more information about what to do before Jessica hits:
- Put away loose items.
- Board up windows and doors.
- Put cars in safe places.

See to it that
- there are flashlights and spare batteries, also for your radio,
- there is enough water,
- there is enough food.

Please help elderly people.

SAVE

The will-future

will	= 'll	He'll be late.
will + not	= won't	She won't come.

You will often find the will-future in texts with information about the future, e.g. weather reports.

The going to-future is for intentions (what you want/are going to do).

G 43

5 What will or won't happen?

Complete the sentences and say what will or won't happen.

1. ... news about Hurricane Jessica.
2. ... the east coast near Miami Beach.
3. ... bad damage.
4. ... roofs and windows.
5. ... emergency services.
6. People ... prepared so that ... too bad.
7. ... turn east or west in the next five or six hours.

6 What will the weather be like?

Make adjectives out of the weather nouns.

Example: 1. There will be a storm in the evening.
The evening will be stormy.

2. There will be winds on the coast.
On the coast it ...
3. There will be no fog tomorrow. Tomorrow ...
4. There will be a lot of sun next week.
5. There won't be any clouds in the mountains.
6. Will there be ice on the roads?

WP 1 The third word

a) *Find the missing word.*

1. most – ? – ghost
2. die – ? – tie
3. day – ? – way
4. shop – ? – stop
5. you – ? – who
6. go – ? – show
7. feed – ? – need
8. bird – ? – word

hurt	read	stay
buy	drop	
coast	snow	shoe

b) *Choose five of the groups and make sentences with the words.*

2 What's the sport?

Work with a partner. Make a list of sports. Then take turns with your examples. You can start like this:

1. Ten players (5 + 5) try to throw a ball into a basket. The sport is … .
2. The players try to get a ball over a high net with their hands. The sport is … .
3. Same game as No. 2 but the players do it on the beach. The sport is … .

3 What next?

What are the people going to do?

Example: 1. She is going to read a newspaper article.

1. A woman is sitting down with a newspaper.
2. Two boys are going into a fish and chip shop.
3. Two girls are going to the cinema.
4. A reporter is taking out her pen.
5. Some musicians are checking their instruments.
6. The cat is jumping into the bed.
7. A man comes in with some new fish food.
8. The pupils are looking for their books.

WP 4 Word pairs

Find the partners for these words and write down the pairs. All your words must come from this unit.

Example: leather – feather, tea – ?

leather	tea	way	word	hand	tie	clock
ghost	save	each	know	get	hide	shift

7

5 How to save your life

Read the texts and look at the pictures. Can you find the right word?

1. … is a ring. It can save people who can't swim.
2. … is a strong boat to help people in danger at sea.
3. … is a long rope. You throw it to someone in danger in the water.
4. … is a person on a beach. Their job is to help people when they are in danger.
5. … is a kind of jacket. You wear it on a boat trip out to sea.

CHECK-IN

news *sing.* [nju:z]	Nachrichten, Neuigkeit(en)
coast [kəʊst]	Küste
Cornish ['kɔ:nɪʃ]	kornisch, aus Cornwall
beachgoer ['bi:tʃˌgəʊə]	Strandurlauber(in)
holidaymaker ['hɒlədiˌmeɪkə]	Urlauber(in)
to **report** [rɪ'pɔ:t]	berichten
oil slick ['ɔɪl slɪk]	Ölteppich
to **rescue** ['reskju:]	retten
feather ['feðə]	Feder, Gefieder
already [ɔ:l'redi]	schon, bereits
dead [ded]	tot, verstorben
Friends of the Earth ['frendz‿əv ði‿'ɜ:θ]	*Name einer Umweltschutzorganisation*
to **spill*** [spɪl]	auslaufen, verschütten
as ... as [æz/əz]	(eben)so ... wie
possible ['pɒsəbl]	möglich
to **reach** [ri:tʃ]	erreichen, gelangen
rocky ['rɒki]	felsig, steinig
bay [beɪ]	Bucht, Bai
volunteer [ˌvɒlən'tɪə]	Freiwillige(r)
coastguard ['kəʊstgɑ:d]	Küstenwache
dangerous ['deɪndʒrəs]	gefährlich
wax content ['wæks ˌkɒntent]	Wachsgehalt
to **destroy** [dɪ'strɔɪ]	zerstören
disaster [dɪ'zɑ:stə]	Katastrophe, Unglück
1 **thousand** ['θaʊznd]	tausend

People who walk along the beach are beachgoers.
People who make holidays are ... .

as good as gold
as old as the hills

What do sea monsters eat?
Fish and ships.

STEP A

assembly hall [ə'sembli ˌhɔ:l]	Aula, Versammlungssaal
rescue ['reskju:]	Rettung
slide [slaɪd]	Dia(positiv)
cliff [klɪf]	Klippe
lovely ['lʌvli]	hübsch, schön
rubbish ['rʌbɪʃ]	Abfall, Müll
beachwatch ['bi:tʃwɒtʃ]	Strandaufsicht, Strandwärter(in)
waste [weɪst]	Abfall, Müll
path [pɑ:θ]	Weg, Pfad
safety ['seɪfti]	Sicherheit
lighthouse ['laɪthaʊs]	Leuchtturm
to **visit** ['vɪzɪt]	besuchen
Penzance [pen'zænts]	*Stadt in Cornwall*
lifeboat ['laɪfbəʊt]	Rettungsboot
British ['brɪtɪʃ]	britisch
Falmouth ['fælməθ]	*Hafenstadt in Cornwall*
1 **dirty** ['dɜ:ti]	schmutzig

From word to word

rock	–	rocky
wind	–	windy
danger	–	dangerous
nature	–	natural
love	–	lovely
safe	–	safety

franz visiter   *lat* visitare
engl to visit

 +  = lighthouse

 + path = ?

coast + path = ?

life + 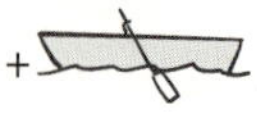 = ?

7

2	**intention** [ɪn'tenʃn]	Absicht, Intention
4	**rock** [rɒk]	Fels
	wet [wet]	nass
	wave [weɪv]	Welle

STEP B

	worst [wɜ:st]	schlechteste(r/s)
	annual ['ænjuəl]	jährlich, Jahres-
	average ['ævrɪdʒ]	Durchschnitt
	piece [pi:s]	Stück, Teil
	dirtiest ['dɜ:tiɪst]	schmutzigste(r/s)
	cleanest ['kli:nɪst]	sauberste(r/s)
	Sennen Cove [ˌsenən 'kəʊv]	*Ort in Cornwall*
	Land's End [ˌlændz 'end]	*westlichster Punkt Englands (in Cornwall)*
	town [taʊn]	(Klein-)Stadt
	to **dump** [dʌmp]	auskippen, hinwerfen
	to **cause** [kɔ:z]	verursachen, anrichten
	danger ['deɪndʒə]	Gefahr
	wildlife ['waɪldlaɪf]	Tierwelt
	among [ə'mʌŋ]	zwischen, unter
	fishing line ['fɪʃɪŋ ˌlaɪn]	Angelschnur
	to **die** [daɪ]	sterben
	to **be responsible** [rɪ'spɒnsəbl]	verantwortlich sein
	easy ['i:zi]	leicht, einfach
	to **throw* (away)** [θrəʊ]	(weg)werfen
	difficult ['dɪfɪklt]	schwierig
	to **dispose of** [dɪ'spəʊzˬɒv]	beseitigen, loswerden
	to **drop** [drɒp]	fallen lassen, abwerfen
	beginning [bɪ'gɪnɪŋ]	Anfang, Beginn
	to **rot** [rɒt]	verrotten, (ver)faulen
	harbour ['hɑ:bə]	Hafen
2	**holiday** ['hɒlədeɪ]	Ferien, Urlaub
	schoolwatch ['sku:lwɒtʃ]	Schulaufsicht, Schulwärter(in),
	result [rɪ'zʌlt]	Ergebnis
	exhibition [ˌeksɪ'bɪʃn]	Ausstellung
4	**scrapbook** ['skræpbʊk]	Sammelalbum

STEP C

1	**Denmark** ['denmɑ:k]	Dänemark
3	to **be rescued** ['reskju:d]	gerettet werden
	sewage ['su:ɪdʒ]	Abwasser
4	**St Ives** [sntˬ'aɪvz]	*Hafenstadt in Cornwall*
	south [saʊθ]	Süden, südlich
	Scilly Isles ['sɪliˬˌaɪlz]	*Inseln vor der Südwestspitze Cornwalls*

good – better – (the) best

bad – worse – (the) worst

Optimists	Pessimists
the best	the worst
the cleanest	the dirtiest
the happiest	the darkest
the ...	the ...

don't dump: chemicals, plastic, bottles, shoes, boxes, ?, ?, ?

What can rot? – Bananas, apples, ...

Opposites

easy	–	difficult
to die	–	to live
to drop	–	to collect
wet	–	dry
dirty	–	clean
dark	–	light

scrapbook: sticker, texts, picture, drawings, cartoons, ?, ?

(DK) is for Denmark.

What are (D) (NL) (F) (E) for?

TRACK 2

1	+**reason** ['ri:zn]	Grund, Ursache
	+**useful** ['ju:sfl]	nützlich, brauchbar
2	+to **birdwatch** ['bɜ:dwɒtʃ]	Vögel beobachten
	+to **enjoy** [ɪn'dʒɔɪ]	genießen, sich (er)freuen
	+to **be proud (of)** [praʊd]	stolz sein (auf)
4	+the **Bahamas** [bə'hɑ:məz]	*Inselgruppe südöstlich von Nordamerika*
	+to **churn** [tʃɜ:n]	sich heftig bewegen, aufwühlen
	+**Florida** ['flɒrɪdə]	*Bundesstaat im Südosten der USA*
	+**Atlantic** [ət'læntɪk]	Atlantik
	+to **hit*** [hɪt]	(auf)treffen (auf), erreichen
	+**east** [i:st]	Osten, östlich
	+**Miami Beach** [maɪˌæmi 'bi:tʃ]	*Stadt in Florida*
	+**resident** ['rezɪdnt]	Bewohner(in), Einwohner(in)
	+**damage** ['dæmɪdʒ]	Schaden
	+**due (to)** [dju:]	zurückzuführen (auf)
	+to **flood** [flʌd]	überfluten, überschwemmen
	+to **upturn** [ʌp'tɜ:n]	umdrehen, umwerfen
	+to **damage** ['dæmɪdʒ]	beschädigen
	+to **uproot** [ʌp'ru:t]	entwurzeln, herausreißen
	+**supply line** [sə'plaɪ ˌlaɪn]	Versorgungsleitung
	+to **be prepared** [prɪ'peəd]	vorbereitet sein
	+**necessary** ['nesəsri]	notwendig, nötig
	+**emergency** [ɪ'mɜ:dʒntsi]	Notfall-, Dringlichkeits-
	+**elderly** ['eldəli]	älter(e/r/s)
	+to **cross** [krɒs]	überqueren, kreuzen
	+**Gulf of Mexico** [ˌgʌlf‿əv 'meksɪkəʊ]	Golf von Mexiko
	+**loose** [lu:s]	lose, locker
	+**item** ['aɪtəm]	Gegenstand, Artikel
	+to **board up** [ˌbɔ:d‿'ʌp]	verschalen, mit Brettern vernageln
	+**safe** [seɪf]	sicher
	+**flashlight** *AE* ['flæʃlaɪt]	(Taschen-)Lampe
	+**spare battery** [ˌspeə 'bætri]	Ersatzbatterie
6	+**foggy** ['fɒgi]	neb(e)lig
	+**icy** ['aɪsi]	eisig

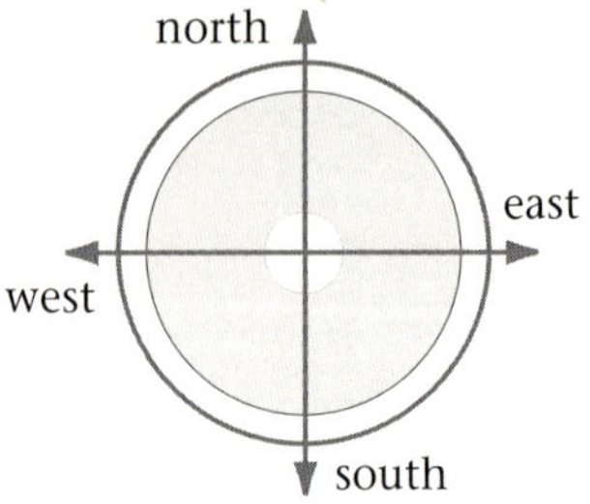

franz raison *lat* ratio
engl reason

Cars can be upturned and damaged.

An uprooted tree has hit a mobile home.

Evacuation: Residents have to leave their homes and go to safer places.

Emergency services have to be prepared for a disaster.

This window is boarded up.

BE: torch
AE: flashlight

CHECK-OUT

2	**basket** ['bɑ:skɪt]	Korb
5	**rope** [rəʊp]	Seil, Tau

a basket

COGNATE WORDS

alphabet ['ælfəbet]	Alphabet
captain ['kæptɪn]	Kapitän
chemical ['kemɪkl]	Chemikalie
+**direction** [dɪ'rekʃn]	Richtung
dream [dri:m]	Traum
to **drift** [drɪft]	(ab)treiben, (ab)driften
+**evacuation** [ɪˌvækju'eɪʃn]	Evakuierung, Räumung
+**expert** ['ekspɜ:t]	Experte/Expertin
fantasy ['fæntəsi]	Fantasie
fish [fɪʃ]	Fisch
+**hurricane** ['hʌrɪkən]	Wirbelsturm, Orkan
illegal [ɪ'li:gl]	ungesetzlich, illegal
information [ˌɪnfə'meɪʃn]	Information, Auskunft
+to **be interested (in)** ['ɪntrəstɪd]	interessiert sein (an)
international [ˌɪntə'næʃnl]	international
kilometre [kɪ'lɒmɪtə]	Kilometer
land [lænd]	Land
meeting ['mi:tɪŋ]	Treffen, Begegnung
million ['mɪljən]	Million
+**mobile home** [ˌməʊbaɪl 'həʊm]	Wohnmobil
+**mountain** ['maʊntɪn]	Berg
museum [mju:'zi:əm]	Museum
natural ['nætʃrl]	natürlich
navigation [ˌnævɪ'geɪʃn]	Navigation, Schiffsverkehr
net [net]	Netz
oil [ɔɪl]	Öl
overboard ['əʊvəbɔ:d]	über Bord
percent [pə'sent]	Prozent
plastic ['plæstɪk]	Plastik
to **produce** [prə'dju:s]	produzieren, herstellen
the **pros and cons** [ˌprəʊz‿n‿'kɒnz]	das Für und Wider, Pro und Contra
radio ['reɪdiəʊ]	Radio
ring [rɪŋ]	Ring
seabird ['si:bɜ:d]	Seevogel
+**service** ['sɜ:rvɪs]	Dienst(leistung), Service
ship [ʃɪp]	Schiff
slogan ['sləʊgən]	Slogan, Werbespruch
+**speed** [spi:d]	Geschwindigkeit
sticker ['stɪkə]	Sticker, Aufkleber
+**storm** [stɔ:m]	Sturm
+**stormy** ['stɔ:mi]	stürmisch
to **swim*** [swɪm]	schwimmen
tanker ['tæŋkə]	Tanker, Tankschiff
team [ti:m]	Team, Mannschaft
tragedy ['trædʒədi]	Tragödie
trip [trɪp]	Reise, Ausflug, Trip
to **warn** [wɔ:n]	warnen

UNIT 8

CONCERT

in School Hall
Fri. 28th April, 7 pm

*

Senior orchestra:
'Spring' from The Four Seasons by Antonio Vivaldi

*

Junior choir:
"Songs of Spring"
– classical, musicals, folk –

*

M. Lee (cello), J. Daly (piano):
Three pieces by L. v. Beethoven

Summer term football

Training:
Senior boys: Tues., Thurs. 6 pm
Junior boys: Tues., Thurs. 5 pm
Girls: Wednesdays, 5 pm

Friendly match:
First 11 against St. Anthony's, Plymouth, Sat., 6th May.
Other matches not yet fixed!

ART COMPETITION

Subject:
The Cornwall coast

You can use water colours, oil paint, pen, pencil, etc. You can get a full list of rules (size of painting, etc.) from Ms Robinson.

Last day: 31st May!

LEARN TO SAIL THIS TERM!

Lessons Tuesdays and Thursdays, 4 pm, Falmouth Harbour

Starting Tuesday, 16th May

And when you have learned to sail:

Come with us on our weekend trips to Plymouth and to the Isles of Scilly!

Apply to: Mr Burns or put your name on the list on the right →

Name	Year
Nora Jones	8
Phil Driver	7
Liam Braden	7

Why not take part in our summer term play? It's –

GALAHAD

A story of his adventures with King Arthur

We need YOU – and not only if you can act!
We need people to:
- make and paint scenery
- make costumes (we've got some great ones, but we need more)
- work the lights
- change the stage between scenes
- write the programme
- sell tickets

etc., etc.

We must be really good this time. We want to win a prize at the Cornwall Drama Festival in July.
YOU CAN HELP!

Come to the Drama Club meeting: 24th April, 5 pm, Room 102

Drama Club notice:
Change of plans – new play for festival!
More work for everybody!

LOST AND FOUND

Lost – small green leather bag.
Lynn, phone 704 509

Has anybody found my silver ring?
MAGGIE, Year 8

Is this your dog?
Marc, Phone 335 643

BUYING AND SELLING

For sale:
Modem, 14,400 bps
Maureen, Year 7

FOR SALE:
Moped, nearly new!
Phone 445 821

Wanted:
CD player
(under £20)
Tony, phone 108 943

Summer term activities

1 What's going on?

a) *Look at the notice board at Penryn School and find out what is going on this term. Then make a list:*

What I would like to take part in:
I'd like ...

b) *Now compare with your partner's list.*
– Are they the same?
– Are they different?

Talk about why you would like to take part in various activities.

nice	boring	I'd like to	hate
awful	silly	wouldn't like to	
don't like	interesting	fun	exciting

2 Work to do

What work must people do before they

a) put on a play?

b) go on a sailing trip?

Start: Before they ...
they must / somebody must ...

3 Listening comprehension: What's the problem?

a) *Look at what the boy and girl in the picture are saying about the activities. What does the girl want to do? What does the boy want to do?*

b) *The boy thinks something is strange. Can you guess what it is?*

c) *Now listen to all of the dialogue and find out:*

1. Were you right?
2. What does the girl think?
3. What does the boy think?

At the Drama Club

They are having a lot of meetings this term.
This dialogue is from the third meeting:

Andrew: Well, we have practised our new play three times already and things are going fine. And we have discussed who does what jobs. So are there any problems?

Brenda: Yes, there are. I don't think everybody in town knows about the new play. A lot of people have asked me about the King Arthur play ...

Andrew: That's strange! Maggie has changed all the posters. Haven't you, Maggie?

Maggie: Er, no. I haven't even collected them from the printers. They're not ready yet.

Andrew: Oh, dear! Can't you talk to them?

Maggie: I've tried. I've phoned them lots of times. In fact, I've just called and explained that we must have them tomorrow or we don't pay them!

Andrew: Good for you!

G 44

1 Can you find the rules?

Find examples of the new tense in the dialogue.

- When do you use 'have'? When do you use 'has'?
- How do you make the past participle of the verbs?

But not all verbs are as easy as this.
Some verbs are irregular ... Read on.

SAVE

The present perfect

have has	+	a form of the verb (past participle)

Use the present perfect when you're only interested in what has happened (not in the exact time).

2 Listening comprehension: A new play?

Oh! You still don't know *why* they have changed the play!
For that we must go back to the first Drama Club meeting in April ...

news, accident, tank, to damage, dirty, grey, to mend, simple, easy, pirates, smugglers, a musical, bits, 'The Pirates of Penzance'

a) *First look at the words on the right and find out what they mean. Then listen to what the kids say at the meeting. Can you now complete this sentence?*

They can't put on the King Arthur play because they have a problem with ...

b) *Look at the present perfect forms from the dialogue and then say:*
- Which past participles are irregular?
- Which verbs do they come from? *(If you're not sure – guess!)*

c) *Some of the kids use short forms of the present perfect. Listen again to find them. (There are four examples.) Write them down. Then pick out two examples of the long form and make them short.*

d) *Now write out in two or three sentences all their problems with the play. Work in pairs.*

Present perfect forms

has happened
have heard
has damaged
have fallen off
has / have done
has tried
have thought
have left

G 44

3 Liz's idea

a) *Find the past participles of these irregular verbs. (There is a list on page 228/229.)*

find say give write

have think read

b) *What does Liz say to Brenda on the phone? Put in the missing participles.*

Brenda – I've just … an idea for a play. Well, you've … it to me, really, with your talk about smugglers! Have you … that Enid Blyton adventure story about smugglers in Cornwall?

Oh, Ms Carey has … she doesn't like Enid Blyton! So what? It's our play! Anyway, I've … about it, and I think we can make a great play out of it. And I've even … a good name for it: The Smugglers of Penryn!

Who, me? But I've never … a script before! You have!

OK, I can help you with it. But first we must ask Andrew and Maggie.

G 45

4 What have they done?

just | already | three/… times | not yet

a) *Look at the first six pictures and say what the people have done. Use the words on the where you can.*

For example, you can start:

John has just …
Liz has already …
… have … three times.

b) *Now look at the last thr pictures and say what the p haven't done yet.*

Example:

Pete hasn't … … yet.

John – paint

Liz – write

Maggie – phone

Pat – learn her part

kids – practise

Mike – put up

Pete – learn his part

Joan – write

kids – sell

YOU

5 Have you ever …?

ever | never | often | three/…/lots of times

a) *Work in pairs. Ask and answer the questions. Give as much information as you can. Example:*

– Have you ever acted in a play?
– Yes, I have. I've acted in … .
– Yes, I've often …
– No, I've never … (but I'd like to).
– No, I haven't. But I've …

b) *Can you think of any more questions to ask? Write them down.*

act in a play | paint a picture | read an adventure story
play in a band | write a script
write a poem | read a comic | go sailing
smuggle something | win a prize
meet a pirate | read an Enid Blyton story
find money in the street

8

Writing a play

Brenda and Liz are working on the script of their play. They have nearly finished Act 1. It has three scenes. Of course they don't use everything in the book. They have printed out the first scene, so you can see how they do it. *Don't worry if you don't understand some new words and forms in the book. You haven't learned them yet – but you can guess a lot, can't you? And you only need to understand the marked bits.*

1 How do they do it?

Look at page 1 of the story:

- What bits of it has Brenda marked?
- Why has she picked out these bits?
- What bits have they changed? Why?

Useful words:	information	facts
	dialogue	action
	understand	easy

CHAPTER ONE

Back to Kirrin Cottage

ONE FINE day, right at the beginning of the Easter holidays, four children and a dog travelled by train together.

"Nearly there now," said Julian, a tall strong boy.

"Woof," said Timmy the dog, getting excited, and trying to look out of the window too.

"Get down, Tim," said Julian. "Let Anne have a look."

Anne was his younger sister. She put her head out of the window. "We're coming into Kirrin Station!" she said. "I hope Aunt Fanny is there to meet us."

"Of course she is!" said Georgina, her cousin. She looked more like a boy than a girl, for she wore her hair very short. She pushed Anne away and looked out of the window. "It's nice to be going home," she said. "I love school – but it's more fun at Kirrin Cottage. We can sail out to Kirrin Island and visit the castle there. We haven't been there since last summer."

"Dick's turn to look out now," said Julian, turning to his younger brother. "We're just coming into sight of Kirrin, Dick. Can't you stop reading for a minute?"

"It's such an exciting book," said Dick. "The most exciting adventure story I've ever read!"

"Pooh! I bet it's not as exciting as some of the adventures we've had!" said Anne.

"Well, I've worked hard at school this term," said Julian. "I need a holiday!"

"You've gone thin," said Georgina. Nobody called her that. They all called her George. She would never answer to any other name. Julian grinned.

"Well, don't you worry! Aunt Fanny is a great cook. It's good that we're meeting your mother again, George. She's really nice."

"Yes, I hope Father is nice to us these hols, too," said George. "He has just finished some new experiments, Mother says, and is very happy about them." George's father was a scientist, always working out new ideas.

Aunt Fanny was there to meet them. The four children jumped out on the platform and rushed to hug her.

1

Act 1
Scene 1: In the train

Julian: Nearly there now!
Timmy: Woof!
Julian: Get down, Tim! Let Anne have a look!
Anne (puts her head out of the window): We're coming into Kirrin station. I hope Aunt Fanny is there to meet us.
George: Of course she's there! *(She pushes Anne away from the window.)* It's nice to go home. I love school, but it's more fun at Kirrin Cottage. We haven't been there since last summer.
Julian: It's Dick's turn to look out now. *(He turns to his younger brother.)* We're coming into Kirrin, Dick. Can't you stop reading for a minute?
Dick: It's such an exciting book! *(He closes the book.)* The best adventure story I've ever read!
Anne: Pooh! I bet it's not as exciting as some of the adventures we've had!
Julian: Well, I've worked hard enough at school this term. I need a holiday!
George: Yes, you've gone thin.
Julian: Well, don't you worry! Aunt Fanny is a great cook. It's good that we're meeting your mother again, George. She's really nice.
George: Yes. And I hope Father is nice to us these holidays, too. He has just finished some new experiments, Mother says, and is very happy about them. *(She looks out of the window again as the train is stopping.)* There she is! *(The children jump up, get their bags and get off the train.)*

2 The characters

The first scene must tell you a lot about the characters. *What have you already found out? Talk with a partner about these questions:*

1. Who is brother or sister of who?
2. One of them is a cousin. Who is it?
3. They talk about two grown-ups. Who are they?
4. The characters are all different. What kind of people are they? What can you guess about them?

The next two scenes in Act 1 are 'A shock in the night' and 'At Smuggler's Top'. They show how a terrible storm damages the roof of Kirrin Cottage, and it isn't safe to stay there any more.
The children must go to a strange, old house a few miles down the coast. It is on a hill with a marsh around it. Mr Lenoir lives there. George's father (Uncle Quentin) knows him, and he is the stepfather of Pete, a schoolfriend of the boys.
The children think they can have some fun there. But there is a problem: Mr Lenoir doesn't like dogs, so Pete hides Timmy in a secret tunnel under the house. And they are afraid of Block, Mr Lenoir's servant ...

3 Write a scene

You have seen how Brenda and Liz do it.
Now help them with the next scene. They want to use the dialogue from Chapter Eight of the book. Work in groups, and start like this:

Act 2
Scene 1: On the cliff-side
Pete (coming out of the tunnel): That other tunnel ...
Anne (still in the tunnel): ...

CHAPTER EIGHT

An exciting walk

THE TUNNEL ran slightly downwards, and smelt nasty in places. Pete flashed his torch.
"That one goes into Barling's house somewhere," he said. "Most of the old houses here have openings into tunnels like ours. Some of them are well hidden too!"
"There's daylight or something in front!" said Anne suddenly. "Oh good! I hate this tunnel."
Sure enough, it was daylight. The children looked out. They were outside the hill, and outside the town, somewhere on the steep cliff-side over the marsh. Pete put his torch into his pocket.
"We must get to that path down there," he said, pointing. "That leads us to a place where the city wall is low, and we can climb over it."
"Come on!" called Pete. "The coast is clear. This is a lonely bit of the town, and no one can see us."
Soon they were all over the wall, Timmy too. They set off for a good walk. The sun felt nice and warm.
"Look out – here's Block!" said Pete suddenly in a low voice. "Don't take any notice of Timmy at all. If he comes around and is jumping up, pretend he is a stray."
"Go away, dog!" said Pete. "Go away! Following us about like this! Go home, can't you?"

64

"Woof, woof!" Timmy thought this was some kind of a game. "Home, dog, home!" yelled Pete.
Then Block came up to them. "The dog bothers you?" he said. "I can throw a stone at him and make him go."
"Don't!" said George immediately. "You go home! The dog is OK. He's a nice one."
"Block's deaf, silly," said Pete. "He can't hear you."
To George's horror Block picked up a big stone, meaning to throw it at Timmy.
"You can't throw stones at a dog!" she yelled. "I'm going to the police."
"Now, now," said a voice nearby. "What's all this about, what's the problem?"
The children turned and saw a tall man standing near them.
"Oh, Mr Barling!" said Pete politely.
"Nothing's wrong, thanks. It's only that this dog is following us, and Block has just thrown a stone at it. And George here likes dogs and is angry about that."
"I see. And who are all these children?" said Mr Barling.
"They've come to stay with us because a tree has fallen on the roof of their uncle's house," explained Pete.
"George's father's house, I mean. At Kirrin."
"Ah – at Kirrin?" said Mr Barling. "That is where that very clever scientist friend of Mr Lenoir's lives?"
"Yes. He's my father," said George. "Why, do you know him?"
"I have heard of him – and of his very interesting experiments," said Mr Barling. "Mr Lenoir knows him well, I believe?"
"Not well," said George puzzled. "They just write, I think."
"And Mr Lenoir, of course, is only too happy to have you!" said Mr Barling. "*Such* a good man, your father, Pete!"
The children stared at Mr Barling, thinking that is was strange of him to say nice things in such a nasty voice.

65

4 Imagine another scene

As you have seen, Brenda and Liz do not always use the words from the book. Sometimes they make up the dialogue. Here you can do the same. Work in pairs and make up the dialogue for:

Act 2, *Scene 2: Who is in the tower?*

The action: One night, Pete comes into Julian's room and wakes him up. He has seen something strange from his bedroom window. Julian wakes Dick, the two brothers go into Pete's room, and they see it too: Somebody is sending light signals from the tower of the house. The signals are going out to sea. The boys talk about who it can be: Pete's mother? No. His stepfather? Maybe – but no, they can hear him in his room. Block? They think yes, because they can't hear anything from his room. But when they open the door of his room, there is Block in his bed. Then they must hide, because a man is coming from the tower. They can't see who it is, but they can hear. The man walks into Block's room and closes the door!

5 Listening comprehension: What is going on?

a) *Before you listen try to answer the questions. It's OK if you just guess. Write out what you think.*

1. Who is sending the signals?
2. Who is he sending the signals to?
3. What do the signals mean?
4. Is Mr Lenoir good or bad?
5. Is Mr Barling good or bad?
6. Why does Mr Barling ask so much about George's father?

b) *Compare your answers with a partner, and talk about why you think you know something. Then make a list of things you still don't know.*

c) *Now listen to a dialogue from the video of the story. When you listen the first time, just try to guess what is going on, who is speaking and where they are. How do you know?*

When you have listened a few times, look at your answers again. Do you want to change any of them?

man woman boy girl
house inside roof sound of birds
angry friendly

6 The programme

It's Joan's job to make the programme for the play.

a) *Help her with the first page. It must give the name of the play, who the story is by, who has written the script, made the costumes, etc. And there must be a list of characters. You know enough now to do this. You don't know yet who plays all the characters – Joan can finish the list when she finds out! (But maybe you can guess who plays Timmy the dog?!) Make sure your design looks good. Work in pairs.*

⟨b)⟩ *The second page of the programme must tell us something about the story, but not too much. When people are watching the play, it isn't exciting if they know how it ends. Work in pairs. Try to make the story interesting and exciting!*

Script by ...
From a story by E...

List of characters
Julian (a boy, about 15) ...
...
...

Costumes: ...
Scenery: ...
Lights: ...
...

G 47

1 Mysteries

Enid Blyton's stories are full of mysteries. Here are some more. And there is an extra mystery – some words are missing!
Can you put in the right ones?

Do you remember the rule for 'some' and 'any'? If not, look it up!

some	any	no	every
something	anything	nothing	everything
somebody / someone	anybody / anyone	nobody / no one	everybody / everyone
somewhere	anywhere	nowhere	everywhere

On the beach, there is a cave. The children can see ... footprints in the sand – they are going into the cave. ... footprints are coming out of the cave. A boy thinks this is strange. "Come on, ..., let's go in and see who is in the cave," he says. But there is ... there! Yes, it's a bit dark in the cave, but they look ..., and can't see ... "There must be ... other way out of the cave!" says the girl. She sees a hole at the back – but it goes ... . "That person must be ...!" she says. But no, they can't find him or her ... .

At the airport, ... is going through customs. It is a man with a big, heavy bag. He takes ... out of the bag, and puts it ... else – into his pocket, or inside his coat. The customs woman thinks he is trying to smuggle ... .
"Have you got ... to declare?" she asks.
"No, I have ... to declare," he answers.
The man must open his bag. The woman looks at ... in it, but she can't find ... bottles, or cigarettes, watches, drugs or ... strange. She looks in ... pocket, and in his jacket, but there is ... there!

2 Role play I: Party talk

At parties, people sometimes want to 'show off' – show how clever they are, what they know, etc. Here you can play the same game!

Have you read the book / seen the film ...?

Oh, yes, of course! It's very like ... . Have you seen / read that one?

Oh, I don't read / like ... (silly adventure stories / action films / ...).

No, I haven't seen / read that one yet. Is it good?

Oh, but it isn't a(n) ... / ... is / are great fun!

Oh, I've never ... such a great ...! You must ... it!

Well, what's so great about ...?

3 Role play II: At the customs

Excuse me, Sir / Madam. Have you got anything to declare?

Oh, no. I've got nothing (haven't got ...) to declare.

Hm. Please open your bags.

OK. / What? All of them?

Yes, please.

Oh, dear!

Hm ... What's this?

Oh, that's just ... !

Well, you must pay duty on that.

Well, yes, I've got this ...

Right. Here's a form. You must write down what it is, the price, and where it's from.

OK. I've written down everything. I hope the duty on it isn't too high ...

That's ... , please.

Oh, dear! / That's not too bad!

Thank you. Have a nice day!

SB

4 ⟨Poetry page⟩

a) Here are two poems – pick one! *Which one do you like best? To answer that, you must look at both of them, of course. But don't try to understand everything at first. (There are a lot of 'nonsense' words in the second poem, for example.)*

b) *Read your poem out loud. You can take turns with different lines.*

c) *Try to learn a verse (or more?) of your poem. Who can say their verse best in your group?*

d) *Now get together in groups and talk about 'your' poem. What is it about? What do you like in it?*
Some words to help you: happy silly funny atmosphere joke sounds same words again

The Garden's Full[1] of Witches[2]

by Colin McNaughton

Mum! The garden's full of witches!
Come quick and see the witches.
There's a full moon[3] out,
And they're flying about,
Come on! You'll miss[4] the witches!

Oh, Mum, you're missing the witches.
You have never seen so many witches.
They're casting spells[5]!
There are horrible smells[6]!
Come on! You'll miss the witches!

Mum, hurry! Come look at the witches.
The shrubbery's[7] bursting[8] with witches.
They've turned[9] our Joan
Into a garden gnome[10].
Come on! You'll miss the witches!

Oh no! You'll miss the witches.
The garden's black with witches.
Come on! Come on!
Too late! They've gone!
Oh, you always miss the witches!

[1][fʊl] *voll (von)* [2][wɪtʃ] *Hexe* [3][ˌfʊlˈmu:n] *Vollmond* [4][ˌju:l'mɪs] *du wirst verpassen* [5][ˌkɑ:st 'spelz] *Zauber machen, verhexen* [6][ˌhɒrəbl 'smelz] *schreckliche Gerüche* [7]['ʃrʌbri] *Gebüsch* [8][bɜ:st] *wimmeln (von)* [9][tɜ:n] *hier: verwandeln* [10][nəʊm] *Gartenzwerg*

Grim and Gloomy[1]

by James Reeves

Oh, grim and gloomy,
So grim and gloomy
Are the caves beneath[2] the sea.
Oh, rare but roomy
And bare and boomy
Those salt sea caverns[3] be.

Oh, slim and slimy
Or grey and grimy[4]
Are the animals of the sea.
Salt and oozy
And safe and snoozy
The caves where those animals be.

Oh, rare but roomy
And bare and boomy
Those caverns under the sea,
And grave and grandiose,
Safe and sandiose
The dens[5] of her denizens[6] be.

[1]['glu:mi] *düster* [2][bɪ'ni:θ] = under [3]['kævn] = cave [4]['graɪmi] = dirty [5][den] *Höhle, Versteck* [6]['denɪzn] *Bewohner*

e) We haven't explained all the new words in this poem. Some are only there for the sound. Some others may sound like a known word (English or German). *Try to guess what they mean.*

8

1 Make a mind map

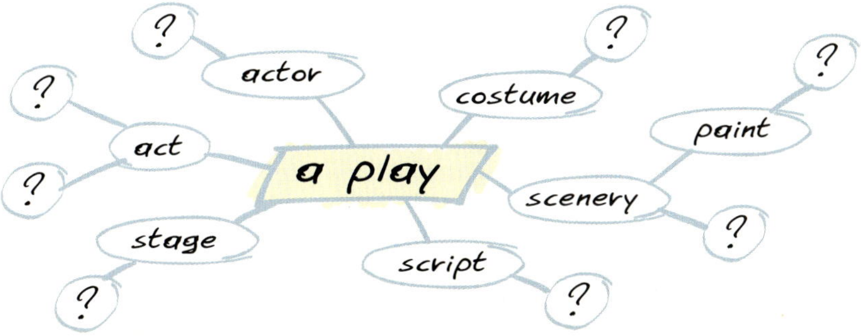

2 Explain

a) *Work in pairs. One of you makes a (sad/happy/angry/...) face, and the other wants to know why.*

Here are some ideas:

You look ...!	happy, tired	I've just ...	hear some good/bad news
Why are you ...?	sad, angry		win a prize, see a ghost
What's wrong?	laughing, crying		hear a very funny story
What's so great?	white in the face		find some money, lose my ...
			have a terrible fight (with ...)
			break a glass/the window/...

b) *Now write out your best dialogues.*

3 Has he done it yet?

Here are some things Liam must do this week:

Jobs to do:
- clean computer
- clean window
- put up shelf
- put books on shelf
- buy present for Grandma
- send present to Grandma
- send 'thank you' e-mail to Uncle George
- translate German text (ice cream maker)

a) *Look at the picture and find out what jobs Liam has or hasn't done. Write out four sentence pairs:*

Liam has already ..., but he hasn't ... yet.

b) *Play the roles. Liam's mother is on the phone from London and wants to know if he has done all his jobs:*

Have you ... ? – Yes, I have. / No, I haven't (but I've ...).

G 46

1 A message from Florida

Hi, Liam!

So the tourists are coming back to Cornwall for the summer. That's nice – or is it? Anyway, it's funny. The tourists have just left Florida – it's too hot here for most of them in the summer. But I like it hot. How hot does it get in Cornwall in the summer? I bet you don't get hurricanes there! Yes, there was a bad one here a few years ago. But people have built things up again.

No, my name isn't Italian. Osceola was a Seminole Indian hero. He fought against the whites when they tried to drive them out of Florida. My Dad is half Seminole, and lots of his aunts, uncles and cousins still live on the reservation in the Everglades. Lots of families there are called Osceola.

And no, I've never been to Disney World. It's too far away. Sure, it's in the middle of Florida, but Florida's a big place. Anyway, it's about 300 miles from where I live, Islamorada, one of the Florida Keys. The Keys are those little islands just off the south coast – only they aren't really islands any more, because the Overseas Highway goes all the way out to Key West. That's where I went on a sailing trip last week. It's the southernmost point in the USA – a bit like your Land's End, I suppose. Anyway, it's a fun place. Liam, when you go on your sailing trip to Plymouth, please take some pictures of the harbor for me. I need them for a school history project. I'll explain later.

Yours,

B. J. Osceola

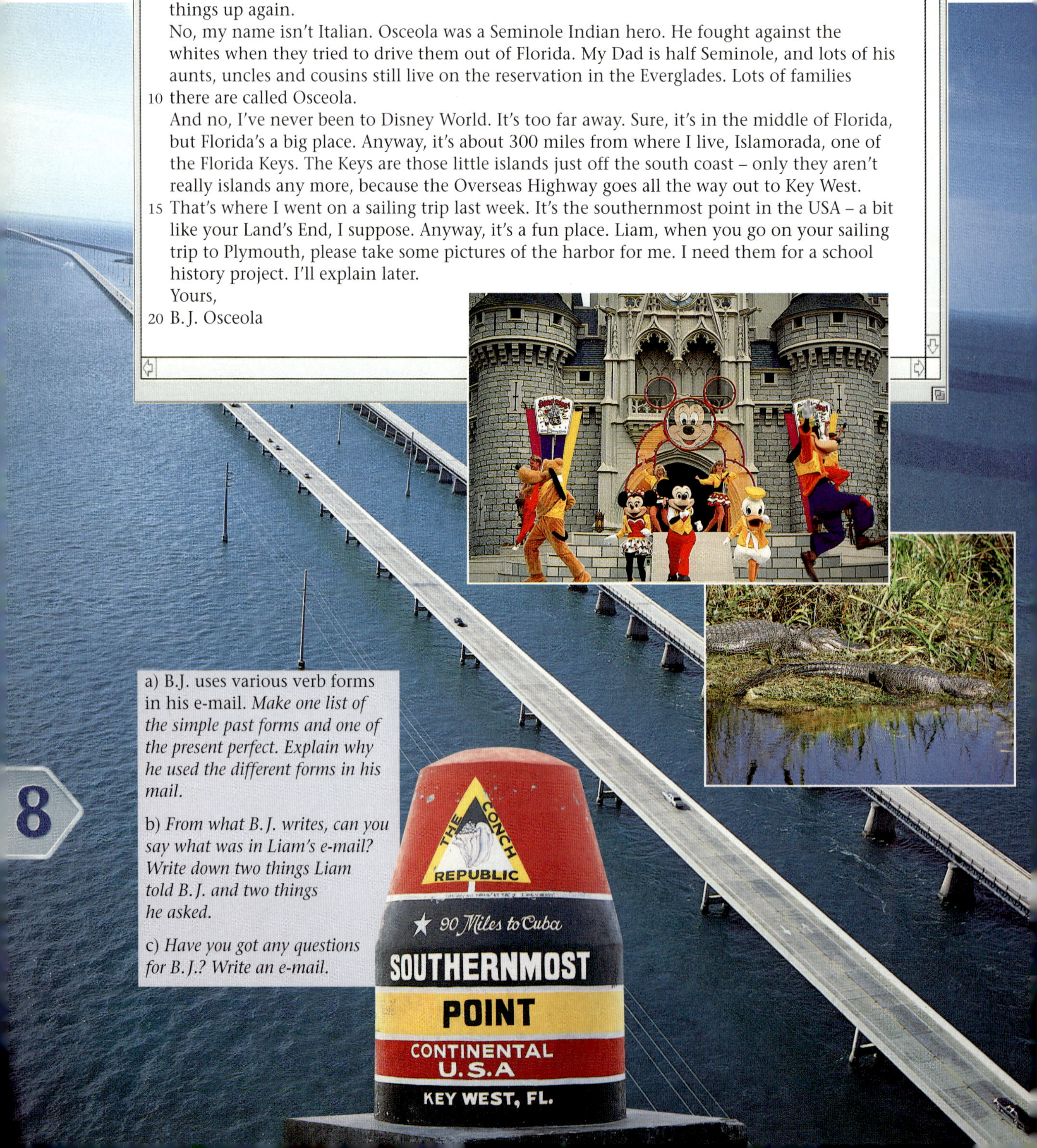

a) B.J. uses various verb forms in his e-mail. *Make one list of the simple past forms and one of the present perfect. Explain why he used the different forms in his mail.*

b) *From what B.J. writes, can you say what was in Liam's e-mail? Write down two things Liam told B.J. and two things he asked.*

c) *Have you got any questions for B.J.? Write an e-mail.*

1 What has he changed?

Mike wants to win the art competition. He is working very carefully on his picture of the Cornwall coast.
Look at his painting and say what new work he has done today.

change the colour of ... finish ... put in ... write ... put ... on the ... make ... better / green / red / blue / ...

WP 2 Verbs and nouns

Which verbs go best with these nouns? (Sometimes there are two or more good 'pairs'.)

to go on | to take part in | to go to | to act in | to win | to have

a play | a prize | an adventure | a concert | a trip | a competition | a meeting | an activity

3 Before the sailing trip ...

Put in the right words.

some	-thing
any	-body
no	-one
every	-where

– Have we packed ..., Ellen?
– Oh, yes, I'm sure I haven't forgotten ... . Let me see. I've put the maps and the guide books in this bag, and ... to read when it gets boring in that one. And here I've got ... extra trousers and jackets for when ... gets wet. I haven't packed ... really warm clothes, but it's summer, and we're going ... very cold. There's ... else on my list. The food is your job, Steve.
– Yes, and I'm not sure if I've got ... . In fact, I think I've forgotten ... important. But I have ... idea what it is! Can ... help me? I've lost the list. And I've looked ... for it!
– Oh, it's the same ... time! But the list must be ...! Hey, listen ... – has ... seen Steve's food list?
– Have you looked in your back pocket, Steve?
– Huh? Oh, yes, there it is – how silly of me! Hm, I've packed nearly ... on this list: the bread, the chocolate, the water, etc. I haven't got ... tea – but ... likes tea, do they?
– Uh-oh! We're not going ... without tea, Steve! ... way!

8

CHECK-IN

	term [tɜ:m]	(Schul-)Trimester, Semester
	senior orchestra [ˌsi:niə‿ˈɔ:kɪstrə]	Orchester der oberen Klassenstufen
	spring [sprɪŋ]	Frühling
	season [ˈsi:zn]	Jahreszeit
	junior choir [ˌdʒu:niə ˈkwaɪə]	Chor der unteren Klassenstufen
	friendly match [ˌfrendli ˈmætʃ]	Freundschaftsspiel
	against [əˈgenst]	gegen
	St. Anthony [snt‿ˈæntəni]	*hier: Name einer Schule*
	Plymouth [ˈplɪməθ]	*Hafenstadt in Südengland*
	competition [ˌkɒmpəˈtɪʃn]	Wettbewerb, Wettkampf
	to **sail** [seɪl]	segeln
	to **apply (to)** [əˈplaɪ]	(sich) wenden (an)
	to **take part (in)** [ˌteɪk ˈpɑ:t]	teilnehmen (an)
	Galahad [ˈgæləhæd]	*Figur der Arthursage*
	adventure [ədˈventʃə]	Abenteuer
	scenery [ˈsi:nəri]	Bühnenbild, Kulisse
	stage [steɪdʒ]	Bühne
	sale [seɪl]	Verkauf
	anybody [ˈenibɒdi]	irgendjemand
1	**notice board** [ˈnəʊtɪs ˌbɔ:d]	schwarzes Brett, Anschlagtafel
	various [ˈveəriəs]	verschiedene
2	to **put on** [ˌpʊt‿ˈɒn]	*hier:* herausbringen, auf die Bühne bringen
	somebody [ˈsʌmbədi]	jemand
3	to **sound** [saʊnd]	klingen
	strange [streɪndʒ]	merkwürdig, sonderbar
	to **imagine** [ɪˈmædʒɪn]	sich vorstellen, annehmen

STEP A

	what [wɒt]	was für eine(r/s), welche(r/s)
	in fact [ɪn ˈfækt]	eigentlich
	to **pay*** [peɪ]	(be)zahlen
2	to **complete** [kəmˈpli:t]	vervollständigen
	to **damage** [ˈdæmɪdʒ]	beschädigen
	accident [ˈæksɪdnt]	Unfall
	grey [greɪ]	grau
	to **mend** [mend]	ausbessern, reparieren
	bit [bɪt]	Stück(chen), Teil
3	**Enid Blyton** [ˌi:nɪd ˈblaɪtn]	*englische Schriftstellerin (1897-1968)*
	script [skrɪpt]	Drehbuch, Textbuch
5	**ever** [ˈevə]	je(mals), immer
	poem [ˈpəʊɪm]	Gedicht

The seasons

spring summer autumn winter

Let's listen to the senior orchestra and to the junior choir.

At big pop concerts or open air concerts they have special stages.

If you've got something for sale, tell people on the notice board.

franz varié *lat* varius
engl various

There's no other way – at the check-out you must pay.

In your workbook you write and complete sentences.

franz compléter *lat* complere
engl to complete

A car with a damaged tank after an accident. Careful!

There's a hole in my T-shirt, I must mend it.

If the script is good, the film can't be too bad.

8

STEP B

A	**marked** [mɑ:kt]	markiert
	Kirrin Cottage [ˌkɪrɪn ˈkɒtɪdʒ]	*Name eines Landhauses*
	since [sɪns]	seit
	it's his/her turn [tɜ:n]	er/sie ist an der Reihe
	younger [ˈjʌŋgə]	jünger(e/r/s)
	such [sʌtʃ]	solch(e/r/s)
	thin [θɪn]	dünn
	cook [kʊk]	Koch/Köchin
	hols (= holidays) [hɒlz]	Ferien
2	**who** [hu:]	wer, wem, wen
	grown-up [ˈgrəʊnˌʌp]	Erwachsene(r)
B	**safe** [seɪf]	sicher
	(a) few [fju:]	wenige, ein paar
	marsh [mɑ:ʃ]	Marschland, Sumpf
	stepfather [ˈstepfɑ:ðe]	Stiefvater
	schoolfriend [ˈsku:lfrend]	Schulfreund(in)
	secret [ˈsi:krət]	geheim, verborgen
	to **be afraid** [əˈfreɪd]	sich fürchten, Angst haben
	servant [ˈsɜ:vnt]	Diener(in)
	cliff-side [ˈklɪfsaɪd]	Klippe(n)
	opening [ˈəʊpnɪŋ]	Eröffnung, Beginn
	ours [ˈaʊəz]	der/die/das Unsere
	to **be hidden** [ˈhɪdn]	versteckt sein
	daylight [ˈdeɪlaɪt]	Tageslicht
	low [ləʊ]	niedrig
	to **climb** [klaɪm]	klettern
	clear [klɪə]	klar, hell
	no one [ˈnəʊwʌn]	niemand
	to **take notice (of)** [ˌteɪk ˈnəʊtɪs]	beachten, Notiz nehmen (von)
	not … at all [ˌnɒt‿əˈtɔ:l]	überhaupt nicht
	to **pretend (to)** [prɪˈtend]	vorgeben (zu), vortäuschen
	to **stray** [streɪ]	herumschweifen, herumstreunen
	to **bother** [ˈbɒðə]	belästigen, plagen
	stone [stəʊn]	Stein
	to **make so. do sth.** [ˈmeɪk ˌsʌmwʌm ˈdu: ˌsʌmθɪŋ]	jmdn veranlassen etw zu tun
	deaf [def]	taub
	silly [ˈsɪli]	Dumme(r), Dummkopf
	nothing [ˈnʌθɪŋ]	nichts
	angry [ˈæŋgri]	ärgerlich, wütend
	scientist [ˈsaɪəntɪst]	Wissenschaftler(in)
4	to **make up** [ˌmeɪk‿ˈʌp]	(sich) ausdenken, erfinden
	tower [ˈtaʊə]	Turm
	light [laɪt]	Licht

Opposites

younger	–	older
smaller	–	bigger
lighter	–	darker
cleverer	–	sillier

My cousin wants to be a cook.

Is this tunnel safe?

Don't tell anybody. It's secret!

This is our car. It's ours.

High up in the north they have daylight for 24 hours.

franz clair *lat* clarus
engl clear

You will never make me play this role.

In this film the actor plays a deaf servant.

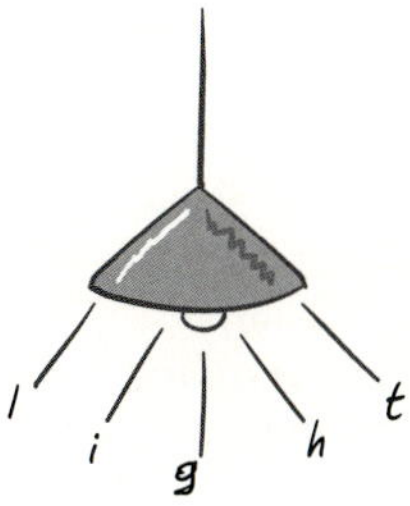

8

STEP C

1	**mystery** ['mɪstri]	Geheimnis, Mysterium
	anyone ['eniwʌn]	irgendjemand
	everyone ['evriwʌn]	jeder
	somewhere ['sʌmweə]	irgendwo
	nowhere ['nəʊweə]	nirgends, nirgendwo
	cave [keɪv]	Höhle
	hole [həʊl]	Loch
	customs ['kʌstəmz]	Zoll *(Verwaltung)*
	coat [kəʊt]	Mantel
	to **declare** [dɪ'kleə]	angeben, deklarieren
	bottle ['bɒtl]	Flasche
2	to **show off** [ˌʃəʊ‿'ɒf]	angeben
3	**where (from / to)** ['weə]	woher / wohin
	duty ['dju:ti]	Zoll *(Gebühr)*
⟨4⟩	**poetry** ['pəʊɪtri]	Dichtung, Poesie, Gedichte
	to **like best** [ˌlaɪk 'best]	am liebsten mögen
	to **be known** [nəʊn]	bekannt sein

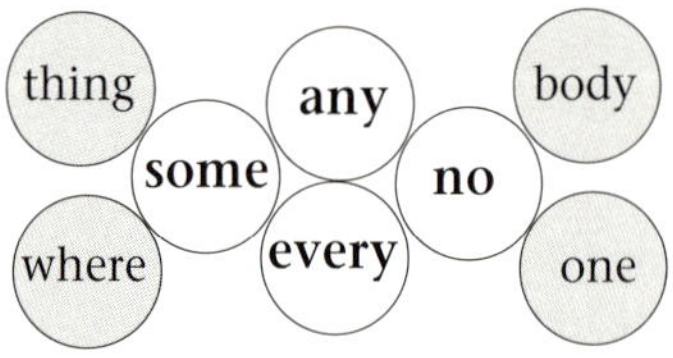

The man from the customs asks: "Anything to declare?"

In winter you wear a coat.

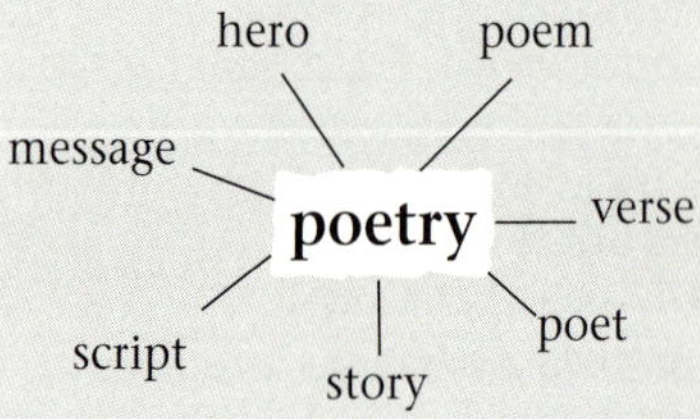

TRACK 1

1	**actor** ['æktə]	Schauspieler
3	**ice cream maker** [aɪs 'kri:m ˌmeɪkə]	Eismaschine

TRACK 2

+**message** ['mesɪdʒ]	Nachricht, Mitteilung
+**Florida** ['flɒrɪdə]	*Bundesstaat im Südosten der USA*
+**ago** [ə'gəʊ]	vor *(zeitlich)*
+to **build*** [bɪld]	bauen
+**Italian** [ɪ'tæliən]	italienisch, Italienisch
+**Seminole Indian** ['semɪnəʊl ˌɪndiən]	*Angehörige(r) eines indianischen Stamms*
+**hero** ['hɪərəʊ]	Held
+the **whites** [waɪts]	die Weißen
+to **drive so. out** [ˌdraɪv‿'aʊt]	jmdn verjagen, hinausjagen
+**Everglades** ['evəgleɪdz]	*Sumpfgebiet im südlichen Florida*
+**Disney World** ['dɪznɪ ˌwɜ:ld]	*Vergnügungspark in Florida*
+**Islamorada** [ˌɪzləmə'rɑ:də]	*Ort in Florida*
+**Keys** [ki:z]	*Inselgruppe südwestlich von Florida*
+**island** ['aɪlənd]	Insel
+**Overseas Highway** [ˌəʊvəsi:z 'haɪweɪ]	*autobahnähnliche Straße, die die Keys verbindet*
+**Key West** [ˌki: 'west]	*Insel und gleichnamige Stadt südwestlich von Florida*

Why didn't you leave a message on my answering machine?

The Keys are islands.

Hemingway's house is on Key West.

	+**sailing trip** ['seɪlɪŋ ˌtrɪp]	Segeltörn
	+**southernmost** ['sʌðənməʊst]	südlichste(r/s)
	harbor *AE* ['hɑ:bə]	Hafen
	+to **suppose** [sə'pəʊz]	vermuten, annehmen

Wonderful,
the experiment
works!

CHECK-OUT

Juggle is to juggler

3	**no way** *coll.* [ˌnəʊ 'weɪ]	auf keinen Fall, keineswegs

COGNATE WORDS

act [ækt]	Akt, Aufzug	**madam** ['mædəm]	gnädige Frau *(Anrede)*
activity [æk'tɪvəti]	Aktivität, Tätigkeit	+**middle** ['mɪdl]	Mitte
⟨**atmosphere**⟩ ['ætməsfɪə]	Atmosphäre	**pirate** ['paɪərət]	Pirat(in)
bps (= bits per second) ['bi:'pi:'es]	*Übertragungsgeschwindigkeit eines Modems*	**poster** ['pəʊstə]	Poster, Plakat
bread [bred]	Brot	to **print (out)** [prɪnt]	(aus)drucken
cigarette [ˌsɪgr'ət]	Zigarette	**printer** ['prɪntə]	Drucker
clever ['klevə]	schlau, klug	**prize** [praɪz]	Preis, Gewinn
concert ['kɒnsət]	Konzert	**program(me)** ['prəʊgræm]	Programm
cousin ['kʌzn]	Cousin(e)	+**reservation** [ˌrezə'veɪʃn]	Reservat
to **end** [end]	(be)enden	**sand** [sænd]	Sand
exact [ɪg'zækt]	exakt, genau	**simple** ['sɪmpl]	einfach, gewöhnlich
experiment [ɪk'sperɪmənt]	Versuch, Experiment	to **smuggle** ['smʌgl]	schmuggeln
fact [fækt]	Tatsache, Fakt	**smuggler** ['smʌglə]	Schmuggler(in)
festival ['festɪvl]	Festival	**storm** [stɔ:m]	Sturm
film [fɪlm]	Film	**tank** [tæŋk]	Tank
folk [fəʊk]	Volksmusik, Folk(-)	**training** ['treɪnɪŋ]	Training
hard [hɑ:d]	hart	**tunnel** ['tʌnl]	Tunnel
job [dʒɒb]	Job, Arbeit	⟨**verse**⟩ [vɜ:s]	Strophe, Vers
⟨**joke**⟩ [dʒəʊk]	Scherz, Spaß, Witz	**video** ['vɪdiəʊ]	Video
		warm [wɔ:m]	warm

UNIT 9

School's out!

Welcome Holiday Camp

Super family fun, non-stop entertainment and activities for all ages. Pools, gym, bouncy castle, organized day-trips. Special bus service to Alton Towers theme park. Clean accommodation. Kids eat for free!

If you want to sit on a beach all day, go to Benidorm. If you want adventure, fun and freedom, walk the 965 kilometres of coastal paths on the edge of South West England (or just a bit of it)!

The landscape is wild in places – but you needn't be super fit. You can be green – with a short walk to and from one of the railway stations or coastal bus stops. And don't think you need to bring everything with you. You can find food, maps, guides, film, and walking gear locally. Get away from it all for the weekend – or the week – or forever!

When you buy a BRITRAIL PASS, your child can travel free if she or he is under 15.

Mumbles View

Comfortable B & B with friendly atmosphere in sunny Swansea. Swimming, sailing and water-skiing on the 'Welsh Riviera'.

FLY-AND-DRIVE USA

Direct flights to major American cities. Rental ca campervans and motorhomes at low prices. For t vacation of a lifetime contact: Flydrive Travel, 0171/123

1 Listening comprehension: Which holiday?

The Wilsons are making plans for their summer holiday, and are looking at some ads.

a) *Listen and take notes. Which of the holidays are they talking about? Say how you know.*

b) *Listen again. Which of the phrases on the right do you hear? Write them down.*

c) *Work in groups of three. Write a dialogue between Jimmy and his parents about the other holidays. Use the phrases on the right.*

d) *Which ads can they throw away now?*

Making suggestions	Reacting to suggestions
Let's …	That's (not) a good idea.
We could …	I'm not sure about …
Why don't we …?	What a great idea!
What about … (-ing)?	Yes, why not?

Boats on the Norfolk Broads

Take a boat down England's most beautiful canal. A holiday with a difference. No experience necessary.

Dingle Bay cottages

Cottages in beautiful countryside. Perfect for family holidays and touring SW Ireland. Close to beach and pubs with live Irish music. 10 minutes' walk to Dingle. Self-catering, satellite TV.
No. of cottages: 20
To sleep: 2-6 people.

YHA Accommodation Guide
Youth hostelling is a great way to get to know a country.
Stay in Youth Hostels and go as you please.

Cycling in Cumbria

Cycle your way across the wild and beautiful areas of the north of England on a 120-mile route which goes along small roads, over unused bridges and through unused tunnels.
Contact: Best of British Bike Tours, 01207-281 259.

Stuart Lodge

Quiet hotel with traditional Scottish charm overlooking Loch Lomond. Fine cuisine and excellent wines. Indoor heated swimming pool. Ideal for walking, fishing, golf and relaxing.
No children / pets.

WP 2 You can guess

Find where the words below are in the texts and read the information on the right. Say what you think each word means, and how you know.

bouncy castle – heated – comfortable – wild
freedom – unused – landscape – coastal – forever
experience – golf – major – lifetime – relaxing
motorhome – wine – water-skiing – charm
rental – overlook – traditional – railway

Understanding new words

You can often guess a new word
- from the context or pictures,
- if you know it in a different form, e.g. an adjective, noun or verb,
- if it looks like a German, French or Latin word you know.

If you can't guess the word, you can
- just try to understand the context,
- look it up,
- ask someone.

YOU 3 What about you?

Which holiday would you choose, and which not? Explain why.

4 Sound check

a) *Copy the words into your exercise book. Read them aloud and divide them into their syllables. Underline the syllable that you stress.*

1. atmosphere
2. adventure
3. entertainment
4. accommodation
5. holiday
6. vacation
7. hotel
8. hostel

Example: nationality = na / (tio)n / al / ity (4 syllables)

b) *Listen and check.*

When you write down new vocabulary, it is useful to
- mark the stress.
- add words in the same family.

national (adj) – nationality (n)

5 Nationality words

What are the adjectives for these nouns?

1. Ireland 3. Wales 5. America 7. Turkey 2. Scotland 4. England 6. Britain 8. France

6 What is Britain?

Its full name is the United Kingdom of Great Britain and Northern Ireland, and it is a member of the European Union.

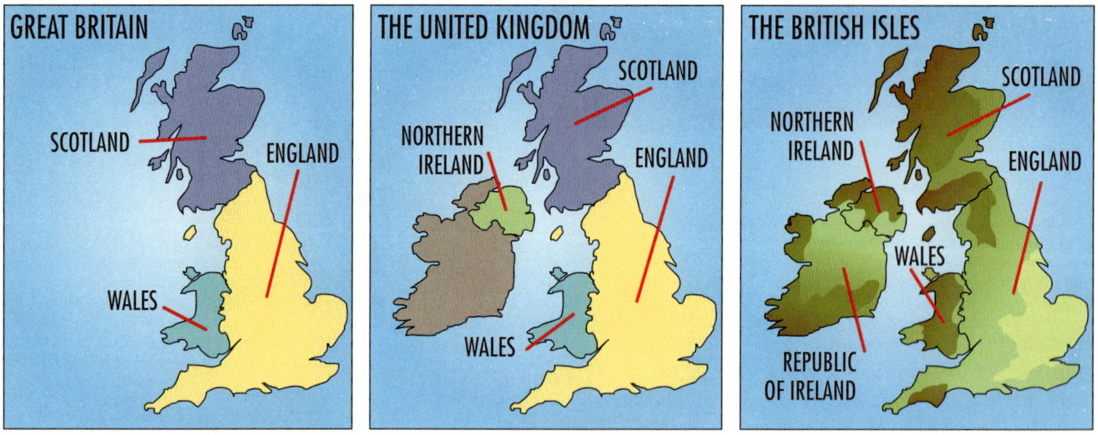

Great Britain = England, Scotland, Wales
United Kingdom = Great Britain and Northern Ireland
The British Isles = the United Kingdom and Ireland

The Republic of Ireland is a separate state and a member of the European Union.

Look at the maps. Which of the four points about each city is wrong?

1. Edinburgh is in a) Britain, b) England, c) the UK, d) Scotland.
2. Dublin is in a) the UK, b) the EU, c) the British Isles, d) the Republic of Ireland.
3. Cardiff is in a) Britain, b) the UK, c) Scotland, d) Wales.
4. Belfast is in a) England, b) the UK, c) Great Britain, d) Northern Ireland.
5. Bristol is in a) Britain, b) England, c) the UK, d) Wales.

9

I've got a better idea

The Wilsons have decided to visit different parts of Britain this summer. The question is how.

Jimmy: Why don't we go by train? I can travel for free, so maybe it's cheaper than going by car.

Mrs Wilson: Yes, and better for the environment. But how do we get to the hotels from the station?

Jimmy: By taxi, of course.

Mr Wilson: Hey, what's all this about hotels and taxis? Money doesn't grow on trees, you know. I think we should go on a camping and walking holiday. It's healthier than sitting in a car all day.

Jimmy: Camping is great, but walking is boring! Cycling is much more fun – and it's faster too.

Mrs Wilson: I don't like the idea of camping. It isn't as easy as you think – I know because I've tried it. The worst holiday of my life – and the wettest!

Mr Wilson: Well, we could stay in youth hostels – then we needn't carry a tent with us.

Jimmy: I've got a better idea. The Cliftons don't need their campervan this year, so maybe we can borrow it. We can still take our bikes!

Mr Wilson: Yes, why not? We can be more independent with a campervan. We can go where we want, and cook our own meals. It's less expensive than hotels or B & Bs.

Mrs Wilson: Well, I don't want to cook all the time! I want a holiday!

Mr Wilson: We can go to restaurants now and then. Campervans give you freedom! That's the most important thing. And they're more comfortable than tents too.

Mrs Wilson: OK, it can't be worse than camping! Have you seen the Cliftons' campervan, Jimmy?

Jimmy: Yes, I have. It's great! Why don't you call the Cliftons now?

1 Right or wrong?

Correct what is wrong.

1. Jimmy thinks going by train is less expensive than going by car.
2. Mrs Wilson thinks going by car is better for the environment.
3. Mrs Wilson thinks sitting in a car is not as healthy as walking.
4. Jimmy thinks a campervan holiday is worse than youth hostelling.
5. Mr Wilson thinks campervans are cheaper than hotels and not as comfortable as tents.
6. Mrs Wilson thinks camping is better than staying in campervans.

SAVE

than + -ing verb

It's health**ier than** sitt**ing**.
It's slow**er than** walk**ing**.

G 49-51

2 You make the rules

a) *Look at the examples in the box. Write the adjectives they are from with their comparative and superlative forms.*

Example: nice – nicer – nicest

SAVE

comparative adjectives	superlative adjectives
nicer	longest
cheaper	coldest
healthier	easiest
hotter	biggest
more / less expensive	most / least comfortable

irregular forms

good – better – (the) best   bad – worse – (the) worst

b) *Work out the rules for making the comparative and superlative of adjectives. Say when you need to:*

– add 'ier' and 'iest',
– add more and most,
– add 'r' and 'st',
– add 'er' and 'est',
– add a consonant,
– use another form / word.

9

3 Easy – easier – easiest

Use your rules to write the comparative and superlative forms of these adjectives.

long	quiet	difficult	wet
funny	boring	strange	heavy

G 52

4 What do you think?

Agree with each sentence in two ways. First use a comparative form. Then use its opposite.

Example: Latin isn't as easy as English.
I agree. English is **easier than** Latin. Latin is **more difficult than** English.

1. Berlin isn't as big as London.
2. B & Bs aren't as cheap as youth hostels.
3. Trains aren't as fast as cars.
4. Dogs aren't as clever as cats.
5. Maths isn't as interesting as History.
6. Summer days aren't as short as winter days.

5 The funniest person in the class

a) *Complete the sentences with superlative adjectives. (You can choose!)*

1. Who is the ... person in our class?
2. Where is the ... country to go on holiday?
3. What is the ... thing in your bag?
4. Which pop star wears the ... clothes?
5. What is the ... thing you have ever done?
6. Who is the ... person you have ever met?

b) *Work in pairs. Ask your partner your questions and write sentences with the answers.*

Example: Christian thinks our teacher is the funniest person in the class.

6 Yoo needn't be super fit!

a) *Put in 'needn't, or 'must'/'mustn't'.*

1. The sea can be dangerous so you ... be careful.
2. You ... swim when the weather is bad.
3. You ... know all about boats, we can teach you.
4. The landscape is wild but you ... be super fit.
5. You ... cycle so fast. It's dangerous.

b) *Now put in 'can'/'can't' or 'may'/'may not'.*

1. ... I see the map please? I think we're lost.
2. ... you help me? I ... find the guide book.
3. You ... swim and sail in sunny Swansea.
4. It says 'No pets' so we ... take our dog with us.
5. No, you ... go out, Jimmy – it's raining!

7 The best way to travel

a) *Work in groups. Copy the grid and put in numbers from 1 to 6. (1 is for the quietest, most expensive, safest, and so on.) Use the phrases in the box for agreeing and disagreeing when you discuss the points.*

b) *Compare your numbers with other groups' numbers.*

Example: Going by train is not as safe as by plane.
I don't agree. Going by train is safer.

	quiet	fast	expensive	safe	easy	interesting
train						
car						
bike						
plane						
boat						
bus						

Agreeing	Disagreeing
I agree.	I don't agree.
That's true.	That's not true.
I think so too.	I don't think so.

9

Jimmy's travel diary

We've come to pick up the campervan from the Cliftons. Mum and Dad aren't too happy about it, but it's comfortable enough for me!

This is my room. I always leave things until the last minute. How can I get everything into one suitcase?

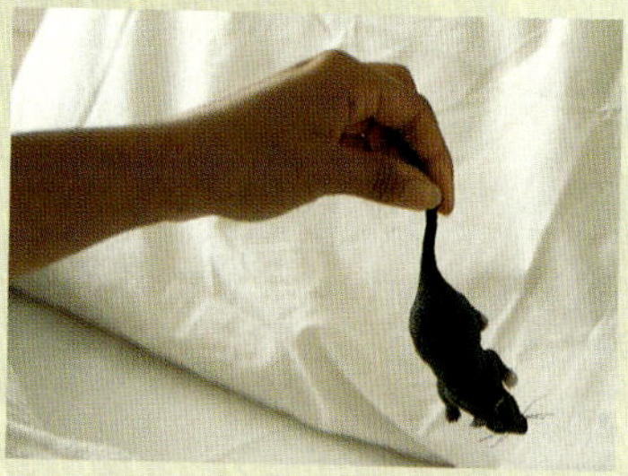

We're getting ready to leave. Mum has just found a dead mouse in one of the beds.

Off we go! Mum is driving and Dad is reading the map. We go round and round for an hour before we leave London.

We've stopped at this motorway café for a sandwich. A typical English castle.

All the campsites are full. It's raining cats and dogs. Our campervan hasn't got a toilet. Help!

We've decided to camp in this wood. Let's hope nobody sees us. Water is coming into the van. Dad is trying to find the hole. Mum is going crazy inside.

Dad has mended the hole, but we can't make tea because there aren't any matches. Dad is rubbing sticks together to start a fire and imagining he's an American pioneer like Daniel Boone. The rain has stopped – but too late for the sleeping bags.

Dad's famous last words before he gets on:
"Maybe I shouldn't eat a third hot dog after all!"

Cycling and walking in the Yorkshire Dales: My bike has got a flat tyre AGAIN! All this healthy activity is a bit too much for Dad.

This is one of Dad's famous 'short-cuts'. I've never seen so many sheep – but where's the sheepdog?

Snowdonia: A 'traditional English breakfast' – in a Welsh B&B! Fried bacon, fried eggs, fried sausages, fried tomatoes and fried bread. Mum calls it a 'heart attack on a plate'.

One whole week without photos – no film in the camera!

The Bradens' new house in Penryn. The campervan has broken down again, but they've invited us to stay with them as long as we like!!! So Mum gets her 'hotel', Dad is having a nice rest, and Liz and Liam have lent me their tent. We go swimming and surfing every day, so it's a perfect holiday!

1 As fast as you can

Work in pairs. Read the texts and see how fast you can find:

five animals, six things to eat, four places to sleep, four hobbies.

2 Good or bad?

a) *Look at the pictures and say who says what, and when.*

b) *Think of things they can say for the other pictures.*

1. This is just like the Wild West!
2. Look what I've just found.
3. This isn't my idea of a relaxing holiday.
4. Maybe it isn't healthy, but it's good!
5. I can't wait much longer!
6. Go left. No! Go right!

3 Creative writing

Write about a funny, fantastic or terrible holiday. It can be a true story, a fantasy story, or a bit of both. Add photos or draw pictures to go with the text if you want.

1 Listening comprehension: Britain and America

The Cliftons are visiting relatives in Washington DC, the capital of the United States. Tessa and her American cousin Nathan are on their way to a shopping mall.

a) *Before you listen, read the sentences below and say whether you think they are correct.*

b) *Listen and find out whether Nathan agrees or disagrees.*

1. Washington DC is an older city than London.
2. The British can learn to drive earlier than Americans.
3. Washington DC is less dangerous than London.
4. The weather is warmer in Washington DC than in London.
5. Americans drive less than the British.
6. Washington DC is further south than London.
7. Jeans are more expensive in the United States.
8. American food is the best in the world.

2 Finding things in common

Tessa and Nathan are finding out what they've got in common.

I love hot dogs!
I've got a computer.
I'm crazy about clothes.
I can't juggle.
I'm in the school swimming team.

So do I!
Have you? I haven't.
Me too!
Neither can I.
So am I!

a) *Work in groups. First make a list of five or six things you like/don't like. Then find out what you've got in common with the others in your group.*

Examples: I like English.	So do I!/Me too!	Do you? I don't.
I don't like homework.	Nor/Neither do I.	Don't you? I do!

b) *Now try the same thing with other verbs, e.g. have, can and forms of 'to be'.*

Example: I can't swim. Neither can I.

3 Word wheels

Work in pairs. Copy both word wheels into your exercise book. One of you compares two things in one of the wheels (e.g. A dog is more useful than a cat), and draws a line between them. Then your partner compares two things in the same position in the other wheel (e.g. England is smaller than Australia). Make as many lines between pairs as you can.

mouse
dog cat
sheep horse
bird seabird
fish

Germany
England Australia
Turkey the US
Italy France
Ireland

Hi there! Thanks for the e-mail. It's great that you can come and see us next summer.
Nathan, can you help me with a school project? I'm looking for info about special days in the US (e.g. Thanksgiving). Could you tell me something about them in your next e-mail? Please!!!
Hope to hear from you soon!
Love,

4 The language of letters

a) *What information does Tessa need, and why? What about Rizwan?*

b) *Which letter is more formal? How do you know? Give examples.*

c) *Make a list of useful phrases for asking for information/help.*

Can you help me?
Please could you ...

5 Asking for information

Do a project on holidays and festivals in the United States. There are many organizations that give free information about the United States. You can find out about them on the Internet or you can ask your teacher for useful addresses. Write to them for information, and follow the steps below in your letter.

- Write the names, addresses, today's date and the beginning with 'Dear ...'.
- Explain why you are writing.
- Say what kind of information/details you need, or how the organization can help you.
- Say you need an answer soon (but be polite!).
- End the letter and sign your name.

Tips for your project
- Work in groups. Each group works on a different topic.
- Collect information and pictures for your topic.
- In your group, decide who does what (e.g. who writes the texts, makes posters or gives a talk to the class).
- Save the information in a special folder.

Rizwan Modi
14 Englefield Road
Islington, N1 3LG

Tourist Information UK
21 Park Lane
London, W1

24 May 2003

Dear Sir or Madam,

My class is doing a project on tourism at school, and I am writing to ask for your help.
Please could you send me some information about tourism in Britain during the last five years. I would like to know the number of tourists for each year, which countries most of them come from, where they stay in Britain and for how long. Do you also have details of how much money they spend and what they spend it on? Brochures of popular tourist attractions would be very useful too.
Please also let me know if you have an e-mail address or Internet homepage.
I would be very grateful for your help, and look forward to hearing from you soon.

Yours faithfully,

Rizwan Modi

Rizwan Modi

Writing to an organization

If you start ...	**You finish ...**
(British English)	
Dear Sir or Madam,	Yours faithfully,
Dear Mr/Mrs/Ms/Miss Bond	Yours sincerely,
(American English)	
Dear Sir or Madam:	Sincerely,
Dear Mr. Bond	Sincerely,

The date
6th May 2003 or 6 May 2003 *(BE)*
May 6th, 2003 *(AE)*
(Write the month as a word, because 5/6/2003 can be 5th June or May 6th)

Style and layout
- Put your name above your address.
- Start the first sentence with a capital letter.
- Don't use short forms. Write 'I am', and not 'I'm'.
- Be polite, e.g. 'I would like', and not 'I want'.

1 School holidays

What do the school holidays mean to you? Freedom? Fun? Or looking at your bedroom walls all day? Yes, it's great to have a break from school, but the holidays can be boring sometimes. Parents aren't much help. If you tell them your problem, they just say "Go and tidy your room!". So here are some ways to make the most of your holidays – things you can do on your own:

- Look at your cassettes and write a list of your favourite songs. Record them together on one cassette. You can use it for a party, or make a copy to give your best friend as a present.
- Do something to collect money for charity.
- Take some 'art' photos with black and white film. Trees, buildings and old people are very interesting.
- Go through old family photos and choose some interesting ones of you at different ages. Stick them into a notebook, write your memories under them and you have the story of your life!
- Paint or draw a picture of your favourite pop, TV or sports star and send it to them as a present.
- Cook dinner one night for your family.
- Write a letter to your best friend or to a penfriend organization.
- Write a diary about your exciting school holiday!
- Ask your mum or dad if you can help out in their place of work for one day.
- Write a crazy cartoon-strip with you and your family as the 'stars'.

(Adapted from *Thirteen Something*, Jane Goldman Puffin Books)

a) *Work in groups. Talk about the ideas in the text. Have you ever done any of these things? Which ideas do you like best? Which do you not like? Maybe you have got some of your own ideas too.*

b) *In your group, write a list of ten tips for 'Things you can do with your friends'.*

2 Punctuation

This is the text of Jimmy's postcard to Sebastian. As you can see, there are no gaps between the words and the punctuation is missing. Write the text as it should look. Start like this:

Dear Sebastian,
I'm having a ...

dearsebastianiamhavingagreattimehereonholidaywith
mymumanddadwerehavingalotoffunithasrainedalotbut
todaytheweatherisbetteratthemomentwerestayingata
reallynicecampsiteandtheresaveryfriendlygirlhereher
nameisjackiethatsallfornowseeyouagainsoonyoursjimmy

3 Having a lovely time

Choose one of the photos on pages 140/141. Imagine you are on holiday there and write a postcard home.

Punctuation

(,)	comma
(?)	question mark
(.)	full-stop
(')	apostrophe
(!)	exclamation mark
(" ")	inverted commas

1 Frequently asked questions

WHITEWATER RAFTING IN COLORADO

A Don't panic. Lie on your back with your feet downstream and 'go with the flow'. When the water moves slowly again, swim quickly to the edge of the river.

B People with no experience start out on slow rivers. But you'll learn fast, and when you can manage the quiet rivers easily, you can try more exciting trips.

C If you want to go on fast rivers with a lot of rapids, it helps if you can swim well. But everyone has to wear a life jacket at all times.

D Whitewater rafting is not dangerous, but make sure you go with a well-managed organization. Listen to their instructions carefully and you should have no problem.

a) *Match the 'frequently asked questions' about whitewater rafting with the tips.*

1. How safe is whitewater rafting?
2. Do I need to be a good swimmer?
3. What happens if I fall in the water?
4. Are there easy trips for beginners?

b) *How should you swim if you fall in the water?*

c) *Go through the text and write down the adjectives and adverbs.*

G 54

2 Adjective or adverb?

1. Nathan drives (careful / carefully). He's a (safe / safely) driver.
2. Jimmy writes to Maike (regular / regularly) but she isn't (good / well) at answering his letters.
3. Tessa was (hungry / hungrily), so she ate her sandwich (quick / quickly).
4. Mr Wilson is (good / well) with numbers and he can explain Maths problems (good / well) too.
5. The Clifton's campervan is (slow / slowly), and it breaks down (frequent / frequently).

YOU

3 How well can you do these things?

Work in pairs. Say how good (or bad) you are at these things.

Examples: Are you a good swimmer?
Yes, I can swim quite well.
I can't run very fast. Are you a fast runner?
I can understand French easily, but I can't speak it very well. What about you?

swimming	running	riding
singing	painting	sailing
playing tennis	speaking languages	writing stories

adjective	adverb
slow	slowly
careful	carefully
easy	easily
good	well

fast, hard, late, early
are adjectives and adverbs

G 55

4 Talking about the weather

How to be an alien is a funny book about the English by George Mikes. He says the most important topic in England is the weather, so you must be good at discussing it. Here are some 'typical conversations':

For good weather

Lovely day, isn't it?
Isn't it beautiful?
The sun ...
Isn't it gorgeous?
Wonderful, isn't it?
It's so nice and hot ...
Personally, I think it's so nice when it's hot – isn't it?
I adore it – don't you?

For bad weather

Nasty day, isn't it?
Isn't it dreadful?
The rain ... I hate rain ...
I don't like it at all. Do you?
Fancy such a day in July. Rain in the morning, then a bit of sunshine, and then rain, rain, rain, all day long. I remember exactly the same July day in 1936.
Yes, I remember it too.
Or was it in 1928?
Yes, that's right.

SAVE

Question tags

+	–	–	+
It's a lovely day,	isn't it?	You aren't 16 yet,	are you?
They live in Stuttgart,	don't they?	He hasn't got a sister,	has he?
You can come,	can't you?	It doesn't help you,	does it?
I'm your best friend,	aren't I?*	I'm not in this group,	am I?
He was late,	wasn't he?	They didn't enjoy it,	did they?

When you say something with a question tag, you hope the other person agrees. Your voice goes down at the end of the tag.

*More natural than 'am I not'.

5 Singing the sentences

a) *Listen to the conversation and how the speakers 'sing' these sentences.*

"Lovely day, isn't it?" "Nasty day, isn't it?"

b) *What happens to the sound at the end of the sentence? Does it go up or down?*

c) *You will hear six more sentences. Listen and repeat them.*

d) *Imagine the weather is terrible and someone says to you: 'Lovely day, isn't it?' Which of the answers below is 1. the most polite, 2. the rudest, 3. the coldest?*
"No, it isn't." "Are you crazy?" "It's wonderful!"

6 Question tags

What are the question tags?

1. Her name is Nicola, ...?
2. You don't wear school uniform, ...?
3. Nathan has got a new car, ...?
4. These sandwiches aren't bad, ...?
5. They didn't help you, ...?
6. Jeans cost less in the USA, ...?
7. You've brought a map with you ...?
8. You met him last year, ...?
9. It doesn't snow much in London, ...?
10. It was a rainy day, ...?
11. Tessa and Nathan like shopping, ...?
12. They were late, ...?

7 A funny dialogue

a) *Work in pairs. Choose an important topic of conversation in Germany and write a funny dialogue. Add question tags where you can.* b) *Act your conversation to the class.*

1 Describe the nouns

a) *Which groups of adjectives can describe which nouns?*

1. expensive, relaxing, comfortable
2. beautiful, wild, coastal
3. long, boring, fun
4. free, useful, easy to read
5. fried, healthy, big
6. heated, long, free

landscape
breakfast
swimming pool
hotel
school holidays
guide

b) *Think of one more adjective for each group.*

2 Comparisons

Make sentences. Use the adjectives with '-er' or 'more'.

Example: Gold is more expensive than silver.

1. gold / expensive / silver
2. water / heavy / ice
3. London / big / Dublin
4. a pair of shoes / useful / one shoe
5. whitewater rafting / dangerous / sailing
6. brown bread / healthy / white bread

3 Three hotels

Put in the adjectives with '-er' / 'more' or '-est' / 'most'.

1. Wonky Towers is ... hotel but it's ... than the Metropolitan. (small, cheap)
2. The Plush is ... than Wonky Towers and it's ... too. (expensive, comfortable)
3. Wonky Towers is the ... hotel but it's not the ... . (old, big)
4. Wonky Towers is the ... hotel, but the Metropolitan is the ... . (crazy, young)

Wonky Towers*
350 years old
Rooms £10
12 rooms

The Plush******
100 years old
Rooms £200
50 rooms

The Metropolitan****
2 years old
Rooms £50
150 rooms

4 Letter quiz

1. When you start with 'Dear Sir or Madam', how do you finish the letter?
2. Write today's date in three ways (one of them American English).
3. Where do you write your address? On the top or bottom, left or right of the page?
4. Write these sentences in a more polite way:
   a) I want some help. b) Send me some information. c) Write back soon.

9

CHECK-IN

A	**needn't** ['ni:dnt]	nicht brauchen
	bed and breakfast (B&B) [ˌbed‿n‿'brekfəst]	Frühstückspension
	Wales [weɪlz]	Wales
	Mumbles View [ˌmʌmblz 'vju:]	*Name eines Hotels*
	Swansea ['swɒnzi]	*Stadt an der Südküste von Wales*
	Welsh [welʃ]	walisisch, Waliser(in)
	Stuart Lodge [ˌstjʊət 'lɒdʒ]	*Name eines Hotels*
	Scottish ['skɒtɪʃ]	schottisch
	to overlook [ˌəʊvə'lʊk]	überschauen, *hier:* mit Blick über/auf
	Loch Lomond [ˌlɒk 'ləʊmənd]	*größter See in Schottland*
	indoor [ˌɪn'dɔ:]	Innen-, Hallen-
	to heat [hi:t]	heizen
	entertainment [ˌentə'teɪnmənt]	Unterhaltung, Animation
	age [eɪdʒ]	Alter
	bouncy castle [ˌbaʊntsi 'kɑ:sl]	(aufblasbare) Hüpfburg
	Alton Towers [ˌɔ:ltn 'taʊəz]	*Ausflugsziel in Mittelengland*
	clean [kli:n]	sauber
	accommodation [əˌkɒmə'deɪʃn]	Unterkunft, Hotelzimmer, Übernachtung
1	**suggestion** [sə'dʒestʃn]	Vorschlag
	could [kʊd]	konnte(n), könnte(n)
	to react [ri'ækt]	reagieren
B	**Norfolk Broads** [ˌnɔ:fək 'brɔ:dz]	*Urlaubsgebiet mit Kanälen im Osten Englands*
	beautiful ['bju:tɪfl]	(wunder)schön
	experience [ɪk'spɪəriənts]	Erfahrung
	necessary ['nesəsri]	nötig, notwendig
	Britrail Pass ['brɪtreɪl ˌpɑ:s]	*Pass der britischen Eisenbahn*
	to travel ['trævl]	reisen
	Cumbria ['kʌmbriə]	*Grafschaft im Norden Englands*
	to cycle ['saɪkl]	Rad fahren, radeln
	across [ə'krɒs]	über, durch
	area ['eəriə]	Gebiet, Region, Areal
	unused [ˌʌn'ju:zd]	unbenutzt, nicht mehr benutzt
	Benidorm ['benɪdɔ:m]	*Feriensiedlung in Spanien*
	freedom ['fri:dəm]	Freiheit
	coastal ['kəʊstl]	Küsten-
	edge [edʒ]	Ufer, Rand (eines Sees)
	landscape ['lændskeɪp]	Landschaft
	railway ['reɪlweɪ]	Eisenbahn
	gear [gɪə]	Ausrüstung
	forever [fə'revə]	für immer
	to fly* [flaɪ]	fliegen
	flight [flaɪt]	Flug
	major ['meɪdʒə]	größter, Haupt-
	rental ['rentl]	Miet-
	campervan ['kæmpəˌvæn]	Wohnwagen

England	–	English
Wales	–	Welsh
Scotland	–	Scottish
Ireland	–	Irish
America	–	American
Australia	–	Australian
Germany	–	German

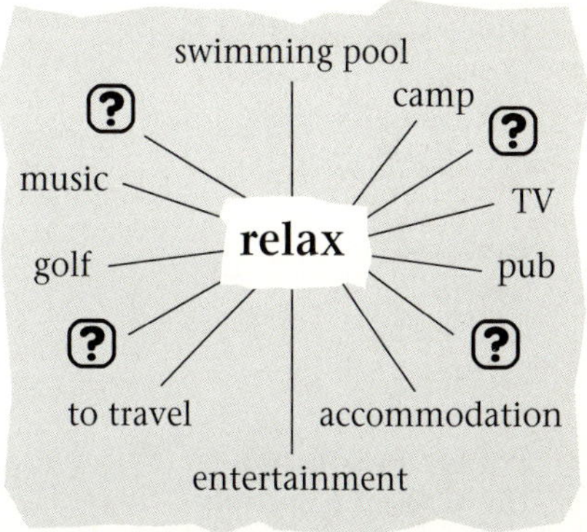

franz nécessaire *lat* necessarius
engl necessary

theme	–	thematic
free	–	freedom
to react	–	reaction
different	–	difference
beautiful	–	beauty
bicycle	–	to cycle
to use	–	unused
to travel	–	traveller
coast	–	coastal

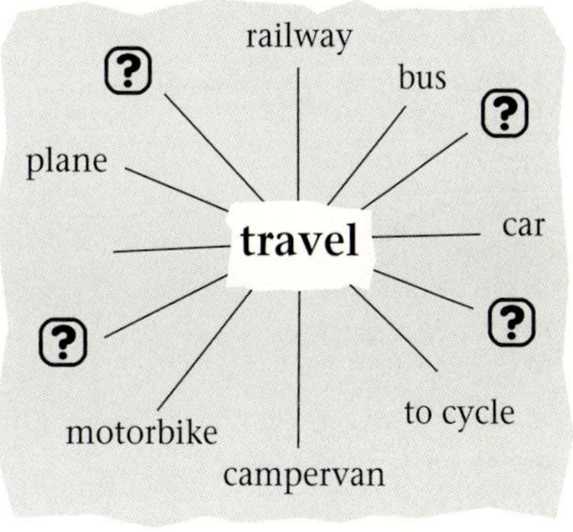

motorhome [ˈməʊtəˌhəʊm]	Wohnmobil
vacation *AE* [vəˈkeɪʃn]	Urlaub, Ferien
lifetime [ˈlaɪftaɪm]	Lebenszeit, Leben
Dingle Bay [ˌdɪŋgl ˈbeɪ]	*Name einer Feriensiedlung an der Küste*
countryside [ˈkʌntriˌsaɪd]	Land, Landschaft
to **tour** [tʊə]	reisen, besichtigen
Ireland [ˈaɪələnd]	Irland
close (to) [kləʊs]	nah, dicht (bei)
self-catering [ˌselfˈkeɪtrɪŋ]	Selbstversorgung
below [bɪˈləʊ]	unterhalb, unten
to **look sth. up** [ˌlʊk‿ˈʌp]	etw nachschlagen
4 **aloud** [əˈlaʊd]	laut
to **divide** [dɪˈvaɪd]	aufteilen, dividieren
syllable [ˈsɪləbl]	Silbe
hostel [ˈhɒstl]	Herberge
to **stress** [stres]	betonen
useful [ˈjuːsfl]	nützlich, brauchbar
stress [stres]	Betonung
5 **Turkey** [ˈtɜːki]	Türkei
Scotland [ˌskɒtlənd]	Schottland
France [frɑːnts]	Frankreich
6 the **United Kingdom** [juːˌnaɪtɪd ˈkɪŋdəm]	das Vereinigte Königreich
Great Britain [ˌgreɪt ˈbrɪtn]	Großbritannien
member [ˈmembə]	Mitglied
European Union [ˌjʊərəˈpiːən ˈjuːnjən]	Europäische Union
the **British Isles** [ˌbrɪtɪʃ‿ˈaɪlz]	die Britischen Inseln
the **Republic of Ireland** [rɪˌpʌblɪk‿əv‿ˈaɪəlnd]	die Republik Irland
state [steɪt]	Staat
above [əˈbʌv]	oberhalb, oben
Edinburgh [ˈedɪnbrə]	*Hauptstadt von Schottland*
Dublin [ˈdʌblɪn]	*Hauptstadt von Irland*
Cardiff [ˈkɑːdɪf]	*Hauptstadt von Wales*
Belfast [belˈfɑːst]	*Hauptstadt von Nordirland*
Bristol [ˈbrɪstl]	*Großstadt in Südwestengland*

STEP A

environment [ɪnˈvaɪərnmənt]	Umwelt
to **grow*** [grəʊ]	wachsen
healthy [ˈhelθi]	gesund
fast [fɑːst]	schnell
to **carry** [ˈkæri]	tragen
tent [tent]	Zelt
independent [ˌɪndɪˈpendənt]	unabhängig
to **cook** [kʊk]	kochen
less [les]	weniger
now and then [ˌnaʊ‿n‿ˈðen]	ab und zu
6 to **agree** [əˈgriː]	zustimmen

You can tour | Ireland. / the coast. / …

We live close to | a pub. / the coast. / a hotel. / …

Names with one syllable:
Jack, Jean, Bill, Ann

Names with two syllables:
Jenny, Henry, Tessa, Tony

Names with three syllables:
Nicola, Jonathan, Stephanie

Names with four syllables:
(In your class?)

UK is short for United Kingdom.
GB is short for Great Britain.
USA is short for United States of America.

The USA has 50 states.

Dublin is to Ireland as London is to …

Cardiff is to Wales as Belfast is to …

Edinburgh is to Scotland as Washington DC is to …

1 syllable	2 syllables	3 syllables
France	England	Germany
golf	football	basketball
drum	keyboard	saxophone

Go on.

Opposites

to agree	–	to disagree
separate	–	united
to live	–	to die
old	–	new
…		

9

	to **disagree** [ˌdɪsəˈgriː]	ablehnen
	true [truː]	wahr

STEP B

	travel [ˈtrævl]	Reise-
	until [ənˈtɪl]	bis
	suitcase [ˈsuːtkeɪs]	Koffer
	motorway café [ˈməʊtəweɪ ˌkæfeɪ]	Cafeteria auf der Autobahn
	castle [ˈkɑːsl]	Burg, Schloss
	campsite [ˈkæmpsaɪt]	Campingplatz
	to **rain cats and dogs** [ˈreɪn ˌkæts‿n‿ˈdɒgz]	heftig regnen, schütten, gießen
	hole [həʊl]	Loch
	match [mætʃ]	Streichholz
	to **rub** [rʌb]	reiben
	Daniel Boone [ˌdænjəl ˈbuːn]	*amerikanischer Pionier*
	sleeping bag [ˈsliːpɪŋ ˌbæg]	Schlafsack
	bill [bɪl]	Rechnung
	Yorkshire Dales [ˌjɔːkʃə ˈdeɪlz]	*Flußtäler in Nordengland*
	flat tyre [ˌflæt ˈtaɪə]	platter Reifen, Plattfuß
	sheep, *pl.* **sheep** [ʃiːp]	Schaf(e)
	sheepdog [ˈʃiːpdɒg]	Schäferhund, Hirtenhund
	without [wɪˈðaʊt]	ohne
	Snowdonia [snəʊˈdəʊniə]	*höchster Berg in Wales*
	to **fry** [fraɪ]	frittieren, braten
	bacon [ˈbeɪkn]	Speck
	egg [eg]	Ei
	sausage [ˈsɒsɪdʒ]	Würstchen
	heart attack [ˈhɑːt‿əˌtæk]	Herzinfarkt
	plate [pleɪt]	Teller
	to **invite** [ɪnˈvaɪt]	einladen

STEP C

1	**relative** [ˈrelətɪv]	Verwandte(r)
	Washington DC [ˌwɒʃɪŋtən ˌdiːˈsiː]	*Hauptstadt der USA*
	capital [ˈkæpɪtl]	Hauptstadt
	shopping mall *AE* [ˈʃɒpɪŋ ˌmɑːl]	Einkaufszentrum
	whether [ˈweðə]	ob
	further [ˈfɜːðə]	weiter
2	**in common** [ɪn ˈkɒmən]	gemeinsam
	neither [ˈnaɪðə]	keine(r) (von beiden), auch nicht
	nor [nɔː]	noch, (und) auch nicht
	neither ... nor [ˈnaɪðə ... ˈnɔː]	weder ... noch
3	**wheel** [wiːl]	Rad
	Australia [ɒsˈtreɪliə]	Australien
	the **United States (US)** [juːˌnaɪtɪd ˈsteɪts]	die Vereinigten Staaten (USA)

You can fry | eggs.
sausages.
tomatoes.
bacon.

one sheep – lots of sheep(!)

Who would you invite to your birthday party?

Your aunts and uncles are your relatives. And what about your cousins?

Washington DC is the capital of the USA. And what's the capital of Australia?

In the USA there are lots of modern shopping malls.

She doesn't know whether he can come.

What do the USA, NZ, GB, IRL, CDN, ... have in common? – The English language.

9

4	**Thanksgiving** [ˌθæŋks'gɪvɪŋ]	*amerikanischer Feiertag (Erntedankfest am 4. Donnerstag im November)*
	to **be grateful** ['greɪtfl]	dankbar sein
	to **look forward (to)** [ˌlʊk 'fɔ:wəd]	sich freuen (auf)
	Yours faithfully, ['feɪθfli]	mit freundlichen Grüßen, hochachtungsvoll (*Briefschluss*)
5	**soon** [su:n]	bald, rasch
	polite [pə'laɪt]	höflich
	to **sign** [saɪn]	unterzeichnen, unterschreiben
	topic ['tɒpɪk]	Thema
	to **give a talk** ['tɔ:k]	ein (Kurz-)Referat halten
	Ms [mɪz/məz]	Frau *(Anrede)*
	Miss [mɪs]	Fräulein *(Anrede)*
	capital letter [ˌkæpɪtl 'letə]	Großbuchstabe

TRACK 1

1	to **make the most of sth.** [məʊst]	das Beste aus etw machen
	to **record** [rɪ'kɔ:d]	aufzeichnen, aufnehmen
	penfriend ['penfrend]	Brieffreund(in)
2	**punctuation** [ˌpʌŋktʃu'eɪʃn]	Zeichensetzung, Interpunktion
	gap [gæp]	Lücke, Abstand

TRACK 2

1	+**frequent** ['fri:kwənt]	häufig, oft
	+**whitewater rafting** [ˌwaɪtwɔ:tə 'rɑ:ftɪŋ]	Wildwasserfahren
	+**Colorado** [ˌkɒlr'ɑ:dəʊ]	*Bundesstaat im Westen der USA*
	+**downstream** [ˌdaʊn'stri:m]	stromabwärts
	+**flow** [fləʊ]	Strömung, Fließen
	+**slow** [sləʊ]	langsam
	+**rapids** ['ræpɪdz]	Stromschnellen
	+**well-managed** [ˌwel'mænɪdʒd]	gut organisiert, gut geführt
	+**instructions** [ɪn'strʌkʃnz]	Anweisungen, Instruktionen
	+**beginner** [bɪ'gɪnə]	Anfänger(in)
2	+**driver** ['draɪvə]	Fahrer(in)
	+**language** ['læŋgwɪdʒ]	Sprache
4	+**alien** ['eɪliən]	Ausländer(in), Fremde(r)
	+**George Mikes** [ˌdʒɔ:dʒ 'mi:keʃ]	*britischer Schriftsteller (ungarischer Abstammung)*
	+**gorgeous** ['gɔ:dʒəs]	prächtig, prachtvoll
	+to **adore** [ə'dɔ:]	anbeten, sehr gern haben
	+**nasty** ['nɑ:sti]	scheußlich, abscheulich
	+**dreadful** ['dredfl]	furchtbar, schrecklich
	+**fancy** ['fæntsi]	seltsam, ausgefallen
	+to **repeat** [rɪ'pi:t]	wiederholen

On Thanksgiving Day many people in America eat turkey.

I'm looking forward to reading your homepage.

Are you giving a talk? What's the topic?

Use capital letters for the heading of your report.

Make the most of your talents!

It's easier to record interviews than to take notes.

Penfriends today often send a fax or an e-mail.

Whitewater rafting, surfing, sailing and water-skiing are all water sports.

franz différence *lat* differentia *engl* difference

In GB young drivers have the **L**-sign on their cars. **L** means learner. So everybody knows that the driver is a beginner.

How many languages do you know?

franz adorer *lat* adorare *engl* to adore

CD-ROM = **R**ead **O**nly **M**emory

CHECK-OUT

2	**comparison** [kəm'pærɪsn]	Vergleich
3	**Wonky Towers** [ˌwɒŋki 'taʊəz]	*Name eines Hotels*
	the Plush [plʌʃ]	*Name eines Hotels*
	Metropolitan [ˌmetrə'pɒlɪtn]	*Name eines Hotels*
4	**at the bottom** ['bɒtəm]	unten

The UNO is an international organization.

franz thème *lat* thema *engl* theme

COGNATE WORDS

to **add** [æd]	hinzufügen, addieren
address [ə'dres]	Adresse
attraction [ə'trækʃn]	Besonderheit, Attraktion
bread [bred]	Brot
brochure ['brəʊʃə]	Broschüre, Prospekt
camera ['kæmrə]	Kamera, Fotoapparat
camp [kæmp]	(Ferien-)Lager
to **camp** [kæmp]	zelten
camping ['kæmpɪŋ]	Zelten
charm [tʃɑ:m]	Charme
comfortable ['kʌmftəbl]	bequem, komfortabel
contact ['kɒntækt]	Kontakt, Verbindung
to **contact** ['kɒntækt]	Kontakt aufnehmen
context ['kɒntekst]	Textzusammenhang, Kontext
+**conversation** [ˌkɒnvə'seɪʃn]	Gespräch, Konversation
correct [kə'rekt]	richtig, korrekt
cuisine [kwɪz'ɪ:n]	Küche
detail ['di:teɪl]	Detail, Einzelheit
difference ['dɪfrnts]	Unterschied, Differenz
dinner ['dɪnə]	Abendessen
direct [dɪ'rekt]	direkt
excellent ['ekslnt]	ausgezeichnet, exzellent
fantastic [fæn'tæstɪk]	fantastisch
festival ['festɪvl]	Festival
film [fɪlm]	Film
to **fish** [fɪʃ]	angeln
formal ['fɔ:ml]	förmlich, formell
free [fri:]	frei, kostenlos
golf [gɒlf]	Golf
homepage ['həʊmpeɪdʒ]	Homepage
ideal [aɪ'dɪəl]	ideal, hervorragend
layout ['leɪaʊt]	Gestaltung, Layout
line [laɪn]	Linie
live [laɪv]	lebendig, direkt, live
+to **manage** ['mænɪdʒ]	bewältigen, schaffen
to **mark** [mɑ:k]	markieren
memory ['memri]	Gedächtnis
mouse [maʊs]	Maus
nationality [ˌnæʃn'æləti]	Nationalität
organization [ˌɔ:gnaɪ'zeɪʃn]	Organisation, Veranstalter
to **organize** ['ɔ:gnaɪz]	organisieren, durchführen
+to **panic** ['pænɪk]	in Panik geraten
+**personal** ['pɜ:snl]	persönlich
pioneer [ˌpaɪə'nɪə]	Pionier
popular ['pɒpjələ]	beliebt, populär
position [pə'zɪʃn]	Position
pub [pʌb]	Pub, Kneipe
to **relax** [rɪ'læks]	ausruhen, erholen
rest [rest]	Rast, Pause
route [ru:t]	Route, Strecke
satellite ['sætlaɪt]	Satellit
separate ['seprət]	getrennt, separat
special ['speʃl]	besondere(r/s)
star [stɑ:]	Stern
stick [stɪk]	Stock
strip [strɪp]	Streifen
style [staɪl]	Stil
sunny ['sʌni]	sonnig
+**sunshine** ['sʌnʃaɪn]	Sonnenschein
super ['su:pə]	super, spitze
surfing ['sɜ:fɪŋ]	Surfen
swimming pool ['swɪmɪŋ ˌpu:l]	Swimmingpool
theme [θi:m]	Thema
tomato, *pl.* **-es** [tə'mɑ:təʊ]	Tomate
tourism ['tʊərɪzm]	Tourismus
traditional [trə'dɪʃnl]	traditionell
to **underline** [ˌʌndə'laɪn]	unterstreichen
water-skiing ['wɔ:təski:ɪŋ]	Wasserskifahren
wild [waɪld]	wild
Wild West [ˌwaɪld 'west]	Wilder Westen
wine [waɪn]	Wein
+**wonderful** ['wʌndəfl]	wunderschön
world [wɜ:ld]	Welt

9

Cats

by Eleanor Farjeon

(after Unit 2)

Cats sleep[1]
Anywhere[2],
Any[3] table,
Any chair,
Top[4] of piano,
Window-ledge[5],
in the middle,
on the edge[6],
Open drawer[7],
Empty[8] shoe,
Anybody's[9]
Lap[10] will[11] do,
Fitted[12] in a
Cardboard box[13],
In the cupboard
With your frocks[14] –
Anywhere!
They don't care[15]!
Cats sleep
Anywhere.

1. *Pick out the words with the same sound at the end (the rhymes). Can you find more rhymes for these words?*

2. *Write your own poem* (Gedicht). *Here are some ideas:*

a) *Start the lines like this, and put in some words from the 'Cats' poem:*

Where's Max, the Bradens' cat?
Is he … … … …?
Or … … … … …?
Or is he … … …?
No, he's … … … … .
… … … … … .

b) *Write about your own cat/dog/hamster/…:*

Where's … … …?
Is he/she … … …?
…

[1][sli:p] *schlafen* [2]['eniweə] *irgendwo* [3]['eni] *irgendein* [4][tɒp] *oben* [5]['wɪndəʊledʒ] *Fensterbrett* [6][edʒ] *Rand, Kante* [7]['drɔ:] *Schublade* [8]['empti] *leer* [9]['enibɒdi] *irgendjemand* [10][læp] *Schoß* [11][wɪl] *werden* [12]['fɪtɪd] *eingerichtet* [13]['kɑ:dbɔ:dˌbɒks] *Pappkarton* [14][frɒks] *Kleider* [15]['keə] *es ist ihnen egal*

Monday's child

(after Unit 3)

Monday's child is fair of face[1],
Tuesday's child is full of grace[2],
Wednesday's child is full of woe[3],
Thursday's child has far[4] to go,
Friday's child is loving and giving,
Saturday's child works hard for a living,
But the child that is born[5] on the Sabbath day
Is bonny[6], and blithe[7], and good, and gay[8].

1. *What day's child are you? Perhaps you can find out from your mum or dad. Then you can talk about the other questions in groups.*

2. *Do you like what the poem says about you? Why?/Why not?*

3. *Say what you think: Is it right/wrong* (falsch)*/funny/silly/…?*

[1][feɪs] *Gesicht* [2][greɪs] *Anmut* [3][wəʊ] *Weh, Leid* [4][fɑ:] *weit* [5][bɔ:n] *geboren sein* [6]['bɒni] *gut aussehend* [7][blaɪð] *vergnügt* [8][geɪ] *fröhlich*

Tuff

I'm tough[1]!
Mighty[2] tough!
T-U DOUBLE F
See!
Good word 'tough' –
Strong! Rough[3]!
Good enough[4]
for me, see!

Don't need[5] anyone,
not me, see!

Nobody[6] loves me.
Love! Huh!
Who needs it!
L-U-V.
Silly word, love ...,
They say "I love you"
then they leave[7].
Empty[8] words –
just deceive[9].

I get by,
Don't cry[10],
not me.
Got enough.
I'm tough.
See!

Plenty[11] friends
on the street[12];
plenty places we can meet[13],
plenty food
for us to eat;
don't need shoes on our feet[14];
we're tough!
T-U DOUBLE F! See!

Friends are mates[15],
there for me.
Special mates;
They care[16] for me. See!

Is that love? ...
Could[17] be ...
We'll[18] see ...
we'll see ...
we'll see ...

1. *You can't find the word 'tuff' in an English dictionary, but it means something here. What? What is the real English word?*

2. *What other word in the poem is not real, like 'tuff'?*

3. *Make two lists:*

a) *what the speaker doesn't need,*
b) *what the speaker likes.*

4. *Do you think the speaker is a boy or a girl? Why?*

5. *Do you think he/she really doesn't want the things in the first list?*

[1][tʌf] *zäh* [2]['maɪti] *mächtig* [3][rʌf] *rau, roh* [4][ɪ'nʌf] *genug* [5][ni:d] *brauchen* [6]['eniwʌn] *irgendjemand* [7]['nəʊbədi] *niemand* [8][li:v] *verlassen* [9]['empti] *leer* [10][kraɪ] *weinen* [11]['plenti] *viele* [12][stri:t] *Straße* [13][mi:t] *treffen* [14][fi:t] *Füße* [15][meɪt] *Kumpel, Kamerad(in)* [16][keə] *sorgen* [17][kʊd] *könnten* [18][wi:l] *wir werden*

Watchwords

by Roger McGough

watch the words
watch words the
watchword is
watch words are
sly[1] as boots[2]
ifyoutakeyoureyes[3]offthemforaminute

up[4]
and they're and
away[5] allover
the place

[1][slaɪ] *hinterhältig* [2][bu:t] *Stiefel* [3][aɪ] *Auge* [4][ʌp] *oben* [5][ə'weɪ] *weg*

1. *There are lots of words here! But what sentences can you find in the poem?*

2. *Write your own poem, and call it 'catchwords'* (Schlagwörter, *to catch* = fangen). *Start with your words 'all over the place', and end it with a sentence (in a box?).*

A Christmas[1] story

(after Unit 4)

Rudolph strikes[2] again!

It's coming up to Christmas, and everybody at the North Pole is busy[3] ...

... and happy.

For example: Dasher, Dancer, Prancer and Vixen ...

But also Comet and Cupid ...

... and Donner and Blitzen.

Well, not quite[5] everybody.

Vixen is half right (after generations of genetic mutation, the family nose is now really bright[10]) ... but also half wrong.

Flashback[12] ...

Santa has got a new toy[13] ...

Now back to the present:
It's December 24th!

[1]['krɪsməs] *Weihnachten* [2][straɪk] *(zu)schlagen* [3]['bɪsi] *beschäftigt (sein)* [4][sleɪ] *Schlitten* [5][kwaɪt] *ganz, wirklich* [6][ˌməʊst 'feɪməs] *berühmteste(r/s)* [7]['reɪndɪə] *Rentier* [8]['grændpɑː] *Großvater* [9]['nəʊz] *Nase* [10][braɪt] *leuchtend, hell* [11][rɪ'membə] *(sich) erinnern (an)* [12]['flæʃbæk] *Rückblick* [12][tɔɪ] *Spielzeug* [13]['gædʒɪt] *Gerät, Apparat* [14][niːd] *Bedarf* [15]['ʃaɪni] *scheinend* [16][nɒt ... ˌeni‿'mɔː] *(überhaupt) nicht mehr* [17][skriːn] *Bildschirm* [18][dɪ'liːt] *löschen* [20][nɒt ... jet] *(noch) nicht* [21]['deɪndʒə] *Gefahr* [22]['hedeɪk] *Kopfweh* [23]['fɒgi] *neb(e)lig* [24]['dæmɪt] *verdammt* [25]['nɔːðn] *nördlich, Nord-* [26][əˌbaʊt'tɜːn] *umdrehen, kehrt machen* [27][ˌɑːftə‿'ɔːl] *trotzdem, dennoch* [28][wɪn] *gewinnen* [29][ˌgəʊ‿'daʊn ɪn 'hɪstri] *in die Geschichte eingehen* [30][ə'rɪdʒnl] *ursprünglich* [31]['kærəktə] *Personen, Charaktere*

1. *Who is Rudolph? And what is his normal job?*
2. *In this story, there are two Rudolphs. What has the one got to do with the other?*
3. *At Christmas, you can often hear the 'Rudolph' song (see pictures 7 and 8). Listen to it. Some parts of it are like this story. Can you find them?*
4. *The original[30] Rudolph story is about a hundred years old. What parts are (must be) different in this new story?*
5. *Which characters[31] in this story do you like? And who do you not like? Say why.*

The shopping rap

(after Unit 5)

Where is the car park?
It's over there!
And where are the trolleys[1]?
In the corner[2] somewhere[3]!
But where can we go now?
I can't see the door!
Where are the radios?
On the lower[4] floor[5].
Do we need any butter?
Yes, half a pound!
Where is the popcorn?
Just turn around!
And coffee and tea,
And a sandwich for me!
OK, and some cheese[6],
And an ice cream, please.
What about biscuits[7]?
They look very nice!
No, no, stop it!
Just look at the price!
And now to the check-out.
Number seven is free!
But where is my purse[8]?
... In the car! Dear me!

[1]['trɒli] *Einkaufswagen*
[2]['kɔːnə] *Ecke*
[3]['sʌmweə] *irgendwo*
[4]['ləʊə] *unterer*
[5][flɔː] *Etage*
[6][tʃiːz] *Käse*
[7]['bɪskɪt] *Gebäck*
[8][pɜːs] *Geldbörse*

1. *Where are the people in the poem? How do you know?*
2. *Pick out the rhymes in the rap – the words with the same sound at the end. When you say the rap out loud, you must make these words very clear.*
3. *You need two or more people to read it out loud. How many is best, do you think? How many people are speaking in the rap? Put 'A' and 'B' (and 'C', 'D', etc. if you want) on the different lines for different speakers.*
4. *Now read it in groups. Clap your hands and tap your feet!*

The sword[1] in the stone

(after Unit 6)

It is a very long time ago[2]. Uther Pendragon is the King of Britain. But Kings do not live for ever[3] … His stepdaughter[4] is the witch, Morgan le Fay.

Merlin has magic powers.

But nobody is strong enough.

So the castle invites knights from all over the land to a tournament[7].

One of these knights is Sir Ector. He brings his sons, Sir Kay and Arthur. It is Sir Kay's first tournament.

But when Arthur gets home …

Arthur doesn't read the words on the stone.

Sir Kay goes to his father.

At the church Arthur puts the sword back in.

Sir Ector has something important to tell Arthur.

A week later there is a big feast[17], as Arthur Pendragon becomes King.

[1][sɔ:d] *Schwert* [2][ə'gəʊ] *vor(her)*
[3]['evə] *immer* [4]['stepˌdɔ:tə] *Stieftochter*
[5][ded] *tot* [6][stʌk] *festgesteckt, geklebt*
[7]['tʊənəment] *Turnier* [8][aɪ'wəʊnt] *ich werde nicht* [9]['pʊld] *gezogen*
[10]['pɒsɪbl] *möglich* [11]['ri:zn] *Grund*
[12]['dɪfɪklt] *schwierig* [13][brɔ:t] *gebracht*
[14][wɜ:] *du warst* [15][wɒz] *es war*
[16] = I will [17][fi:st] *Fest(mahl), Bankett*

1. *Make a list of all the people in the story.*

2. *Say what you now know about each of them:*

Uther Pendragon is ...
But he ...
Morgan le Fay is ...

Go on.

3. *What else do you know about King Arthur? Make a list and put the information under headings or key words.*

4. *If you are interested in further information, you can go to your library and ask for books about King Arthur.*

Of course, you can find material on the Internet too.

+Bijon's story

From *The Guardian*

MY NAME is Bijon. I am nearly nine years old. Poverty[1] means you don't have what you need. We weren't always poor[2]. Before, when Mum and Dad lived together we had money, but it is more peaceful[3] now and there is a lot of happiness[4] in our house.

At first we lived in a hostel[5]. I liked it. We had a little room and there were lots of children to play with. When we got our council[6] house we had to do a lot of decorating[7]. That was fun! I liked some things about being poor. I liked doing homework with a torch[8] or having Christmas dinner by candle-light[9]. But now I'm fed up[10] and bored with poverty.

Before we were poor I went riding and swimming, and my Mum took me to concerts and to see friends and relations[11]. That's all stopped.

Mum says that poverty kills people all the time, all over the world. For us, being poor means you have less[12] and less. When things break you can't mend[13] them or get new ones. First the lawnmower[14] broke so the grass is very long. I call it the field. Then Mum's bike was stolen[15], and the iron[16], the television, vacuum cleaner[17] and the kettle[18] broke.

This summer we have to move to London. I don't want to go. I like the seaside[19] here and my school and I've got a lot of friends here. But if Mummy gets a good job, then there won't[20] be so much poverty in our life.

1. *Why is Bijon poor? Is it because*

a) *his parents were always poor*
b) *they live in a very poor country*
c) *his dad went away*
d) *his mum lost her job?*

2. *What was it like for Bijon before they were so poor?*

3. *What does Bijon not like about being poor?*

4. *Being poor wasn't always bad. What good things did he like?*

5. *Is it good or bad that they have to move to London?*

[1]['pɒvəti] *Armut* [2][pɔ:] *arm* [3]['pi:sfl] *friedlich* [4]['hæpɪnəs] *Glück, Fröhlichkeit* [5]['hɒstl] *Wohnheim* [6]['kaʊntsl,haʊs] *Sozialwohnung* [7]['dekreɪtɪŋ] *Verschönerung* [8][tɔ:tʃ] *Taschenlampe* [9]['kændllaɪt] *Kerzenlicht* [10][,fed'ʌp] *es satt haben* [11][rɪ'leɪʃn] *Verwandte(r)* [12][les] *weniger* [13][mend] *reparieren* [14]['lɔ:n,məʊə] *Rasenmäher* [15][sti:l] *stehlen* [16]['aɪən] *Bügeleisen* [17]['vækju:m,kli:nə] *Staubsauger* [18]['ketl] *(Wasser-)Kessel* [19]['si:saɪd] *Küste* [20][wəʊnt] *wird nicht*

The famous Five

by Enid Blyton

(after Unit 8)

Julian, the eldest[1] of the five characters, and older brother to Dick and Anne, usually takes the role of the group leader. He is strong and clever, and helps the children through many dangerous moments.

Anne is the sister of both Julian and Dick, and is the youngest of the group. She likes nothing better than cooking[2], cleaning and looking after other people. She is more emotional that the others. However, she has lots of ideas and is often strong when they're in danger.

Dick is the younger brother of Julian. He is the funny one of the Five, and is always playing games. He is clever, and loves mysteries.

George's real name is Georgina. She is the cousin of Julian, Dick and Anne. She is the tomboy[3] of the group and always wants to show that she's just as good as a boy. She is often stubborn[4], strong-willed and hot-tempered[5], but she is a real friend to her cousins. By far her best friend is her dog Timmy.

Timmy is never happier than when he is with his master George. His second favourite thing is running after rabbits[6]. He has lots of adventures with George, Anne, Dick and Julian.

1. *Put in one extra sentence about each of the Five, and say what they do in the 'Smugglers' story.*

2. *Which of the Five do you like best? Why?*

[1]['eldɪst] *älteste(r)* [2]['kʊkɪŋ] *Kochen* [3]['tɒmbɔɪ] *Wildfang* [4]['stʌbən] *stur, störrisch* [5]['hɒt,tempəd] *jähzornig* [6]['ræbɪt] *Kaninchen*

An Internet yearbook

Project

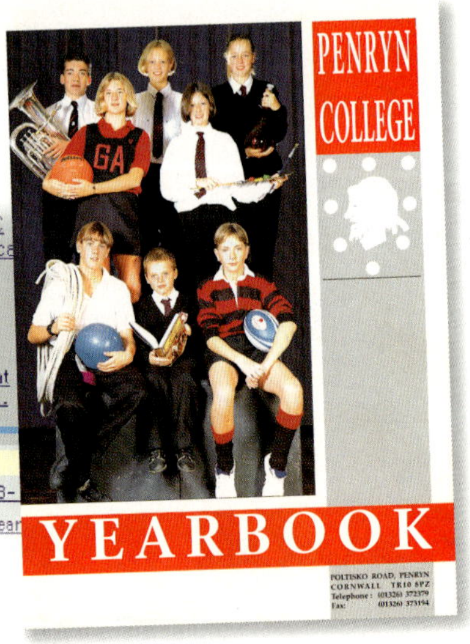

Would you like to create[1] an Internet yearbook for your English class? It can be fun, and you can get to know people in other countries. Here is what you can do:

1. Before you start, have a look at the yearbooks already on the Internet. You will find a list of them at ... or you can type in the word 'yearbook'.

2. Look at them carefully and make two lists: the things that you like about them and the things that you don't like. Discuss your lists in class and decide what you want in *your* yearbook.

3. A number of different types of layout are possible. Discuss which layout is best for what you want to do.

4. Perhaps you want to create a page for each pupil in your class. Discuss what information you want to give about each person and make a list or form on a sheet[2] of paper. Each person then starts to produce his / her own individual page.

5. And what do you do together? Some people can write about the subjects and projects that you have done, and the excursions you have gone on during[3] the last year.

6. Collect photos of your class and your teachers. Or take new photos or make drawings if you want to. Scan in pictures of all the people in your group.

7. Now choose the layout from the web package and enter[4] the information in the layout. Add the photos and drawings if you have a scanner.

8. Your English teacher, your IT teacher or the 'expert' in your class can then publish all the pages on the Internet. If you want it in book form, you can print it out and take it home or send to your family and friends.

This is what you need:

Software: Netscape 3 or higher, sound-recording software (it comes with the soundcard), a graphics program (for example Photoshop) and a web package.

Hardware: Windows-based PCs or Macs with 16 MB RAM, 100 MB free space on the hard disk, a graphics card to support at least 800 x 600 pixels 24 Bit (2 MB card), a soundcard and a connection to the Internet. *Optional:* a scanner and a printer.

Of course, there are other ways. The important thing is: it should be *your* yearbook and it should be FUN!!!

[1] [kri'eɪt] *gestalten* [2] [ʃi:t] *Blatt* [3] ['djʊərɪŋ] *während* [4] ['entə] *eingeben*

Picture postcards from L.A.[1]

Project

1 When it's time for closing, I play while Rachel cleans.

2 She listens to my music, I listen to her dreams.

3 I'm the piano player down at Eddie's bar.

4 do I really think she's pretty[2], do I like the way she sings?

5 She'll even buy a ticket and pack her things to leave.

6 And still no picture postcards from L.A.

7 and she'll send me picture postcards from L.A.

8 When Rachel shares[3] my pillow[4] she always asks me things like

9 and does a scene from the late show.

10 She swears[5] she's gonna[6] make it, she's going all the way.

11 and says, "Next week. I'm gonna go."

12 Rachel, if you find me one, I'd love a picture of the California sun.

13 But something always comes up, something always makes her stay.

14 I don't know how to answer, so I always smile and say,

15 Though we all know the story we pretend that we believe

16 and I say, "Send me picture postcards from L.A."

17 and Rachel she's the waitress[7] who wants to be a star

18 She swears she's gonna make it, make it big someday.

19 Picture postcards from L.A. to hang on my refrigerator[8] door.

20 we all clap our hands as she puts her apron[9] on

21 Sometimes Rachel stands up in the middle of the bar

22 I say, "Send me picture postcards from L.A."

23 Send me postcards from L.A. signed[10] with love forevermore[11].

24 I'm the piano player down at Eddie's bar, and Rachel she's the waitress who wants to be a star.

1. This is Joshua Kadison's[12] famous song *Picture Postcards from L.A.* It tells an interesting story, but the lines of the song are all mixed up. First you must put the words together the right way. You can do it this way: prepare[13] large strips[14] of paper, one for each line. Then each of you writes down one line on his or her strip of paper – as big as possible. Decide who does which line (24 strips = 24 people).

2. Now it's time to listen to the song. While[15] you are listening, you must identify[16] your line. When you hear your line, hold it up. You can stand in a long line or in a circle. Or you can put the lines down on the floor in the middle of the classroom. Be careful with lines 6, 7, 16 and 22: they are very similar[17]. When Kadison has finished his song, all the lines will be in the right order[18]. Maybe you want to have the whole text in writing. What can you do?

3. Is there anything that you can say about the words of the song? Go and get a sheet[19] of paper. You can work with a partner. Go through the text and choose one word or sentence which you think is very important[20] for Kadison's message. Write it down in big letters. Then put all the papers on the floor in the middle of the classroom.

4. One of you begins and puts his / her word (or sentence) down, and says in one or two sentences why he / she has chosen this word. Imagine someone has the word 'dream' on his / her paper. He / she puts it down on the floor and says: "I think the word 'dream' is important in the song." Then another pupil says: "My paper can go with his / her paper because I've got the word 'star'. Rachel dreams of becoming[21] a star." The others go on, and paper by paper a new kind of mind map appears[22] on the classroom floor. It could look like this:

California ? famous star rich dream ? love L.A. ?

5. Have you got an interesting mind map? Do you want to keep it? Then some of you should copy it and make a poster. Or can anybody take a photo of the mind map?

6. What else do you know about California and Los Angeles? Bring some pictures, picture postcards, leaflets[23] , maps and other songs. You can also get some information from the Internet. Add all your material to the mind map poster or make more posters to go with the first one. You can also write or draw things that have to do with the words in the mind map or the text of the song: poems, graffiti, pictures, comics, cartoons, jokes, stickers, ...

7. When you have finished your project, you will have something interstesting for the walls of your classroom. Have fun!

[1]['el͜'eɪ] *Los Angeles* [2]['prɪti] *hübsch* [3][ʃeə] *teilen* [4]['pɪləʊ] *Kissen* [5][sweə] *schwören* [6]['gɒnə] = going to [7]['weɪtrəs] *Kellnerin* [8][rɪ'frɪdʒəreɪtə] *Kühlschrank* [9]['eɪprn] *Schürze* [10][saɪn] *unterschreiben* [11][fə'revəˌmɔ:] *für immer und ewig* [12]['dʒɒʃʊə 'kædɪsn] [13][prɪ'peə] *vorbereiten* [14][strɪp] *Streifen* [15][waɪl] *während* [16][aɪ'dentɪfaɪ] *erkennen, identifizieren* [17]['sɪmɪlə] *ähnlich* [18]['ɔ:də] *Reihenfolge* [19][ʃi:t] *Blatt* [20][ɪm'pɔ:tnt] *wichtig* [21][bɪ'kʌm] *werden* [22][ə'pɪə] *erscheinen* [23]['li:flət] *Prospekt*

Translation

Mit diesen Übersetzungsübungen kannst du überprüfen, ob der Wortschatz und die Grammatik, die du in den einzelnen *Units* gelernt hast, ‚sitzen'. Wenn du nicht mehr weiter weißt, hilft dir ein Blick in die Texte der jeweiligen *Unit* oder in die entsprechenden Kapitel im Grammatikanhang. In den Kästchen zwischen den Übersetzungsübungen findest du Tipps, die dich auf besondere Schwierigkeiten beim Übersetzen aufmerksam machen. Also dann, viel Spaß!

T Beim Übersetzen ist es meist nicht sinnvoll, jedes Wort einzeln zu übersetzen, da der gleiche Sachverhalt in zwei Sprachen häufig unterschiedlich ausgedrückt wird. Wenn du also etwas ins Englische übersetzen willst, dann überlege zunächst, wie Tessa Clifton oder Liz und Liam Braden dazu sagen würden.

Willkommen in England.	*Welcome to England.*
Viel Spaß!	*Have a good time. / Have fun!*
Wie heißt du?	*What's your name?*

1 Willkommen in Islington! — Unit 1 Step B

Bei der Ankunft in Islington kommen Fiona und Matthias ins Gespräch. Sie unterhalten sich natürlich auf Englisch. Übersetze **nicht** *Wort für Wort!*

Fiona: Hallo! Ich heiße Fiona. Und du?
Matthias: Ich heiße Matthias. Mein Name steht auf meinem T-Shirt.
Fiona: Seid ihr alle aus Neustadt?
Matthias: Nein. Ich nicht. Ich bin aus Altdorf.
Fiona: Aber ihr seid alle von einer Schule?
Matthias: Ja.
Fiona: Welche Instrumente spielt ihr?
Matthias: Ich spiele E-Gitarre. Und Mehmet spielt Schlagzeug.
Fiona: Ist Mehmet ein deutscher Name?
Matthias: Nein, es ist ein türkischer Name.
Fiona: Nur noch eine Frage: Wie heißt eure Band?
Matthias: Wir sind die ‚Rolling Phones'.
Fiona: Viel Spaß in England!

2 Bei wem wohnst du? — Unit 2 Step B

Ein paar Tage nach ihrer Ankunft in Islington unterhält sich Florian mit Barry über seine Gasteltern. Versetze dich an Florians Stelle und übersetze.

Barry: Who are you with?
Florian: Ich wohne bei den Holdens. Sie haben ein großes Haus mit einer grünen Tür. Welche Farbe hat eure Tür?
Barry: It's red. Is your room nice?
Florian: Oh ja! Ich habe ein schönes Zimmer unter dem Dach. Es ist auch der Hobbyraum der Holdens.
Barry: What hobby have they got?
Florian: Sie haben zwei Hobbys, klassische Musik und Computer. In meinem Zimmer stehen ein Klavier, ein Cello und ein neuer Computer.
Barry: Have they got a modem too?

Florian: Ja! Wir können im Internet surfen und E-Mails verschicken.
Barry: That's great!
Florian: Was für Hobbys hast denn du?
Barry: I'm interested in football and I've got a dog, a girl dog.
Florian: Wie heißt sie denn?
Barry: Her name is Susie.

3 Sandras Fragen

Unit 3 Step B

Vor dem Interview hat sich Sandra einige Fragen auf Deutsch zurechtgelegt, die sie noch übersetzen muss.

Wie heißt du?
Wie alt bist du?
Habt ihr ein Haustier?
Wer sind deine Freunde?
Gibt es an eurer Schule *bullies*?
Wann beginnt die 1. Stunde?
Was sind deine Lieblingsfächer?
Magst du Mathe?
Wer ist dein Englischlehrer?
Machst du deine Hausaufgaben am Abend?
Was arbeitet deine Mutter?
Wo ist Wimbledon?
Rauchen englische Schüler an der Schule?
Nehmen englische Schüler Drogen?

T Die Wortstellung ist im Englischen in der Regel weniger flexibel als im Deutschen.

Du kannst im Deutschen sagen:	Im Englischen gibt es meist nur eine Möglichkeit:
Ich gehe **normalerweise** um 9 ins Bett.	
Normalerweise gehe ich um 9 ins Bett.	*I **usually** go to bed at 9 o'clock.*
Ins Bett gehe ich **normalerweise** um 9.	

Wenn du das Häufigkeitsadverb besonders betonen möchtest, kannst du *usually, often* und *sometimes* (aber nicht *never* oder *always*) auch an den Satzanfang stellen: ***Usually** I go to bed at 9 o'clock.* Achte bei der folgenden Übersetzung besonders auf die Wortstellung (SVO) und die Stellung von *always, often, usually* usw. **vor** dem Verb.

4 Meine neuen Freunde aus Islington Green

Unit 3 Step B

Sandra hat einen ersten Entwurf ihres Beitrags für die Schülerzeitung geschrieben. Er soll aber auf Englisch erscheinen. Hilf ihr beim Übersetzen.

Meine neuen Freunde aus Islington Green

Joanna ist 14 und wohnt mit ihren Eltern und ihrem kleinen Bruder in einem kleinen Haus in Islington. Ihre Lieblingsfächer sind Mathe und Sport. Sie findet, dass sie oft zu viele Hausaufgaben aufbekommen.

James ist auch 14. Weil seine Eltern getrennt leben, wohnt er bei seiner Mutter. Sie arbeitet im Schichtdienst und ist manchmal nicht zu Hause. Er mag Tiere und möchte er eines Tages Tierarzt werden. Die meiste Zeit verbringt er gewöhnlich mit seinem Hund.

Stephanie ist 15 und findet die Schule in Ordnung. Sie glaubt nicht, dass es an der Schule Drogen gibt. Die Lehrer klären sie über Drogen auf, aber sie sind nicht besonders auf dem Laufenden. Viele Schüler an der Schule rauchen, sie aber nicht, wegen des Sports. Sie ist nämlich verrückt auf Sport: Sie spielt Hockey und Volleyball und schaut sich immer Fußball im Fernsehen an.

T Wie du sicher schon festgestellt hast, werden manche Dinge in beiden Sprachen unterschiedlich ausgedrückt. Dazu gehören auch *there is (+ singular) / there are (+ plural).*

Es gibt viel Verkehr.	*There is a lot of traffic.*
Es gibt viele Geschäfte.	*There are lots of shops.*
die Themse	*the River Thames*
mitten durch London	*through the heart of London*
Man kann dort Getränke kaufen.	*You can buy drinks there.*

5 Informationen über München

Unit 4 Check-in

Ferdinand zeigt seinen Gasteltern ein Prospekt über München und übersetzt für sie einige Passagen ins Englische.

Hier habe ich ein Prospekt mit vielen Sehenswürdigkeiten von München.
- Hier (in der Fußgängerzone) kann man alles Mögliche kaufen, aber es ist normalerweise ziemlich teuer.
- Das hier ist der ‚Alte Peter'. Er hat auch eine Glocke.
- In München gibt es auch eine U-Bahn. Mit ihr kann man schnell von einem Ort zum anderen kommen, aber man kann nichts sehen.
- München besteht nicht nur aus Geschäften, Verkehr und Lärm. Es gibt Parks, in denen man ein Picknick machen, Vögel füttern oder sich einfach ausruhen kann.
- Das ist das Olympiastadion[1]. Es hat 64.000 Sitzplätze[2]. Bayern München spielt dort.

[1] *Olympic Stadium* [2]*seats*

6 Was machen sie gerade?

Unit 4 Step A

Jimmy ist mit den 'Good Vibes' unterwegs in Covent Garden. Es herrscht eine großartige Atmosphäre. Eine Menge Leute stehen um einen Jongleur herum und applaudieren. Übersetze das Gespräch für Jimmy.

Max: Was machen all die Leute da?
Sandra: Sie sehen einem Jongleur zu.
Max: Ich kann nichts sehen. Womit jongliert er denn?
Sandra: Er jongliert mit einem Fußball.
Tarkan: Das kann ich auch.
Max: Wirklich? Schaut, jetzt läuft er auf einem Nagelbett! Kannst du das auch?
Tarkan: Ja, aber nur mit Schuhen.
Max: Was macht er jetzt?
Sandra: Er geht mit einem Hut herum und sammelt (Geld).
Tarkan: Nichts wie weg!

7 Eine Postkarte aus London

Unit 4 Track 1

Schreibe deiner Brieffreundin/deinem Brieffreund in New York eine Postkarte aus London mit folgendem Inhalt (Vergiss Anrede und Schluss nicht!):

- Du amüsierst dich großartig hier in London.
- Es gibt hier so viele Sehenswürdigkeiten (du nennst den Tower mit den Kronjuwelen und drei weitere).
- Man kann hier so viele aufregende Sachen unternehmen.
- Das Wetter ist nicht besonders, aber es regnet gerade nicht.
- Heute Abend wollen dich deine englischen Freunde in ‚Phantom der Oper' mitnehmen, du kannst es gar nicht erwarten.

8 Souvenirs vom Camden Market

Unit 5 Step A

Du bist als Austauschschüler(in) in Islington und sprichst mit deinen Gasteltern über Souvenirs und Geschenke für Freunde daheim.

- Du erklärst deinen Gasteltern, dass du einige Souvenirs für deine Freunde in Deutschland kaufen möchtest und fragst sie, wo es günstige CDs gibt.
- *Well, you can go to Virgin Megastore or HMV.*
- Du fragst, wo sie sind.
- *They're near Oxford Street.*
- Du möchtest wissen, wie du da hinkommst.
- *You can go by bus or by Underground.*
- Du möchtest wissen, ob sie Schallplatten haben. Für deinen Vater suchst du nämlich eine Platte von den Beatles.
- *I'm not sure, but you can try to find one in Camden Market.*
- Du möchtest wissen, was Camden Market ist.
- *It's a great street market quite near here.*
- Du möchtest gleich hin.
- *You must wait, I'm afraid. The stalls aren't open today.*

Du bist jetzt an einem Schallplattenstand in Camden Market und redest mit einer Händlerin.

- Du fragst, ob sie Schallplatten von den Beatles hat.
- *Of course, are you looking for something special?*
- Du weißt nicht genau und fragst, ob du einige Platten anschauen kannst.
- *Sure you can.*
- Du deutest auf eine Platte und fragst, ob du sie haben kannst.
- *Sure. It's £4.50.*
- Du bist erstaunt über den Preis und sagst, dass dir das zu teuer ist.
- *Well, I can give you three for only £10.*
- Du bedauerst, du hast insgesamt nur £5 und möchtest noch Schals für deine Mutter und deine Schwester kaufen. Du verabschiedest dich.

Jetzt brauchst du erst einmal ein Eis.

- Du schlägst deinem englischen Freund vor, ein Eis zu essen und bestellst einmal Vanille und einmal Schokolade.
- *Sorry, we haven't got any vanilla, but we've got some banana.*
- Du lehnst dankend ab, denn du magst kein Bananeneis. Dann bestellst du zweimal Schokoladeneis.

T Wie du bereits weißt, ist es oft nicht richtig, Wort für Wort aus dem Deutschen ins Englische zu übersetzen. Besonders aufpassen musst du, wenn Ausdrücke und Formulierungen in beiden Sprachen sehr ähnlich sind. Die Unterschiede sind oft nur gering, also genau hinschauen!

zweimal **pro** Woche	*twice **a** week*
Was **für** ein Film!	*What • a film!*
Welche Farbe **hat** dein T-Shirt?	*What colour **is** your T-shirt?*
Deine Hose• **ist** zu kurz.	*Your trousers are too short.*
Die Schule fängt um 8 Uhr an.	*• School starts at 8 o'clock.*
zu viele Hausaufgabe**n**	*too much homework•*

9 Andenken an London

Unit 5 Track 2

Sandra hat in ihr Tagebuch geschrieben, was beim Einkaufen passiert ist. Sie übersetzt für Liz, was sie über den Vorfall im Computergeschäft notiert hat.

Heute sind Sebastian und ich in diesen tollen Computerladen gegangen, wo man alle Spiele ausprobieren kann. Sebastian hat ein Spiel ganz besonders gefallen, aber er hat nicht genügend Geld gehabt um es zu kaufen. Er hat mich gebeten, ihm etwas Geld zu leihen, aber ich habe ‚nein' gesagt. Dann haben wir Liam getroffen. Ich habe ihm alle meine lustigen Andenken gezeigt. Er hat gelacht, aber Sebastian ist zu den Spielen hinübergegangen. Er hat die Gelegenheit beim Schopf gepackt und das Spiel in die Tasche gesteckt. Dann wollte er plötzlich gehen. Liam hat ihm gesagt, dass er ein Vollidiot ist, und ich habe ihn gebeten, es wieder zurückzulegen, weil ich keinen Ärger wollte. Als wir den Laden verlassen wollten, hat ein Mann Sebastian die Hand auf die Schulter gelegt und gesagt: „Komm hier entlang, bitte." Es war ein Kaufhausdetektiv und Sebastians Gesicht wurde knallrot. In einem kleinen Raum konnten wir auf einem großen Fernsehgerät die lustige Szene mit den Andenken sehen. Aber wir haben nicht gelacht. Dann haben sie uns aufgefordert, unsere Einkaufstaschen herzuzeigen und alles, was wir in unseren Hosentaschen hatten. Aber sie haben nichts gefunden. Eine Zeitlang hat der Mann geschwiegen, dann hat er gesagt: „Entschuldigt das Versehen."

10 E-Mail

Unit 6 Step A

Jonas ist als Austauschschüler in Cornwall. Er sitzt bei seinen Gasteltern am Computer und schreibt eine E-Mail an seine Freunde in Berlin. Mike will wissen, was er schreibt. Jonas übersetzt für ihn.

Hallo Kumpels!
Ich bin jetzt endlich in Cornwall. Das Leben auf dem Land macht Spaß und das Haus von Mikes Familie ist toll! Es liegt drei Meilen vom Dorf entfernt und es fahren nur zwei Busse pro Tag, aber der Strand ist sehr nah. Von seinem Schlafzimmerfenster aus kann Mike das Meer sehen. Was für eine Aussicht! Am Montag fängt die Schule an. Mikes Schule ist gar nicht so schlecht. Einige Lehrer sind ganz in Ordnung, aber sie geben manchmal zu viele Hausaufgaben auf. Mike hat eine Schuluniform. Er behauptet, sie hat eine scheußliche Farbe. Ich finde sie aber ganz okay. Seine Sportausrüstung ist jedenfalls super!
Das wär's für heute!
Euer Freund Jonas

T Bei einer E-Mail wird kein besonderer Wert auf die äußere Form gelegt. Wenn du aber einen persönlichen Brief auf Englisch schreiben willst, musst du – ähnlich wie im Deutschen – auch auf die Form achten.

- Wenn du an Freunde oder gute Bekannte schreibst, verwendest du als Anrede
  Dear Liam, oder *Dear Liz,*
- dann beginnst du eine neue Zeile und schreibst den ersten Buchstaben **groß**
  Thank you for your letter ...
- Als Grußformel am Schluss kannst du verwenden
  Love, oder *Yours,* oder *Best Wishes,*
- Wenn du mit jemandem per Sie bist, schreibst du als Anrede
  Dear Mr Bean, oder *Dear Ms Bean,*
- und als Schluss
  Yours sincerely,
- ... und vergiss das Komma nicht!

11 Sandras Brief an Liz

Unit 6 Step A

Sandra möchte den Brief von Liz beantworten. Sie hat ihn zunächst auf Deutsch aufgesetzt, aber wie du weißt, soll man ja nicht Wort für Wort übersetzen, sondern gleich überlegen, wie sich ein(e) englische(r) Sprecher(in) ausdrücken würde.

Liebe Liz,
vielen Dank für Deinen Brief mit den lustigen Fotos von Dir in Deiner neuen Schuluniform. Du siehst wirklich großartig aus. In Deutschland gibt es keine Schuluniformen, aber viele Schüler tragen die gleichen modischen Klamotten: Sweatshirts, Jeans und Turnschuhe. Es freut mich sehr, dass dir die Kassette unserer Band gefällt. Wir treten jeden Samstag Nachmittag im Jugendclub auf. Tarkan und die anderen üben gerade, aber ich kann heute nicht singen, weil ich fürchterlich erkältet bin. In deinem Brief schreibst du, dass in Cornwall draußen alles weiß ist. Es schneit zwar ziemlich viel in dieser Gegend von Deutschland, aber momentan ist alles grau; es regnet in Strömen.
Antworte bald!
Viele Grüße
Sandra

P.S. Vergiss nicht, Deine Eltern, Deinen Bruder und Deine Freunde von mir zu grüßen!

12 Was machst du am Projekttag?

Unit 7 Step A

Du nimmst an einem Schüleraustausch mit einer englischen Schule teil. Dein(e) Austauschpartner(in) steht mit dir vor dem schwarzen Brett. Ihr seht euch an, wer sich schon in die Teilnehmerlisten eingetragen hat, und unterhaltet euch über die verschiedenen Projekte, die angeboten werden.

- *Oh look here, Peter and Sally are going to go camping on the Isles of Scilly!*
- Du fügst hinzu, dass Andy das Leuchtturmmuseum in Penzance besucht und Helen vorhat, Karate[1] zu lernen. Das ist nichts für dich. Du wirst doch im Sommer keine Hallensportart[2] machen!
- *Oh yes, you're right ... Oh look over there! 25 people are interested in the project on the coast!*
- Du fragst, ob sie wirklich die verschmutzen Strände saubermachen.
- *I don't know. What are we going to do? How about the drama workshop?*
- Du entgegnest, dass ihr eine Theatergruppe an eurer Schule habt, und dass dir die Schauspielerei nicht besonders gefällt. Du schlägst das Computerprojekt vor. Eine Homepage zu verfassen ist doch sehr interessant.
- *Sorry, but I hate computers.*
- Du würdest gerne einen Videofilm über englische Schulen machen.
- *That's a good idea! But the course is already full! Hm ... And what about this project here? A camping trip to the Isles of Scilly!*
- Du sagst, dass das sehr interessant klingt.

[1]*karate* [2]*indoor sport*

T Um einen deutschen Text sinngemäß im Englischen wiederzugeben, ist es nicht nötig, jede Formulierung haarklein in die andere Sprache zu übertragen. Es genügt, die wichtigsten Informationen des Textes wiederzugeben.

die zunehmende Verschmutzung	*there is more and more pollution*
aus aller Herren Länder	*from countries all over the world*
die Vögel gehen zugrunde	*the birds die*
auf hoher See Abfall entsorgen	*to dump rubbish overboard*
Öl ins Meer leiten	*to spill oil into the sea*

13 Die Nordsee in Gefahr? Unit 7 Step B

Dein(e) englische(r) Austauschpartner(in) hat einen interessanten Zeitungsartikel gefunden, der allerdings einige schwierige Passagen enthält. Gemeinsam bemüht ihr euch, die wichtigsten Informationen des Artikels sinngemäß ins Englische zu übertragen.

Greenpeace:

Maßnahmen gegen die Verschmutzung der Nordsee[1] gefordert

Die Umweltschutzorganisation warnt vor drohendem Desaster

Hamburg.
Die Umweltschutzorganisation Greenpeace hat auf die zunehmende Verschmutzung der Nordsee hingewiesen, die eine Gefahr für die Menschen und vor allem für die Tierwelt darstellt. Die Verschmutzung ist darauf zurückzuführen, dass Schiffe aus aller Herren Länder bis zu 260.000 Tonnen[2] Abfall pro Jahr auf hoher See entsorgen. Tanker und andere Schiffe leiten Öl ins Meer.
Dieses Öl bildet einen Teppich auf der Meeresoberfläche. Dabei genügen nach Aussage von Umweltexperten zwei Liter Öl um einen Ölteppich zu verursachen, der so groß ist wie fünf Fußballfelder. Vögel, die auf diesem Teppich landen, können nicht mehr fliegen, da sich ihr Gefieder verklebt. Auf diese Weise gehen Jahr für Jahr mehr als 200.000 Vögel zugrunde. Die toten Vögel werden nun zusammen mit anderem Abfall, der zum großen Teil aus Plastik besteht, an Land geschwemmt. Plastik ist schwierig zu entsorgen, weil dieses Material nur sehr schwer biologisch abbaubar ist. Greenpeace appelliert daher an alle Verursacher, Kapitäne, Bootsbesitzer und Strandurlauber, keinen Abfall im Meer zu entsorgen.

[1]*North Sea* [2]*tons of*

T Im Deutschen kann man mit dem Präsens Handlungen und Sachverhalte ausdrücken, die gewohnheitsmäßig oder gerade im Moment oder aber in der Zukunft (Vorhaben oder Ereignis, das man nicht beeinflussen kann) stattfinden. Im Englischen muss man je nach Situation das *simple present, present progressive, going to-future* oder *will-future* verwenden.

Fiona schreibt (oft) Briefe.	*Fiona often writes letters.*
Sie schreibt (jetzt) Einladungskarten.	*She is writing invitations now.*
Nächsten Samstag gibt sie eine Party. *(Vorhaben = Zukunft)*	*She is going to have a party next Saturday.*
Dann wird sie vierzehn. *(Ereignis = Zukunft)*	*She will be fourteen then.*

14 Ein Orkan über Florida Unit 7 Track 2

Guten Morgen! Hier ist Radio Fort Lauderdale mit den neuesten Nachrichten. Von den Westindischen Inseln[1] her kommt ein Orkan und bewegt sich schnell auf Florida zu. Orkane erreichen manchmal eine Geschwindigkeit von bis zu 120 Meilen pro Stunde. Sichern Sie also ihre Türen und Fenster mit Brettern und stellen Sie Ihren Wagen an einem sicheren Ort ab. Sorgen Sie dafür, dass Sie genügend Essensvorräte und Trinkwasser haben. Unsere Wetterexperten sagen, dass der Orkan am Nachmittag noch an Geschwindigkeit zunimmt und um fünf Uhr die Küste erreicht. Zur Zeit bewegt er sich mit einer Geschwindigkeit von 50 Meilen pro Stunde nordwärts. Sie sind nicht sicher, ob er sich nach Osten in Richtung offenes Meer bewegt, oder Florida überquert und in Richtung Golf von Mexiko wegzieht. Seien Sie jedoch auf der Hut, denn Orkane richten oft Schäden an Fenstern und Dächern an und entwurzeln Bäume. Und hören Sie immer Radio Fort Lauderdale. Wir informieren Sie alle 30 Minuten.

[1]*West Indies*

15 Das Verfassen eines neuen Theaterstücks — Unit 8 Step B

Mit den Kostümen für das König Arthur Theaterstück ist etwas Schreckliches passiert: Sie sind alle durch Wasser beschädigt worden. Sie sind so verschmutzt, dass man sie nicht reinigen oder wiederherrichten kann. Die Schüler haben daran gedacht, neue zu kaufen, aber das kommt zu teuer. Doch Liz hat eine Idee: Man könnte doch ein leichtes Stück mit einfachen Kostümen aufführen[1]! Sie hat gerade eine aufregende Abenteuergeschichte gelesen – es handelt sich um ein Fünf-Freunde-Buch von Enid Blyton über Schmuggler in Cornwall – und sie meint, dass sie und Brenda daraus ein Theaterstück machen können.
Die drei Szenen des ersten Akts haben sie schon fertiggestellt. Natürlich haben sie nicht alles aus dem Buch verwendet. Sie haben einige interessante Stellen herausgenommen und einige schwierige Stellen abgeändert. Im Moment arbeiten sie an der zweiten Szene des zweiten Akts. Sie versuchen, einen spannenden Dialog zwischen Pete und Julian zu verfassen.

[1]*to perform*

16 Noch eine E-Mail aus Cornwall :-) — Unit 8 Track 2

Liam sitzt (schon wieder) am Computer und antwortet auf B. J.s E-Mail aus Florida.

Hallo B. J.,
anscheinend kommen gerade alle Touristen nach Cornwall! Es ist ganz schön heiß hier, ungefähr 28° (natürlich Celsius, nicht Fahrenheit) und so wimmelt[1] es an meinem Strand nur so von Menschen!
Deine Wette über Orkane in Großbritannien hast Du übrigens verloren! 1987 gab es hier einen fürchterlichen Orkan. Der ist über den südlichen Landesteil mit einer Geschwindigkeit von mehr als 100 Meilen pro Stunde hereingebrochen und hat Millionen von Bäumen entwurzelt.
Ich kann einfach nicht verstehen, dass Du noch nie in Disney World warst! Ich war schon dreimal in Eurodisney in der Nähe von Paris. Wir sind mit dem Zug durch den Ärmelkanaltunnel[2] nach Frankreich gefahren – das war aufregender als mit der Fähre[3] (meine Schwester hatte fürchterliche Angst!).
Als wir letzte Woche in Plymouth waren, habe ich natürlich an Dich gedacht und jede Menge Fotos gemacht. Ich schicke sie Dir mit der ‚Schneckenpost'[4]. Worüber geht Euer Schulprojekt eigentlich?
Lass bald was von Dir hören!

Liam

[1]*teem with* [2]*Channel Tunnel* [3]*ferry* [4]*snail mail*

17 Die Urlaubspläne der Shiltons — Unit 9 Step B

Die Shiltons schmieden gerade Pläne für den Sommerurlaub ...

Mrs S.: Wir könnten in eines dieser kleinen, ruhigen Hotels in Schottland gehen. Schaut her – Nessies Lodge: Komfortables Hotel mit exquisiter Küche. Wir könnten Angeln gehen und Golf spielen.
Peter: Aber könnt ihr denn nicht lesen? Da steht ‚Kinder und Hunde nicht erwünscht'!
Mr S.: Ja, Peter hat Recht. Ich meine, wir sollten in eine Frühstückspension gehen. Die ist billiger als ein Hotel ...
Peter: Wie wär's denn mit einem Camping- und Rad-Urlaub? Das macht viel mehr Spaß als den ganzen Tag in einem Hotel herumzusitzen.
Mrs S.: Oh nein! Ich habe nicht vor, ein Zelt auf dem Fahrrad herumzuschleppen.
Mr S.: Ich habe eine bessere Idee: Mieten wir doch ein Boot in den Norfolk Broads. „Der etwas andere Urlaub ... Keine Vorkenntnisse erforderlich." Das klingt doch interessant!

Mrs S.: Nein danke! Das ist schwieriger als du glaubst. Ich habe es einmal ausprobiert: Der feuchteste Urlaub meines Lebens! Warum mieten wir eigentlich kein Wohnmobil? Das kommt zwar teurer als Camping, ist aber auch bequemer.
Mr S.: Eine tolle Idee! Den ganzen Tag in einem Auto sitzen und fahren. Ohne mich! Ich denke, wir wollen nicht die ganze Zeit kochen?
Mrs S.: Nun, wir können ja ab und zu ins Restaurant gehen.
Peter: Und wir können beim Alton Towers Freizeitpark Halt machen. Schaut euch mal diesen Prospekt hier an: „Riesenspaß für die ganze Familie, organisierte Tagesausflüge und Kinder essen umsonst." Da gehen wir hin!
Mr und Mrs S.: Ja, warum eigentlich nicht!?

18 Informationen über einen Urlaub in Schottland — Unit 9 Step C

Du hast deine Eltern soweit, dass sie mit dir im Sommer nach Schottland fahren wollen. Allerdings liegt es bei dir, Informationen über Unterbringung und Sehenswürdigkeiten zu besorgen. Daher verfasst du einen förmlichen Brief ... natürlich auf Englisch!

Scottish Tourist Board
23 Ravelston Terrace
Edinburgh EH4 3EU

Sehr geehrte Damen und Herren,

meine Eltern und ich möchten unseren Sommerurlaub in Schottland verbringen. Wir interessieren uns insbesondere für Burgen, Angeln und Wandern. Könnten Sie uns bitte einige Informationen über Frühstückspensionen und über besondere Veranstaltungen im August zusenden? Prospekte von beliebten Touristenattraktionen wären auch sehr hilfreich. Teilen Sie mir bitte auch mit, ob sie eine E-Mail-Adresse oder eine Internet-Homepage haben.

Für Ihre Bemühungen bedanke ich mich bereits jetzt und freue mich darauf, von Ihnen zu hören.

Mit freundlichen Grüßen

19 Ein faszinierender Sport — Unit 9 Track 2

Tessa und Nathan unterhalten sich über das Wildwasserfahren ...

Tessa: Wildwasserfahren ist gefährlich, oder?
Nathan: Naja, so gefährlich wie das Bungee-Springen ist es nicht. Wenn du die Anweisungen genau[1] befolgst, kriegst du keine Probleme.
Tessa: Aber ihr nehmt nur gute Schwimmer, oder?
Nathan: Klar hilft es, wenn du gut schwimmen kannst, aber du musst sowieso eine Schwimmweste anziehen.
Tessa: Wenn ich ins Wasser falle, dann lachst du mich nicht aus, oder?
Nathan: Natürlich nicht, aber du darfst den Kopf nicht verlieren. Leg dich auf den Rücken und lass dich einfach treiben. Wenn das Wasser wieder langsam fließt, schwimmst du schnell ans Ufer.
Tessa: Es gibt schon leichte Touren für Leute wie mich, oder?
Nathan: Sicher! Anfänger gehen erst mal an langsame Flüsse. Aber du lernst schnell und dann kannst du schwierigere Touren ausprobieren.

[1] *hier:* vorsichtig

Grammar

Wie du weißt, gibt es in jeder Sprache grammatische Regeln. Die Regeln der englischen Sprache unterscheiden sich in manchen Punkten von den deutschen. In der *Grammar* sind die Unterschiede übersichtlich zusammengestellt, erklärt und mit Beispielen erläutert. Hier kannst du nachlesen, wenn du
- etwas vergessen hast,
- etwas genau wissen willst,
- dich auf einen Test oder eine Klassenarbeit vorbereitest.

Damit dir das Lernen so leicht wie möglich gemacht wird, gibt es Wegweiser, an denen du dich orientieren kannst. Ab und zu ist es hilfreich, Regeln gleich anzuwenden. Deshalb haben wir an einigen Stellen kurze Übungen aufgenommen. Die Lösungen dazu findest du auf Seite 232. Grammatikpunkt mit hochgestelltem + behandeln die neuen Strukturen im *Track* 2. Da alles immer wieder in anderen Zusammenhängen vorkommt, kannst du dich auf die ständige Wiederholung und Absicherung verlassen.

S = Sehen: Die Übersichten zeigen, was zusammengehört.

M = Merken: Die Merkhilfen unterstützen das Gedächtnis.

W = Wissen: Die Zusammenhänge und Hintergründe erleichtern das Verstehen und Behalten.

A = Anwenden: In den Übungen kannst du die Regeln gleich anwenden.

Also dann, viel Spaß!

UNIT 1

1 Der unbestimmte Artikel – The indefinite article

a	keyboard guitar ticket

Der unbestimmte Artikel besteht im Englischen normalerweise aus dem kurzen Wörtchen *a*.

Merken musst du dir allerdings, dass bei Wörtern, die mit einem Vokal (a, e, i, o, u) beginnen – *airport, electric, instrument, open* usw. – zur leichteren Aussprache ein *-n* an das *a* angehängt wird. *A window* ist richtig, aber bei *open window* muss es *an* heißen: *an open window*.

a	window guitar band	an	open window electric guitar English band

Eine Besonderheit musst du noch wissen: Viele Wörter, die mit *u* beginnen, z.B. *unit*, brauchen **kein** eingeschobenes *-n*, weil man im Anlaut nicht den Vokal, sondern ein j hört: *a unit.*

W Den vielen deutschen Formen *ein, eine, einer, eines, einem, einen* entspricht im Englischen der eine unbestimmte Artikel *a/an.*

2 Der bestimmte Artikel – The definite article

Auch beim bestimmten Artikel hast du es im Englischen viel einfacher als im Deutschen. Den vielen deutschen Formen (der, die, das, den, dem) entspricht im Englischen immer der Artikel *the*.

	window		airport
the [ðə]	guitar	**the** [ði]	electric instruments
	minibus		open door

Allerdings musst du wieder darauf achten, ob das folgende Wort mit einem Konsonanten oder einem Vokal beginnt. Anders als beim unbestimmten Artikel siehst du den Unterschied diesmal nicht im Schriftbild. Der bestimmte Artikel wird immer *the* geschrieben, aber unterschiedlich gesprochen.

3 Substantive und Personalpronomen – Nouns and personal pronouns

Im Englischen werden alle Substantive kleingeschrieben, außer wenn sie am Satzanfang stehen oder Eigennamen sind. Das Geschlecht der Substantive erkennst du nicht wie im Deutschen am Artikel (vgl. Punkt 2). Englische Substantive werden nach ihrem natürlichen Geschlecht unterschieden. Die Personalpronomen *he, she* und *it* zeigen das Geschlecht.

Tony Clifton, Sebastian, ...	**he**	(er)
Tessa, Sandra, Maike, ...	**she**	(sie)
instrument, door, dog, ...	**it**	(es)

Für eine Sache verwendest du immer *it*. Auch Tiere sind normalerweise *it*. Wenn du ein Tier aber gut kennst und den Eigennamen benutzt, sagst du *he* oder *she*.

Die Personalpronomen *I, you, he, she, it* stehen stets nur für **eine** Person, **eine** Sache oder **ein** Tier. Die Personalpronomen *we, you, they* stehen dagegen für **mehrere** Personen, Sachen oder Tiere.

S

	I	(ich)
	you	(du)
singular	**he**	(er)
	she	(sie)
	it	(es)
	we	(wir)
plural	**you**	(ihr / Sie)
	they	(sie)

Das Personalpronomen *I* wird im Englischen **immer** großgeschrieben.

You kann sowohl *du* (Singular) als auch *ihr* (Plural) oder *Sie* (höfliche Anrede) heißen.

Tarkan, **you** are OK.	(du)
Are **you** the two singers in the band?	(ihr)
You are nice, Mr Clifton.	(Sie)

4 Kurzformen – Short forms

1 *I'm* ist die Kurzform von *I am* (ich bin ... / ich heiße ...). Mit *I'm* ... kannst du dich z.B. vorstellen oder sagen, wie es dir geht. *I am* ... hört man seltener, da die Langform *am* eine starke Betonung ausdrückt.

Let's ... ist aus *let us* ... entstanden (lass/t uns ...). Die Langform *let us* ... hört man nur noch selten. Sie klingt veraltet, etwa wie das deutsche *lasset uns* ... Mit *let's* ... kannst du Vorschläge machen: *Let's go.*

2 Wann verwendet man die Kurzform, und wann die Langform?

Kurzform	Langform
– beim Sprechen – beim Aufschreiben von Gesprächen – in persönlichen Briefen an Freunde	– beim Schreiben von Aufsätzen und Berichten – in offiziellen Briefen an nicht näher bekannte Personen

We're in Islington. → **Are we** in Islington?
He's a good friend. → **Is he** a good friend?

Wenn du Fragen stellst, musst du **immer** die Langform verwenden. Wie im Deutschen werden auch im Englischen bei einer Frage mit *to be* (sein) Subjekt und Prädikat umgestellt. Man nennt das Inversion.

5 Das Präsens von *to be* – The simple present of *to be*

1 S

	Kurzform	Langform	Frage?	Verneinung
singular	I'm ...	I am ...	Am I ...?	I'm not ...
	You're ...	You are ...	Are you ...?	You aren't ...
	He's ...	He is ...	Is he ...?	He isn't ...
	She's ...	She is ...	Is she ...?	She isn't ...
	It's ...	It is ...	Is it ...?	It isn't ...
plural	We're ...	We are ...	Are we ...?	We aren't
	You're ...	You are ...	Are you ...?	You aren't ...
	They're ...	They are ...	Are they ...?	They aren't ...

2 She **isn't** a singer.
You **aren't** English.
They **aren't** in the minibus.
I'm not from London.

Bei der Verneinung von *to be* brauchst du eine weitere Kurzform. *Not* wird zu *n't* verkürzt und direkt an die Form von *to be* angehängt: *isn't, aren't.* Beachten musst du allerdings, dass in der 1. Person **immer** die Langform von *not* verwendet wird.

A

Forme die Aussagen so um, dass daraus Fragen werden.

They're from Islington. She's a friend.
You're at the check-in. Tarkan is OK.
It's a bus. He's English.

6 Der Plural der Substantive (regelmäßige Formen) – The plural of nouns (regular forms)

1

one / a ticket	three tickets
one / a dog	two dogs

Die Pluralformen der Substantive sind im Englischen leicht zu bilden. Bei den meisten Substantiven wird einfach ein *-s* an die Singularform angehängt.

2

pilot	pilots	['paɪləts]
snack	snacks	[snæks]
shop	shops	[ʃɒps]

Bei der Aussprache des Plural-*s* musst du allerdings gut aufpassen. Nach stimmlos gesprochenen Lauten wie [t], [p] oder [k] wird das Plural-*s* ebenfalls stimmlos gesprochen.

3

dog	dogs	[dɒgz]
girl	girls	[gɜ:lz]
door	doors	[dɔ:z]
taxi	taxis	['tæksɪz]
window	windows	['wɪndəʊz]

Nach stimmhaft gesprochenen Konsonanten wie [g], [l] oder [r] sowie nach den Vokalen *a, e, i, o, u* und deren Verbindungen mit *-y* (z.B. *boy*) wird das Plural-*s* immer stimmhaft gesprochen. Es entscheidet grundsätzlich immer das, was man zuletzt hört. Bei *window* beispielsweise hört man am Schluss ein *-o* (oder genauer, ein [əʊ]), deshalb wird das Plural-*s* stimmhaft gesprochen.

7 Kurzantworten auf Fragen mit *to be* – Short answers with *to be*

Anstatt auf eine Frage nur mit *yes* oder *no* zu antwortet, benutzt man im Englischen meist eine Kurzantwort mit dem Verb oder Hilfsverb. Kurzantworten klingen höflicher als ein knappes *yes* oder *no*.

S

Frage	Bestätigung	Verneinung
Are you Mr Clifton?	Yes, I am.	No, I'm not.
Am I late (*spät*)?	Yes, you are.	No, you aren't.
Is he a pilot?	Yes, he is.	No, he isn't
Is Tessa in the minibus?	Yes, she is.	No, she isn't.
Is the dog OK?	Yes, it is.	No, it isn't.
Are you from Germany?	Yes, we are.	No, we aren't.
Are we in Islington?	Yes, you are.	No, you aren't.
Are they at the check-in?	Yes, they are.	No, they aren't.

8 Die Possessivbegleiter (Singular) – The possessive determiners (singular)

Wenn man sagt, wer etwas besitzt oder (zu) wem etwas gehört, verwendet man Possessivbegleiter.

My instrument is the guitar.	I	**my**
Is Tessa **your** friend?	you	**your**
Oh, look! Tony and **his** minibus.	he	**his**
Look, Maike with **her** band.	she	**her**

Your klingt fast genauso wie die Kurzform *you're*. Deshalb musst du genau auf den Inhalt einer Frage oder Aussage achten.

UNIT 2

9 *There is/there are*

Mit *there is/there are* kannst du Sätze einleiten, wenn du auf Personen, Sachen oder Tiere hinweisen willst. Im Deutschen kann man dafür *es ist/es sind* bzw. *es gibt* verwenden.

S	Aussage	Verneinung	Frage
singular	There is ... (There's ...)	There isn't ...	Is there ...?
plural	There are ...	There aren't ...	Are there ...?

There's a tree in front of the Cliftons' house.
Vor dem Haus der Cliftons ist (steht) ein Baum.

There are five terminals at Heathrow Airport.
Am Flughaften Heathrow gibt es fünf Terminals.

Wenn es sich um nur **eine** Person, **eine** Sache oder **ein** Tier handelt, steht *there is* (Kurzform: *there's*). Bei **mehreren** Personen, Sachen oder Tieren brauchst du *there are*. Aus Aussprachegründen gibt es keine Kurzform von *there are*.

Is there a tree in the front garden?
Yes, **there is**.

Are there flowers in the window?
No, **there aren't**.

Zur Fragebildung stellt du wieder um: *Is there ...? / Are there ...?* Und bei der Beantwortung der Fragen verwendest du die höflichen Kurzantworten anstelle von *yes* oder *no* (vgl. Punkt 7).

10 Der Plural der Substantive (unregelmäßige Formen) – The plural of nouns (irregular forms)

1 Die regelmäßige Pluralbildung bei Substantiven kennst du bereits (vgl. Punkt 6). Es wird einfach ein *-s* an den Singular angehängt. Es gibt aber auch einige Substantive mit unregelmäßiger Pluralbildung. Diese Formen musst du einfach auswendig lernen – es sind nicht sehr viele.

one man	lots of **men**
one woman	lots of **women**
one child	lots of **children**

Achte auf die Aussprache: woman ['wʊmən], aber women ['wɪmɪn], child [tʃaɪld], aber children ['tʃɪldrən].

2 Neben den unregelmäßigen Formen, die du einfach lernen musst, gibt es noch ein paar Besonderheiten, die bei den regelmäßigen Pluralformen zu beachten sind.

one bus [bʌs]	lots of bus**es** ['bʌsɪz]
one box [bɒks]	lots of box**es** ['bɒksɪz]
one sandwich [sænwɪdʒ]	lots of sandwich**es** [sænwɪdʒɪz]

Generell gilt, dass das Plural-*s* zu hören sein muss. Das einfache Anhängen des *-s* führt aber bei Substantiven, die auf *-s, -z* oder einen Zischlaut (z.B. *ch, tch, sh*) auslauten, zu Ausspracheschwierigkeiten. Um das Plural-*s* hörbar zu machen, wird deshalb ein *-e-* vor dem *-s* eingeschoben.

one house [haʊs(!)]	lots of houses ['haʊzɪz]
one garage ['gærɑːʒ]	lots of garages ['gærɑːʒɪz]

Bei anderen Substantiven ist am Wortende bereits ein stummes *-e* vorhanden. Das Plural-*s* macht dieses *-e* hörbar.

3

one baby	lots of bab**ies**
one hobby	lots of hobb**ies**
one family	lots of famil**ies**
one country	lots of countr**ies**

Bei Substantiven, die auf *-y* enden, kann sich im Plural die Schreibweise verändern. Die Aussprache bleibt davon unberührt. Wenn du die Beispiele anschaust, stellst du fest, dass vor dem *-y* immer ein Konsonant steht.

one boy	lots of boys
one way	lots of ways

Anders ist es, wenn ein Vokal vor dem *-y* steht. Hier ändert sich beim Anhängen des Plural-*s* nichts.

11 Der s-Genitiv – The s-genitive

Tessa**'s** friends	*Tessas Freunde/Freundinnen*
the pilot**'s** hobby	*das Hobby des Piloten/der Pilotin*
the Cliftons**'** house	*das Haus der Cliftons*
the boys**'** T-shirts	*die T-Shirts der Jungen*

W

Noch kein Plural-*s* da?
Dann Apostroph + *s*.
Schon ein Plural-*s* da?
Dann nur ein Apostroph.

Wenn du sagen willst, dass jemand oder etwas zu einer oder mehreren Personen gehört, brauchst du den s-Genitiv. Im Singular hängt man zuerst ein Apostroph und dann ein *s* an das Substantiv an: *The girl's bedroom.*

An Pluralformen mit der Endung *-s* wird nur ein Apostroph angehängt: *The Cliftons' baby.* Bei der Aussprache ändert sich nichts. Deshalb musst du beim Zuhören gut aufpassen, ob von **einem** oder von **mehreren** Besitzern die Rede ist.

Endet ein Substantiv oder ein Name auf *s, z* oder einen Zischlaut (z.B. *ch, tch, sh*), wird die Genitivendung [ɪz] ausgesprochen: *Liz's hobby is pop music.* [ˌlɪzɪz 'hɒbi]

the man**'s** bike	the men**'s** bikes
the woman**'s** magazine	the women**'s** magazines
the child**'s** bag	the children**'s** bags

Bei Substantiven mit unregelmäßigen Pluralformen (vgl. Punkt 10) wird ebenfalls erst ein Apostroph und dann ein *s* angehängt.

12 *Has got/have got*

1

Liam **has got** a computer.
Has he **got** a modem too?
Yes, he **has.**

Mrs Braden **has got** a computer too.
And **has** she **got** a modem?
No, she **hasn't.**

he**'s got**	he **has got**
she**'s got**	she **has got**
it**'s got**	it **has got**

Wenn man sagen will, dass jemand etwas besitzt oder dass bestimmte Teile zu etwas gehören, benutzt man *he/she/it has got.* Bei *has got* gibt es wieder eine Kurz- und eine Langform.

Bei Fragen brauchst du immer die Langform (vgl. Punkt 4.2). Mit *Has* … leitest du die Fragen ein, *got* steht immer nach der Personen- oder Sachbezeichnung: *Has Liam got …?/Has it got …?*

Bei der Verneinung verwendest du *hasn't got*. Die Kurzform wird genau wie bei *isn't/aren't* gebildet (vgl. Punkt 5.2). Aus *has not* wird *hasn't*.

2 Bislang ging es nur um die 3. Person Singular in Verbindung mit *has got*. Bei allen anderen Personen steht *have got*. Auch hier gibt es Kurzformen: *I've got* … Die verneinte Form lautet: *I haven't got* … Fragen bildet man genau wie bei *has got: Have you got …?*

S

	Aussage	Verneinung	Frage
	I**'ve got**	I **haven't got**	**have** I **got?**
	you**'ve got**	you **haven't got**	**have** you **got?**
singular	he**'s got**	he **hasn't got**	**has** he **got?**
	she**'s got**	she **hasn't got**	**has** she **got?**
	it**'s got**	it **hasn't got**	**has** it **got?**
	we**'ve got**	we **haven't got**	**have** we **got?**
plural	you**'ve got**	you **haven't got**	**have** you **got?**
	they**'ve got**	they **haven't got**	**have** they **got?**

has	Yes, she **has.**	No, she **hasn't.**
have	Yes, I **have.**	No, I **haven't.**

Auf Fragen mit *has got/have got* antwortest du wieder mit den höflichen Kurzantworten. Dabei entfällt *got*.

13 Attributiver und prädikativer Gebrauch von Adjektiven – Attributive and predicative use of adjectives

The Cliftons have got a **big** fireplace.

The Cliftons' fireplace is **big.**

Ein Adjektiv kann entweder **vor** einem Substantiv (= attributiver Gebrauch) oder **nach** einer Form von *to be* stehen (= prädikativer Gebrauch).

Anders als im Deutschen, Französischen und Lateinischen verändert sich das Adjektiv im Englischen weder in attributiver noch in prädikativer Stellung.

A

Du willst sagen / fragen,

- dass Liam ein neues Modem hat.
- ob die Wilsons eine große Garage haben.
- dass die Bradens keinen großen Garten haben.
- ob Sandra ein grünes T-Shirt hat.

- dass Liams Modem neu ist.
- ob die Garage der Wilsons groß ist.
- dass der Garten der Bradens nicht groß ist.
- ob Sandras T-Shirt grün ist.

14 Die Possessivbegleiter – The possessive determiners

1

Where's my Beatles CD?
It's in **its** box.

This is a nice cat!
What's **its** name?

Die Possessivbegleiter *my, your, his, her* kennst du bereits (vgl. Punkt 8). Mit den Possessivbegleitern kannst du sagen bzw. fragen, zu wem oder was etwas gehört. Eine Singularform fehlt noch, und zwar *its*. Vorsicht, nicht verwechseln: *It's (it is) my CD. It's in its box.* Mit *its* kannst du ausdrücken, was zu einer Sache oder einem Tier gehört. Wenn du ein Tier allerdings gut kennst, sagst du nicht mehr *its*, sondern *his* oder *her* (vgl. Punkt 3).

2

Our house is new.
Is **your** cat in the garden?
Their friends are nice.

Jetzt fehlen noch die Possessivbegleiter *our, your, their*. Mit ihnen kannst du ausdrücken, was zu mehreren Personen gehört.

S

	my bedroom	I	–	**my**
	your computer	you	–	**your**
singular	**his** T-shirt	he	–	**his**
	her CD	she	–	**her**
	its box	it	–	**its**
	our garden	we	–	**our**
plural	**your** family	you	–	**your**
	their garage	they	–	**their**

Hello! What's **your** name? (dein)
Hey, boys, where are **your** CDs? (euere)
Your hobby is nice, Mr Braden. (Ihr)

Für *your* gilt das gleiche wie für *you* (vgl. Punkt 3). Es kann *dein(e/r/s), euer(e/r/s)* oder *Ihr(e/r/s)* bedeuten.

15 Das Hilfsverb *can* – The modal auxiliary *can*

1

I **can** play the guitar.
She **can** send an e-mail.
You **can** wait for him.

Mit *can* drückst du aus, dass eine Person oder ein Tier etwas kann, d.h. eine Fähigkeit besitzt. Das Hilfsverb *can* ist in allen Personen gleich. Es verändert sich nicht. Direkt nach *can* steht das Vollverb im Infinitiv ohne *to*.

I **can't** see you.
He **can't** say the word.
We **can't** play the music.

Die verneinte Langform von *can* [kæn] heißt *cannot* ['kænɒt] und wird zusammengeschrieben: *can + not = cannot*. Die Kurzform lautet *can't* [kɑːnt]. *Not* wird wieder zu *n't* verkürzt. Auch die verneinte Form ist in allen Personen gleich.

2

Can you play the guitar?
Kannst du Gitarre spielen?

Can they speak English?
Können sie Englisch (sprechen)?

Zur Fragebildung musst du den Aussagesatz wieder umstellen (Inversion), sodass das Hilfsverb *can* am Anfang des Satzes steht.

She can play the guitar.
Can she play the guitar?

Auf eine Frage mit *can* antwortest du wieder mit einer höflichen Kurzantwort (vgl. Punkte 7 und 9).

S

Frage	Bestätigung	Verneinung
Can you hear that sound?	Yes, I **can.**	No, I **can't.**
Can we give you the box?	Yes, you **can.**	No, you **can't.**
Can he guess her name?	Yes, he **can.**	No, he **can't.**

A

Stelle Fragen mit *can.*

Du willst wissen, of Hunde rot, grün und gelb sehen können.
Du fragst, ob deine Freunde einen neuen Besitzer für deinen Hund finden können.
Du willst herausfinden, ob dein(e) Freund(in) dir eine E-Mail schicken kann.

UNIT 3

16 Die Fragewörter *who/what/where/how* – The question words *who/what/where/how*

Bei der Verbindung der Fragewörter *who, what* und *where* mit *is* kannst du auch in der Frage die Kurzform verwenden. Ansonsten steht in der Fragestellung immer die Langform.

W

who = wer
where = wo

S

Frage (Langform)	Frage (Kurzform)	Antwort
Who is in the garden?	Who's in the garden?	Liz.
What is in the box?	What's in the box?	A dog.
Where is the CD?	Where's the CD?	On the table.
How old is he?	–	He's 15.
What can we say?	–	Let's say hello.
Where can we play?	–	In the garage.

17 Die Uhrzeit – The time

It's five **o'clock.**

It's four minutes **past** five.
It's five **past** five.
It's (a) **quarter past** five.
It's **half past** five.

It's ten **to** six.
It's nine minutes **to** six.

9.30	7.50	11.25

Nur bei der Angabe der vollen Stunde verwendest du *o'clock.*
Bei Zeitangaben in den ersten 30 Minuten nach der vollen Stunde sagst du *past.* Bei den Fünferschritten (5, 10, 15 usw.) wird *minutes* meistens ausgelassen.

M

o	**a**
t **o**	p **a** st
v **o** *r*	*n* **a** *ch*

Nach *half past* zählst du mit *to* zur nächsten vollen Stunde.

Du kannst die Uhrzeit auch ‚digital' angeben: *nine thirty, seven fifty, eleven twenty-five.* Solche Zeitangaben findest du vorwiegend bei Programmansagen und Fahrplanangaben.

18 Das Präsens (einfache Form) – The simple present

1 S

I	play	the guitar.
You	play	tennis.
He	plays	in the garage.
She	plays	with the dog.
It	plays	with a ball.
We	play	hockey at school.
You	play	in a band.
They	play	at the weekends.

Bei *I, you, we, they* hat das Verb die gleiche Form wie der Infinitiv (ohne *to*). Bei *he, she, it* wird ein *-s* angehängt. Die Aussprache und Schreibung der Verben in der 3. Person Singular erfolgen nach den gleichen Regeln wie die Pluralformen der Substantive (vgl. Punkt 6).

M

He, she, it, das -s muss mit.

I go [gəʊ]	he go**es** [gəʊz]
I say [seɪ]	she says [sez]
I do [du:]	it do**es** [dʌz]

Achte auf die Besonderheiten in der Schreibung bzw. Aussprache bei diesen Verben.

I play	She plays the keyboard.
I bully	He bull**ies** the girls.

Auch bei den Verben auf *-y* musst du aufpassen. In der 3. Person Singular gelten die gleichen Regeln wie bei den Pluralformen der Substantive.

2 S

Aussprachevarianten in der 3. Person Singular

-s [s]	-es [ɪz]	-s [z]
likes	chases	gives
barks	watches	listens
helps	changes	sings
eats		
nach den Lauten [f][k][p][t]	*nach allen Zischlauten, z.B.* [s][tʃ][dʒ]	*nach allen anderen Lauten*

Tarkan usually goes to school on his bike.
He often does his homework in the kitchen.

Das *simple present* brauchst du um über Gewohnheiten und gewohnheitsmäßige, d.h. immer wiederkehrende Handlungen zu sprechen und zu schreiben.

After school Liz goes to her uncle's garage.
She says hello to Milly.
Then she gives her something to drink.

Außerdem wird das *simple present* verwendet um Geschichten zu erzählen, in denen eine Sache nach der anderen geschieht.

I think it's great.
I hate hot dogs.

Mit dem *simple present* kannst du außerdem Vorlieben und Abneigungen ausdrücken.

19 Das Wortstellung in Aussagesätzen im Präsens – The word order in statements in the simple present

Subjekt	Verb	Objekt
Liam	has got	a new computer.
Sandra	can use	the modem.
The boy	bullies	the girls.
The man	plays	an instrument.

Die Wortstellung im englischen Aussagesatz lautet: **Subjekt – Verb – Objekt = SVO**.

	S	V	O
	Liz	plays	with Milly every day.
Every day	Liz	plays	with Milly.

Anders als im Deutschen kannst du diese Reihenfolge nicht verändern. Auch Zeitangaben wie *after school, every day* usw. ändern nichts daran. Sie stehen entweder am Anfang oder am Ende des Satzes. Dagegen im Deutschen: *Liz spielt jeden Tag mit Milly./Jeden Tag spielt Liz mit Milly.*

20 Adverbien der Häufigkeit – Adverbs of frequency

Subjekt	Satzergänzung (Adverb)	Verb	Objekt
The dog	**sometimes**	chases	the cat.
Liz	**never**	forgets	Milly's food.

Im *simple present* stehen die Adverbien der Häufigkeit (*sometimes, often, never, usually, always*) meistens zwischen Subjekt und Verb. Verb und Objekt bilden eine feste Einheit. Es können keine anderen Wortarten oder Satzteile eingeschoben werden. Dagegen im Deutschen: *Der Hund jagt manchmal die Katze. Liz vergisst nie Millys Futter.*

21 Verneinte Sätze mit *do* und *does* – Negative sentences with *do* and *does*

	Hilfsverb	Vollverb				Hilfsverb	Vollverb	
I	–	play	the guitar	but	I	**don't**	play	the saxophone.
She	–	likes	cats	but	she	**doesn't**	like	dogs.

do + not (n't) = **don't**
does + not (n't) = **doesn't**

Wenn du etwas verneinen willst, brauchst du in der Regel dazu ein Hilfsverb und den Infinitiv eines Vollverbs. Gibt es im Aussagesatz kein Hilfsverb (*I play the guitar*), musst du eines ergänzen. Das ist immer das Hilfsverb *do* bzw. *does*. Von diesen beiden Wörtern bildest du die verneinten Formen.

Wenn es im Aussagesatz bereits ein Hilfsverb gibt (*I can play the guitar*), brauchst du *do* bzw. *does* zur Verneinung nicht: *I can play the guitar but can't play the saxophone.*

A

a) Verneine die Sätze.

Our dog barks a lot.
She likes homework.
He plays with the cat.
They go for a walk with Milly.

b) Du willst sagen, dass

– du das Saxophon nicht magst,
– deine Freundin nicht mit ihrem Hund spielt,
– die Kinder nicht zur Schule gehen wollen,
– Lehrer keine *bullies* mögen.

22 Fragen und Kurzantworten mit *do/don't* und *does/doesn't* – Questions and short answers with *do/don't* and *does/doesn't*

S

Frage	Bestätigung	Verneinung
Do you like cats?	Yes, I **do.**	No, I **don't.**
Do children like homework?	Yes, they **do.**	No, they **don't.**
Does Liz play with Milly?	Yes, she **does.**	No, she **doesn't.**
Does a dog like hot dogs?	Yes, it **does.**	No, it **doesn't.**

Do und *don't* stehen bei den Personalpronomen *I, you, we, they.* In der 3. Person Singular brauchst du wieder *does* und *doesn't.* Das gilt auch für die Fragen und die entsprechenden Kurzantworten. In den Kurzantworten auf Entscheidungsfragen (*yes/no*-Fragen) wird immer die Form von *do* wiederholt, nicht das Vollverb.

Hilfsverb	Subjekt	Verb	Objekt
Do	you	like	Maths?
Does	James	love	dogs?
Does	Joanna	hate	sports?
Do	they	want	more homework?

Wie bei der Verneinung (vgl. Punkt 21) brauchst du auch bei der Frage ein Hilfsverb und den Infinitiv eines Vollverbs. Ist in dem Aussagesatz (*I like Maths*) kein Hilfsverb vorhanden, musst du wieder *do* bzw. *does* ergänzen. Das Hilfsverb steht **immer** vor dem Subjekt, das Vollverb danach (Regel: **SVO**).

A

a) Bilde aus diesen Aussagesätzen Fragen.

Sandra plays the cello.
Nicola reads her magazine.
The Modis help the children.

b) Übertrage diese Fragen ins Englische.

Hilft Ihnen Ihr Freund oft?
Wissen Hundebesitzer viel über Tiere?
Mag eine Katze Musik?

23 Fragen mit Fragewörtern und *do/don't* und *does/doesn't* – Questions with question words and *do/don't* and *does/doesn't*

Die Wortstellung **SVO** bleibt auch bei Fragen mit Fragewörtern unverändert.

Fragewort	Hilfsverb	Subjekt	Verb	Objekt
What	**do**	you	like?	
Why	**don't**	they	want	a hot dog?
When	**does**	Ben	do	his homework?
Why	**doesn't**	Joanna	like	bullies?
Who	**do**	you	love?	

W

Beachte:

Who loves Stephanie?
(who = *wer/Subjekt)*

Who **does** Stephanie love?
(who = *wen/Akkusativobjekt)*

24 *This/that* und *these/those*

S

	here	over there
singular	**this**	**that**
plural	**these**	**those**

This is my book here and **that**'s your picture over there.

These are my friends here and **those** are your friends over there.

Im Englischen steht immer zuerst *this* und dann *that*. *This* deutet auf etwas Nahes hin, *that* auf etwas Entfernteres. *This* steht deshalb häufig zusammen mit *here, that* dagegen mit *over there*. Sind zwei Dinge gleich weit weg und werden sie einander gegenübergestellt, wird ebenfalls *this* vor *that* verwendet: *Look at these books: this is old and that is new.* Aus Aussprachegründen steht nach *this* immer die Langform (*this is*), nach *that* die Kurzform (*that's*). Zu *this* und *that* gibt es die entsprechenden Pluralformen *these* und *those*. Nach *these* und *those* steht immer *are*.

W

Die Menschen neigen – unabhängig von der Sprache – dazu, ein Wort mit einem *i* vor einem Wort mit einem *a* oder *o* auszusprechen: *zick-zack, ritsch-ratsch, tick-tack; ding-dong, ping-pong, King Kong*. Deshalb heißt es auch: *this – that* und *these – those*.

A

a) Übersetze ins Englische.

Dieses hier sind meine Bücher.
Ist das da drüben euer Hund?

b) Übersetze ins Deutsche.

That's my friend over there.
Let's listen to this CD here.

UNIT 4

25 Die Verlaufsform des Präsens (Aussage und Verneinung) – The present progressive (statements and negations)

1

	Form von *to be*	Verb + *-ing*		
A man	**is**	eat**ing**	fire.	*Ein Mann schluckt (gerade) Feuer.*
Lots of people	**are**	watch**ing**	him.	*Die Leute schauen ihm (gerade) zu.*

Wenn du erzählen willst, was jemand gerade macht (oder nicht macht), verwendest du die Verlaufsform des Präsens: *am/is/are + verb + -ing*. Im Deutschen gibt es keine vergleichbare Form. Es wird einfach das Präsens verwendet. Die entsprechende Bedeutung wird oft mit *gerade, im Augenblick* oder *im Moment* wiedergegeben.

Natürlich gibt es auch hier wieder einige Ausnahmen. Du kannst z.B. von Verben wie *know, think, like, love* oder *want* in der Regel keine *progressive form* bilden, da diese Verben Wissen, Meinung, Gefühle oder Wünsche ausdrücken und sich deshalb nicht nur auf den Augenblick der Aussage beziehen.

S

	Aussage	Verneinung
	I'm listen**ing** to my new CD.	I'm not listen**ing** ...
	You're stand**ing** on my foot.	You aren't stand**ing** ...
singular	He's eat**ing** fire.	He isn't eat**ing** ...
	She's juggl**ing** with some balls.	She isn't juggl**ing** ...
	It's happen**ing** near Covent Garden.	It isn't happen**ing** ...
	We're watch**ing** TV.	We aren't watch**ing**...
plural	You're sitt**ing** on my books, girls!	You aren't sitt**ing** ...
	They're sing**ing** a new song.	They aren't sing**ing** ...

2 Bei der Bildung der Verlaufsform musst du einige Besonderheiten in der Schreibung beachten.

Liam is writ**ing** an e-mail. Maike is mak**ing** a poster.	writ~~e~~ + ing mak~~e~~ + ing	Endet der Infinitiv auf ein stummes *-e*, entfällt das *-e* in der Verlaufsform.
Jimmy is sitt**ing** on the table. They are runn**ing** around the tree.	sit + t + ing run + n + ing	Steht im Infinitiv ein kurzer, betonter Vokal vor dem Endkonsonanten, wird der Konsonant verdoppelt.
Milly is ly**ing** on the floor.	l~~ie~~ + y + ing	Steht am Ende des Infinitivs ein *-ie*, wird es zu *-y*.

A

Wie lauten die Sätze auf Englisch?

1. Der Mann spielt (gerade) mit dem Baby.
2. Das Mädchen isst (gerade) ein Eis.
3. Meine Schwester schreibt (gerade) eine Postkarte.
4. Die Leute klatschen (jetzt gerade).
5. Jimmy trägt heute neue Schuhe.
6. Die Kinder machen gerade Hausaufgaben.
7. Der Ball liegt auf dem Tisch.
8. Eine Frau fotografiert (gerade).

26 Die Verlaufsform des Präsens (Frage und Kurzantwort) – The present progressive (questions and short answers)

Is the man eating fire?
Are the people watching him?

Um Fragen mit der Verlaufsform zu bilden, stellst du die konjugierte Form von *to be* an den Satzanfang.

Bei den Antworten werden in der Regel die Kurzantworten mit *to be* verwendet.

	Bestätigung	Verneinung
Are you wear**ing** new shoes?	Yes, I am.	No, I'm not.
Am I sitt**ing** on your book?	Yes, you are.	No, you're not.
Is he go**ing** out today?	Yes, he is.	No, he isn't.
Is Maike sitt**ing** in your bedroom?	Yes, she is.	No, she isn't.
Is the dog drink**ing** water?	Yes, it is.	No, it isn't.
Are you (two) talk**ing** about that man?	Yes, we are.	No, we aren't.
Are we go**ing** to assembly too?	Yes, you are.	No, you aren't.
Are they runn**ing** around the tree?	Yes, they are.	No, they aren't.

27 Präpositionen für Ortsangaben – Prepositions of places

28 Präpositionen für Richtungsangaben – Prepositions for directions

UNIT 5

29 *I'd like* und *I want*

I'd like an ice cream, please.
Ich hätte gerne ein Eis, bitte.

Wenn du höflich um etwas bitten oder einen Wunsch äußern möchtest, brauchst du die Form: *I'd like* ... Es ist die Kurzform von *I would like* ... (*Ich hätte/möchte gern* ...). Nicht verwechseln mit: *I like ice cream* (*Ich esse/mag gern Eis.*)!

I want an ice cream!
Ich will (aber) ein Eis!

Du kannst auch mit *I want* ... (*Ich will* ...) einen Wunsch oder eine Bitte äußern, nur klingt das – genau wie im Deutschen – sehr bestimmt und dadurch unhöflich.

No, thank you, **I don't want** an ice cream.

Willst du aber ein Angebot ablehnen, dann musst du *I don't want* ... verwenden.

30 Das Stützwort *one/ones* – The propword *one/ones*

Give me that blue book from the shelf, please.
(Which blue book, the little blue book or the big blue book?)

Which blue book, the little **one** or the big **one?**

Die Rückfrage nach dem Buch klingt durch die Wiederholungen stilistisch nicht besonders gut. Das Stützwort *one/ones* hilft dir, solche Sätze zu vermeiden. *One/ones* kann ein zählbares Substantiv ersetzen..

This ball is very small.
Do you want a bigger **one?**

Look at that girl over there.
Which **one** – the **one** with the bike?

One steht für Substantive im Singular.

I like Ben's CDs, the old **ones** and the new **ones.**

My uncle knows lots of school jokes.
I like the **ones** about the teachers best.

Ones verwendest du für Substantive im Plural.

M

Merke dir, dass im Englischen – anders als im Deutschen – ein Adjektiv nicht alleine nach *a* oder *the* stehen kann (vgl. ‚Gibt es eine Kleinere?'). Es muss ‚gestützt' werden, wenn das Substantiv entfällt. Das übernimmt das Stützwort *one/ones*.

31 Der Plural der Substantive (unregelmäßige Formen) – The plural of nouns (irregular forms)

In Punkt 10 hast du bereits einige unregelmäßige Pluralformen kennen gelernt. Es kommen noch einige (wenige) dazu.

knife	–	knives
scarf	–	scarves
shelf	–	shelves

In diesen Pluralformen wird *-f* durch *-ves* ersetzt. Da das aber nicht bei allen Substantive auf *-f* der Fall ist (z.B. *roof – roofs*), musst du dir die Formen einfach merken.

32 *Some* und *any*

S

Aussage: ***some***	**Frage:** ***any***	**Verneinung:** ***any***
They've got **some** cheap watches.	Are there **any** sweets in the kitchen?	I can't find **any** shoes for my big feet.

Mit *some* und *any* kannst du eine unbestimmte Menge oder Anzahl ausdrücken. Im Deutschen werden *some* und *any* durch *etwas, einige* oder *ein paar* wiedergegeben. In bejahten Sätzen brauchst du *some,* in Fragen und verneinten Sätzen meistens *any.*

Can I have **some** ice cream, please?

Kann ich bitte etwas Eis haben?
(Es ist klar, dass es Eis gibt.)

In Fragen kann aber auch *some* stehen, und zwar dann, wenn du davon ausgehst, dass die Antwort ‚ja' lautet.

Do you need **any** help?

Brauchst du Hilfe?

Hier weißt du nicht, ob die Antwort ‚ja' oder ‚nein' sein wird. Im Deutschen werden *some* und *any* oft gar nicht wiedergegeben.

M

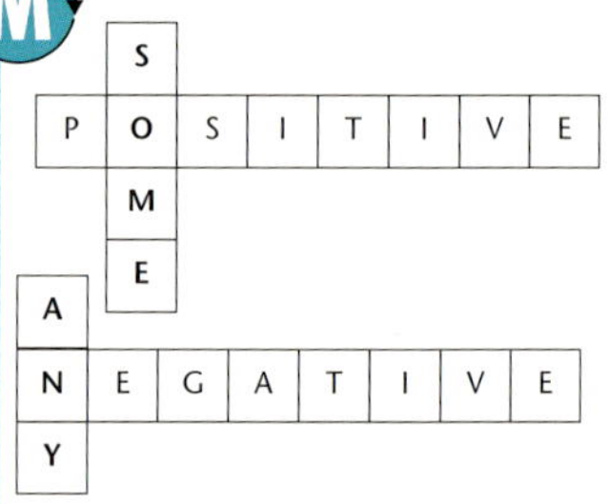

A

Wie kann man das ausdrücken?

1. Du bist in einem kleinen Ledergeschäft und willst wissen, ob sie denn auch Lederjacken in deiner Größe haben. — Du fragst: ...?
2. Du bist in einem großen Uhrengeschäft und siehst, dass sie auch billige Uhren haben. — Du fragst: ...?
3. Du bist mit einem Freund / einer Freundin im Restaurant und möchtest wissen, ob er / sie auch etwas Essig haben möchte. — Du fragst: ...?
4. Dein Freund / deine Freundin winkt ab. Er / Sie möchte keinen. — Er / Sie sagt: ...

I'd like	a pair	of	boots, please?
Can I have	a glass	of	water, please?
Give me	a box	of	those sweets, please?

Bei Paarwörtern verwendest du für Mengenangaben immer *a pair of.* Bei der Mengenangabe von Substantiven, die nur im Singular stehen, umschreibst du die Menge mit *of: a piece of paper, a pound of butter, a cup of tea, etc.* Dies gilt auch für Sachen, die normalerweise nicht gezählt werden: *two packets of cornflakes, a box of sweets.* Zahlenangaben werden natürlich ohne *of* gemacht: *six sweets.*

33 *Much* und *many*

How **much** time have we got? – Not **much.**
Don't put so **much** salt on your chips!
We don't eat **much** ice cream.
Thank you very **much.**

Much verwendest du bei nicht zählbaren Substantiven. Es hat die Bedeutung *viel.* *Much* steht meist in Fragen und Verneinungen. In bejahten Sätzen kommt es vor allem in den Verbindungen *so much, too much* oder *very much* vor, ansonsten steht immer *a lot of* oder *lots of:* *We spend a lot of money on CDs.*

I haven't bought **many** computer games this year.
How **many** T-shirts have you got?

Bei den Pluralformen von zählbaren Substantiven kannst du nur *many* verwenden. Es bedeutet *viele.*

34 Das Datum – The date

Zur Angabe des Datums brauchst du auch im Englischen die Ordnungszahlen. Anstelle des Punktes, den wir im Deutschen setzen, werden im Englischen die letzten beiden Buchstaben des Ordnungszahlworts an die Ziffer angehängt: *1st, 2nd, 3rd, 4th, ...*

First, second, third sind Ausnahmen, ab *fourth* wird immer *-th* an die Grundzahl angehängt. Bei einigen Ordnungszahlen verändert sich dabei die Schreibweise (z.B. *twelve – twelfth, twenty – twentieth*).

31st January	=	the thirty-first of January
January 31st	=	January the thirty-first

Beide Formen der Datumsangabe existieren nebeneinander. Allerdings überwiegt im britischen Englisch (BE) die erste Form, im amerikanischen Englisch (AE) dagegen die zweite Variante.

Es wird beim Schreiben des Datums in England zunehmend auf die letzten beiden Buchstaben der Ordnungszahl verzichtet: *31 January*. Beachte, dass auch dann kein Punkt steht, der Monatsname in Worten geschrieben ist und trotzdem *thirty-first of January* gesprochen wird.

35 +Das Präteritum von *to be* und *to have* – The simple past of *to be* and *to have*

1 Das *simple past* brauchst du um Geschichten zu erzählen oder über Ereignisse zu berichten, die in der Vergangenheit liegen.

S

Today	I am happy but ...	... yesterday	I **was** unhappy.
	you are funny but ...		you **were** not funny.
	she is at home but ...		she **was** at school.
	we are early but ...		we **were** late.
	they have two modems but ...		they **had** only one.

Das *simple past* von *to be* lautet: **was** (mit *I, he, she, it*), **were** (mit *you, we, they*).
Das *simple past* von *to have* lautet: **had** (bei allen Personen).

W Signalwörter für das *simple past* sind: *yesterday, ago, last week/month/year, in 1998, etc.*

2 Die Verneinung von *was, were* und *had* funktioniert genauso wie bei *isn't/aren't* und *hasn't/haven't*. Die Kurzform von *not* = *n't* wird direkt angehängt: *wasn't, weren't, hadn't.*

3

	Bestätigung	Verneinung
Was it in his pocket?	Yes, it was.	No, it wasn't.
Were they angry?	Yes, they were.	No, they weren't.

Auf Fragen mit *was* und *were* antwortest du wieder mit den Kurzantworten. Sie sind höflicher als ein einfaches *yes* oder *no*.

36 +Das Präteritum (regelmäßige Formen) – The simple past (regular forms)

S

	I	walk**ed**	into the store.
	You	look**ed**	at me.
singular	He	watch**ed**	it all on TV.
	She	wait**ed**	behind the door.
	The video	stopp**ed**.	
	We	open**ed**	the box.
plural	You	ask**ed**	us a lot of questions.
	They	show**ed**	us everything.

Das *simple past* von regelmäßigen Verben bildest du, indem du die Endung *-ed* an die Stammform des Verbs anhängst: *walk + ed = walked*.

Bei der Aussprache und Schreibung der *simple past*-Formen musst du einige Besonderheiten beachten.

Beachte beim Sprechen

show – show**ed** play – play**ed** turn – turn**ed**	Nach Vokalen und stimmhaften Konsonanten spricht man [d].
walk – walk**ed** watch – watch**ed** ask – ask**ed**	Nach stimmlosen Konsonanten spricht man [t].
wait – wait**ed** want – want**ed**	Nach den Endkonsonanten *-t* und *-d* spricht man [ɪd].

Beachte beim Schreiben

like – like**d** phone – phone**d** save – save**d**	Endet der Infinitiv auf ein stummes *-e*, wird nur ein *-d* angehängt.
stop – sto**pped**	Nach einem kurzen, betonten Vokal wird der Endkonsonant verdoppelt.
try – tr**ied**	Verben, die auf Konsonant + *-y* enden, erhalten die Endung *-ied*. Aber: *play – played*!

37 +Das Präteritum (unregelmäßige Formen) – The simple past (irregular forms)

Du kennst auch im Deutschen regelmäßige und unregelmäßige Präteritumformen: *weinen – weinte, singen – sang*. Ähnlich ist es im Englischen.

I **saw** them in the store.	see –	saw
They **went** to the computer games.	go –	went
We **thought** they were shoplifters.	think –	thought

Zur Bildung der unregelmäßigen Formen gibt es keine Regel. Du musst sie einfach auswendig lernen. Eine Liste mit den unregelmäßigen Verben findest du auf den Seiten 228/229.

Am besten kannst du die Verben gruppenweise nach Lautung oder Schreibweise lernen: *bring – brought, think – thought, buy – bought* usw. Genau wie bei den regelmäßigen Verben (vgl. Punkt 36) sind auch bei den unregelmäßigen Verben die Formen für alle Personen gleich.

38 +Die Verneinung im *simple past* mit *didn't* – Negative sentences with *didn't*

I **saw** your brother but I **didn't see** your sister.

Most of the children **understood** the story but two boys **didn't understand** it.

Die Verneinung mit *didn't* funktioniert genauso wie *don't/doesn't* (vgl. Punkt 21). Die Form *didn't* ist für alle Personen gleich. Nach *didn't* steht immer der Infinitiv des Vollverbs.

UNIT 6

39 *Present progressive* und *simple present*

The girls **are** play**ing** football in the gym.

It **is** rain**ing** at the moment.

Mit dem *present progressive* drückst du aus, was gerade geschieht und zum Zeitpunkt der Aussage noch nicht beendet ist.

W Signalwörter für das *present progressive* sind: *now, at the moment, just, etc.*

They usually **play** outside.

It often **rains** in winter.

Das *simple present* verwendest du, wenn du sagen willst, was regelmäßig, manchmal, oft oder nie geschieht.

First Liam **puts** on his hat and scarf.
Then he **runs** downstairs.
After that he **checks** his purse.
Then he **calls** Liz.
After that he ...

Mit dem *simple present* schilderst du aber auch Handlungen die nacheinander geschehen.

W Signalwörter für das *simple present* sind: *always, sometimes, often, usually, never, etc.*

UNIT 7

40 Das *going to*-Futur – The going to-future

Zukünftiges kannst du im Englischen mit unterschiedlichen Strukturen ausdrücken. Welche Form du verwenden musst, hängt von den Sprechabsichten ab. Mit dem *going to*-Futur kannst du ausdrücken, was jemand vorhat oder zu tun beabsichtigt. Oft handelt es sich um kurzfristige Vorhaben, die sich auf die nahe Zukunft beziehen.

Das *going to*-Futur wird gebildet aus: *am/is/are* + *going to* + Infinitiv. Meistens werden die Kurzformen von *to be* verwendet.

S

I'**m**	**going to**	help	the Beachwatch volunteers.
What **are** you	**going to**	do	today?
Mr Clifford **is**	**going to**	start	a project.
The girl'**s**	**going to**	talk	to the tourist.
We'**re**	**going to**	visit	the museum.
They'**re**	**going to**	have	fish and chips.

Liz is **going to** visit her friends in Islington next week.

Mit dem *going to*-Futur kann auch eine Absicht in fernerer Zukunft ausgedrückt werden. Allerdings muss dann eine entsprechende Zeitangabe erfolgen.

Look, Liz is coming out of the house with Milly.

Yes, she's **going to** take her for a walk.

Das *going to*-Futur verwendest du außerdem, wenn ein Ereignis mit großer Gewissheit zu erwarten ist. Dabei geht es in der Regel um eine logische Schlussfolgerung, die Absicht ist hier unwichtig.

M

Verwechsle das *going to*-future nicht mit der Verlaufsform des Präsens.

They're going to Camden Market.
Sie gehen (gerade) zum Camden Market.

They're **going to** go to Camden Market.
Sie haben vor (in Kürze) zum Camden Market zu gehen.

41 Stellung der Präpositionen in Fragen – Position of prepositions in questions

What else are they talking about?
What are you looking at?
What are you proud of?
Where are you from?
Who are you waiting for?
Which animals are you afraid of?

Bei der Verbindung von bestimmten Verben, Hilfsverben und Adjektiven mit Präpositionen stellst du die Präposition in der Fragestellung an das Satzende:
What do you need this for? – I need it for my fax.

42 +Das Gerundium – The gerund

Substantive bezeichnen in der Regel konkrete Gegenstände (*a tanker*), Personen (*a reporter*), Tiere (*a seabird*) oder abstrakte Sachverhalte (*a dialogue*). Du kannst aber auch Tätigkeiten mit Substantiven benennen: (das) Lesen, Schwimmen, Klettern usw. Im Englischen verwendest du dazu die *ing*-Form des Verbs*: reading, swimming, climbing* usw. Sie heißt *gerund.*

Reading is fun.
Lesen macht Spaß.

Hier handelt es sich bei *reading* um ein *gerund.*

Jim is **reading** a letter.
Jim liest (gerade) einen Brief.

In diesem Beispiel ist *reading* die Verlaufsform, die du in Punkt 25 kennen gelernt hast.

Wie bei der Bildung des Partizips Präsens musst du auch beim *gerund* auf die Schreibung achten.

swim	–	swimm**ing**	smil~~e~~	–	smil**ing**
sit	–	sitt**ing**	rid~~e~~	–	rid**ing**
shut	–	shutt**ing**	rescu~~e~~	–	rescu**ing**

1 **Birdwatching** can be interesting.
Sailing is fun.

Da das Gerundium die Eigenschaften eines Substantivs hat, kann es Subjekt eines Satzes sein.

2

I	like	**birdwatching.**
Do you	enjoy	**running?**
Mr Clifford	loves	**reading.**
They	hate	**working.**

Das Gerundium kann auch das Objekt eines Satzes sein. Es steht häufig nach Verben, die eine Vorliebe oder Abneigung ausdrücken, z.B. *like, enjoy, love, hate* usw.

S

Subjekt		Objekt
Walking	is fun.	
Climbing	is dangerous.	
Mr Clifford	likes	**walking.**
Liz's dog	enjoys	**chasing** cats.

M

Merke dir, dass das *gerund* entweder Subjekt oder Objekt eines Satzes sein kann.

3 My sister is crazy about **biking.**

Mr Clifford is good at **explaining** things.

Einer Reihe von Adjektiven sind Präpositionen fest zugeordnet: *crazy about, good at, proud of, interested in, famous for* usw. Nach Präpositionen steht immer das *gerund.* Das gilt auch für Verben, die mit Präpositionen verbunden sind: *I am thinking about buying a new computer.*

43 +Das *will-future* – The will-future

1 S

	will	
I / you / he / she / it / we / you / they	**'ll**	start tomorrow.
	won't	

Das *will-future* wird aus *will* + Infinitiv gebildet. Das gilt für alle Personen. Häufig wird die Kurzform verwendet: *he will – he'll.* Die Kurzform in der Verneinung (*will not*) lautet *won't.*

2 Während das *going to-future* (vgl. Punkt 40) zum Ausdruck von Absichten und Vorhaben in der Zukunft verwendet wird, benutzt du das *will-future,* wenn du sagen willst, was in der Zukunft geschehen wird.

There **will** be emergency services.
They'**ll** help elderly people.

Das *will-future* brauchst du, wenn ein fester Entschluss oder eine feste Verabredung vorliegt.

The storm **will** hit the coast. It'**ll** churn east. We hope that the damage **won't** be too bad.	Das *will-future* verwendest du auch, wenn ein Ereignis von äußeren Umständen, z.B. vom Wetter abhängt und nicht unmittelbar beeinflusst werden kann.
You haven't got a spare battery? I'**ll** give you one of my batteries. Is your homework difficult? I'**ll** help you with it.	Und wenn du spontan zu etwas bereit bist, ohne es vorher geplant zu haben, benutzt du ebenfalls das *will-future*.

UNIT 8

44 Das Perfekt – The present perfect

Das *present perfect* wird aus *has/have* und dem *past participle* (Partizip Perfekt) gebildet: *has/have packed*.

S

I'	**ve**	just	pack**ed**	my lunch.
They	**have**		chang**ed**	the play.
She	**has**		phon**ed**	him.
I'	**ve**		**written**	a new dialogue.
We	**haven't**		**heard**	about it.
He	**has**		**given**	me his comic.

Neben den regelmäßigen Formen auf *-ed* gibt es eine Reihe unregelmäßiger Verben, deren Formen du auswendig lernen musst, z.B.: *has/have written*. Für die Bildung der unregelmäßigen Formen gibt es keine Regeln. Du findest auf den Seiten 228/229 eine Liste aller unregelmäßigen Verben, die in **Swift 1** vorkommen.

Bei der Aussprache der regelmäßigen Formen auf *-ed* gibt es ein paar Besonderheiten zu beachten (vgl. Punkt 36):

pack**ed** [t]	phon**ed** [d]	collect**ed** [ɪd]
nach stimmlosen Konsonanten	nach stimmhaften Konsonanten	nach *-t* oder *-d*

A

Sprich die folgenden Beispiele laut aus.

happen	–	happened	pack	–	packed	make	–	made
damage	–	damaged	look	–	looked	have	–	had
change	–	changed	pick	–	picked	try	–	tried
compare	–	compared	work	–	worked	pay	–	paid
explain	–	explained	paint	–	painted	read	–	read
practise	–	practised	collect	–	collected	write	–	written

Maggie **has** collect**ed** all the posters.
(Here they are.)

Mr Bean **has** just clean**ed** his car.
(It is clean now.)

Das *present perfect* verwendest du, wenn eine vergangene Handlung zu einem Ergebnis geführt hat, das sich auf die Gegenwart auswirkt.
Das gilt auch für Handlungen, die gerade erst abgeschlossen wurden (*just*).

45 Das Perfekt in Frage, Verneinung und Kurzantwort – The present perfect in questions, negations and short answers

S

Frage *has/have*	*subject*	*past participle*	**Kurzantwort / Verneinung**	*subject*	*has/have*
Has	Brenda	collect**ed** the posters?	Yes,	she	**has.**
Have	the people	hear**d** the news yet?	No,	they	**haven't.**
Has	Andrew	phone**d** his family yet?	Yes,	he	**has.**
Has	Maggie	**lost** the posters?	No,	she	**hasn't.**

Have you done your homework **yet?**
Hast du deine Hausaufgaben schon gemacht?

No, I have**n't** done it **yet.**
Nein, ich habe sie noch nicht gemacht.

Wenn du fragen möchtest, ob etwas schon geschehen ist, kannst du zum *present perfect* das Wort *yet* hinzufügen.

Willst du ausdrücken, dass etwas noch nicht geschehen ist, ergänzt du *not yet.* Das Wort *yet* steht immer am Ende des Frage- oder Antwortsatzes.

Have you **ever** heard that story?
Hast du diese Geschichte schon je(mals) gehört?

Wenn du wissen möchtest, ob jemand etwas überhaupt schon einmal getan hat, fügst du das Wort *ever* hinzu.

Has he written the dialogue?
Hat er den Dialog geschrieben?

Beachte die unterschiedliche Wortstellung im Englischen und im Deutschen. Das gilt auch für den Aussagesatz: *He has written the dialogue. (Er hat den Dialog geschrieben.)*

A

Du fragst / sagst,

- ob die anderen das Gedicht schon gelernt haben?
- ob Liz das Fünf-Freunde-Video gesehen hat?
- ob die anderen die Nachrichten gehört haben?
- dass deine Schwester dein Buch eingepackt hat.
- dass du deine Hausaufgaben gemacht hast.
- dein Vater diese Geschichte schon gehört hat.

46 +*Present perfect* und *simple past*

Jetzt musst du nur noch wissen, wann du das *present perfect* verwendest und wann das *simple past.*

She **has written** the story.
Now she is reading it to the class.

David **wrote** a story last week.
He got a good mark for it.

Das *present perfect* brauchst du, wenn eine Handlung der Vergangenheit noch in einer Beziehung zur Gegenwart steht.

Das *simple past* verwendest du dagegen, wenn die Handlung in der Vergangenheit abgeschlossen wurde und jetzt vorbei ist.

47 Die Zusammensetzungen von *some* und *any* – The compounds of *some* and *any*

Something, somewhere, anybody, anyone usw. sind Zusammensetzungen von *some* und *any*. Die zusammengesetzten Wörter werden nach den gleichen Regeln verwendet wie *some* und *any* (vgl. Punkt 32).

S

Aussage: *some...*	Frage: *any...*	Verneinung: *any...*
I want to buy **something** for his party.	Can you think of **anything?**	No, sorry. I can't think of **anything.**
My comic must be **somewhere.**	Have you seen it **anywhere?**	No, sorry. We can't find it **anywhere.**

M

someone	something		anyone	anything
some			**any**	
somebody	somewhere		anybody	anywhere

48 Der Gebrauch von *you* – The use of *you*

S

You	*du*	–	Mum, where are **you**?
	dir	–	Can I help **you**, Dad?
	dich	–	When can I phone **you**, Brenda?
	ihr	–	Hi, you two! **You** can start now.
	euch	–	Liz! Liam! I can't hear **you**!
	Ihnen	–	Can I give **you** the book, Ms Carey?
	Sie	–	Have **you** ever heard this song, Mr Wilson?

Soweit ist alles ganz einfach: Insgesamt sieben deutsche Pronomen drückst du im Englischen mit dem einen Wort *you* aus.

You must pay customs on that.
Dafür muss man Zoll zahlen.

It's not easy but **you** can find out.
Es ist nicht (ganz) leicht, aber man kann es herausfinden.

Es kommt noch eine weitere Bedeutung von *you* hinzu. Das Pronomen *you* kann auch für das unpersönliche *man* stehen.

UNIT 9

49 Die Steigerung der Adjektive auf *-er* und *-est* – The comparison of adjectives with *-er* and *-est*

Im Englischen hängt die Form der Steigerung von der Länge eines Adjektivs ab. Kurze, einsilbige Adjektive (*short*) werden anders gesteigert als z.B. dreisilbige Adjektive (*expensive*). Die Steigerung auf *-er* und *-est* funktioniert ähnlich wie die Bildung von Komparativ und Superlativ im Deutschen:
kurz – kürzer – am kürzesten.

Monica's story is **short.**

But Andrew's story is much **shorter.**

And Nicola has written the **shortest** story.

Den Komparativ bildest du, indem du *-er* an die Grundform eines Adjektivs anhängt:
old + er = older.
Beim Superlativ hängst du *-est* an die Grundform an:
cold + est = coldest.

S

Adjektiv	Komparativ	Superlativ
dark	dark**er**	(the) dark**est**
fast	fast**er**	(the) fast**est**
old	old**er**	(the) old**est**
small	small**er**	(the) small**est**
ugly	ugl**ier**	(the) ugl**iest**
clever	clever**er**	(the) clever**est**

Auf diese Weise werden gesteigert:

- alle einsilbigen Adjektive: *big, cheap, fast* usw.
- alle zweisilbigen Adjektive, die auf *-y* enden: *easy, crazy, tidy, funny, heavy* usw.
- manche anderen zweisilbigen Adjektive, die du dir einfach merken musst, z.B.: *clever, quiet.*

Auch bei der Bildung der Steigerungsformen musst du wieder auf die Schreibung achten.

big
bigger

Nach betontem, einfachem Vokal wird der Endkonsonant verdoppelt: *hot, wet* usw.

nice
nic**er**
nic**est**

Auf ein stummes *-e* folgt nur *-r* oder *-st*: *late, safe* usw.

crazy
craz**ier**
craz**iest**

Bei Adjektiven, die auf *-y* enden, wird das *-y* zu *-i*: *hungry, silly, heavy* usw.

50 Die Steigerung der Adjektive mit *more* und *most* – The comparison of adjectives with more and *most*

Look at these T-shirts. They're **expensive.**

Yes, they are. But these blue ones are **more expensive**.

And those lovely red ones over there are the **most expensive** T-shirts in the shop.

Neben der Steigerung mit *-er* und *-est* gibt es auch die Steigerung mit *more* und *most*. Alle Adjektive, die mehr als zwei Silben haben, werden auf diese Weise gesteigert: *expensive – more expensive – most expensive (teuer – teurer – am teuersten).*

S

Adjektiv	Komparativ	Superlativ
expensive	**more** expensive	**most** expensive
positive	**more** positive	**most** positive
interesting	**more** interesting	**most** interesting
helpful	**more** helpful	**most** helpful

Alle Adjektive auf *-ing* werden ebenfalls mit *more* und *most* gesteigert: *boring.*
Ebenso die meisten zweisilbigen Adjektive, die nicht auf *-y* enden: *useful, famous.*

51 Unregelmäßige Steigerung der Adjektive – Irregular comparison of adjectives

These chips are **good.**
But the hot dogs are **better.**
And the ice cream is the **best** of all.

Genauso wie im Deutschen die Adjektive *gut* und *schlecht,* werden im Englischen auch *good* und *bad* unregelmäßig gesteigert: *bad – worse – worst (schlecht – schlechter – am schlechtesten).*

52 Der Vergleich im Satz – Sentences with comparisons

Es gibt drei Grundmuster, mit denen du Gleichheit bzw. Ungleichheit ausdrücken kannst.

The green pullover is **as nice as** the blue one.	*genauso hübsch wie*
But the blue one is **not as cheap as** the green one.	*nicht so billig wie*
The blue pullover is **more expensive than** the green one.	*teurer als*

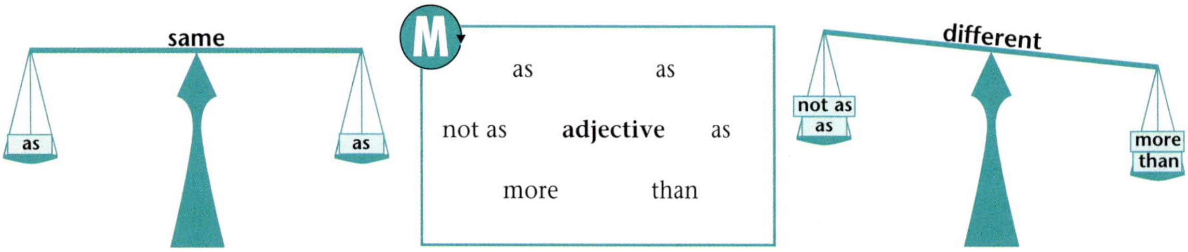

53 Modale Hilfsverben – Modal auxiliaries

Can / May I go now? No, you **can't / may not.**	*Can / can't (cannot)* und *may / may not* (Vorsicht: keine Kurzform!) verwendest du, wenn du um Erlaubnis für etwas bittest, oder eine Erlaubnis erteilst bzw. verweigerst. In der Alltagssprache wird *can* häufiger verwendet als *may.*
Anyone **can** sail a boat.	Mit *can* drückst du auch eine Fähigkeit aus.
You **must** go now.	*Must* bedeutet, dass etwas notwendig ist oder sein muss.
You **mustn't** miss the train.	*Mustn't* steht, wenn man etwas nicht tun soll oder darf.
You **needn't** wait for me.	*Needn't* verwendest du, wenn jemand etwas nicht zu tun braucht.

54 +Adverbien und ihr Gebrauch – The use of adverbs

Adverbien beschreiben die Art und Weise, in der etwas getan wird. Im Englischen musst du zwischen abgeleiteten und nicht abgeleiteten Adverbien unterscheiden.

She is a careful driver.	She drives careful**ly**.
Our dog is so hungry.	He eats his food hungr**ily**.
Jimmy is happy.	He sings happ**ily**.

Viele Adverbien sind von Adjektiven abgeleitet. Du erkennst sie an der Endung *-ly*, die an das Adjektiv angehängt ist: *slow – slowly, bad – badly, careful – carefully* usw.
Bei Adjektiven auf *-y* wird das *-y* vor der Endung *-ly* zu *-i*: *easy – easily.*

Adjektiv	Adverb
Peter is **fast.**	Peter runs **fast.**
You are **late.**	You often come **late.**
She is **early.**	She always gets up **early.**

Bei den nicht abgeleiteten Adverbien sind die Formen mit den Adjektivformen identisch. Sie können je nach Kontext entweder als Adjektiv oder als Adverb verwendet werden

Our teacher is very **good** at grammar.
She explains grammar very **well.**

Das Adverb zu *good* heißt *well.*

55 +Bestätigungsfragen – *Question tags*

In der gesprochenen englischen Sprache gibt es sogenannte Frageanhänger (*question tags*), mit denen du Bestätigung oder Zustimmung zu einer Frage einholen kannst. Solche Fragen werden Bestätigungsfragen genannt. Im Deutschen verwendest du: *..., nicht wahr?/..., oder?/..., gell?*

S

Aussagesatz bejaht (+)	Bestätigungsfrage verneint (–)
You are new here,	**aren't you?**
She is with you,	**isn't she?**
You've got time now,	**haven't you?**
He's got your book,	**hasn't he?**
We must stop,	**mustn't we?**
It works,	**doesn't it?**
They lived here,	**didn't they?**

Die Bestätigungsfrage greift das Hilfsverb und das Subjekt des Aussagesatzes wieder auf, wobei das Subjekt immer als Personalpronomen erscheint.

Steht im Aussagesatz kein Hilfsverb, wird in der Bestätigungsfrage eine Form von *do* verwendet: *do/does/did* bzw. *don't/doesn't/didn't.*

S

Aussagesatz verneint (–)	Bestätigungsfrage bejaht (+)
You aren't from here,	**are you?**
Dad wasn't at home,	**was he?**
They haven't finished,	**have they?**
He hasn't got your book,	**has he?**
It doesn't work,	**does it?**
They won't come,	**will they?**

Das gleiche gilt für den verneinten Aussagesatz.

Merke dir, dass in Sätzen mit Bestätigungsfragen immer ein bejahter und ein verneinter Satzteil vorhanden sein muss.

It's six o'clock, **isn't it?** ↗

That sounds good, **doesn't it?** ↘

Bestätigungsfragen sprichst du mit steigender Satzmelodie (Intonation), wenn du nicht sicher bist, ob deine Aussage richtig oder falsch ist.

Bist du deiner Sache aber ganz sicher und erwartest keine Antwort, verwendest du eine fallende Intonation.

Grammar list

German / Latin	English	Example	Number
Adjektive	adjectives		
– attributiver und prädikativer Gebrauch	– attributive and predicative use	They have got a **big** house. The Cliftons' house is **big**.	13
– Steigerung auf *-er* / *-est*	– comparison with *-er* / *-est*	cheap – cheap**er** – cheap**est**	49
– Steigerung mit *more* / *most*	– comparison with *more* / *most*	interesting – **more** interesting – **most** interesting	50
– unregelmäßige Steigerung	– irregular comparisons	good – **better** – **best**	51
Adverbien	adverbs		
– der Häufigkeit	– of frequency	Their dog **always** barks at me.	20
– Gebrauch der Adverbien	– use of adverbs	She is singing **happily**.	54
Artikel	article		
– bestimmter Artikel	– definite article	**the** window / **the** airport	2
– unbestimmter Artikel	– indefinite article	**a** guitar / **an** instrument	1
+Bestätigungsfragen	question tags	It works, **doesn't it**?	55
Datum	date	23**rd** July / 28**th** August	34
s-Genitiv	*s*-genitive	Tessa**'s** hobbies / the girls**'** friends	11
Fragen mit Fragewörtern und *do* / *don't* und *does* / *doesn't*	questions with question words and *do* / *don't* and *does* / *doesn't*	**What do** you like? / **Who does** he love?	23
Fragen und Kurzantworten mit *do* / *don't* und *does* / *doesn't*	questions and short answers with *do* / *don't* and *does* / *doesn't*	**Do** you like music? – **Yes, I do.** / **No, I don't.** / **Does** he sing? – **Yes, he does.** / **No, he doesn't.**	22
Fragewörter *who* / *what* / *where* / *how*	question words *who* / *what* / *where* / *how*	**What**'s this? / **How** old are you?	16
Gebrauch von *you*	use of *you*	Can I help **you**? / **You** must wait here.	48
+Gerundium	gerund	I hate **climbing**. / **Climbing** is fun.	42
going to-Futur	going to-future	He's **going to** help us. / We're **going to** visit them.	40
has got / *have got*	*has got* / *have got*	**Has** she **got** a hobby? / They **haven't got** it.	12
Hilfsverb *can*	modal auxiliary *can*	**Can** he come today? – No, he **can't**.	15, 53
Hilfsverb *must*	modal auxiliary *must*	You **must** be careful. / You **mustn't** go.	53
I'd like und *I want*	I'd like and I want	**I'd like** an ice cream, please. / **I don't want** an ice cream.	29
Kurzantworten auf Fragen mit *to be*	short answers with *to be*	Is she back? – **Yes, she is.** / Are we late? – **No, you aren't**.	7
Kurzformen	short forms	I'**m** / we'**re** / let'**s**	4
modale Hilfsverben	modal auxiliaries *can* / *may* / *must* / *need*	**May** I help you? You **neen't** wait for me.	53
much und *many*	*much* and *many*	There's not **much** work to do. / How **many** kids are there?	33
Perfekt	present perfect	She **has phoned** us. / We **have heard** it.	44
– in Frage, Verneinung und Kurzantwort	– in questions, negations and short answers	**Has** she **lost** her bag? – **Yes, she has.** / **No, she hasn't.**	45
– +und *simple past*	– and simple past	I've **done** my homework. I **did** it last night.	46

German / Latin	English	Example	Number
Plural der Substantive	plural of nouns		
– regelmäßige Formen	– regular forms	girl / girl**s**, shop / shop**s**	6
– unregelmäßige Formen	– irregular forms	child / child**ren**, knife / kni**ves**	10, 31
Possessivbegleiter	possessive determiners		
– Singular	– singular	**I / my – you(r) – he / his – she / her – it(s)**	8
– Plural	– plural	**our(s) – your(s) – their(s)**	14
Präpositionen	prepositions		
– für Ortsangaben	– of place	The cat is sitting **under** the table.	27
– für Richtungsangaben	– of direction	They are running **around** the tree.	28
– Stellung in Fragen	– position in questions	Where are you **from?**	41
Präsens (einfache Form)	simple present	She **plays** the guitar. / We **play** in a band.	18
Präsens von *to be*	simple present of *to be*	she **is** / he**'s** / we **are** / **are** you?	5
+Präteritum	simple past		
– regelmäßige Formen	– regular forms	They **walked** along the coast.	36
– unregelmäßige Formen	– irregular forms	He **saw** them in the store.	37
– und *present perfect*	– and present perfect	I**'ve done** my homework. I **did** it last night.	46
+Präteritum von *to be* und *to have*	simple past of *to be* and *to have*	Yesterday we **were** late. / Last week we **had** no time.	35
some und *any*	*some* and *any*	I'd like **some** ice cream. / Sorry, we don't have **any**.	32
Stützwort *one / ones*	propword *one / ones*	Which **one** do you want? / The blue **ones**, please.	30
Substantive und Personalpronomen	nouns and personal pronouns	**Mr Clifton / he, Tessa / she**	3
there is / there are	*there is / there are*	**There's** a tree in the garden. / **Are there** any flowers too?	9
this und *that* – *these* und *those*	*this* and *that* – *these* and *those*	**This** is my book. / Are **those** your pens?	24
Uhrzeit	time	It's five **o'clock**. / It's (a) **quarter past** five.	17
Vergleich im Satz	sentences with comparisons	The blue jacket is **more expensive than** the red one, but **not as expensive as** the green one.	52
Verlaufsform des Präsens	present progressive	A man **is juggling**. / **Are** you **having** fun?	25, 26
– und *simple present*	– and simple present		39
Verneinte Sätze mit *do* und *does*	negative sentences with *do* and *does*	They like music but they **don't** play an instrument.	21
+Verneinung im *simple past* mit *didn't*	negative sentences with *didn't*	I **didn't see** your brother.	38
+*will-future*	will-future	I**'ll** help you. / I think it**'ll** rain.	43
Wortstellung in Aussagesätzen im Präsens	word order in statements in the simple present	They bully the girls **every day**.	19
Zusammensetzungen von *some* und *any*	compounds of *some* and *any*	I can't find **anything**. But it must be **somewhere**.	47

Dictionary

In dieser alphabetischen Liste ist das gesamte Vokabular von **Swift 1** enthalten.
Namen werden in gesonderten Listen am Ende dieses *Dictionary* aufgeführt.
Mit ° versehene Wörter sind rezeptiv, Einträge in ⟨ ⟩ fakultativ.
Ein + vor dem Eintrag bedeutet, dass das Wort zum Wortschatz in *Track* 2 gehört.
Die Belegstelle nach den Einträgen bezieht sich auf das erstmalige Vorkommen der Wörter:

to **add** [æd] hinzufügen, addieren **I 9**, 142 = **Swift 1**, *Unit* 9, Seite 142

A

a(n) [ə(n)] ein/eine **I 1**, 10
a bit [ə 'bɪt] ein wenig, ein bisschen **I 3**, 44
(a) few [fju:] wenige, ein paar **I 8**, 129
a lot [ə 'lɒt] viel, eine Menge **I 1**, 15
about [ə'baʊt] über (etw), von (etw) **I 1**, 12; ungefähr, etwa **I 4**, 63
to talk *(about)* ['tɔ:k‿əˌbaʊt] sprechen, reden (über) **I 2**, 27
What about ...? [ˌwɒt‿ə'baʊt] Was ist mit ...? **I 1**, 11
above [ə'bʌv] oberhalb, oben **I 9**, 142
accident ['æksɪdnt] Unfall **I 8**, 126
accommodation [əˌkɒmə'deɪʃn] Unterkunft, Hotelzimmer, Übernachtung **I 9**, 140
across [ə'krɒs] über, durch, darüber **I 9**, 141
°**acrostic** [ə'krɒstɪk] Akrostichon (nacheinander zu lesende Buchstaben, die ein Wort ergeben) **I 3**, 50
act [ækt] Akt, Aufzug **I 8**, 128
to **act** [ækt] darstellen, vorführen **I 4**, 62
action ['ækʃn] Aktion, Handlung **I 4**, 62
activity [æk'tɪvəti] Aktivität, Tätigkeit **I 8**, 124
actor ['æktə] Schauspieler **I 8**, 133
ad (advertisement) [æd (əd'vɜ:tɪsmənt)] Anzeige **I 2**, 32
to **add** [æd] hinzufügen, addieren **I 9**, 142
address [ə'dres] Adresse **I 9**, 148
+to **adore** [ə'dɔ:] anbeten, sehr gern haben **I 9**, 151
adventure [əd'ventʃə] Abenteuer **I 8**, 124
to be **afraid** [ə'freɪd] sich fürchten, Angst haben **I 8**, 129
after ['ɑ:ftə] nach **I 3**, 43
after all [ˌɑ:ftə‿'ɔ:l] schließlich, letztendlich **I 5**, 79
to look after [ˌlʊk‿'ɑ:ftə] schauen nach, sorgen für **I 2**, 32
afternoon [ˌɑ:ftə'nu:n] Nachmittag **I 3**, 43
again [ə'gen] wieder **I 1**, 17
against [ə'genst] gegen **I 8**, 124
age [eɪdʒ] Alter **I 9**, 140
+**ago** [ə'gəʊ] vor *(zeitlich)* **I 8**, 134
to **agree** [ə'gri:] zustimmen **I 9**, 144
+**air** [eə] Luft **I 1**, 19
airport ['eəpɔ:t] Flughafen **I 1**, 8
alcohol ['ælkəhɒl] Alkohol **I 3**, 48
+**alien** ['eɪliən] Ausländer(in), Fremde(r) **I 9**, 151
all [ɔ:l] alle(s) **I 1**, 14
(not) after all [ˌɑ:ftə‿'ɔ:l] doch (nicht) **I 2**, 32
after all [ˌɑ:ftə‿'ɔ:l] schließlich, letztendlich **I 5**, 79
all right [ɔ:l 'raɪt] in Ordnung **I 3**, 45
not ... at all [ˌnɒt‿ə'tɔ:l] überhaupt nicht **I 8**, 129
along [ə'lɒŋ] entlang, längs **I 4**, 63
⟨along *(with)*⟩ [ə'lɒŋ (wɪð)] zusammen (mit) **I 2**, 34
aloud [ə'laʊd] laut **I 9**, 142
alphabet ['ælfəbet] Alphabet **I 7**, 114
already [ɔ:l'redi] schon, bereits **I 7**, 108
also ['ɔ:lsəʊ] auch, ebenfalls **I 3**, 44
always ['ɔ:lweɪz] immer **I 3**, 44
am [æm] bin **I 1**, 9
I'm *(I am)* [aɪm] ich bin **I 1**, 9
+**American** [ə'merɪkən] amerikanisch, Amerikaner(in) **I 5**, 86
among [ə'mʌŋ] zwischen, unter **I 7**, 112
°**amplifier** ['æmplɪfaɪə] Verstärker **I 1**, 13
and [ænd/ənd] und **I 1**, 11
angry ['æŋgri] wütend, ärgerlich **I 8**, 129
animal ['ænɪml] Tier **I 2**, 33
annual ['ænjuəl] jährlich, Jahres- **I 7**, 112
another [ə'nʌðə] ein(e) andere(r/s) **I 6**, 97
answer ['ɑ:nsə] Antwort **I 1**, 20
to **answer** ['ɑnsə] antworten **I 2**, 27
antique [æn'ti:k] Antik-, Antiquitäten **I 5**, 75
any ['eni] irgendeine(r/s), etwas **I 5**, 76
any time [ˌeni 'taɪm] jederzeit **I 3**, 44
anybody ['enibɒdi] irgendjemand **I 8**, 124
anyone ['eniwʌn] irgendjemand **I 8**, 131
anything ['eniθɪŋ] etwas **I 4**, 60
anyway ['eniweɪ] ohnehin, sowieso **I 3**, 45
anywhere ['eniweə] irgendwohin **I 6**, 93
to **apply** *(to)* [ə'plaɪ] (sich) wenden (an) **I 8**, 124
April ['eɪprl] April **I 5**, 78
aquarium [ə'kweəriəm] Aquarium **I 4**, 63
are [ɑ:] sind **I 1**, 11
aren't *(are not)* [ɑ:nt] sind nicht **I 1**, 15
area ['eəriə] Gebiet, Region, Areal **I 9**, 141
arm [ɑ:m] Arm **I 6**, 97
around [ə'raʊnd] um ... herum, umher **I 4**, 59
arrival [ə'raɪvl] Ankunft **I 1**, 8
°**Art** [ɑ:t] Kunst **I 3**, 43
article ['ɑ:tɪkl] (Zeitungs-)Artikel **I 3**, 44
+**artist** ['ɑ:tɪst] Künstler(in) **I 5**, 86
as ... as [æz/əz] (eben)so ... wie **I 7**, 108
to **ask** [ɑ:sk] fragen **I 1**, 13
assembly [ə'sembli] (Schul-)Versammlung **I 3**, 42
assembly hall [ə'sembli ˌhɔ:l] Aula, Versammlungssaal **I 7**, 110
astronomy [ə'strɒnəmi] Astronomie **I 2**, 28
at [æt/ət] an/am, in/im, bei **I 1**, 8
at home [ət‿'həʊm] zu Hause, daheim **I 2**, 28
at the moment ['məʊmənt] im Moment, zur Zeit **I 4**, 67
⟨**atmosphere**⟩ ['ætməsfɪə] Atmosphäre **I 8**, 132
heart **attack** ['hɑ:t‿əˌtæk] Herzinfarkt **I 9**, 146

⁺to pay **attention** [ˌpeɪ‿əˈtenʃn] aufmerksam sein, achtsam sein **I 3**, 52
⁺**attic** [ˈætɪk] Dachboden **I 2**, 36
attraction [əˈtrækʃn] Besonderheit, Attraktion **I 9**, 148
August [ˈɔːgəst] August **I 5**, 78
aunt [ɑːnt] Tante **I 5**, 78
⁺**autumn** (*BE*) [ˈɔːtəm] Herbst **I 4**, 68
⁺**avenue** [ˈævənjuː] Allee, (breite) Straße **I 5**, 86
average [ˈævrɪdʒ] Durchschnitt **I 7**, 112
away [əˈweɪ] weg, fort **I 5**, 79
to throw* (*away*) [θrəʊ] (weg)werfen **I 7**, 112
awful [ˈɔːfl] scheußlich, fürchterlich **I 6**, 92

B

baby [ˈbeɪbi] Baby **I 2**, 29
baby sister [ˌbeɪbi ˈsɪstə] (ganz) kleine Schwester **I 3**, 46
back [bæk] zurück, Hinter- **I 3**, 45
backgammon [ˈbækgæmn] *Name eines Brettspiels* **I 3**, 44
bacon [ˈbeɪkn] Speck **I 9**, 146
bad [bæd] böse, schlecht **I 2**, 32
bag [bæg] Tüte, Tasche **I 4**, 63
sleeping bag [ˈsliːpɪŋ ˌbæg] Schlafsack **I 9**, 145
baggage [ˈbægɪdʒ] Gepäck **I 1**, 8
ball [bɔːl] Ball **I 3**, 51
banana [bəˈnɑːnə] Banane **I 5**, 77
band [bænd] Musikgruppe, Band **I 1**, 10
bandleader [ˈbændˌliːdə] Leiter(in) einer Musikgruppe **I 1**, 14
bank [bæŋk] Bank, Geldinstitut **I 4**, 63
bank robber [ˈbæŋk ˌrɒbə] Bankräuber(in) **I 4**, 64
⁺**bar** [bɑː] Bar **I 5**, 86
coffee bar [ˈkɒfi ˌbɑː] (kleines) Café **I 1**, 9
⁺**bargain** [ˈbɑːgɪn] günstiges Angebot, Gelegenheitskauf **I 5**, 86
to **bark** [bɑːk] bellen **I 3**, 45
baseball [ˈbeɪsbɔːl] Baseball **I 6**, 94
basket [ˈbɑːskɪt] Korb **I 7**, 119
basketball [ˈbɑːskɪtbɔːl] Basketball **I 3**, 47
°**bass** [beɪs] Bass **I 1**, 13
bathroom [ˈbɑːθrʊm] Bad, Badezimmer **I 2**, 29
⁺spare **battery** [ˌspeə ˈbætri] Ersatzbatterie **I 7**, 118
bay [beɪ] Bucht, Bai **I 7**, 108
to **be*** [biː] sein **I 1**, 10
to be afraid [əˈfreɪd] sich fürchten, Angst haben **I 8**, 129
to be busy [ˈbɪzi] beschäftigt sein **I 6**, 93
to be grateful [ˈgreɪtfl] dankbar sein **I 9**, 148
to be hidden [ˈhɪdn] versteckt sein **I 8**, 129
⁺to be interested (*in*) [ˈɪntrəstɪd] interessiert sein (an) **I 7**, 117
⟨to be known⟩ [nəʊn] bekannt sein **I 8**, 132
to be lost [lɒst] sich verlaufen **I 6**, 97
⁺to be prepared [prɪˈpeəd] vorbereitet sein **I 7**, 118
⁺to be proud (*of*) [praʊd] stolz sein (auf) **I 7**, 117
to be rescued [ˈreskjuːd] gerettet werden **I 7**, 114
to be responsible [rɪˈspɒnsəbl] verantwortlich sein **I 7**, 112
⁺to be scared [ˈskeəd] Angst haben, verschreckt sein **I 6**, 102
to be tired [ˈtaɪəd] müde (sein) **I 4**, 63

beach [biːtʃ] Strand **I 6**, 93
beachgoer [ˈbiːtʃˌgəʊə] Strandurlauber(in) **I 7**, 108
beachwatch [ˈbiːtʃwɒtʃ] Strandaufsicht, Strandwärter(in) **I 7**, 110
teddy **bear** [ˈtedi ˌbeə] Teddybär **I 5**, 79
beautiful [ˈbjuːtɪfl] schön **I 5**, 75
because [bɪˈkɒz] weil, da **I 3**, 53
bed [bed] Bett **I 2**, 28
bed and breakfast (*B&B*) [ˌbed‿n‿ˈbrekfəst] Frühstückspension **I 9**, 140
bedroom [ˈbedrʊm] Schlafzimmer **I 2**, 29
before [bɪˈfɔː] vor **I 3**, 43
⁺**beginner** [bɪˈgɪnə] Anfänger(in) **I 9**, 150
beginning [bɪˈgɪnɪŋ] Anfang, Beginn **I 7**, 112
behind [bɪˈhaɪnd] hinter **I 4**, 63
to **believe** [bɪˈliːv] glauben **I 4**, 64
bell [bel] Glocke **I 4**, 59
below [bɪˈləʊ] unterhalb, unten **I 9**, 141
best [best] beste(r/s), der/die Beste **I 3**, 44
⟨to like best⟩ [ˌlaɪk ˈbest] am liebsten mögen **I 8**, 132
to **bet*** [bet] wetten **I 3**, 49
better [ˈbetə] besser **I 3**, 46
between [bɪˈtwiːn] zwischen **I 4**, 65
bhangra [ˈbæŋgrə] *Musikrichtung aus Indien* **I 5**, 77
big [bɪg] groß **I 2**, 26
bike [baɪk] (Fahr-)Rad **I 4**, 59
mountain bike [ˈmaʊntɪn ˌbaɪk] Geländefahrrad, Mountainbike **I 1**, 10
bill [bɪl] Rechnung **I 9**, 146
Biology [baɪˈɒlədʒi] Biologie **I 6**, 96
bird [bɜːd] Vogel **I 4**, 59
⁺to **birdwatch** [ˈbɜːdwɒtʃ] Vögel beobachten **I 7**, 117
biro [ˈbaɪərəʊ] Kuli, Kugelschreiber **I 6**, 99
birthday [ˈbɜːθdeɪ] Geburtstag **I 4**, 62
bit [bɪt] Stück(chen), Teil **I 8**, 126
a bit [ə ˈbɪt] ein wenig, ein bisschen **I 3**, 44
°to **bite** [baɪt] beißen **I 3**, 51
black [blæk] schwarz **I 2**, 27
blackboard [ˈblækbɔːd] Tafel **I 6**, 99
⁺**blind** [blaɪnd] blind **I 3**, 52
⁺colour-blind [ˈkʌləblaɪnd] farbenblind **I 3**, 52
blue [bluː] blau **I 2**, 27
board [bɔːd] Brett, Tafel **I 6**, 99
notice board [ˈnəʊtɪs ˌbɔːd] schwarzes Brett, Anschlagtafel **I 8**, 125
⁺to **board up** [ˌbɔːd‿ˈʌp] verschalen, mit Brettern vernageln **I 7**, 118
boat [bəʊt] Boot **I 4**, 59
book [bʊk] Buch **I 3**, 48
exercise book [ˈeksəsaɪz ˌbʊk] Übungsheft, Heft **I 6**, 99
guide book [ˈgaɪd bʊk] Reiseführer *(Buch)* **I 4**, 63
bookshop [ˈbʊkʃɒp] Buchhandlung **I 5**, 75
boot [buːt] Stiefel **I 5**, 74
boring [ˈbɔːrɪŋ] langweilig **I 2**, 34
to **borrow** [ˈbɒrəʊ] (aus)leihen **I 6**, 99
both [bəʊθ] beide **I 5**, 76
to **bother** [ˈbɒðə] belästigen, plagen **I 8**, 129
bottle [ˈbɒtl] Flasche **I 8**, 131
bottom [ˈbɒtəm] unteres Ende, Fuß **I 9**, 152
bouncy castle [ˌbaʊntsi ˈkɑːsl] (aufblasbare) Hüpfburg **I 9**, 140
box [bɒks] Kiste, Schachtel **I 2**, 31
boy [bɔɪ] Junge **I 1**, 10

boyfriend ['bɔɪfrend] Freund **I 3**, 47
bps (=**bits per second**) ['bi:'pi:'es]
Übertragungsgeschwindigkeit eines Modems **I 8**, 124
bread [bred] Brot **I 8**, 135
break [breɪk] Pause **I 3**, 43
+to **break*** [breɪk] brechen, knacken **I 5**, 85
breakfast ['brekfəst] Frühstück **I 5**, 83
bed and breakfast (*B&B*) [ˌbed‿n‿'brekfəst] Frühstückspension **I 9**, 140
bridge [brɪdʒ] Brücke **I 5**, 79
+**bright** [braɪt] hell, leuchtend **I 2**, 36
to **bring*** [brɪŋ] bringen **I 4**, 63
British ['brɪtɪʃ] britisch **I 7**, 110
brochure ['brəʊʃə] Broschüre, Prospekt **I 9**, 140
brother ['brʌðə] Bruder **I 2**, 30
brown [braʊn] braun **I 2**, 26
+to **build*** [bɪld] bauen **I 8**, 134
building ['bɪldɪŋ] Gebäude **I 4**, 63
bully, pl. -ies ['bʊli] Schlägertyp, Angeber(in) **I 3**, 46
bus [bʌs] Bus **I 1**, 8
bus stop ['bʌs stɒp] Bushaltestelle **I 1**, 8
double decker bus [ˌdʌbl dekə 'bʌs] Doppeldeckerbus **I 4**, 59
but [bʌt] aber **I 1**, 13
to **buy*** [baɪ] kaufen **I 4**, 63
buzz-game ['bʌzˌgeɪm] *Name eines Spiels* **I 1**, 17
by [baɪ] an, neben, bis **I 3**, 47

C

café ['kæfeɪ] Café **I 4**, 67
motorway café ['məʊtəweɪ ˌkæfeɪ] Cafeteria auf der Autobahn **I 9**, 145
cafeteria [ˌkæfə'tɪəriə] Cafeteria **I 3**, 46
+**cage** [keɪdʒ] Käfig **I 6**, 102
calendar ['kæləndə] Kalender **I 5**, 75
(phone) **call** [('fəʊn) kɔ:l] Anruf **I 3**, 45
to **call** [kɔ:l] nennen, (an)rufen **I 2**, 29
camera ['kæmrə] Kamera, Fotoapparat **I 9**, 146
camp [kæmp] (Ferien-)Lager **I 9**, 140
to **camp** [kæmp] zelten **I 9**, 145
campervan ['kæmpəˌvæn] Wohnwagen **I 9**, 141
camping ['kæmpɪŋ] Zelten **I 9**, 143
campsite ['kæmpsaɪt] Campingplatz **I 9**, 145
can [kæn] kann **I 1**, 16
canal [kə'næl] Kanal **I 5**, 77
cap [kæp] Kappe, (Schirm-)Mütze **I 6**, 94
capital ['kæpɪtl] Hauptstadt **I 9**, 147
capital letter [ˌkæpɪtl 'letə] Großbuchstabe **I 9**, 148
captain ['kæptɪn] Kapitän **I 7**, 108
car park ['kɑ: pɑ:k] Parkplatz **I 1**, 8
car rental ['kɑ: ˌrentl] Autovermietung **I 1**, 9
careful ['keəfʊl] vorsichtig **I 1**, 10
to **carry** ['kæri] tragen **I 9**, 143
cartoon [kɑ:'tu:n] Witzzeichnung **I 1**, 17
pencil **case** ['pensl ˌkeɪs] Federmäppchen **I 6**, 99
cassette [kə'set] Kassette **I 3**, 51
castle ['kɑ:sl] Burg, Schloss **I 6**, 93
bouncy castle [ˌbaʊntsi 'kɑ:sl] (aufblasbare) Hüpfburg **I 9**, 140
cat [kæt] Katze **I 2**, 29
to rain cats and dogs ['reɪn ˌkæts‿n‿'dɒgz] heftig regnen, schütten, gießen **I 9**, 145

to **cause** [kɔ:z] verursachen, anrichten **I 7**, 112
cave [keɪv] Höhle **I 8**, 131
+**cellar** ['selə] Keller **I 2**, 36
cello ['tʃeləʊ] Cello **I 1**, 10
+**Celsius** ['selsiəs] Celsius **I 4**, 68
centre ['sentə] Zentrum **I 5**, 76
sports centre ['spɔ:ts ˌsentə] Sportzentrum, Sportanlage **I 4**, 65
chair ['tʃeə] Stuhl **I 2**, 28
chalk [tʃɔ:k] Kreide **I 6**, 99
to **change** [tʃeɪndʒ] ändern; umsteigen **I 4**, 64
character ['kærəktə] Charakter **I 6**, 97
charity ['tʃærɪti] Wohltätigkeit **I 6**, 95
charm [tʃɑ:m] Charme **I 9**, 140
to **chase** [tʃeɪs] (herum)jagen **I 3**, 45
cheap [tʃi:p] billig **I 4**, 59
check [tʃek]
check-in ['tʃekɪn] Abfertigungsschalter (am Flughafen), Einchecken **I 1**, 8
check-out ['tʃekaʊt] Abschlusskontrolle, Auschecken **I 1**, 20
sound check ['saʊn(d) tʃek] Klang-, Tonkontrolle **I 1**, 12
to **check** [tʃek] kontrollieren, überprüfen **I 5**, 80
cheer [tʃɪə] Jubel, Beifall **I 3**, 42
chemical ['kemɪkl] Chemikalie **I 7**, 112
chemist's ['kemɪsts] Apotheke, Drogerie **I 4**, 65
child, (*pl.*) **children** [tʃaɪld/'tʃɪldrn] Kind(er) **I 2**, 29
+**Chinese** [tʃaɪ'ni:z] chinesisch, Chinesisch **I 5**, 86
chips (*pl.*) [tʃɪps] Pommes frites **I 5**, 77
chocolate ['tʃɒklət] Schokolade **I 5**, 77
junior **choir** [ˌdʒu:niə 'kwaɪə] Chor der unteren Klassenstufen **I 8**, 124
to **choose*** [tʃu:z] wählen, aussuchen **I 6**, 93
Christmas ['krɪstməs] Weihnachten **I 6**, 93
church [tʃɜ:tʃ] Kirche **I 4**, 65
+to **churn** [tʃɜ:n] sich heftig bewegen, aufwühlen **I 7**, 118
cigarette [ˌsɪgr'et] Zigarette **I 8**, 131
cinema ['sɪnəmə] Kino **I 4**, 65
city ['sɪti] Großstadt, Innenstadt **I 1**, 12
city shuttle ['sɪti ˌʃʌtl] Pendelverkehr zur Innenstadt **I 1**, 9
to **clap** [klæp] klatschen, applaudieren **I 4**, 60
clapping ['klæpɪŋ] Klatschen, Applaus **I 3**, 42
class [klɑ:s] Klasse **I 1**, 17
classical music ['klæsɪkl 'mju:zɪk] klassische Musik **I 1**, 17
classroom ['klɑ:srʊm] Klassenzimmer **I 4**, 61
to **clean** [kli:n] reinigen, putzen **I 6**, 95
clean [kli:n] sauber **I 9**, 140
cleanest ['kli:nɪst] sauberste(r/s) **I 7**, 112
cleaning lady ['kli:nɪŋ ˌleɪdi] Zugehfrau, Putzfrau **I 6**, 93
clear [klɪə] klar, hell, einleuchtend **I 8**, 129
clever ['klevə] schlau, klug **I 8**, 129
cliff [klɪf] Klippe **I 7**, 110
cliff-side ['klɪfsaɪd] Klippe(n) **I 8**, 129
to **climb** [klaɪm] (hoch)klettern **I 8**, 129
clock [klɒk] Uhr **I 4**, 59
to **close** [kləʊz] schließen **I 4**, 64
close (*to*) [kləʊs] nah, dicht (bei) **I 9**, 141
clothes ['kləʊðz] Kleidung, Kleider **I 5**, 74
+**cloudy** ['klaʊdi] wolkig **I 4**, 68

club [klʌb] Klub, Verein **I 3**, 44
night club ['naɪt klʌb] Nachtclub **I 6**, 93
coast [kəʊst] Küste **I 7**, 108
coastal ['kəʊstl] Küsten- **I 9**, 141
coastguard ['kəʊstgɑ:d] Küstenwache **I 7**, 108
coat [kəʊt] Mantel **I 8**, 131
code [kəʊd] Kode **I 3**, 53
coffee ['kɒfi] Kaffee **I 4**, 61
coffee bar ['kɒfi ˌbɑ:] (kleines) Café **I 1**, 9
cold [kəʊld] kalt **I 6**, 96
collar ['kɒlə] Hundehalsband **I 5**, 74
to **collect** [kə'lekt] sammeln **I 4**, 60
colour ['kʌlə] Farbe **I 2**, 27
+colour-blind ['kʌləblaɪnd] farbenblind **I 3**, 52
to **come*** [kʌm] kommen **I 2**, 29
to come round [ˌkʌm 'raʊnd] vorbeikommen, herüberkommen **I 3**, 44
comfortable ['kʌmftəbl] bequem, komfortabel **I 9**, 140
comic ['kɒmɪk] Comic(heft) **I 4**, 61
+**command** [kə'mɑ:nd] Befehl, Kommando **I 3**, 52
in **common** [ɪn 'kɒmən] gemeinsam **I 9**, 147
to **compare** [kəm'peə] vergleichen **I 3**, 45
comparison [kəm'pærɪsn] Vergleich **I 9**, 152
competition [ˌkɒmpə'tɪʃn] Wettbewerb, Wettkampf **I 8**, 124
to **complete** [kəm'pli:t] vervollständigen **I 8**, 126
listening **comprehension** ['lɪsnɪŋ ˌkɒmprɪ'henʃn] Hörverstehen **I 1**, 16
computer [kəm'pju:tə] Computer, Rechner **I 2**, 30
drum computer ['drʌm kəmˌpju:tə] Rhythmusgerät **I 1**, 10
the pros and **cons** [ˌprəʊz‿n‿'kɒnz] das Für und Wider, Pro und Contra **I 7**, 116
concert ['kɒnsət] Konzert **I 5**, 83
+to **confuse** [kən'fju:z] verwirren, irritieren **I 3**, 52
+to **connect** [kə'nekt] verbinden, zusammenfügen **I 3**, 52
contact ['kɒntækt] Kontakt, Verbindung **I 9**, 141
to **contact** ['kɒntækt] Kontakt aufnehmen (mit) **I 9**, 141
wax **content** ['wæks ˌkɒntent] Wachsgehalt **I 7**, 108
context ['kɒntekst] Textzusammenhang, Kontext **I 9**, 141
+**conversation** [ˌkɒnvə'seɪʃn] Gespräch, Konversation **I 9**, 151
cook [kʊk] Koch/Köchin **I 8**, 128
to **cook** [kʊk] kochen **I 9**, 143
+**cooking** ['kʊkɪŋ] Kochen, Essen **I 5**, 86
copy ['kɒpi] Kopie **I 6**, 96
corner ['kɔ:nə] Ecke **I 4**, 59
Cornish ['kɔ:nɪʃ] kornisch, aus Cornwall **I 7**, 108
to **correct** [kə'rekt] korrigieren, verbessern **I 5**, 80
correct [kə'rekt] richtig, korrekt **I 9**, 147
costume ['kɒstju:m] Kostüm **I 6**, 97
could [kʊd] konnte(n), könnte(n) **I 9**, 140
country ['kʌntri] Land **I 2**, 30
countryside ['kʌntriˌsaɪd] Land, Landschaft **I 9**, 141
of **course** [əv 'kɔ:s] natürlich, selbstverständlich **I 2**, 29
cousin ['kʌzn] Cousin(e) **I 8**, 128
to **crack** [kræk] knacken, aufbrechen **I 3**, 53
crazy ['kreɪzi] verrückt **I 6**, 95
ice **cream** [aɪs 'kri:m] Eiskrem, (Speise-)Eis **I 4**, 61
ice cream maker [aɪs 'kri:m ˌmeɪkə] Eismaschine **I 8**, 133
+to **cross** [krɒs] überqueren, kreuzen **I 7**, 118
crown jewels [ˌkraʊn 'dʒu:əlz] Kronjuwelen **I 4**, 63
to **cry** [kraɪ] rufen, schreien; weinen **I 4**, 63
cuisine [kwɪz'ɪ:n] Küche **I 9**, 140
cupboard ['kʌbəd] Schrank **I 2**, 28
curry ['kʌri] Curry(gericht) **I 4**, 67
customs ['kʌstəmz] Zoll *(Verwaltung)* **I 8**, 131
to **cycle** ['saɪkl] Rad fahren, radeln **I 9**, 141

D

dad [dæd] Papa, Vati **I 2**, 29
+**damage** ['dæmɪdʒ] Schaden **I 7**, 118
to **damage** ['dæmɪdʒ] beschädigen **I 8**, 126
danger ['deɪndʒə] Gefahr **I 7**, 112
dangerous ['deɪndʒrəs] gefährlich **I 7**, 108
dark [dɑ:k] dunkel **I 6**, 97
up to **date** [ˌʌp tə 'deɪt] modern, aktuell **I 3**, 47
day [deɪ] Tag **I 3**, 46
daylight ['deɪlaɪt] Tageslicht **I 8**, 129
dead [ded] tot, verstorben **I 7**, 108
deaf [def] taub **I 8**, 129
Oh, **dear!** [əʊ 'dɪə] Oh je! **I 2**, 30
December [dɪ'sembə] Dezember **I 5**, 78
to **decide** [dɪ'saɪd] entscheiden **I 6**, 98
to **declare** [dɪ'kleə] angeben, deklarieren **I 8**, 131
+**degree** [dɪ'gri:] Grad **I 4**, 68
+**delicatessen, deli** [ˌdelikə'tesn, deli] Delikatessengeschäft, -lokal **I 5**, 86
demo tape ['deməʊ ˌteɪp] Demo(nstrations)band **I 6**, 96
department [dɪ'pɑ:tmənt] Abteilung **I 5**, 79
department store [dɪ'pɑ:tmənt ˌstɔ:] Kaufhaus **I 4**, 59
departure [dɪ'pɑ:tʃə] Abflug, Abfahrt **I 1**, 8
to **describe** [dɪ'skraɪb] beschreiben **I 6**, 94
description [dɪ'skrɪpʃn] Beschreibung **I 6**, 96
design [dɪ'zaɪn] Design **I 6**, 96
°Design and Technology [dɪ'zaɪn‿ən tek'nɒlədʒi] Gestalten und Technik **I 3**, 43
+**designer** [dɪ'zaɪnə] Designer(in) **I 5**, 86
desk [desk] Schreibtisch **I 6**, 99
to **destroy** [dɪ'strɔɪ] zerstören **I 7**, 108
detail ['di:teɪl] Detail, Einzelheit **I 9**, 148
detective [dɪ'tektɪv] Detektiv(in) **I 5**, 79
to **dial** ['daɪəl] wählen **I 4**, 64
dialogue ['daɪəlɒg] Dialog, Gespräch **I 5**, 76
diary ['daɪəri] Tagebuch **I 6**, 92
dictionary ['dɪkʃənəri] Wörterbuch **I 1**, 13
to **die** [daɪ] sterben **I 7**, 112
difference ['dɪfrnts] Unterschied, Differenz **I 9**, 141
different ['dɪfrnt] verschieden, anders(artig) **I 2**, 29
difficult ['dɪfɪklt] schwierig **I 7**, 112
+**dining room** ['daɪnɪŋ ˌrʊm] Esszimmer **I 2**, 36
dinner ['dɪnə] Abendessen **I 9**, 149
direct [dɪ'rekt] direkt **I 9**, 141
+**direction** [dɪ'rekʃn] Richtung **I 7**, 118
dirtiest ['dɜ:tiɪst] schmutzigste(r/s) **I 7**, 112
dirty ['dɜ:ti] schmutzig **I 7**, 110
to **disagree** [ˌdɪsə'gri:] ablehnen **I 9**, 144
disaster [dɪ'zɑ:stə] Katastrophe, Unglück **I 7**, 108
disco ['dɪskəʊ] Disko(thek) **I 6**, 93
to **discuss** [dɪ'skʌs] diskutieren, besprechen **I 3**, 49
to **dispose of** [dɪ'spəʊz‿ɒv] beseitigen, loswerden **I 7**, 112

+**district** ['dɪstrɪkt] Bezirk, (Stadt-)Viertel **I 5**, 86
to **divide** [dɪ'vaɪd] aufteilen, dividieren **I 9**, 142
to **do*** [du:] tun, machen **I 2**, 29
dog [dɒg] Hund **I 2**, 32
+guide dog ['gaɪd dɒg] Blindenhund **I 3**, 52
hot dog ['hɒt dɒg] Hotdog (*langes weiches Brötchen mit Würstchen*) **I 1**, 10
to rain cats and dogs ['reɪn ˌkæts‿n‿'dɒgz] heftig regnen, schütten, gießen **I 9**, 145
dollar ['dɒlə] *amerikanische Währung* **I 4**, 63
door [dɔ:] Tür **I 1**, 10
double ['dʌbl] doppelt(e/r) **I 1**, 18
double decker bus [ˌdʌbl dekə 'bʌs] Doppeldeckerbus **I 4**, 59
+**down** [daʊn] herunter, nieder **I 1**, 19
to note (*down*) [ˌnəʊt 'daʊn] notieren, (auf)schreiben **I 3**, 42
to turn down [ˌtɜ:n 'daʊn] herunterdrehen, leiser stellen **I 2**, 34
to write* (*down*) [ˌraɪt 'daʊn] (auf)schreiben **I 2**, 27
to **download** [ˌdaʊn'ləʊd] herunterladen, downloaden **I 5**, 80
downstairs [ˌdaʊn'steəz] unten; Erdgeschoss **I 6**, 93
+**downstream** [ˌdaʊn'stri:m] stromabwärts **I 9**, 150
+**downtown** (*AE*) [ˌdaʊn'taʊn] *südlicher Teil der Insel Manhattan in New York; sonst:* Stadtzentrum **I 5**, 86
°**Drama** ['drɑ:mə] Theaterspielen (*Fach*) **I 3**, 43
to **draw*** [drɔ:] zeichnen **I 6**, 96
+**dreadful** ['dredfl] furchtbar, schrecklich **I 9**, 151
dress [dres] Kleid **I 6**, 98
to **drift** [drɪft] (ab)treiben, (ab)driften **I 7**, 112
to **drink*** [drɪŋk] trinken **I 3**, 44
to **drive*** [draɪv] fahren **I 4**, 63
+to drive so. out [ˌdraɪv‿'aʊt] jmdn verjagen, hinausjagen **I 8**, 134
+**driver** ['draɪvə] Fahrer(in) **I 9**, 150
to **drop** [drɒp] fallen lassen, abwerfen **I 7**, 112
drug [drʌg] Droge **I 3**, 46
drum [drʌm] Trommel **I 1**, 10
drum computer ['drʌm kəmˌpju:tə] Rhythmusgerät **I 1**, 10
°drum kit ['drʌm kɪt] Schlagzeugausrüstung **I 1**, 13
+**due** (*to*) [dju:] zurückzuführen (auf) **I 7**, 118
to **dump** [dʌmp] auskippen, hinwerfen **I 7**, 112
duty ['dju:ti] Zoll *(Gebühr)* **I 8**, 131

E

e-mail ['i:meɪl] elektronische Post, E-Mail **I 2**, 30
each [i:tʃ] jede(r/s) Einzelne **I 4**, 62
early ['ɜ:li] früh **I 2**, 31
+**east** [i:st] östlich, Osten **I 7**, 118
easy ['i:zi] leicht, einfach **I 7**, 112
to **eat*** [i:t] essen **I 3**, 45
edge [edʒ] Ufer, Rand (eines Sees) **I 9**, 141
egg [eg] Ei **I 9**, 146
+**elderly** ['eldəli] älter(e/r/s) **I 7**, 118
electric [ɪ'lektrɪk] elektrisch **I 1**, 10
electricity [ˌelɪk'trɪsəti] Elektrizität, Strom **I 2**, 31
+**elevator** *(AE)* ['elɪveɪtə] Aufzug, Fahrstuhl **I 4**, 68
else [els] (sonst) noch, außerdem **I 4**, 59
+**emergency** [ɪ'mɜ:dʒntsi] Notfall-, Dringlichkeits- **I 7**, 118
end [end] Ende, Schluss **I 2**, 31
to **end** [end] (be)enden **I 8**, 130
English ['ɪŋglɪʃ] englisch, Englisch **I 1**, 11
+to **enjoy** [ɪn'dʒɔɪ] genießen, sich (er)freuen **I 7**, 117
enough [ɪ'nʌf] genug, ausreichend **I 4**, 64
entertainment [ˌentə'teɪnmənt] Unterhaltung, Animation **I 9**, 140
environment [ɪn'vaɪərnmənt] Umwelt **I 9**, 143
+**evacuation** [ɪˌvækju'eɪʃn] Evakuierung, Räumung **I 7**, 118
even ['i:vn] sogar **I 2**, 30
evening ['i:vnɪŋ] Abend **I 3**, 47
ever ['evə] je(mals), immer **I 8**, 127
every ['evri] jede(r/s) **I 3**, 49
everybody ['evriˌbɒdi] jeder, alle (zusammen) **I 1**, 11
everyone ['evriwʌn] jeder **I 8**, 131
everything ['evriθɪŋ] alles **I 3**, 45
everywhere ['evriweə] überall **I 6**, 92
exact [ɪg'zækt] exakt, genau **I 8**, 126
example [ɪg'zɑ:mpl] Beispiel **I 1**, 10
excellent ['ekslnt] ausgezeichnet, exzellent **I 9**, 140
exciting [ɪk'saɪtɪŋ] aufregend, spannend **I 5**, 80
excuse me [ɪk'skju:z mi:] entschuldigen Sie **I 4**, 65
exercise book ['eksəsaɪz ˌbʊk] Übungsheft, Heft **I 6**, 99
exhibition [ˌeksɪ'bɪʃn] Ausstellung **I 7**, 112
expensive [ɪk'spensɪv] teuer **I 4**, 59
experience [ɪk'spɪəriənts] Erfahrung **I 9**, 141
experiment [ɪk'sperɪmənt] Versuch, Experiment **I 8**, 128
+**expert** ['ekspɜ:t] Experte/Expertin **I 7**, 118
to **explain** [ɪk'spleɪn] erklären **I 5**, 80
extra ['ekstrə] zusätzlich, extra **I 3**, 47

F

face [feɪs] Gesicht **I 5**, 79
fact [fækt] Tatsache, Fakt **I 8**, 128
in fact [ɪn 'fækt] eigentlich **I 8**, 126
Yours **faithfully,** ['feɪθfli] mit freundlichen Grüßen, hochachtungsvoll (*Briefschluss*) **I 9**, 148
+**fall** (*AE*) [fɔ:l] Herbst **I 4**, 68
to **fall*** [fɔ:l] fallen, stürzen **I 4**, 63
family, (*pl.*) -ies ['fæməli] Familie **I 2**, 26
famous ['feɪməs] berühmt **I 4**, 59
+**fancy** ['fæntsi] seltsam, ausgefallen **I 9**, 151
fantastic [fæn'tæstɪk] fantastisch **I 9**, 146
fantasy ['fæntəsi] Fantasie **I 7**, 112
far [fɑ:] weit **I 5**, 81
farm [fɑ:m] Bauernhaus, Farm **I 6**, 93
fashion ['fæʃn] Mode **I 5**, 81
fast [fɑ:st] schnell, rasch **I 9**, 143
father ['fɑ:ðə] Vater **I 4**, 69
favorite (*AE*) ['feɪvrɪt] bevorzugt, Lieblings- **I 6**, 101
favourite ['feɪvrɪt] bevorzugt, Lieblings- **I 3**, 49
feather ['feðə] Feder, Gefieder **I 7**, 108
February ['februri] Februar **I 5**, 78
to **feed*** [fi:d] füttern **I 4**, 59
festival ['festɪvl] Festival **I 8**, 124
to **fetch** [fetʃ] (ab)holen **I 6**, 97
(a) **few** [fju:] wenige, ein paar **I 8**, 129
field [fi:ld] Feld **I 6**, 92
to **fight*** [faɪt] streiten, kämpfen **I 3**, 45
to **fill** [fɪl] einfügen, auffüllen **I 6**, 98

film [fɪlm] Film **I 8**, 131
to **find*** [faɪnd] finden **I 2**, 28
fine [faɪn] gut, prima **I 1**, 17
finger ['fɪŋgə] Finger **I 6**, 93
to **finish** ['fɪnɪʃ] beenden **I 6**, 98
fire ['faɪə] Feuer **I 4**, 60
fireplace ['faɪəpleɪs] (offener) Kamin **I 2**, 29
first ['fɜ:st] erste(r/s), der/die Erste **I 3**, 43
fish [fɪʃ] Fisch **I 7**, 110
to **fish** [fɪʃ] angeln **I 9**, 140
fishing line ['fɪʃɪŋ ˌlaɪn] Angelschnur **I 7**, 112
to **fit** [fɪt] passen **I 6**, 94
fit [fɪt] gesund, in Form **I 3**, 47
to **fix** [fɪks] befestigen, reparieren **I 2**, 31
in a **flash** [flæʃ] blitzschnell **I 4**, 63
+**flashlight** (*AE*) ['flæʃlaɪt] (Taschen-)Lampe **I 7**, 118
flat [flæt] (Etagen-)Wohnung **I 2**, 26
flat tyre [ˌflæt 'taɪə] platter Reifen, Plattfuß **I 9**, 146
flight [flaɪt] Flug **I 9**, 141
+to **flood** [flʌd] überfluten, überschwemmen **I 7**, 118
+**floor** [flɔ:] Fußboden **I 3**, 52; Stockwerk, Etage **I 4**, 68
+**flow** [fləʊ] Strömung, Fließen **I 9**, 150
flower ['flaʊə] Blume **I 2**, 26
to **fly*** [flaɪ] fliegen **I 9**, 141
fog [fɒg] Nebel **I 6**, 97
+**foggy** ['fɒgi] neb(e)lig **I 7**, 118
folder ['fəʊldə] Mappe, Ordner **I 6**, 99
folk [fəʊk] Volksmusik, Folk(-) **I 8**, 124
Irish folk [ˌaɪərɪʃ 'fəʊk] *Musikrichtung aus Irland* **I 5**, 77
to **follow** ['fɒləʊ] folgen **I 4**, 63
food [fu:d] Essen, Nahrung **I 2**, 32
foot [fʊt] Fuß **I 4**, 60
football ['fʊtbɔ:l] Fußball **I 3**, 44
footpath ['fʊtpɑ:θ] Fußweg, Pfad **I 6**, 97
footprint ['fʊtprɪnt] Fußstapfen **I 6**, 97
footwear ['fʊtweə] Schuhe **I 6**, 94
for [fɔ:] für **I 1**, 14
forever [fə'revə] für immer **I 9**, 141
to **forget*** [fə'get] vergessen **I 3**, 45
form [fɔ:m] Form, Art **I 4**, 59
formal ['fɔ:ml] förmlich, formell, offiziell **I 9**, 148
+**forward** ['fɔ:wəd] vorwärts **I 3**, 52
to look forward (*to*) [ˌlʊk 'fɔ:wəd] sich freuen (auf) **I 9**, 148
found [faʊnd] gefunden **I 2**, 33
frame [freɪm] (Bilder-)Rahmen **I 5**, 74
freak [fri:k] Fan, Anhänger(in) **I 2**, 30
free [fri:] frei, kostenlos **I 9**, 140
freedom ['fri:dəm] Freiheit **I 9**, 141
°**French** ['frentʃ] französisch, Französisch **I 3**, 43
+**frequent** ['fri:kwənt] häufig, oft **I 9**, 150
Friday ['fraɪdeɪ] Freitag **I 3**, 43
fridge [frɪdʒ] Kühlschrank **I 6**, 92
friend [frend] Freund(in) **I 1**, 11
friendly ['frendli] freundlich, angenehm **I 3**, 45
friendly match [ˌfrendli 'mætʃ] Freundschaftsspiel **I 8**, 124
+**friendship** ['fren(d)ʃɪp] Freundschaft **I 1**, 19
from [frɒm] von **I 1**, 11
in **front** [ɪn 'frʌnt] davor, vorn **I 2**, 26
front [frʌnt] Vor-, Vorder- **I 2**, 26
to **fry** [fraɪ] frittieren, braten **I 9**, 146
full [fʊl] voll **I 4**, 64
fun [fʌn] Spaß **I 1**, 17
funny ['fʌni] witzig, spaßig **I 2**, 31
further ['fɜ:ðə] weiter **I 9**, 147

G

+**gallery** ['gæləri] Galerie **I 5**, 86
game [geɪm] Spiel **I 1**, 16
°**Games** [geɪmz] (Mannschafts-)Sport **I 3**, 43
gap [gæp] Lücke, Abstand **I 9**, 149
garage ['gærɑ:ʒ] Garage **I 2**, 30
garden ['gɑ:dn] Garten **I 2**, 26
gear [gɪə] Ausrüstung **I 9**, 141
+ladies and **gentlemen** ['leɪdiz‿ən 'dʒentlmən] (meine) Damen und Herren **I 4**, 68
°**Geography** [dʒi'ɒgrəfi] Erdkunde, Geographie **I 3**, 43
German ['dʒɜ:mən] deutsch, Deutsch **I 1**, 11
to **get*** [get] bekommen, haben **I 1**, 15
to get on (*well with so.*) [ˌget‿ɒn 'wel] (gut mit jmdm) zurechtkommen **I 3**, 47
ghost [gəʊst] Geist, Gespenst **I 6**, 93
+**giant** ['dʒaɪənt] Riese, Gigant **I 6**, 102
girl [gɜ:l] Mädchen **I 1**, 10
girlfriend ['gɜ:lfrend] Freundin **I 3**, 47
to **give*** [gɪv] geben **I 1**, 14
to give a talk ['tɔ:k] ein (Kurz-)Referat halten **I 9**, 148
glass [glɑ:s] Glas **I 5**, 76
glove [glʌv] Handschuh **I 6**, 93
to **go*** [gəʊ] gehen **I 1**, 9
to go on [ˌgəʊ‿'ɒn] weitermachen, fortsetzen **I 1**, 12
to go shopping [ˌgəʊ 'ʃɒpɪŋ] Einkaufen gehen **I 5**, 79
+**gold** [gəʊld] Gold **I 1**, 19
golden ['gəʊldn] golden **I 6**, 98
golf [gɒlf] Golf **I 9**, 140
gone [gɒn] ausgegangen, zu Ende gegangen **I 2**, 32
good [gʊd] gut **I 1**, 9
goodbye, bye [(ˌgʊd)'baɪ] (auf) Wiedersehen, tschüs, servus (*regional*) **I 1**, 14
+**gorgeous** ['gɔ:dʒəs] prächtig, prachtvoll **I 9**, 151
+**gorilla** [gə'rɪlə] Gorilla **I 6**, 102
to have* **got** [ˌhæv 'gɒt] haben **I 2**, 26
graffiti [grə'fi:ti] Graffiti **I 3**, 51
grandma ['grænmɑ:] Großmutter, Oma **I 3**, 47
to be **grateful** ['greɪtfl] dankbar sein **I 9**, 148
great [greɪt] großartig, spitze **I 2**, 34
green [gri:n] grün **I 2**, 27
grey [greɪ] grau **I 8**, 126
°**grid** [grɪd] Netz, Gitter **I 3**, 50
group [gru:p] Gruppe **I 2**, 34
to **grow*** [grəʊ] wachsen **I 9**, 143
grown-up ['grəʊn‿ʌp] Erwachsene(r) **I 8**, 128
to **guess** [ges] raten, vermuten **I 2**, 31
guest [gest] Gast **I 4**, 62
guide book ['gaɪd bʊk] Reiseführer *(Buch)* **I 4**, 63
+**guide dog** ['gaɪd dɒg] Blindenhund **I 3**, 52
guitar [gɪ'tɑ:] Gitarre **I 1**, 10
+**guy** [gaɪ] Freund, Kumpel **I 5**, 85
gym(nasium) [dʒɪm('neɪziəm)] Sporthalle **I 6**, 95

H

hair [heə] Haar **I 4**, 63
half [hɑ:f] halb **I 3**, 43
hall [hɔ:l] Diele, (Eingangs-) Halle **I 7**, 110
assembly hall [əˈsembli ˌhɔ:l] Aula, Versammlungssaal **I 7**, 110
village hall [ˌvɪlɪdʒ ˈhɔ:l] Gemeindehaus **I 6**, 97
hand [hænd] Hand **I 5**, 79
handbag [ˈhændbæg] Handtasche **I 5**, 74
to **happen** [ˈhæpn] geschehen, passieren **I 4**, 60
happy [ˈhæpi] froh, glücklich **I 2**, 30
+**harbor** *(AE)* [ˈhɑ:bə] Hafen **I 8**, 134
harbour [ˈhɑ:bə] Hafen **I 7**, 112
hard [hɑ:d] hart **I 8**, 128
+leather **harness** [ˌleðə ˈhɑ:nɪs] Ledergeschirr, -gurtwerk **I 3**, 52
hat [hæt] Hut **I 4**, 60
to **hate** [heɪt] nicht mögen, hassen **I 3**, 46
to **have*** [hæv] haben **I 1**, 9
to have got [ˌhæv ˈgɒt] haben **I 2**, 26
he [hi:] er **I 1**, 12
head [hed] Kopf **I 4**, 60
heading [ˈhedɪŋ] Überschrift **I 6**, 100
headteacher [ˌhedˈti:tʃə] Schulleiter(in) **I 3**, 42
°**Health** [helθ] Gesundheitslehre **I 3**, 43
healthy [ˈhelθi] gesund **I 9**, 143
to **hear*** [hɪə] hören **I 5**, 79
+**heart** [hɑ:t] Herz **I 6**, 102
heart attack [ˈhɑ:t‿əˌtæk] Herzinfarkt **I 9**, 146
+to learn by heart [ˌlɜ:n baɪ ˈhɑ:t] auswendig lernen **I 5**, 85
to **heat** [hi:t] heizen **I 9**, 140
heating [ˈhi:tɪŋ] Heizung **I 6**, 92
heavy [ˈhevi] schwer **I 4**, 60
hello [həˈləʊ] hallo **I 1**, 9
help [help] Hilfe **I 6**, 93
to **help** [help] helfen **I 3**, 48
helpless [ˈhelpləs] hilflos **I 3**, 49
her [hɜ:] ihr/ihre **I 1**, 15; sie *(Akk.)*; ihr *(Dat.)* **I 2**, 32
here [ˈhɪə] hier **I 1**, 9
+**hero** [ˈhɪərəʊ] Held **I 8**, 134
hey! [heɪ] He! **I 2**, 31
hi [haɪ] hallo **I 1**, 9
to be **hidden** [ˈhɪdn] versteckt sein **I 8**, 129
to **hide*** [haɪd] (sich) verstecken, verbergen **I 4**, 63
high [haɪ] hoch **I 2**, 28
hill [hɪl] Hügel **I 6**, 92
him [hɪm] ihn, ihm **I 3**, 44
himself [hɪmˈself] sich (selbst) **I 6**, 101
his [hɪz] sein/seine **I 1**, 15
°**History** [ˈhɪstri] Geschichte **I 3**, 43
+to **hit*** [hɪt] (auf)treffen (auf), erreichen **I 7**, 118
hobby, *(pl.)* -ies [ˈhɒbi] Hobby **I 2**, 28
hockey [ˈhɒki] Hockey **I 3**, 47
hole [həʊl] Loch **I 2**, 31
holiday [ˈhɒlədeɪ] Ferien, Urlaub **I 7**, 112
holidaymaker [ˈhɒlədiˌmeɪkə] Urlauber(in) **I 7**, 108
hols (= **holidays**) [hɒlz] Ferien **I 8**, 128
at **home** [ət‿ˈhəʊm] zu Hause, daheim **I 2**, 28
+mobile home [ˌməʊbaɪl ˈhəʊm] Wohnmobil **I 7**, 118
homepage [ˈhəʊmpeɪdʒ] Homepage **I 9**, 148
homework *(sing.)* [ˈhəʊmwɜ:k] Hausaufgaben **I 3**, 44
to **hope** [həʊp] hoffen **I 6**, 93
horse [hɔ:s] Pferd **I 6**, 98
hostel [ˈhɒstl] Herberge **I 9**, 142
hot [hɒt] heiß; scharf (gewürzt) **I 2**, 33
hot dog [ˈhɒt dɒg] Hotdog *(langes weiches Brötchen mit Würstchen)* **I 1**, 10
hotel [həʊˈtel] Hotel **I 1**, 10
hour [ˈaʊə] Stunde **I 3**, 46
house [haʊs] Haus **I 2**, 26
how [haʊ] wie **I 2**, 32
How are you? [ˌhaʊ‿ˈɑ: ju:] Wie geht's (dir/euch/Ihnen)? **I 1**, 17
how many? [ˈhaʊ ˌmeni] wie viele? **I 3**, 43
how much? [ˈhaʊ ˌmʌtʃ] wie viel? **I 3**, 53
+**huge** [hju:dʒ] riesig **I 5**, 86
hungry [ˈhʌŋgri] hungrig **I 2**, 32
+**hurricane** [ˈhʌrɪkən] Wirbelsturm, Orkan **I 7**, 118
in a **hurry** [ˈhʌri] in Eile, eilig **I 4**, 63
to **hurry** *(up)* [ˌhʌri‿ˈʌp] (sich) beeilen **I 6**, 97
to **hurt*** [hɜ:t] wehtun, schmerzen **I 4**, 60

I

I [aɪ] ich **I 1**, 8
I don't know [aɪ ˌdəʊnt ˈnəʊ] ich weiß (es) nicht **I 2**, 31
I'd (= *I would*) like [aɪd ˈlaɪk] ich hätte gerne **I 5**, 76
I'm (*I am*) [aɪm] ich bin **I 1**, 9
I'm into ... [ˈɪntə] ich stehe auf .../ ich bin begeistert von ... **I 2**, 34
ice [aɪs] Eis **I 6**, 93
ice cream [aɪs ˈkri:m] Eiskrem, (Speise-)Eis **I 4**, 61
ice cream maker [aɪs ˈkri:m ˌmeɪkə] Eismaschine **I 8**, 133
+**icy** [ˈaɪsi] eisig **I 7**, 118
idea [aɪˈdɪə] Idee, Einfall **I 2**, 30
ideal [aɪˈdɪəl] ideal, hervorragend **I 9**, 140
idiot [ˈɪdiət] Idiot **I 4**, 63
if [ɪf] wenn, falls **I 2**, 32
illegal [ɪˈli:gl] ungesetzlich, illegal **I 7**, 108
to **imagine** [ɪˈmædʒɪn] sich vorstellen, annehmen **I 8**, 125
+**important** [ɪmˈpɔ:tnt] wichtig **I 3**, 52
in [ɪn] in/im **I 1**, 12
in a flash [flæʃ] blitzschnell **I 4**, 63
in a hurry [ˈhʌri] in Eile, eilig **I 4**, 63
in common [ɪn ˈkɒmən] gemeinsam **I 9**, 147
in fact [ɪn ˈfækt] eigentlich **I 8**, 126
in front [ɪn ˈfrʌnt] davor, vorn **I 2**, 26
+in return [ɪn rɪˈtɜ:n] dafür **I 5**, 86
independent [ˌɪndɪˈpendənt] unabhängig **I 9**, 143
Indian [ˈɪndiən] Inder(in) **I 2**, 32
+Seminole Indian [ˈsemɪnəʊl ˌɪndiən] *Angehörige(r) eines indianischen Stamms* **I 8**, 134
indoor [ˌɪnˈdɔ:] Innen-, Hallen- **I 9**, 140
information [ˌɪnfəˈmeɪʃn] Information **I 7**, 110
inside [ˌɪnˈsaɪd] im Inneren (von) **I 3**, 49
+**instructions** [ɪnˈstrʌkʃnz] Anweisungen, Instruktionen **I 9**, 150
instrument [ˈɪnstrəmənt] Instrument **I 1**, 10
intention [ɪnˈtenʃn] Absicht, Intention **I 7**, 111
+to be **interested** *(in)* [ˈɪntrəstɪd] interessiert sein (an) **I 7**, 117
interesting [ˈɪntrəstɪŋ] interessant **I 2**, 28
international [ˌɪntəˈnæʃnl] international **I 7**, 112

Internet ['ɪntənet] Internet **I 2**, 30
interview ['ɪntəvju:] Interview **I 1**, 10
to **interview** ['ɪntəvju:] interviewen, befragen **I 3**, 46
into ['ɪntə] in ... hinein **I 4**, 63
I'm into ... ['ɪntə] ich stehe auf .../ ich bin begeistert von ... **I 2**, 34
to **invite** [ɪn'vaɪt] einladen **I 9**, 146
Irish folk [ˌaɪərɪʃ 'fəʊk] *Musikrichtung aus Irland* **I 5**, 77
+**irregular** [ɪ'regjələ] unregelmäßig **I 5**, 85
is [ɪz] ist **I 1**, 11
'**s** (*is*) [ɪz] ist **I 1**, 11
isn't (*is not*) ['ɪznt] ist nicht **I 1**, 14
+**island** ['aɪlənd] Insel **I 6**, 102
°**IT** (*Information Technology*) [ˌaɪ'ti: (ˌɪnfə'meɪʃn tek'nɒlədʒi)] Informatik **I 3**, 43
it [ɪt] es **I 1**, 12
+**Italian** [ɪ'tæliən] italienisch, Italienisch **I 8**, 134
+**item** ['aɪtəm] Gegenstand, Artikel **I 7**, 118

J

jacket ['dʒækɪt] Jacke, Jackett **I 4**, 62
January ['dʒænjuri] Januar **I 5**, 78
jazz [dʒæz] Jazz (*Musikrichtung*) **I 1**, 17
+**jeans** [dʒi:nz] Jeans **I 5**, 86
crown **jewels** [ˌkraʊn 'dʒu:əlz] Kronjuwelen **I 4**, 63
+**jewelry** (*AE*) ['dʒu:əlri] Schmuck **I 5**, 86
+**Jewish** ['dʒu:ɪʃ] jüdisch **I 5**, 86
job [dʒɒb] Job, Arbeit, Stelle **I 2**, 30
⟨**joke**⟩ [dʒəʊk] Scherz, Spaß, Witz **I 8**, 132
to **juggle** ['dʒʌgl] jonglieren **I 4**, 60
July [dʒʊ'laɪ] Juli **I 5**, 78
to **jump** [dʒʌmp] springen **I 4**, 64
jumper ['dʒʌmpə] Strickjacke **I 6**, 92
June [dʒu:n] Juni **I 5**, 78
junior choir [ˌdʒu:niə 'kwaɪə] Chor der unteren Klassenstufen **I 8**, 124
just [dʒʌst] gerade, eben **I 1**, 14

K

to **keep*** [ki:p] (be)halten **I 5**, 79
key word ['ki: wɜ:d] Schlüsselbegriff **I 3**, 42
keyboard ['ki:bɔ:d] elektronische Orgel, Keyboard **I 1**, 10
keyboarder ['ki:bɔ:də] Keyboardspieler(in) **I 1**, 12
kid [kɪd] Kind **I 3**, 46
+to **kill** [kɪl] töten, umbringen **I 6**, 102
kilometre [kɪ'lɒmɪtə] Kilometer **I 7**, 112
kind [kaɪnd] Art, Sorte **I 5**, 74
What kind (*of*) ...? Was für eine/welche Art ...? **I 2**, 34
king [kɪŋ] König **I 4**, 65
°drum **kit** ['drʌmkɪt] Schlagzeugausrüstung **I 1**, 13
kitchen ['kɪtʃɪn] Küche **I 2**, 29
knife, (*pl.*) -ves [naɪf] Messer **I 5**, 76
knight [naɪt] Ritter **I 6**, 98
°to **knock** [nɒk] klopfen **I 3**, 51
to **know*** [nəʊ] wissen, kennen **I 1**, 13
I don't know [aɪ ˌdəʊnt 'nəʊ] ich weiß (es) nicht **I 2**, 31
⟨to be **known**⟩ [nəʊn] bekannt sein **I 8**, 132
kung fu film [ˌkʊŋ 'fu: fɪlm] Kung-Fu-Film **I 3**, 44

L

lady ['leɪdi] Dame, Frau **I 6**, 93
cleaning lady ['kli:nɪŋ ˌleɪdi] Zugehfrau, Putzfrau **I 6**, 93
+ladies and gentlemen ['leɪdiz‿ən 'dʒentlmən] (meine) Damen und Herren **I 4**, 68
land [lænd] Land **I 7**, 110
+to **land** [lænd] landen **I 4**, 68
landscape ['lændskeɪp] Landschaft **I 9**, 141
+**language** ['læŋgwɪdʒ] Sprache **I 9**, 150
last [lɑ:st] letzte(r/s), der/die Letzte **I 3**, 43
late [leɪt] spät **I 4**, 60
later ['leɪtə] später **I 2**, 29
latest ['leɪtɪst] neueste(r/s), zuletzt erschienene(r/s) **I 5**, 74
+**Latin** ['lætɪn] lateinisch, Latein **I 4**, 68
to **laugh** [lɑ:f] lachen **I 5**, 79
+**lawn** [lɔ:n] Rasen **I 2**, 36
layout ['leɪaʊt] Gestaltung, Layout **I 9**, 148
to **learn*** [lɜ:n] lernen **I 3**, 53
+to learn by heart [ˌlɜ:n baɪ 'hɑ:t] auswendig lernen **I 5**, 85
learning tip ['lɜ:nɪŋ ˌtɪp] Lerntipp **I 3**, 50
leather ['leðə] Leder **I 5**, 77
+leather harness [ˌleðə 'hɑ:nɪs] Ledergeschirr, -gurtwerk **I 3**, 52
to **leave*** [li:v] weggehen, verlassen **I 4**, 60
left [left] links **I 1**, 15
legend ['ledʒənd] Legende **I 6**, 97
to **lend*** [lend] (ver)leihen **I 6**, 99
less [les] weniger **I 9**, 143
lesson ['lesn] Unterrichtsstunde **I 3**, 43
let's (*let us*) [lets] lass(t) uns **I 1**, 9
letter ['letə] Buchstabe; Brief **I 1**, 18
capital letter [ˌkæpɪtl 'letə] Großbuchstabe **I 9**, 148
library ['laɪbri] Bibliothek, Bücherei **I 6**, 95
to **lie*** [laɪ] liegen **I 3**, 51
life, (*pl.*) -ves [laɪf] Leben **I 6**, 103
lifebelt ['laɪfbelt] Rettungsgurt, Rettungsring **I 7**, 119
lifeboat ['laɪfbəʊt] Rettungsboot **I 7**, 110
lifeguard ['laɪfgɑ:d] Rettungsschwimmer(in) **I 7**, 119
lifejacket ['laɪfˌdʒækɪt] Schwimmweste **I 7**, 119
lifeline ['laɪflaɪn] Rettungsleine **I 7**, 119
lifetime ['laɪftaɪm] Lebenszeit, Leben **I 9**, 141
light [laɪt] Licht **I 8**, 130
traffic light ['træfɪk ˌlaɪt] Ampel **I 4**, 65
lighthouse ['laɪthaʊs] Leuchtturm **I 7**, 110
to **like** [laɪk] mögen, gerne haben **I 3**, 44
I'd (= *I would*) like [aɪd 'laɪk] ich hätte gerne **I 5**, 76
⟨to like best⟩ [ˌlaɪk 'best] am liebsten mögen **I 8**, 132
would you like to? [ˌwʊd ju: 'laɪk tə] möchtest du?/möchtet ihr/möchten Sie? **I 3**, 45
like [laɪk] (ebenso) wie **I 2**, 37
line [laɪn] Linie **I 9**, 147
fishing line ['fɪʃɪŋ ˌlaɪn] Angelschnur **I 7**, 112
+supply line [sə'plaɪ ˌlaɪn] Versorgungsleitung **I 7**, 118
list [lɪst] Liste **I 1**, 14
to **listen** ['lɪsn] zuhören **I 1**, 12

listening comprehension ['lɪsnɪŋ ˌkɒmprɪ'henʃn] Hörverstehen **I 1**, 16
little ['lɪtl] klein **I 1**, 14
to **live** [lɪv] wohnen, leben **I 3**, 44
live [laɪv] lebendig, direkt, live **I 9**, 141
living room ['lɪvɪŋ ˌrʊm] Wohnzimmer **I 2**, 29
ll. (= **lines**) [laɪnz] Zeilen **I 4**, 64
local ['ləʊkl] lokal, örtlich, Orts- **I 5**, 83
logo ['ləʊgəʊ] Logo, Emblem **I 6**, 93
long [lɒŋ] lang **I 1**, 12
to **look** [lʊk] schauen, betrachten **I 2**, 28
to look after [ˌlʊk‿'ɑ:ftə] schauen nach, sorgen für **I 2**, 32
to look forward (*to*) [ˌlʊk 'fɔ:wəd] sich freuen (auf) **I 9**, 148
to look sth. up [ˌlʊk‿'ʌp] etw nachschlagen **I 9**, 141
⁺**loose** [lu:s] lose, locker **I 7**, 118
to **lose*** [lu:z] verlieren **I 6**, 97
lost [lɒst] verloren **I 2**, 33
to be lost [lɒst] sich verlaufen **I 6**, 97
a **lot** [ə 'lɒt] viel, eine Menge **I 1**, 15
lots of ['lɒts‿əv] viele (von) **I 1**, 13
loud [laʊd] laut **I 4**, 64
love [lʌv] (in) Liebe; herzlichst **I 4**, 67
to **love** [lʌv] lieben, gern haben, mögen **I 3**, 48
lovely ['lʌvli] hübsch, schön **I 7**, 110
low [ləʊ] niedrig **I 8**, 129
luck [lʌk] Glück **I 6**, 93
lunch [lʌntʃ] Mittagessen **I 3**, 43

M

mad [mæd] verrückt, wahnsinnig **I 3**, 47
madam ['mædəm] gnädige Frau (*Anrede*) **I 8**, 131
magazine [ˌmægə'zi:n] Zeitschrift **I 1**, 10
major ['meɪdʒə] größter, Haupt- **I 9**, 141
to **make*** [meɪk] machen **I 1**, 12
to make so. do sth. ['meɪk ˌsʌmwʌn 'du: ˌsʌmθɪŋ] jmdn veranlassen etw zu tun **I 8**, 129
to make sure [ˌmeɪk 'ʃʊə] sicherstellen **I 3**, 47
to make the most of sth. [məʊst] das Beste aus etw machen **I 9**, 149
to make up [ˌmeɪk‿'ʌp] (sich) ausdenken, erfinden **I 8**, 130
ice cream **maker** [aɪs 'kri:m ˌmeɪkə] Eismaschine **I 8**, 133
shopping **mall** (*AE*) ['ʃɒpɪŋ ˌmɑ:l] Einkaufszentrum **I 9**, 147
man, (*pl.*) men [mæn/men] Mann / Männer **I 2**, 31
⁺to **manage** ['mænɪdʒ] bewältigen, schaffen **I 9**, 150
how **many?** ['haʊ ˌmeni] wie viele? **I 3**, 43
map [mæp] Stadtplan, Landkarte **I 4**, 63
mind map ['maɪnd mæp] *etwa:* Gedankennetz **I 1**, 20
Marathon ['mærəθn] Marathon **I 5**, 74
March [mɑ:tʃ] März **I 5**, 78
to **mark** [mɑ:k] markieren **I 9**, 142
marked [mɑ:kt] markiert **I 8**, 128
market ['mɑ:kɪt] Markt **I 4**, 64
marsh [mɑ:ʃ] Marschland, Sumpf **I 8**, 129
match [mætʃ] Streichholz **I 9**, 145
friendly match [ˌfrendli 'mætʃ] Freundschaftsspiel **I 8**, 124
to **match** [mætʃ] zuordnen **I 4**, 59
°**Maths** [mæθs] Mathe(matik) **I 3**, 43
May [meɪ] Mai **I 5**, 78
may [meɪ] dürfen, können **I 6**, 99
maybe ['meɪbi] vielleicht **I 4**, 63
me [mi:] mich **I 2**, 29
meal [mi:l] Mahlzeit, Essen **I 6**, 95
to **mean*** [mi:n] bedeuten; meinen **I 3**, 51
to **meet*** [mi:t] treffen, begegnen **I 5**, 79
meeting ['mi:tɪŋ] Treffen, Begegnung **I 7**, 110
member ['membə] Mitglied **I 9**, 142
memory ['memri] Gedächtnis **I 6**, 99
to **mend** [mend] ausbessern, reparieren **I 8**, 126
⁺**message** ['mesɪdʒ] Nachricht, Mitteilung **I 8**, 134
⁺**microphone** ['maɪkrəfəʊn] Mikrofon **I 1**, 19
⁺**mid-town** ['mɪdtaʊn] *mittlerer Teil der Insel Manhattan in New York* **I 5**, 86
⁺**middle** ['mɪdl] Mitte **I 8**, 134
mile [maɪl] Meile *(Längenmaß = 1,61 km)* **I 6**, 93
million ['mɪljən] Million **I 7**, 112
mind map ['maɪnd mæp] *etwa:* Gedankennetz **I 1**, 20
minibus ['mɪnɪbʌs] Kleinbus **I 1**, 10
⁺**minus** ['maɪnəs] minus **I 4**, 68
minute ['mɪnɪt] Minute **I 3**, 44
Miss [mɪs] Fräulein (*Anrede*) **I 9**, 148
to **miss** [mɪs] verpassen, versäumen **I 6**, 97
mistake [mɪ'steɪk] Fehler **I 5**, 79
⁺**mobile home** [ˌməʊbaɪl 'həʊm] Wohnmobil **I 7**, 118
mobile phone [ˌməʊbaɪl 'fəʊn] Mobiltelefon, Handy **I 4**, 63
model ['mɒdl] Modell **I 5**, 79
modem ['məʊdem] Modem **I 2**, 30
at the **moment** ['məʊmənt] im Moment, zur Zeit **I 4**, 67
Monday ['mʌndeɪ] Montag **I 3**, 43
money ['mʌni] Geld **I 3**, 46
pocket money ['pɒkɪt ˌmʌni] Taschengeld **I 3**, 47
⁺**moon** [mu:n] Mond **I 2**, 36
⁺**moped** ['məʊped] Moped, Kleinkraftrad **I 3**, 52
more [mɔ:] mehr **I 1**, 13
morning ['mɔ:nɪŋ] Morgen, Vormittag **I 3**, 43
most (*of*) ['məʊst‿əv] meiste(r/s) **I 3**, 46
to make the most of sth. [məʊst] das Beste aus etw machen **I 9**, 149
mother ['mʌðə] Mutter **I 4**, 61
motorbike ['məʊtəˌbaɪk] Motorrad **I 4**, 59
motorhome ['məʊtəˌhəʊm] Wohnmobil **I 9**, 141
motorway café ['məʊtəweɪ ˌkæfeɪ] Cafeteria auf der Autobahn **I 9**, 145
⁺**motto** ['mɒtəʊ] Motto, Leitsatz **I 4**, 68
⁺**mountain** ['maʊntɪn] Berg **I 7**, 118
mountain bike ['maʊntɪn ˌbaɪk] Geländefahrrad, Mountainbike **I 1**, 10
mouse [maʊs] Maus **I 9**, 145
°**mouth** [maʊθ] Mund **I 3**, 51
to **move** [mu:v] (sich) bewegen; umziehen **I 3**, 45
movie (*AE*) ['mu:vi] Film **I 6**, 101
Mr ['mɪstə] Herr (*Anrede*) **I 1**, 12
Mrs ['mɪsɪz] Frau (*Anrede für verheiratete Frauen*) **I 2**, 28
Ms [mɪz/məz] Frau (*Anrede*) **I 9**, 148
much [mʌtʃ] viel **I 3**, 44
how much? ['haʊ ˌmʌtʃ] wie viel? **I 3**, 53
mum [mʌm] Mama, Mutti **I 2**, 29
museum [mju:'zi:əm] Museum **I 7**, 110
music ['mju:zɪk] Musik **I 1**, 17
classical music ['klæsɪkl 'mju:zɪk] klassische Musik **I 1**, 17

pop music ['pɒp ˌmju:zɪk] Popmusik **I 2**, 30
rock music ['rɒk ˌmju:zɪk] Rockmusik **I 3**, 45
musical ['mju:zɪkl] Musical **I 4**, 59
musician [mju:'zɪʃn] Musiker(in) **I 5**, 78
must [mʌst] müssen **I 3**, 45
my [maɪ] mein/meine **I 1**, 11
mystery ['mɪstri] Geheimnis, Mysterium **I 8**, 131

N

nail [neɪl] Nagel **I 4**, 60
name [neɪm] Name **I 1**, 11
+**nasty** ['nɑ:sti] scheußlich, abscheulich **I 9**, 151
nationality [ˌnæʃn'æləti] Nationalität **I 9**, 142
+**native** ['neɪtɪv] Eingeborene(r), Ureinwohner(in) **I 6**, 102
natural ['nætʃrl] natürlich **I 7**, 108
navigation [ˌnævɪ'geɪʃn] Navigation, Schiffsverkehr **I 7**, 114
near [nɪə] in der Nähe, nah **I 5**, 74
+**nearer** ['nɪərə] näher **I 5**, 85
nearly ['nɪəli] fast, beinahe **I 3**, 51
necessary ['nesəsri] nötig, notwendig **I 9**, 141
to **need** [ni:d] brauchen **I 6**, 94
needn't ['ni:dnt] nicht brauchen **I 9**, 140
negative ['negətɪv] negativ, verneinend **I 5**, 77
neither ['naɪðə] keine(r) (von beiden), auch nicht **I 9**, 147
neither ... nor ['naɪðə...'nɔ:] weder ... noch **I 9**, 147
net [net] Netz **I 7**, 119
never ['nevə] nie(mals) **I 3**, 44
new [nju:] neu **I 2**, 26
news (*sing.*) [nju:z] Nachrichten, Neuigkeit(en) **I 7**, 108
newspaper ['nju:speɪpə] Zeitung **I 4**, 61
next [nekst] nächste(r/s), der/die Nächste **I 3**, 44
+**next to** ['nekst tu:] neben, in der Nähe von **I 2**, 36
nice [naɪs] hübsch, nett **I 2**, 26
night [naɪt] Nacht **I 3**, 46
night club ['naɪt klʌb] Nachtclub **I 6**, 93
no [nəʊ] nein; kein/keine **I 1**, 11
no one ['nəʊwʌn] niemand **I 8**, 129
no way (*coll.*) [ˌnəʊ 'weɪ] auf keinen Fall, keineswegs **I 8**, 135
nobody ['nəʊbədi] niemand **I 3**, 46
+**noise** [nɔɪz] Geräusch, Lärm **I 3**, 52
noisy [nɔɪzi] laut, geräuschvoll **I 6**, 92
nor [nɔ:] noch, (und) auch nicht **I 9**, 147
neither ... nor ['naɪðə...'nɔ:] weder ... noch **I 9**, 147
normal ['nɔ:ml] normal **I 6**, 97
north [nɔ:θ] Norden, nördlich **I 2**, 26
nose [nəʊz] Nase **I 6**, 95
not [nɒt] nicht **I 1**, 11
(*not*) after all [ˌɑ:ftə‿'ɔ:l] doch (nicht) **I 2**, 32
not ... at all [ˌnɒt‿ə'tɔ:l] überhaupt nicht **I 8**, 129
not ... yet [jet] noch nicht **I 5**, 79
to **note** (*down*) [ˌnəʊt'daʊn] notieren, (auf)schreiben **I 3**, 42
vocabulary **notebook** [vəʊˌkæbjəlri 'nəʊtbʊk] Vokabelheft **I 4**, 65
nothing ['nʌθɪŋ] nichts **I 4**, 59
notice board ['nəʊtɪs ˌbɔ:d] schwarzes Brett, Anschlagtafel **I 8**, 125
to take notice [ˌteɪk 'nəʊtɪs] beachten, Notiz nehmen (von) **I 8**, 129

November [nəʊ'vembə] November **I 5**, 78
now [naʊ] nun, jetzt **I 2**, 37
now and then [ˌnaʊ‿n‿'ðen] ab und zu **I 9**, 143
nowhere ['nəʊweə] nirgends, nirgendwo **I 8**, 131
number (*No.*) ['nʌmbə] Zahl, Nummer (Nr.) **I 1**, 12

O

10 **o'clock** [ə'klɒk] 10 Uhr **I 3**, 43
+to **obey** [ə'beɪ] gehorchen **I 3**, 52
October [ɒk'təʊbə] Oktober **I 5**, 78
odd one out [ˌɒd wʌn‿'aʊt] das Nichtdazupassende scheidet aus **I 1**, 15
of [ɒv/əv] von/vom **I 2**, 31
of course [əv 'kɔ:s] natürlich, selbstverständlich **I 2**, 29
off [ɒf] weg, fort **I 4**, 60
to show off [ˌʃəʊ‿'ɒf] angeben **I 8**, 131
to take off [ˌteɪk‿'ɒf] starten, abheben **I 5**, 83
office ['ɒfɪs] Arbeitszimmer, Büro **I 2**, 29
official [ə'fɪʃl] offiziell **I 4**, 58
often ['ɒfn] oft, öfters **I 3**, 44
Oh, dear! [əʊ 'dɪə] Oh je! **I 2**, 30
oil [ɔɪl] Öl **I 7**, 108
oil slick ['ɔɪl slɪk] Ölteppich **I 7**, 108
OK [əʊ'keɪ] in Ordnung, okay **I 1**, 9
old [əʊld] alt **I 2**, 26
older ['əʊldə] älter(e/r/s) **I 6**, 101
on [ɒn] auf, an/am **I 1**, 14
to go on [ˌgəʊ‿'ɒn] weitermachen, fortsetzen **I 1**, 12
to put on [ˌpʊt‿'ɒn] herausbringen, auf die Bühne bringen **I 8**, 125
one [wʌn] eins **I 1**, 12
the only ones [wʌnz] die Einzigen **I 4**, 64
only ['əʊnli] nur **I 3**, 44
to **open** ['əʊpn] öffnen, aufmachen **I 2**, 31
open ['əʊpn] offen **I 1**, 10
opening ['əʊpnɪŋ] Eröffnung, Beginn **I 8**, 129
opposite ['ɒpəzɪt] Gegenteil; gegenüber **I 3**, 51
or [ɔ:] oder **I 1**, 10
senior **orchestra** [ˌsi:niə‿'ɔ:kɪstrə] Orchester der oberen Klassenstufen **I 8**, 124
+**order** ['ɔ:də] Reihenfolge **I 6**, 102
organization [ˌɔ:gnaɪ'zeɪʃn] Organisation, Veranstalter **I 9**, 148
to **organize** ['ɔ:gnaɪz] organisieren, durchführen **I 9**, 140
other ['ʌðə] andere(r/s) **I 1**, 15
ouch! [aʊtʃ] au!, autsch! **I 4**, 60
our ['aʊə] unser **I 1**, 14
ours ['aʊəz] der/die/das Unsere **I 8**, 129
out (*of*) [aʊt] hinaus, heraus **I 4**, 64
outside [ˌaʊt'saɪd] draußen **I 6**, 92
over [əʊvə] hinüber **I 3**, 47
over there [ˌəʊvə 'ðeə] da drüben **I 2**, 31
to push so. over [ˌpʊʃ‿'əʊvə] jmdn umstoßen **I 3**, 46
overboard ['əʊvəbɔ:d] über Bord **I 7**, 112
to **overlook** [ˌəʊvə'lʊk] überschauen; mit Blick über/auf **I 9**, 140
own [əʊn] eigene(r/s) **I 6**, 98
owner ['əʊnə] Eigentümer(in), Besitzer(in) **I 2**, 32

P

p (*pence, pl. of penny*) [pens] *britische Währung (100 pence = £1)* **I 5**, 76
to **pack** [pæk] packen **I 5**, 83
page [peɪdʒ] Seite **I 5**, 78
paint [peɪnt] Farbe **I 6**, 92
to **paint** [peɪnt] anmalen, streichen **I 6**, 92
+**painting** ['peɪntɪŋ] Gemälde, Bild **I 5**, 86
pair [peə] Paar **I 1**, 18
+to **panic** ['pænɪk] in Panik geraten **I 9**, 150
parents ['peərnts] Eltern **I 3**, 44
car **park** ['kɑː pɑːk] Parkplatz **I 1**, 8
part [pɑːt] Teil **I 2**, 31
  to take part (in) [ˌteɪk 'pɑːt] teilnehmen (an) **I 8**, 124
partner ['pɑːtnə] Partner(in) **I 4**, 61
party ['pɑːti] Party, Fest **I 4**, 62
past [pɑːst] nach **I 3**, 43; +vorbei (an) **I 5**, 86
+**pastrami** [pæs'trɑːmi] geräuchertes Rindfleisch **I 5**, 86
path [pɑːθ] Weg, Pfad **I 7**, 110
to **pay*** [peɪ] (be)zahlen **I 8**, 126
  +to pay attention [ˌpeɪ‿ə'tenʃn] aufmerksam sein, achtsam sein **I 3**, 52
°**PE** (*Physical Education*) [ˌpiː'iː: ('fɪzɪkl ˌedʒʊ'keɪʃn)] Sport, Turnen **I 3**, 43
pen [pen] Füller, Füllfederhalter **I 6**, 99
pencil ['pensl] Bleistift **I 6**, 99
  pencil case ['pensl ˌkeɪs] Federmäppchen **I 6**, 99
  pencil sharpener ['pensl ˌʃɑːpnə] Bleistiftspitzer **I 6**, 99
penfriend ['penfrend] Brieffreund(in) **I 9**, 149
people ['piːpl] Leute, Menschen **I 2**, 31
percent [pə'sent] Prozent **I 7**, 112
perfect ['pɜːfɪkt] perfekt, vollkommen **I 6**, 96
perhaps [pə'hæps] vielleicht **I 2**, 32
person ['pɜːsn] Person **I 3**, 49
+**personal** ['pɜːsnl] persönlich **I 9**, 151
petrol station ['petrl ˌsteɪʃn] Tankstelle **I 4**, 65
phew! [fjuː] puh! **I 4**, 60
phone [fəʊn] Telefon **I 2**, 37
  (phone) call [('fəʊn) kɔːl] Anruf **I 3**, 45
to **phone** [fəʊn] telefonieren, anrufen **I 2**, 33
photo ['fəʊtəʊ] Foto **I 1**, 14
phrase [freɪz] Phrase, kurzer Satz **I 5**, 76
+**piano** [pi'ænəʊ] Klavier, Piano **I 1**, 19
piccolo ['pɪkələʊ] Piccolo(-flöte) **I 1**, 17
to **pick** (*out*) [ˌpɪk‿'aʊt] (heraus)picken, (heraus)suchen **I 5**, 83
picnic ['pɪknɪk] Picknick **I 4**, 59
picture ['pɪktʃə] Bild **I 1**, 12
piece [piːs] Stück, Teil **I 7**, 112
pilot ['paɪlət] Pilot(in) **I 1**, 10
pink [pɪŋk] pink **I 6**, 93
pioneer [ˌpaɪə'nɪə] Pionier **I 9**, 145
pirate ['paɪərət] Pirat(in) **I 8**, 126
place [pleɪs] Ort, Platz **I 2**, 30
plain [pleɪn] schlicht, einfach **I 6**, 94
plan [plæn] Plan **I 5**, 78
to **plan** [plæn] planen, vorhaben **I 3**, 47
plane [pleɪn] Flugzeug **I 4**, 59
+**planet** ['plænɪt] Planet **I 2**, 36
plastic ['plæstɪk] Plastik **I 7**, 112
plate [pleɪt] Teller **I 9**, 146
play [pleɪ] Theaterstück **I 4**, 59
  role play ['rəʊl pleɪ] Rollenspiel **I 2**, 33
to **play** [pleɪ] spielen **I 1**, 17
player ['pleɪə] Spieler(in) **I 1**, 11
please [pliːz] bitte **I 1**, 12
pm [ˌpiː'em] nachmittags *(12-24 Uhr)* **I 6**, 97
pocket ['pɒkət] (Hosen-/Jacken-)Tasche **I 4**, 64
  pocket money ['pɒkɪt ˌmʌni] Taschengeld **I 3**, 47
poem ['pəʊɪm] Gedicht **I 8**, 127
⟨**poetry**⟩ ['pəʊɪtri] Dichtung, Poesie, Gedichte **I 8**, 132
point [pɔɪnt] Punkt **I 6**, 101
police [pə'liːs] Polizei **I 4**, 64
polite [pə'laɪt] höflich **I 9**, 148
polo shirt ['pəʊləʊ ˌʃɜːt] Polohemd **I 6**, 93
swimming **pool** ['swɪmɪŋ ˌpuːl] Swimmingpool **I 9**, 140
pop music ['pɒp ˌmjuːzɪk] Popmusik **I 2**, 30
popular ['pɒpjələ] beliebt, populär **I 9**, 148
position [pə'zɪʃn] Position **I 9**, 147
positive ['pɒzətɪv] positiv, bejahend **I 5**, 77
possible ['pɒsəbl] möglich **I 7**, 108
postcard ['pəʊstkɑːd] Postkarte **I 4**, 61
poster ['pəʊstə] Poster, Plakat **I 8**, 126
£ (pound sterling) [paʊnd] Pfund *(britische Währung)* **I 5**, 76
practical ['præktɪkl] praktisch **I 3**, 46
to **practise** ['præktɪs] üben, proben **I 5**, 78
+to be **prepared** [prɪ'peəd] vorbereitet sein **I 7**, 118
present ['preznt] Geschenk **I 5**, 79
to **pretend** (*to*) [prɪ'tend] vorgeben (zu), vortäuschen **I 8**, 129
+**pretty** ['prɪti] hübsch, nett **I 6**, 102
price [praɪs] Preis **I 5**, 79
to **print** (*out*) [prɪnt] (aus)drucken **I 8**, 128
printer ['prɪntə] Drucker **I 8**, 126
prize [praɪz] Preis, Gewinn **I 8**, 124
the **pros and cons** [ˌprəʊz‿n‿'kɒnz] das Für und Wider, Pro und Contra **I 7**, 116
problem ['prɒbləm] Problem **I 2**, 30
to **produce** [prə'djuːs] produzieren, herstellen **I 7**, 112
+**program** ['prəʊgræm] (Computer-) Programm **I 5**, 85
project ['prɒdʒekt] Projekt **I 6**, 96
+to be **proud** (*of*) [praʊd] stolz sein (auf) **I 7**, 117
pub [pʌb] Kneipe, Pub, Lokal **I 4**, 65
to **pull** [pʊl] ziehen **I 4**, 64
punctuation [ˌpʌŋktʃu'eɪʃn] Zeichensetzung, Interpunktion **I 9**, 149
pupil ['pjuːpl] Schüler(in) **I 3**, 45
purse [pɜːs] Portmonee, Geldbörse **I 6**, 97
to **push so. over** [ˌpʊʃ‿'əʊvə] jmdn umstoßen **I 3**, 46
to **put*** [pʊt] setzen, stellen, legen **I 2**, 30
  to put on [ˌpʊt‿'ɒn] herausbringen, auf die Bühne bringen **I 8**, 125
  to put up [ˌpʊt‿'ʌp] aufgeben, aufhängen **I 2**, 32

Q

quarter (*to/past*) ['kwɔːtə] Viertel (vor/nach) **I 3**, 43
queen [kwiːn] Königin **I 4**, 65
question ['kwestʃən] Frage **I 1**, 14
quick [kwɪk] schnell, rasch **I 4**, 59
quiet ['kwaɪət] ruhig **I 6**, 92
quite [kwaɪt] ziemlich **I 5**, 76
quiz [kwɪz] Fragespiel, Quiz **I 1**, 13

R

radio ['reɪdiəʊ] Radio **I 7**, 109
+whitewater **rafting** [ˌwaɪtwɔ:tə 'rɑ:ftɪŋ] Wildwasserfahren **I 9**, 150
railway ['reɪlweɪ] Eisenbahn **I 9**, 141
to **rain** ['reɪn] regnen **I 4**, 67
to rain cats and dogs ['reɪn ˌkæts‿n‿'dɒgz] heftig regnen, schütten, gießen **I 9**, 145
+**rapids** ['ræpɪdz] Stromschnellen **I 9**, 150
to **reach** [ri:tʃ] erreichen, gelangen **I 7**, 108
to **react** [ri'ækt] reagieren **I 9**, 140
to **read*** [ri:d] lesen **I 4**, 61
ready ['redi] fertig, bereit (sein) **I 5**, 83
real [rɪəl] echt, wirklich **I 5**, 79
really ['rɪəli] wirklich **I 3**, 45
+**reason** ['ri:zn] Grund, Ursache **I 7**, 117
record ['rekɔ:d] Schallplatte **I 5**, 74
to **record** [rɪ'kɔ:d] aufzeichnen, aufnehmen **I 9**, 149
recorder [rɪ'kɔ:də] (Video-/Kassetten-)Rekorder **I 5**, 74
recording [rɪ'kɔ:dɪŋ] Aufzeichnung, (Ton-)Aufnahme **I 3**, 46
red [red] rot **I 2**, 26
+**regular** ['regjələ] regelmäßig **I 5**, 85
to **rehearse** [rɪ'hɜ:s] proben, üben **I 6**, 95
relative ['relətɪv] Verwandte(r) **I 9**, 147
to **relax** [rɪ'læks] ausruhen, sich erholen **I 9**, 140
to **remember** [rɪ'membə] sich erinnern (an), denken (an) **I 6**, 97
car **rental** ['kɑ: ˌrentl] Autovermietung **I 1**, 9
rental ['rentl] Miet- **I 9**, 141
to **repeat** [rɪ'pi:t] wiederholen **I 6**, 99
report [rɪ'pɔ:t] Bericht **I 6**, 100
to **report** [rɪ'pɔ:t] berichten **I 7**, 108
reporter [rɪ'pɔ:tə] Reporter(in), Journalist(in) **I 1**, 14
rescue ['reskju:] Rettung **I 7**, 110
to **rescue** ['reskju:] retten **I 7**, 108
to be **rescued** ['reskju:d] gerettet werden **I 7**, 114
+**reservation** [ˌrezə'veɪʃn] Reservat **I 8**, 134
+**resident** ['rezɪdnt] Bewohner(in), Einwohner(in) **I 7**, 118
to be **responsible** [rɪ'spɒnsəbl] verantwortlich sein **I 7**, 112
rest [rest] Rast, Pause **I 9**, 146
restaurant ['restrɔ:ŋ] Restaurant **I 2**, 33
result [rɪ'zʌlt] Ergebnis **I 7**, 112
+in **return** [ɪn rɪ'tɜ:n] dafür **I 5**, 86
to **ride*** [raɪd] fahren, reiten **I 6**, 103
right [raɪt] rechts; richtig **I 1**, 15
all right [ɔ:l 'raɪt] in Ordnung **I 3**, 45
ring [rɪŋ] Ring **I 7**, 119
to **ring* so. up** [ˌrɪŋ‿'ʌp] jmdn anrufen **I 3**, 46
river ['rɪvə] Fluss **I 4**, 63
road [rəʊd] Straße **I 3**, 47
bank **robber** ['bæŋk ˌrɒbə] Bankräuber(in) **I 4**, 64
rock [rɒk] Fels **I 7**, 111
rock music ['rɒk‿ˌmju:zɪk] Rockmusik **I 3**, 45
rocky ['rɒki] felsig, steinig **I 7**, 108
role [rəʊl] Rolle **I 2**, 33
role play ['rəʊl pleɪ] Rollenspiel **I 2**, 33
roof [ru:f] Dach **I 2**, 26
room [rʊm] Zimmer **I 2**, 28
+dining room ['daɪnɪŋ ˌrʊm] Esszimmer **I 2**, 36
living room ['lɪvɪŋ ˌrʊm] Wohnzimmer **I 2**, 29
rope [rəʊp] Seil, Tau **I 7**, 119
to **rot** [rɒt] verrotten, (ver)faulen **I 7**, 112
to come* **round** [ˌkʌm 'raʊnd] vorbeikommen, herüberkommen **I 3**, 44
route [ru:t] Route, Strecke **I 9**, 141
row [rəʊ] Reihe **I 4**, 67
to **rub** [rʌb] reiben **I 9**, 145
rubber ['rʌbə] Radiergummi **I 6**, 99
rubbish ['rʌbɪʃ] Abfall, Müll **I 7**, 110
rule [ru:l] Regel **I 2**, 28
ruler [ru:lə] Lineal **I 6**, 99
to **run*** [rʌn] rennen, laufen **I 3**, 51

S

sad [sæd] traurig **I 6**, 98
safe [seɪf] sicher **I 8**, 129
safety ['seɪfti] Sicherheit **I 7**, 110
to **sail** [seɪl] segeln **I 8**, 124
+**sailing trip** ['seɪlɪŋ ˌtrɪp] Segeltörn **I 8**, 134
sale [seɪl] Verkauf **I 8**, 124
salt [sɔ:lt] Salz **I 5**, 77
same [seɪm] gleich, dasselbe **I 3**, 43
sand [sænd] Sand **I 8**, 130
+**sandwich** ['sænwɪdʒ] Sandwich, belegtes Brot **I 5**, 86
satellite ['sætlaɪt] Satellit **I 9**, 141
Saturday ['sætədeɪ] Samstag **I 3**, 43
sausage ['sɒsɪdʒ] Würstchen **I 9**, 146
to **save** [seɪv] sichern, abspeichern **I 1**, 11; +retten **I 6**, 102
saxophone ['sæksəfəʊn] Saxophon **I 1**, 10
to **say*** [seɪ] sagen, reden **I 1**, 12
+to be **scared** ['skeəd] Angst haben, verschreckt sein **I 6**, 102
scarf, (*pl.*) -ves [skɑ:f] Schal, Halstuch **I 5**, 74
scene [si:n] Szene **I 5**, 79
scenery ['si:nəri] Bühnenbild, Kulisse **I 8**, 124
school [sku:l] Schule **I 1**, 12
schoolfriend ['sku:lfrend] Schulfreund(in) **I 8**, 129
schoolwatch ['sku:lwɒtʃ] Schulaufsicht, Schulwärter(in), **I 7**, 112
°**Science** ['saɪəns] (Natur-)Wissenschaften **I 3**, 43
scientist ['saɪəntɪst] Wissenschaftler(in) **I 8**, 129
scissors ['sɪzəz] Schere **I 6**, 99
Scottish ['skɒtɪʃ] schottisch **I 9**, 140
scrapbook ['skræpbʊk] Sammelalbum **I 7**, 113
script [skrɪpt] Drehbuch, Textbuch **I 8**, 127
sea [si:] Meer, (die) See **I 3**, 45
seabird ['si:bɜ:d] Seevogel **I 7**, 108
season ['si:zn] Jahreszeit **I 8**, 124
+**second-hand** ['sekndˌhænd] gebraucht, aus zweiter Hand **I 5**, 86
secret ['si:krət] geheim, verborgen **I 8**, 129
to **see*** [si:] sehen, erblicken **I 1**, 16
to **seem** [si:m] (er)scheinen **I 3**, 44
self-catering [ˌself'keɪtrɪŋ] Selbstversorgung **I 9**, 141
to **sell*** [sel] verkaufen **I 4**, 59
+**Seminole Indian** ['semɪnəʊl ˌɪndiən] *Angehörige(r) eines indianischen Stamms* **I 8**, 134
to **send*** [send] schicken, senden **I 2**, 30
senior orchestra [ˌsi:niə‿'ɔ:kɪstrə] Orchester der oberen Klassenstufen **I 8**, 124
sentence ['sentns] Satz **I 1**, 12

separate ['seprət] getrennt, separat I 9, 142
September [sep'tembə] September I 5, 78
servant ['sɜ:vnt] Diener(in) I 8, 129
+**service** ['sɜ:rvɪs] Dienst(leistung), Service I 7, 118
to **set*** (*up*) [ˌset‿'ʌp] (auf)stellen, (auf)bauen I 5, 83
sewage ['su:ɪdʒ] Abwasser I 7, 114
shape [ʃeɪp] Gestalt, (äußere) Form I 6, 97
pencil **sharpener** ['pensl ˌʃɑ:pnə] Bleistiftspitzer I 6, 99
she [ʃi:] sie (*sing.*) I 1, 12
sheep, (*pl.*) sheep [ʃi:p] Schaf(e) I 9, 146
sheepdog ['ʃi:pdɒg] Schäferhund, Hirtenhund I 9, 146
+**shelf**, (*pl.*) -ves [ʃelf] Regal(brett) I 5, 85
+**shepherd** ['ʃepəd] Schäferhund; Schäfer I 3, 52
to work **shift** [ˌwɜ:k 'ʃɪft] Schicht arbeiten, Schichtdienst machen I 3, 46
ship [ʃɪp] Schiff I 7, 108
polo **shirt** ['pəʊləʊ ˌʃɜ:t] Polohemd I 6, 93
shock [ʃɒk] Schreck, Schock I 5, 80
shoe [ʃu:] Schuh I 4, 60
shop [ʃɒp] Geschäft, Laden I 2, 29
video shop ['vɪdiəʊ ˌʃɒp] Videothek, Videoladen I 4, 65
+**shoplifter** ['ʃɒpˌlɪftə] Ladendieb(in) I 5, 85
shopping ['ʃɒpɪŋ] Einkaufen I 4, 67
shopping mall (*AE*) ['ʃɒpɪŋ ˌmɑ:l] Einkaufszentrum I 9, 147
to go shopping [ˌgəʊ 'ʃɒpɪŋ] Einkaufen gehen I 5, 79
short-cut ['ʃɔ:tkʌt] Abkürzung I 6, 97
short [ʃɔ:t] kurz I 1, 12
shorts [ʃɔ:ts] kurze Hose, Shorts I 6, 94
should [ʃʊd/ʃəd] sollen I 6, 97
shoulder ['ʃəʊldə] Schulter I 4, 60
to **shout** [ʃaʊt] rufen I 6, 97
show [ʃəʊ] Show I 6, 96
to **show*** [ʃəʊ] zeigen I 5, 79
to show off [ˌʃəʊ‿'ɒf] angeben I 8, 131
to **shut*** [ʃʌt] schließen I 3, 45
city **shuttle** ['sɪti ˌʃʌtl] Pendelverkehr zur Innenstadt I 1, 9
sick [sɪk] krank, übel I 3, 46
side [saɪd] Seite I 6, 98
sight [saɪt] Sehenswürdigkeit I 4, 58
sightseeing ['saɪtˌsi:ɪŋ] Besichtigung von Sehenswürdigkeiten I 4, 58
to **sign** [saɪn] unterzeichnen, unterschreiben I 9, 148
signal ['sɪgnl] Signal I 6, 95
signpost ['saɪnpəʊst] Wegweiser I 6, 97
silly ['sɪli] dumm, kindisch I 2, 29
silly ['sɪli] Dumme(r), Dummkopf I 8, 129
silver ['sɪlvə] Silber I 5, 76
simple ['sɪmpl] einfach, gewöhnlich I 8, 126
since [sɪns] seit I 8, 128
to **sing** [sɪŋ] singen I 3, 44
singer ['sɪŋə] Sänger(in) I 1, 12
sir [sɜ:] mein Herr (*Anrede*) I 5, 80
sister ['sɪstə] Schwester I 2, 30
baby sister [ˌbeɪbi 'sɪstə] (ganz) kleine Schwester I 3, 46
to **sit*** [sɪt] sitzen I 4, 60
size [saɪz] Größe I 5, 76
skirt [skɜ:t] Rock I 6, 94
+**sky** [skaɪ] Himmel I 2, 36
+**skyline** ['skaɪlaɪn] (Stadt-)Silhouette, Skyline I 4, 68
to **sleep*** [sli:p] schlafen I 4, 61
sleeping bag ['sli:pɪŋ ˌbæg] Schlafsack I 9, 145
oil **slick** ['ɔɪl slɪk] Ölteppich I 7, 108
slide [slaɪd] Dia(positiv) I 7, 110
slogan ['sləʊgən] Slogan, Wahl-/Werbespruch I 3, 50
+**slow** [sləʊ] langsam I 9, 150
small [smɔ:l] klein I 2, 26
+**smell** [smel] Geruch I 5, 86
smile [smaɪl] Lächeln I 1, 14
to **smile** [smaɪl] lächeln I 4, 60
to **smoke** [sməʊk] rauchen I 3, 44
smoking ['sməʊkɪŋ] (das) Rauchen I 3, 46
to **smuggle** ['smʌgl] schmuggeln I 8, 127
smuggler ['smʌglə] Schmuggler(in) I 8, 126
snack [snæk] Imbiss I 1, 9
snow [snəʊ] Schnee I 6, 97
to **snow** [snəʊ] schneien I 6, 92
so [səʊ] so (sehr); so, also I 2, 32
sock [sɒk] Socke I 6, 93
sofa ['səʊfə] Sofa, Couch I 3, 51
software ['sɒftweə] Software I 5, 74
some [sʌm] einige I 2, 32
somebody ['sʌmbədi] jemand I 8, 125
someone ['sʌmwʌn] jemand I 6, 94
+**something** ['sʌmθɪŋ] etwas I 5, 85
sometimes ['sʌmtaɪmz] manchmal I 3, 44
somewhere ['sʌmweə] irgendwo I 8, 131
⟨**song**⟩ [sɒŋ] Lied, Song I 1, 16
soon [su:n] bald, rasch I 9, 148
sorry ['sɒri] (es) tut mir Leid I 2, 31
sound [saʊnd] Klang, Ton I 2, 31
sound check ['saʊn(d) tʃek] Klang-, Tonkontrolle I 1, 12
to **sound** [saʊnd] klingen I 8, 125
south [saʊθ] südlich, Süden I 7, 115
+**southernmost** ['sʌðənməʊst] südlichste(r/s) I 8, 134
souvenir [ˌsu:vn'ɪə] Souvenir, Andenken I 5, 79
+**spare battery** [ˌspeə 'bætri] Ersatzbatterie I 7, 118
to **speak*** [spi:k] sprechen I 3, 51
°**speaker** ['spi:kə] Lautsprecher I 1, 13
special ['speʃl] besondere(r/s) I 9, 148
+**speed** [spi:d] Geschwindigkeit I 7, 118
to **spell** [spel] buchstabieren I 6, 101
to **spend*** [spend] verbrauchen, ausgeben; verbringen I 3, 46
to **spill*** [spɪl] auslaufen, verschütten I 7, 108
to **split* up** [ˌsplɪt‿'ʌp] sich (voneinander) trennen I 3, 46
sponge [spʌndʒ] Schwamm I 6, 99
sport [spɔ:t] Sport I 3, 47
sports centre ['spɔ:ts ˌsentə] Sportzentrum, Sportanlage I 4, 65
sportsfield ['spɔ:tsfi:ld] Sportplatz I 6, 95
to **spot** [spɒt] entdecken I 6, 98
spring [sprɪŋ] Frühling I 8, 124
°**spy**, (*pl.*) spies [spaɪ] Spion(in), Spitzel I 4, 62
staffroom ['stɑ:frʊm] Lehrerzimmer I 6, 95
stage [steɪdʒ] Bühne I 8, 124
+**stairs pl.** [steəz] Treppe I 2, 36
stall [stɔ:l] (Verkauf-)Stand I 5, 76
to **stand*** [stænd] stehen I 4, 60
star [stɑ:] Stern I 9, 149
to **start** [stɑ:t] anfangen, beginnen I 2, 27
state [steɪt] Staat I 9, 142
station ['steɪʃn] Haltestelle, Station I 4, 58
petrol station ['petrl ˌsteɪʃn] Tankstelle I 4, 65

to **stay** [steɪ] bleiben **I 2**, 30
step [step] Schritt, Stufe, Abschnitt **I 1**, 11
stepfather ['stepfɑːðe] Stiefvater **I 8**, 129
stick [stɪk] Stock **I 9**, 145
to **stick*** [stɪk] kleben **I 6**, 101
sticker ['stɪkə] Sticker, Aufkleber **I 7**, 113
still [stɪl] noch **I 3**, 45
stone [stəʊn] Stein **I 8**, 129
stop [stɒp] Halt, Stopp **I 4**, 63
bus stop ['bʌs stɒp] Bushaltestelle **I 1**, 8
to **stop** [stɒp] anhalten, stoppen **I 4**, 60
store ['stɔː] (großes) Geschäft, Laden **I 5**, 75
department store [dɪ'pɑːtmənt ˌstɔː] Kaufhaus **I 4**, 59
storm [stɔːm] Sturm **I 8**, 129
+**stormy** ['stɔːmi] stürmisch **I 7**, 118
story ['stɔːri] Geschichte **I 2**, 31
straight ['streɪt] geradeaus **I 4**, 65
strange [streɪndʒ] merkwürdig, sonderbar **I 8**, 125
straw [strɔː] Stroh **I 2**, 31
to **stray** [streɪ] herumschweifen, herumstreunen **I 8**, 129
street [striːt] Straße **I 4**, 63
stress [stres] Betonung **I 9**, 142
to **stress** [stres] betonen **I 9**, 142
string [strɪŋ] Faden; Saite **I 5**, 79
strip [strɪp] Streifen **I 9**, 149
+**strong** [strɒŋ] streng, rauh **I 4**, 68
stronger ['strɒŋgə] stärker **I 1**, 15
stupid ['stjuːpɪd] dumm, dämlich **I 6**, 96
style [staɪl] Stil **I 9**, 148
subject ['sʌbdʒɪkt] (Unterrichts-)Fach; Thema **I 3**, 43
+**subway** *(AE)* ['sʌbweɪ] U-Bahn **I 5**, 86
such [sʌtʃ] solch(e/r/s) **I 8**, 128
suddenly ['sʌdnli] plötzlich **I 6**, 97
suggestion [sə'dʒestʃn] Vorschlag **I 9**, 140
suitcase ['suːtkeɪs] Koffer **I 9**, 145
summer ['sʌmə] Sommer **I 6**, 93
Sunday ['sʌndeɪ] Sonntag **I 3**, 43
sunny ['sʌni] sonnig **I 9**, 140
+**sunshine** ['sʌnʃaɪn] Sonnenschein **I 9**, 151
super ['suːpə] super, spitze **I 9**, 140
+**supply line** [sə'plaɪ ˌlaɪn] Versorgungsleitung **I 7**, 118
+to **suppose** [sə'pəʊz] vermuten, annehmen **I 8**, 134
sure [ʃʊə] sicher, klar **I 2**, 29
to make sure [ˌmeɪk 'ʃʊə] sicherstellen **I 3**, 47
surfing ['sɜːfɪŋ] Surfen **I 9**, 146
sweatshirt ['swetʃɜːt] Sweatshirt **I 6**, 92
sweet [swiːt] süß, niedlich **I 2**, 37
sweets *(pl.)* [swiːts] Süßigkeiten **I 5**, 77
to **swim*** [swɪm] schwimmen **I 7**, 111
swimming pool ['swɪmɪŋ ˌpuːl] Swimmingpool **I 9**, 140
syllable ['sɪləbl] Silbe **I 9**, 142

T

T-shirt ['tiːʃɜːt] T-Shirt **I 1**, 14
table [teɪbl] Tisch **I 2**, 28
to **take*** [teɪk] nehmen, (hin)bringen **I 3**, 45
to take notice [ˌteɪk 'nəʊtɪs] beachten, Notiz nehmen (von) **I 8**, 129
to take off [ˌteɪk 'ɒf] starten, abheben **I 5**, 83
to take part (in) [ˌteɪk 'pɑːt] teilnehmen (an) **I 8**, 124
to take turns [tɜːnz] (sich) miteinander abwechseln **I 6**, 98
talk [tɔːk] Gespräch **I 6**, 99
to give a talk [tɔːk] ein (Kurz-)Referat halten **I 9**, 148
to **talk** *(about)* ['tɔːk‿əˌbaʊt] sprechen, reden (über) **I 2**, 27
+**tall** [tɔːl] hohe(r/s) **I 4**, 68
tank [tæŋk] Tank **I 8**, 126
tanker ['tæŋkə] Tanker, Tankschiff **I 7**, 108
demo **tape** ['deməʊ ˌteɪp] Demo(nstrations)band **I 6**, 96
taxi ['tæksi] Taxi **I 1**, 8
tea [tiː] Tee **I 5**, 79
teacher ['tiːtʃə] Lehrer(in) **I 2**, 26
+**team** [tiːm] Mannschaft, Team **I 3**, 52
teapot ['tiːpɒt] Teekanne **I 5**, 79
°Design and **Technology** [dɪ'zaɪn‿ˌən tek'nɒlədʒi] Gestalten und Technik **I 3**, 43
teddy bear ['tedi ˌbeə] Teddybär **I 5**, 79
telephone ['telɪfəʊn] Telefon **I 4**, 65
+**telescope** ['telɪskəʊp] Teleskop, Fernrohr **I 2**, 36
to **tell*** [tel] erzählen **I 3**, 44
telly ['teli] Fernseher **I 3**, 47
+**temperature** ['temprətʃə] Temperatur **I 4**, 68
+**tennis** ['tenɪs] Tennis **I 1**, 19
tent [tent] Zelt **I 9**, 143
term [tɜːm] (Schul-)Trimester, Semester **I 8**, 124
terminal ['tɜːmɪnl] Terminal **I 1**, 8
terrible ['terəbl] schrecklich, furchtbar **I 2**, 30
test [test] Test **I 6**, 96
to **test** [test] testen **I 6**, 98
+**text** [tekst] Text **I 2**, 36
than [ðæn/ðn] als **I 6**, 93
°to **thank** [θæŋk] danken **I 3**, 51
thank you ['θæŋk jʊ] danke **I 1**, 14
thanks [θæŋks] danke **I 3**, 42
that [ðæt] das; dass **I 1**, 14
the [ðə/ði] der/die/das **I 1**, 8
theatreland ['θɪətəˌlænd] Theaterviertel **I 4**, 58
their [ðeə] ihr/ihre *(pl.)* **I 2**, 26
them [ðem] sie *(Akk.)*; ihnen *(Dat.)* **I 5**, 76
theme [θiːm] Thema **I 9**, 140
now and **then** [ˌnaʊ‿n‿'ðen] ab und zu **I 9**, 143
+**then** [ðen] dann, danach **I 3**, 52
there is / are [ðeə(r)‿'ɪz / 'ɑː] es gibt, da ist/sind **I 2**, 26
these [ðiːz] dies (sind), das (sind); diese(r/s) *(pl.)* **I 1**, 13
they [ðeɪ] sie *(pl.)* **I 1**, 12
thick [θɪk] dick, dicht **I 6**, 97
thin [θɪn] dünn **I 8**, 128
thing [θɪŋ] Sache, Ding **I 1**, 12
to **think*** [θɪŋk] denken, glauben, meinen **I 3**, 45
this [ðɪs] dies (ist), das (ist); diese(r/s) *(sing.)* **I 1**, 15
those [ðəʊz] jene, diese *(pl.)* **I 3**, 50
thousand ['θaʊznd] tausend **I 7**, 109
through [θruː] durch, über **I 3**, 48
to **throw*** *(away)* [θrəʊ] (weg)werfen **I 7**, 112
Thursday ['θɜːzdeɪ] Donnerstag **I 3**, 43
ticket ['tɪkət] Flugschein, Fahrkarte **I 1**, 18
tie [taɪ] Krawatte **I 6**, 94
tights [taɪts] Strumpfhose **I 6**, 92
time [taɪm] (Uhr-)Zeit **I 1**, 14
any time [ˌeni 'taɪm] jederzeit **I 3**, 44
timetable ['taɪmˌteɪbl] Stundenplan **I 3**, 43
learning **tip** ['lɜːnɪŋ ˌtɪp] Lerntipp **I 3**, 50
to be **tired** ['taɪəd] müde (sein) **I 4**, 63
title ['taɪtl] Titel, Überschrift **I 6**, 98
to [tʊ/tu] in/im, zu **I 1**, 9

today [tə'deɪ] heute **I 6**, 95
together [tə'geðə] zusammen **I 3**, 47
toilet ['tɔɪlɪt] Toilette **I 6**, 103
tomato, (*pl.*) -oes [tə'mɑ:təʊ] Tomate **I 9**, 146
tomorrow [tə'mɒrəʊ] morgen **I 5**, 83
tonight [tə'naɪt] heute Abend, heute Nacht **I 4**, 67
too [tu:] auch, ebenfalls **I 1**, 14; zu (sehr, viel) **I 2**, 32
top [tɒp] Top, ärmelloses T-Shirt **I 6**, 93
top [tɒp] oben **I 4**, 59
topic ['tɒpɪk] Thema **I 9**, 148
+to **touch** [tʌtʃ] berühren, anfassen **I 3**, 52
to **tour** [tʊə] reisen, besichtigen **I 9**, 141
tourism ['tʊərɪzm] Tourismus **I 9**, 148
tourist ['tʊərɪst] Tourist(in) **I 4**, 59
toward(*s*) [tə'wɔ:d(z)] auf ... zu, in Richtung auf, (ent)gegen **I 6**, 97
tower ['taʊə] Turm **I 8**, 130
town [taʊn] (Klein-)Stadt **I 7**, 112
track [træk] Spur, Weg, Pfad **I 1**, 18
traditional [trə'dɪʃnl] traditionell **I 9**, 140
traffic ['træfɪk] Verkehr **I 4**, 59
traffic light ['træfɪk ˌlaɪt] Ampel **I 4**, 65
tragedy ['trædʒədi] Tragödie **I 7**, 108
train [treɪn] (U-Bahn-)Zug **I 4**, 59
trainer ['treɪnə] Turnschuh **I 6**, 94
training ['treɪnɪŋ] Training **I 8**, 124
to **translate** [træns'leɪt] übersetzen **I 3**, 51
transport ['trænspɔ:t] Transport, Beförderung **I 4**, 59
travel ['trævl] Reise- **I 9**, 145
to **travel** ['trævl] reisen **I 9**, 141
tree [tri:] Baum **I 2**, 26
trip [trɪp] Kurzreise, Trip **I 7**, 112
+sailing trip ['seɪlɪŋ ˌtrɪp] Segeltörn **I 8**, 134
trousers ['traʊzəz] Hose(n) **I 6**, 94
true [tru:] wahr **I 9**, 144
+**trumpet** ['trʌmpɪt] Trompete **I 1**, 19
to **try** [traɪ] versuchen, probieren **I 2**, 31
tube [tju:b] *Name der Londoner U-Bahn* (*wörtlich:* Röhre) **I 4**, 58
Tuesday ['tju:zdeɪ] Dienstag **I 3**, 43
tunnel ['tʌnl] Tunnel **I 8**, 129
Turkish ['tɜ:kɪʃ] türkisch, Türkisch **I 1**, 14
to take **turns** [tɜ:nz] (sich) miteinander abwechseln **I 6**, 98
it's his/her turn [tɜ:n] er/sie ist an der Reihe **I 8**, 128
to **turn** [tɜ:n] (um)drehen, wenden **I 5**, 79
to turn down [ˌtɜ:n 'daʊn] herunterdrehen, leiser stellen **I 2**, 34
TV [ˌti:'vi:] Fernseher **I 3**, 44
twice [twaɪs] zweimal **I 6**, 93
two [tu:] zwei **I 1**, 12
typical ['tɪpɪkl] typisch **I 6**, 93
flat **tyre** [ˌflæt 'taɪə] platter Reifen, Plattfuß **I 9**, 146

U

ugly ['ʌgli] hässlich **I 6**, 97
uncle ['ʌŋkl] Onkel **I 2**, 31
under ['ʌndə] unter **I 2**, 28
Underground ['ʌndəgraʊnd] U-Bahn **I 1**, 8
to **underline** [ˌʌndə'laɪn] unterstreichen **I 9**, 142
to **understand*** [ˌʌndə'stænd] verstehen **I 3**, 45
uniform ['ju:nɪfɔ:m] Uniform **I 6**, 92
unit ['ju:nɪt] Lektion, Einheit **I 1**, 8
until [ən'tɪl] bis **I 9**, 145
unused [ˌʌn'ju:zd] unbenutzt, nicht mehr benutzt **I 9**, 141
up [ʌp] oben (auf); hinauf **I 4**, 63
+to board up [ˌbɔ:d‿'ʌp] verschalen, mit Brettern vernageln **I 7**, 118
to hurry (*up*) [ˌhʌri‿'ʌp] (sich) beeilen **I 6**, 97
to look sth. up [ˌlʊk‿'ʌp] etw nachschlagen **I 9**, 141
to make* up [ˌmeɪk‿'ʌp] (sich) ausdenken, erfinden **I 8**, 130
to put* up [ˌpʊt‿'ʌp] aufgeben, aufhängen **I 2**, 32
to ring* so. up [ˌrɪŋ‿'ʌp] jmdn anrufen **I 3**, 46
to set* (*up*) [ˌset‿'ʌp] (auf)stellen, (auf)bauen **I 5**, 83
to split* up [ˌsplɪt‿'ʌp] sich (voneinander) trennen **I 3**, 46
to wake* (*up*) [ˌweɪk‿'ʌp] (auf)wachen **I 6**, 92
up to date [ˌʌp tə 'deɪt] modern, aktuell **I 3**, 47
+to **uproot** [ʌp'ru:t] entwurzeln, herausreißen **I 7**, 118
+**upstairs** [ˌʌp'steəz] oben; Obergeschoss **I 2**, 36
+to **upturn** [ʌp'tɜ:n] umdrehen, umwerfen **I 7**, 118
us [ʌs] uns **I 2**, 37
to **use** [ju:z] benutzen, gebrauchen **I 2**, 37
useful ['ju:sfl] nützlich, brauchbar **I 9**, 142
usually ['ju:ʒli] gewöhnlich, normalerweise **I 3**, 44

V

vacation (*AE*) [və'keɪʃn] Urlaub, Ferien **I 9**, 141
van [væn] Kleinlaster, Lieferwagen **I 2**, 29
vanilla [və'nɪlə] Vanille **I 5**, 76
various ['veəriəs] verschiedene **I 8**, 125
+**vegetable** ['vedʒtəbl] Gemüse **I 5**, 86
⟨**verse**⟩ [vɜ:s] Strophe, Vers **I 8**, 132
⟨**version**⟩ [vɜ:ʃn] Version, Fassung **I 2**, 34
very ['veri] sehr **I 2**, 33
vet (veterinarian) [vet (ˌvetrɪ'neəriən)] Tierarzt/-ärztin **I 2**, 32
vibes (**vibrations**) [vaɪbz (vaɪ'breɪʃnz)] Vibrationen, Schwingungen **I 1**, 14
video ['vɪdiəʊ] Video **I 8**, 130
video shop ['vɪdiəʊ ˌʃɒp] Videothek, Videoladen **I 4**, 65
view [vju:] Aussicht, Blick, Ansicht **I 6**, 92
village ['vɪlɪdʒ] Dorf, Ortschaft **I 6**, 93
village hall [ˌvɪlɪdʒ 'hɔ:l] Gemeindehaus **I 6**, 97
vinegar ['vɪnɪgə] Essig **I 5**, 77
+**violin** [ˌvaɪə'lɪn] Geige, Violine **I 1**, 19
to **visit** ['vɪzɪt] besuchen **I 7**, 110
vocabulary notebook [vəʊˌkæbjəlri 'nəʊtbʊk] Vokabelheft **I 4**, 65
voice [vɔɪs] Stimme **I 4**, 64
volleyball ['vɒlibɔ:l] Volleyball **I 3**, 47
volunteer [ˌvɒlən'tɪə] Freiwillige(r) **I 7**, 108

W

to **wait** [weɪt] warten **I 2**, 32
to **wake*** (*up*) [ˌweɪk‿'ʌp] (auf)wachen **I 6**, 92
walk [wɔ:k] Spaziergang **I 3**, 45
to **walk** [wɔ:k] spazierengehen **I 4**, 60
wall [wɔ:l] Wand **I 2**, 28

to **want** [wɒnt] wollen, wünschen **I 3**, 42
warm [wɔ:m] warm **I 8**, 135
to **warn** [wɔ:n] warnen **I 7**, 110
to **wash** [wɒʃ] waschen, putzen **I 6**, 95
waste [weɪst] Abfall, Müll **I 7**, 110
watch [wɒtʃ] Armbanduhr **I 5**, 76
to **watch** [wɒtʃ] anschauen, zuschauen **I 3**, 44
to watch TV [ˌwɒtʃ ti:'vi:] fernsehen **I 3**, 44
water ['wɔ:tə] Wasser **I 4**, 67
water-skiing ['wɔ:təski:ɪŋ] Wasserskifahren **I 9**, 140
wave [weɪv] Welle **I 7**, 111
wax content ['wæks ˌkɒntent] Wachsgehalt **I 7**, 108
way [weɪ] Art und Weise, Weg **I 3**, 42
no way (*coll.*) [ˌnəʊ 'weɪ] auf keinen Fall, keineswegs **I 8**, 135
we [wi:] wir **I 1**, 12
to **wear*** [weə] anhaben, tragen **I 4**, 60
weather ['weðə] Wetter **I 4**, 67
Wednesday ['wenzdeɪ] Mittwoch **I 3**, 43
week [wi:k] Woche **I 2**, 30
weekend [ˌwi:k'end] Wochenende **I 3**, 48
welcome ['welkəm] willkommen **I 1**, 9
+**well-managed** [ˌwel'mænɪdʒd] gut organisiert, gut geführt **I 9**, 150
well [wel] nun gut, na ja **I 1**, 14
Welsh [welʃ] walisisch, Waliser(in) **I 9**, 140
west [west] westlich, Westen **I 4**, 64
wet [wet] nass **I 7**, 111
what [wɒt] was? **I 1**, 11; welche(r/s), was für eine(r/s) **I 8**, 126
What about ...? [ˌwɒt‿ə'baʊt] Was ist mit ...? **I 1**, 11
What kind (*of*) ...? Was für eine/welche Art ...? **I 2**, 34
wheel [wi:l] Rad **I 9**, 147
when [wen] wenn, wann **I 2**, 32
where [weə] wo, wohin, woher **I 1**, 17
where (*from/to*) [weə] woher/wohin **I 8**, 131
whether ['weðə] ob **I 9**, 147
which [wɪtʃ] welche(r/s) **I 4**, 59
+**while** [waɪl] (eine) Weile; während **I 5**, 85
white [waɪt] weiß **I 2**, 26
+the whites [waɪts] die Weißen **I 8**, 134
+**whitewater rafting** [ˌwaɪtwɔ:tə 'rɑ:ftɪŋ] Wildwasserfahren **I 9**, 150
who [hu:] der/die/das, welche(r/s) **I 3**, 46; wer, wem, wen **I 2**, 26
whole [həʊl] ganz, komplett **I 4**, 63
whose [hu:z] wessen **I 6**, 102
why [waɪ] warum **I 2**, 26
wild [waɪld] wild **I 9**, 141
wildlife ['waɪldlaɪf] Tierwelt **I 7**, 112
+**will** [wɪl] werden **I 1**, 19
to **win*** [wɪn] gewinnen **I 6**, 101
+**wind** [wɪnd] Wind **I 4**, 68
window ['wɪndəʊ] Fenster **I 1**, 10
+**windy** ['wɪndi] windig **I 4**, 68
wine [waɪn] Wein **I 9**, 140
winter ['wɪntə] Winter **I 6**, 93
witch [wɪtʃ] Hexe **I 6**, 97
with [wɪð] mit **I 1**, 10
without [wɪ'ðaʊt] ohne **I 9**, 146
woman, (*pl.*) women ['wʊmən/'wɪmɪn] Frau(en) **I 2**, 31
+**wonderful** ['wʌndəfl] wunderbar, wundervoll **I 9**, 151
woods [wʊdz] Wald **I 6**, 92
word [wɜ:d] Wort **I 1**, 12
key word ['ki: wɜ:d] Schlüsselbegriff **I 3**, 42
work [wɜ:k] Arbeit **I 2**, 31
to **work** [wɜ:k] arbeiten **I 2**, 29
to work shift [ˌwɜ:k 'ʃɪft] Schicht arbeiten, Schichtdienst machen **I 3**, 46
world [wɜ:ld] Welt **I 9**, 147
to **worry** ['wʌri] sich Sorgen machen **I 4**, 60
worst [wɜ:st] schlechteste(r/s) **I 7**, 112
would you like to? [ˌwʊd ju: 'laɪk tə] möchtest du?/möchtet ihr/möchten Sie? **I 3**, 45
I'd (= *I would*) like [aɪd 'laɪk] ich hätte gerne **I 5**, 76
wow! [waʊ] *Ausruf der Bewunderung* **I 1**, 14
to **write*** (*down*) [ˌraɪt 'daʊn] (auf)schreiben **I 2**, 27
wrong [rɒŋ] falsch **I 4**, 64

Y

yeah [jeə] ja **I 5**, 80
year [jɪə] (Schul-)Jahr; Jahrgang, Klasse **I 3**, 42
yellow ['jeləʊ] gelb **I 2**, 27
yes [jes] ja **I 1**, 11
+**yesterday** ['jestədeɪ] gestern **I 5**, 85
not ... **yet** [jet] noch nicht **I 5**, 79
yoga ['jəʊgə] Joga **I 5**, 78
you [ju:] du, ihr, Sie **I 1**, 9
young [jʌŋ] jung **I 5**, 79
younger ['jʌŋgə] jünger(e/r/s) **I 8**, 128
your [jɔ:] dein/deine, euer/eure, Ihr/Ihre **I 1**, 14
+**yours** [jɔ:z] deine(r/s), eure(r/s), Ihre(r/s) **I 5**, 86
Yours faithfully, ['feɪθfli] mit freundlichen Grüßen, hochachtungsvoll (*Briefschluss*) **I 9**, 148
yourself [jɔ:'self] dich (selbst) **I 6**, 101

Z

+**zero** ['zɪərəʊ] null **I 1**, 12

Boys' names

Andrew ['ændru:]
Ben [ben]
B.J. ['bi: 'dʒeɪ]
Bruce [bru:s]
Dick [dɪk]
Farrukh ['færuk]
Gary ['gæri]
George [dʒɔ:dʒ]
Glen [glen]
Hassan [hə'sɑ:n]
Jake [dʒeɪk]
James [dʒeɪmz]
Jimmy ['dʒɪmi]
John [dʒɒn]
Jonathan ['dʒɒnəθn]
Julian ['dʒu:liən]
Kevin ['kevɪn]
Lance [lɑ:ns]
Liam ['lɪəm]
Marc [mɑ:k]
Mark [mɑ:k]

Mike [maɪk]
Nathan ['neɪθən]
Pete [pi:t]
Peter ['pi:tə]
Phil [fɪl]
Rizwan ['rɪzwən]
Steve [sti:v]
Tim [tɪm]
Timmy ['tɪmi]
Timothy ['tɪməθi]
Tony ['təʊni]
Trevor ['trevə]
Wayne [weɪn]
William ['wɪljəm]

Girls' names

Abby ['æbi]
Angela ['ændʒlə]
Ann(e) [æn]
Brenda ['brendə]
Diana [daɪ'ænə]
Elizabeth [ɪ'lɪzəbəθ]
Fanny ['fæni]
Georgina [dʒɔ:'dʒi:nə]
Gina ['dʒi:nə]
Hamida [hæ'mɪdə]
Hilary ['hɪlri]
Jean [dʒi:n]
Jessica ['dʒesɪkə]
Joanna [dʒəʊ'ænə]
Karen ['kærən]
Kate [keɪt]
Lauren ['lɔ:rən]
Linda ['lɪndə]
Liz [lɪz]
Lynn [lɪn]
Maggie ['mægi]
Mary Ann [ˌmeəri‿'æn]
Maureen ['mɔ:ri:n]
Molly ['mɒli]
Nicola ['nɪkələ]
Nora ['nɔ:rə]
Pamela ['pæmlə]
Pramila [præ'mɪlə]
Rukshana ['rʌkʃɑ:nə]
Samantha [sə'mænθə]
Shamira [ʃə'mi:rə]
Stella ['stelə]
Stephanie ['stefəni]
Susan ['su:zn]
Susie ['su:zi]
Tara ['tɑ:rə]
Tessa ['tesə]

Surnames

Barling ['bɑ:lɪŋ]
Blake [bleɪk]
Block [blɒk]
Braden ['breɪdn]
Burns [bɜ:nz]
Clifford ['klɪfəd]
Clifton ['klɪftən]
Cummings ['kʌmɪŋz]
Daly ['deɪli]
Dawson ['dɔ:sn]
Driver ['draɪvə]
Grimsby ['grɪmzbi]
Harrington ['hærɪŋtən]
Harrison ['hærɪsn]
Howard ['haʊəd]
James [dʒeɪmz]
Jones [dʒəʊnz]
Kapadia [kə'pædɪə]
Kwang [kwæŋ]
Lee [li:]
Lenoir [lə'nwɑ:]
Macintosh ['mækɪntɒʃ]
Manning ['mænɪŋ]
McBride [mək'braɪd]
Mills [mɪlz]
Modi ['məʊdi]
Morton ['mɔ:tn]
Norton ['nɔ:tn]
O'Brien [əʊ'braɪən]
Osceola [ˌɒskɪ'əʊlə]
Patel [pə'tel]
Pollard ['pɒlɑ:d]
Quentin ['kwentɪn]
Smith [smɪθ]
Todd [tɒd]
Wilson ['wɪlsn]
Wong [wɒŋ]

Geographical names

Alton Towers [ˌɔ:ltn 'taʊəz]
America [ə'merɪkə]
+Atlantic [ət'læntɪk]
Australia [ɒs'treɪliə]
+the Bahamas [bə'hɑ:məz]
Belfast [bel'fɑ:st]
Benidorm ['benɪdɔ:m]
Bristol ['brɪstl]
Britain ['brɪtn]
the British Isles [ˌbrɪtɪʃ‿'aɪlz]
Cardiff ['kɑ:dɪf]
+Chicago [ʃɪ'kɑ:gəʊ]
+Colorado [ˌkɒlr'ɑ:dəʊ]
Cornwall ['kɔ:nwɔ:l]
Cumbria ['kʌmbriə]
Denmark ['denmɑ:k]
Dingle Bay [ˌdɪŋgl 'beɪ]
Dublin ['dʌblɪn]
Edgecombe ['edʒkəm]
Edinburgh ['edɪnbrə]
England ['ɪŋglənd]
European Union [ˌjʊərə'pi:ən 'ju:njən]
+Everglades ['evəgleɪdz]
Falmouth ['fælməθ]
+Florida ['flɒrɪdə]
France [frɑ:nts]
Germany ['dʒɜ:məni]
Great Britain [ˌgreɪt 'brɪtn]

+**Gulf of Mexico** [ˌgʌlf‿əv 'meksɪkəʊ]
Hampstead Heath [ˌhæmstəd 'hi:θ]
Helston ['helstən]
India ['ɪndiə]
Ireland ['aɪələnd]
+**Islamorada** [ˌɪzləmə'rɑ:də]
Islington ['ɪzlɪŋtən]
+**Key West** [ˌki: 'west]
+**Keys** [ki:z]
+**Lake Michigan** [ˌleɪk 'mɪʃɪgən]
Land's End [ˌlændz‿'end]
Liverpool ['lɪvəpu:l]
Loch Lomond [ˌlɒk 'ləʊmənd]
London ['lʌndən]
+**Miami Beach** [maɪˌæmi 'bi:tʃ]
Munich ['mju:nɪk]
New York [ˌnju: 'jɔ:k]
Norfolk Broads [ˌnɔ:fək 'brɔ:dz]
+**Overseas Highway** [ˌəʊvəsi:z 'haɪweɪ]
Penzance [pen'zænts]
Plymouth ['plɪməθ]
the Republic of Ireland [rɪˌpʌblɪk‿əv‿'aɪəlnd]
Riviera [ˌrɪvi'eərə]
Scilly Isles ['sɪli‿ˌaɪlz]
Scotland ['skɒtlənd]
Sennen Cove [ˌsenən 'kəʊv]
Snowdonia [snəʊ'dəʊniə]
St Ives [snt‿'aɪvz]
Swansea ['swɒnzi]
Tokyo ['təʊkiəʊ]
Turkey ['tɜ:ki]
the United Kingdom [ju:ˌnaɪtɪd 'kɪŋdəm]
the United States (*US*) [ju:ˌnaɪtɪd 'steɪts]
Wales [weɪlz]
Washington DC [ˌwɒʃɪŋtən ˌdi:'si:]
Yorkshire Dales [ˌjɔ:kʃə 'deɪlz]

Other names

+**American Airlines** [ə'merɪkən‿'eəˌlaɪnz]
Angel ['eɪndʒl]
+**Barnes and Noble** ['bɑ:nz‿ən 'nəʊbl]
Beano ['bi:nəʊ]
⟨**Beatles**⟩ ['bi:tlz]
Big Ben [ˌbɪg 'ben]
+**Blacky** ['blæki]
Britrail Pass ['brɪtreɪl ˌpɑ:s]
Brixton ['brɪkstn]
+**Calvin Klein** [ˌkælvɪn 'klaɪn]
Camden Lock [ˌkæmdən 'lɒk]
Camden Passage [ˌkæmdən 'pæsɪdʒ]
Chicago Cub [ʃɪ'kɑ:gəʊ 'kʌb]
+**Chinatown** ['tʃaɪnətaʊn]
Circle Line ['sɜ:kl ˌlaɪn]
Covent Garden [ˌkɒvnt 'gɑ:dn]
Daniel Boone [ˌdænjəl 'bu:n]
+**Disney World** ['dɪzni ˌwɜ:ld]
Doc Martens [ˌdɒk 'mɑ:tɪnz]
+**Empire State Building** [ˌempaɪə 'steɪt ˌbɪldɪŋ]
Enid Blyton [ˌi:nɪd 'blaɪtn]
Friends of the Earth ['frendz‿əv ði‿'ɜ:θ]
Galahad ['gæləhæd]
+**George Mikes** [ˌdʒɔ:dʒ 'mi:keʃ]
Girlzone ['gɜ:lzəʊn]
Gosforth & Sons ['gɒsfɔ:θ‿ən ˌsʌnz]
Harrods ['hærədz]
Heathrow [ˌhi:θ'rəʊ]
High Street ['haɪ stri:t]
Islington Green [ˌɪslɪŋtən 'gri:n]
Jack the Ripper [ˌdʒæk ðə 'rɪpə]
Jennifer Kolby [ˌdʒenɪfə 'kɒlbi]
King Arthur [ˌkɪŋ 'ɑ:θə]
King Kong [ˌkɪŋ 'kɒŋ]
Kirrin Cottage [ˌkɪrɪn 'kɒtɪdʒ]
Lancelot ['lɑ:ntsəlɒt]
+**Little Italy** [ˌlɪtl 'ɪtli]
London Dungeon [ˌlʌndən 'dʌndʒn]
+**Lower East Side** [ˌləʊə‿'i:st saɪd]
+**Macy's** ['meɪsiz]
Madonna [mə'dɒnə]
Merlin the Magician [ˌmɜ:lɪn ðə mə'dʒɪʃn]
Metropolitan [ˌmetrə'pɒlɪtn]
Michael Jackson [ˌmaɪkl 'dʒæksn]
Milly ['mɪli]
the Monument ['mɒnjəmənt]
Morgan le Fay [ˌmɔ:gn lə 'feɪ]
Mumbles View [ˌmʌmblz 'vju:]
+**O'Hare** [əʊ'heə]
+**Orchard Street** ['ɔ:tʃəd ˌstri:t]
Oxford Street ['ɒksfəd ˌstri:t]
Penryn College [penˌrɪn 'kɒlɪdʒ]
Petticoat Lane [ˌpetɪkəʊt 'leɪn]
the Plush [plʌʃ]
Princess Elaine [prɪn'ses‿ɪ'leɪn]
Red Nose Day [ˌred 'nəʊz ˌdeɪ]
Rolling Stones [ˌrəʊlɪŋ 'stəʊnz]
+**Saks Fifth Avenue** ['sæks ˌfɪfθ 'ævənju:]
+**Sears Tower** [ˌsɪəz 'taʊə]
Sloane Square [ˌsləʊn 'skweə]
+**SoHo** ['səʊhəʊ]
St. Anthony [snt‿'æntəni]
Starlight Express [ˌstɑ:laɪt‿ɪk'spres]
Stuart Lodge [ˌstjʊət 'lɒdʒ]
Superman ['su:pəmæn]
Temple ['templ]
Thanksgiving [ˌθæŋks'gɪvɪŋ]
+**Tiffany's** ['tɪfniz]
Top Girls ['tɒp ˌgɜ:lz]
Tottenham Court Road [ˌtɒtnəm kɔ:t 'rəʊd]
Tower Hill station ['taʊə ˌhɪl 'steɪʃn]
Tower of London [ˌtaʊə‿əv 'lʌndən]
Trafalgar Square [trəˌfælgə 'skweə]
Victoria Line [vɪk'tɔ:riə ˌlaɪn]
the West End [ˌwest‿'end]
Wild West [ˌwaɪld 'west]
Wonky Towers [ˌwɒŋki 'taʊəz]

Irregular verbs

infinitive	simple past	past participle	German
be [bi:]	was, were [wɒz, wɜ:]	been [bi:n]	sein
bet [bet]	bet [bet]	bet [bet]	wetten
break [breɪk]	broke [brəʊk]	broken ['brəʊkn]	brechen
bring [brɪŋ]	brought [brɔ:t]	brought [brɔ:t]	bringen
build [bɪld]	built [bɪlt]	built [bɪlt]	bauen
buy [baɪ]	bought [bɔ:t]	bought [bɔ:t]	kaufen
choose [tʃu:z]	chose [tʃəʊz]	chosen ['tʃəʊzn]	(aus)wählen
come [kʌm]	came [keɪm]	come [kʌm]	kommen
cost [kɒst]	cost [kɒst]	cost [kɒst]	kosten
do [du:]	did [dɪd]	done [dʌn]	machen, tun
draw [drɔ:]	drew [dru:]	drawn [drɔ:n]	zeichnen
drink [drɪŋk]	drank [dræŋk]	drunk [drʌŋk]	trinken
drive [draɪv]	drove [drəʊv]	driven ['drɪvn]	fahren
eat [i:t]	ate [et]	eaten ['i:tn]	essen
fall [fɔ:l]	fell [fel]	fallen ['fɔ:ln]	fallen
feed [fi:d]	fed [fed]	fed [fed]	füttern
fight [faɪt]	fought [fɔ:t]	fought [fɔ:t]	kämpfen
find [faɪnd]	found [faʊnd]	found [faʊnd]	finden
fly [flaɪ]	flew [flu:]	flown [fləʊn]	fliegen
forget [fə'get]	forgot [fə'gɒt]	forgotten [fə'gɒtn]	vergessen
get [get]	got [gɒt]	got [gɒt]	holen, bekommen
give [gɪv]	gave [geɪv]	given ['gɪvn]	geben
go [gəʊ]	went [went]	gone [gɒn]	gehen
grow [grəʊ]	grew [gru:]	grown [grəʊn]	wachsen, (an)bauen
have [hæv]	had [hæd]	had [hæd]	haben
hear [hɪə]	heard [hɜ:d]	heard [hɜ:d]	hören
hide [haɪd]	hid [hɪd]	hidden ['hɪdn]	(sich) verstecken
hit [hɪt]	hit [hɪt]	hit [hɪt]	schlagen
hurt [hɜ:t]	hurt [hɜ:t]	hurt [hɜ:t]	verletzen, wehtun
keep [ki:p]	kept [kept]	kept [kept]	(be)halten
know [nəʊ]	knew [nju:]	known [nəʊn]	wissen, kennen
learn [lɜ:n]	learned [lɜ:nt], learnt [lɜ:nt]	learned [lɜ:nt], learnt [lɜ:nt]	lernen
leave [li:v]	left [left]	left [left]	(ver)lassen
lend [lend]	lent [lent]	lent [lent]	(ver)leihen
let [let]	let [let]	let [let]	lassen
lie [laɪ]	lay [leɪ]	lain [leɪn]	liegen
lose [lu:z]	lost [lɒst]	lost [lɒst]	verlieren
make [meɪk]	made [meɪd]	made [meɪd]	machen
mean [mi:n]	meant [ment]	meant [ment]	bedeuten
meet [mi:t]	met [met]	met [met]	treffen, begegnen
pay [peɪ]	paid [peɪd]	paid [peɪd]	zahlen, bezahlen
put [pʊt]	put [pʊt]	put [pʊt]	setzen, stellen, legen
read [ri:d]	read [red]	read [red]	lesen
ride [raɪd]	rode [rəʊd]	ridden ['rɪdn]	reiten, fahren
ring [rɪŋ]	rang [ræŋ]	rung [rʌŋ]	klingeln, anrufen
run [rʌn]	ran [ræn]	run [rʌn]	laufen, rennen
say [seɪ]	said [sed]	said [sed]	sagen

infinitive	simple past	past participle	German
see [siː]	saw [sɔː]	seen [siːn]	sehen
sell [sel]	sold [səʊld]	sold [səʊld]	verkaufen
send [send]	sent [sent]	sent [sent]	schicken, senden
set [set]	set [set]	set [set]	setzen, stellen, legen
show [ʃəʊ]	showed [ʃəʊd]	shown [ʃəʊn]	zeigen
shut [ʃʌt]	shut [ʃʌt]	shut [ʃʌt]	schließen
sing [sɪŋ]	sang [sæŋ]	sung [sʌŋ]	singen
sit [sɪt]	sat [sæt]	sat [sæt]	sitzen
sleep [sliːp]	slept [slept]	slept [slept]	schlafen
speak [spiːk]	spoke [spəʊk]	spoken ['spəʊkn]	sprechen
spell [spel]	spelled [spelt], spelt [spelt]	spelled [spelt], spelt [spelt]	buchstabieren
spend [spend]	spent [spent]	spent [spent]	ausgeben (*Geld*), verbringen (*Zeit*)
spill [spɪl]	spilled [spɪlt], spilt [spɪlt]	spilled [spɪlt], spilt [spɪlt]	ausschütten, vergießen
split [splɪt]	split [splɪt]	split [splɪt]	aufsplitten, trennen
stand [stænd]	stood [stʊd]	stood [stʊd]	stehen
stick [stɪk]	stuck [stʌk]	stuck [stʌk]	kleben, stecken
swim [swɪm]	swam [swæm]	swum [swʌm]	schwimmen
take [teɪk]	took [tʊk]	taken ['teɪkn]	nehmen, (hin)bringen
tell [tel]	told [təʊld]	told [təʊld]	erzählen, sagen
think [θɪŋk]	thought [θɔːt]	thought [θɔːt]	denken
throw [θrəʊ]	threw [θruː]	thrown [θrəʊn]	werfen
understand [ˌʌndə'stænd]	understood [ˌʌndə'stʊd]	understood [ˌʌndə'stʊd]	verstehen
wake [weɪk]	woke [wəʊk]	woken ['wəʊkn]	wecken, aufwachen
wear [weə]	wore [wɔː]	worn [wɔːn]	tragen (*Kleidung*)
win [wɪn]	won [wʌn]	won [wʌn]	gewinnen
write [raɪt]	wrote [rəʊt]	written ['rɪtn]	schreiben

It's rhyme time with irregular verbs

sell – sold – sold and
tell – told – told

fly – flew – flown and
know – knew – known

Can you make more rhymes?

Classroom phrases

What you can say to your friends or to your teacher:

I'm / We're against it. That's not the same at all. How do you know? I don't agree with you.	**Ablehnen**	Ich bin / Wir sind dagegen. Das ist überhaupt nicht dasselbe. Woher willst du/wollt ihr das wissen? Ich stimme nicht zu. / Da bin ich anderer Meinung.
Can I get the OHP ready? Can I get the cassette recorder/ CD player / video / ...? Can I play / rewind / ... the tape? Can I operate the video recorder?	**Arbeitsmittel**	Kann ich den OHP fertig machen? Kann ich den Rekorder / ... / holen? Kann ich das Band / ... / abspielen / zurückspulen ...? Kann ich den Videorekorder bedienen?
Can we ... do this / that? Let's read / sing / act / ... Can we play / clap / ...? Can I start / go on / ...? Can we do that in pairs / in groups / together / ...?	**Arbeitsvorschläge**	Können wir das / dieses hier machen? Lass(t) uns lesen / singen / spielen / ... Können wir spielen / klatschen / ...? Kann ich anfangen / weitermachen / ...? Können wir das zu zweit / in Gruppen / zusammen / ... machen?
Hi (there)! Hello everybody/you two / ... Good morning.	**Begrüßen**	Hallo, ihr da (alle)! Guten Morgen.
Can I open the window? Can I go out for a moment? Can we act this story? Can't we do something else?	**Bitten**	Darf ich das Fenster öffnen? Kann ich mal kurz hinausgehen? Können wir diese Geschichte spielen? Können wir nicht etwas anderes machen?
Thank you (very much). Thanks. Thanks a lot.	**Danken**	Danke schön / sehr. Vielen Dank.
I'm sorry! / Sorry! I'm so / very sorry. I'm sorry I'm late.	**Entschuldigen**	Entschuldigung. Es tut mir (sehr) Leid. Tut mir Leid, dass ich zu spät komme.
What's the matter with you? Are you feeling ill? What's wrong with you? Are you better now?	**Erkundigen**	Was ist mit dir? Fühlst du dich krank? Stimmt etwas nicht? Geht es dir jetzt besser?
That's wrong, I'm afraid. Sorry, that's not right. I think you're wrong there. I think he / she's got it all wrong.	**Falsch**	Das ist leider falsch. Tut mir Leid, aber das ist nicht richtig. Ich glaube, da irrst du. Ich glaube, er / sie hat das alles nicht richtig mitgekriegt.
Finished! / I've finished. I've done it already.	**Fertig**	Fertig! / Ich bin fertig. Ich habe das schon gemacht.

What's that in English / German? What does that mean? Can I ask a question, please? What's next? Who's next?	**Fragen**	Wie heißt das auf Englisch / Deutsch? Was heißt / bedeutet das? Kann ich bitte etwas fragen? Was ist als Nächstes dran? Wer kommt als Nächste(r)?
What must we do for homework? What's for homework? Have you done your homework?	**Hausaufgaben**	Was sollen wir zu Hause machen? Was sind die Hausaufgaben? Hast du/Habt ihr deine / eure Hausaufgaben gemacht?
Can / Could you help me, please? Can I have your ...? How do you do this exercise? How do you pronounce this word? Could you spell that? Could you write it down for me?	**Hilfe**	Kannst du / Könnten Sie mir bitte helfen? Kann ich dein(e) / euer(e)/ Ihr(e) ... haben? Wie geht diese Übung? Wie spricht man dieses Wort aus? Könntest du / Könnten Sie das buchstabieren? Könntest du / Könnten Sie das für mich aufschreiben?
Sorry, I can't hear/see that! It's so / too loud in here. Sorry, that's too fast. That's very / too difficult.	**Klagen**	Tut mir Leid. Ich kann das nicht hören / sehen. Es ist so laut hier drinnen. Tut mir Leid, das ist zu schnell. Das ist sehr / zu schwierig.
Could you repeat that, please? I'm sorry, I don't understand this! Pardon! Could you explain that again?	**Nicht verstanden**	Könntest du / Könnten Sie das bitte wiederholen? Tut mir Leid, das verstehe ich nicht. Wie bitte? Könntest du / Könnten Sie das noch einmal erklären?
(Very) Good! / That's good! Well done! Fantastic! Correct! / That's right. / You're right.	**Richtig**	(Sehr) Gut! / Das ist gut! Gut gemacht! Fantastisch! Korrekt. / Das ist richtig. / Du hast Recht.
Quiet, please. / Silence, please. Be quiet.	**Ruhe**	Ruhig, bitte! / Ruhe, bitte! Sei(d) ruhig!
Where's my ... I can't find my ... Has anyone seen / taken my ...? I must look for my ...	**Suchen**	Wo ist mein(e) ...? Ich kann mein(e) ... nicht finden. Hat jemand mein(e) ... gesehen / genom men? Ich muss mein(e) ... suchen.
I'm not feeling well. I've got a headache. Can I go to the toilet, please.	**Unwohl**	Ich fühle mich nicht gut. Ich habe Kopfschmerzen. Kann ich mal zur Toilette gehen?
Bye. Goodbye. See you.	**Verabschieden**	Tschüs. Auf Wiedersehen. Bis bald.
Sorry, I've forgotten it. I'm afraid I've forgotten my ... Sorry, I can't / don't remember it. Sorry, I don't know. Sorry, no idea.	**Vergessen**	Tut mir Leid, ich hab's vergessen. Ich fürchte, ich hab mein(e) ... vergessen. Tut mir Leid, es fällt mir nicht ein. Das weiß ich leider nicht. Tut mir Leid. Keine Ahnung.

Quellenverzeichnis

Bildquellen

S. 8 o. li.: Bygott; mi.: J. Allan Cash Ltd.; o. re.: Topham Picturepoint; Fond: VCL/Bavaria; S 9: Bygott; S. 11: Jürgen Kleine; u. li.: Duncan Smith; Cartoon: From *The Fanatics Guide to Dogs*, Exley Publications, Watford, © Roland Fiddy 1991; S. 16: Topham Picturepoint; S. 17 o. li.: Mauritius/SST; o. re: Mauritius/C. Bayer; Cartoon li: From *Roundabout* by C. Gutknecht et. al., © Winklers Verlag/Gebr. Grimm, Darmstadt 1991; re: © OUP 1972; S. 26/27: Noreen O'Donovan; S. 30: Duncan Smith; u. li.: Jürgen Kleine; S. 33: Mauritius/fm; S. 34: From *The Music Makers*, © Christian Verlag, München 1979/Foto: Erich Auerbach; m. li.: Jürgen Kleine; m. re.; Duncan Smith; Cartoon li: © Punch 1981; re: © *The Best of Heath*, David & Charles 1984; S. 42: Greenhill; S. 46/47: Bavaria (46 o.: Prince; m., u.: TCL; 47 o.: March; u.: TCL); S. 52: Bavaria/Picture Finders; S. 58 o. li.: Harding/Nigel Blythe; 2. v. o. li.: J. Allan Cash Ltd.; o. re.: Bygott; u. re.: Harding; u. li.: © RV-Verlag; S. 59: J. Allen Cash Ltd.; S. 63: Harding/Walter Rawlings; S. 67: Topham Picturepoint; S. 68 o. li.: Silvestris/The Telegraph Colour Library; o. re.: Mauritius/Elsen; 2. v. o. re.: Bavaria/Segal; 2. v. o. li.: Bilderberg/Michael Engler; u.: Silvestris/Lenz; S. 68: Mauritius Superstock; S. 74: Bygott; S. 75 o. li.: Noreen O'Donovan; o. re.: Bygott; m. re.: Harding/Vicky Skeet; m. u.: J. Allen Cash Ltd.; S. 76: Greenhill; S. 77: Harding/Walter Rawlings; S. 81: Elsie Lennox; S. 83 o. re.: Harding; S. 86 o. re.: Mauritius/Vidler; m. re.: Mauritius/Macia; 3. v. o. re.: Mauritius/Lindner; u. re.: Sebastian Hartz; li.: Noreen O'Donovan; S. 92 o. li: Tom Sobolik/Black Star/PNE; u. li.: Patrick Ward; S. 93 o. re.: Snowdon/Hoyer; m. re.: Focus; S. 95: Andrew Hutchins; S. 102: Kinoarchiv Peter W. Engelmeier, Hamburg; Cartoon: © McLachlan, Punch; S. 108 li.: J. Allan Cash Ltd.; S. 109 re.: Bavaria/VCL; S. 110 o. re.: J. Allan Cash Ltd.; u. re.: Greenhill; o. li., u.: Photodisc; S. 114 re.: dpa; Fond: Photodisc; Cartoons: From *Three Sheets in the Wind*, Methuen Paperbacks Ltd. London, © 1973 by Norman Thelwell; S. 117: © Greenpeace, From *Greenpeace – Making Waves* by Biederstädt et. al., Klett; S. 118: Fond u. o. re: dpa; u. re.: Noreen O'Donovan; S. 129/130: Eileen A. Soper, © Hodder & Stoughton 1945; S. 134: Fond: Heinz Steenmans; m. o.: Klaus Andrews/argus-Fotoarchiv; 2. v. o. mi.: Guido Steenmans; mi. u.: Heinz Steenmans; S. 140 li: Alton Towers, Staffordshire (brochure); re.: British Tourist Authority; S. 141 o., u. re.: British Tourist Authority; u. li.: J. Allan Cash Ltd.; S. 145/146: Duncan Smith; S. 147: Mauritius/Torino; S. 150: Photodisc; S. 152: Topham Picturepoint; S. 168: Penryn College, S. 169: Music + Show: Nanna Botsch

Textquellen

S. 16: Words and music by J.Guldberg / T. Stahl © SING-A-SONG Publ. Polygram Songs Musikverlag GmbH, Hamburg; S. 19: © June Factor, from *Far Out, Brussel Sprout!*, Hodder Headline Australia Pty. Ltd., 1992. S. 34: Words and music by John Lennon and Paul McCartney © Music Sales Ltd., London; S. 46/47: © The Guardian Education 14/5/96; S. 49: From *Sister's sweets'/ Fighting, Teasing and Bullying* by John Pierce, © HarperCollins Publishers Ltd., London; S. 50: Words by R. Baumann / A. Breitung © Edition Capricorn - EAMS Musikverlag, Deggendorf; S. 66: From *Walking the Bridge of Your Nose* by Michael Rosen. Published by Kingfisher, an imprint of Larousse, London; S. 83: Graham McPherson/Michael Barson (Text + Melodie), © EMI Music Publishing Ltd. Für D/A/CH/Osteuropa: EMI Music Publishing Germany GmbH, Hamburg; Sänger: Suggs 1995 (The Lone Ranger); S. 94: © Penryn College; S. 100: From *Excuses, Excuses* by John Foster, OUP, Oxford, © Jack Ousbey; S. 112: © The Guardian 6/5/98; S. 114: Words and music by G. Sutherland © Island Music Ltd., Polygram Songs Musikverlag GmbH, Hamburg; S. 128/129/131: From *The Famous Five: Five Go To Smuggler's Top*, Hodder Children's Books, London 1997, © Enid Blyton; Illustrations by Eileen A. Soper, © Hodder & Stoughton 1945; S. 132 o.: From *There's An Awful Lot of Weirdos in Our Neighbourhood*, Walker Books Ltd., © Colin McNaughton 1987; u.: From *Complete Poems for Children*, Heinemann, by permission of Laura Cecil Literary Agency on behalf of the Estate of the author, © James Reeves; S. 149: From *Thirteensomething*, Puffin Books, London, © Jane Goldman; S. 151: From *How to be an Alien*, Andre Deutsch Ltd. London, © George Mikes; S. 158 o.: From *Silver Sand and Snow* by Michael Joseph, by permission of David Higham, © Eleanor Farjeon; S. 159 o.: © 1994 by Annette Kosseris et. al., Southwood Press Ltd, Marrickville; u.: Reprinted by permission of Peter Fraser & Dunlop, © Roger McGough; S. 166: © The Guardian 5/4/89; S. 167: © Enid Blyton Homepage; S. 169: Words and music by Joshua Kadison © Joshuasongs / Seymour Glass Songs / EMI Blackwood Music Inc. / EMI Music Publishing GmbH, Hamburg

Grammar exercises

5 Are they from Islington? / Is she a friend? / Are you at the check-in? / Is Tarkan OK? / Is it a bus? / Is he English?

13 Liam has got a new modem. – Liam's modem is new. / Have the Wilsons got a big garage? – Is the Wilsons' garage big? / The Bradens haven't got a big garden. – The Bradens' garden is not big. / Has Sandra got a green T-shirt? – Is Sandra's T-shirt green?

15 Can dogs see red, green and yellow? / Can my friends find a new owner for my dog? / Can my friend send me an e-mail?

21 a) Our dog doesn't bark a lot. / She doesn't like homework. / He never plays with the cat. / They don't go for a walk with Milly. / b) I don't like the saxophone. / My friend doesn't play with her dog. / The children don't want to go to school. / Teachers don't like bullies.

22 a) Does Sandra play the cello? / Does Nicola read her magazine? / Do the Modis help the children? / b) Does your friend often help you? / Do (Must) dog owners know a lot about animals? / Does a cat like music?

24 a) These are my books here. / Is that your dog over there? / b) Das da drüben ist mein(e) Freund(in). / Lass(t) uns diese CD (hier) anhören.

25 1. The man is playing with the baby. / 2. The girl is eating an ice cream. / 3. My sister is writing a postcard. / 4. The people are clapping. / 5. Jimmy is wearing new shoes today. / 6. The children are doing (their) homework (at the moment). / 7. The ball is lying on the table. / A woman is taking photos.

32 1. Have you got any leather jackets in my size? / 2. Can you show me some cheap watches? / 3. Would you like some vinegar? / 4. I don't want any.

45 Have they learnt the poem yet? / Has Liz watched the 'Five friends' video? / Have the others heard the news yet? / My sister has packed my book. / I've already done my homework. / My father has already heard the story.

THE UNITED STATES OF AMERICA

CT = Connecticut
DE = Delaware
MA = Massachusetts
MD = Maryland
NH = New Hampshire
NJ = New Jersey
RI = Rhode Island
VT = Vermont

35 major highways
4^{00} time zones, compared with Central European Time 12^{00} (noon)

Countries in which English is the / an official language

NAME Independent states